The Writer's Handbook

Allan B. Lefcowitz

United States Naval Academy

Prentice-Hall, Inc.

Englewood Cliffs, New Jersey

Library of Congress Cataloging in Publication Data

Lefcowitz, Allan B.
  The writer's handbook.

  Includes index.
  1. English language—Rhetoric. I. Title.
PE1408.L387   808′.042   75-33333
ISBN 0-13-969923-6

Printed in the United States of America

10 9 8 7 6 5 4 3 2 1

PRENTICE-HALL INTERNATIONAL, INC., London
PRENTICE-HALL OF AUSTRALIA PTY. LTD., Sydney
PRENTICE-HALL OF CANADA, LTD., Toronto
PRENTICE-HALL OF INDIA PRIVATE LIMITED, New Delhi
PRENTICE-HALL OF JAPAN, INC., Tokyo
PRENTICE-HALL OF SOUTHEAST ASIA PTE. LTD., Singapore

Acknowledgments for quoted works begin on page 381.

Contents

Contents

3

Paragraphs (¶) 69

4

Sentences 111

Contents

5

Diction (d)   151

6

Conventions of Writing (ms)   193

Contents

7

Punctuation (p)   241

Contents

8

Grammar (Gr)   **275**

Contents

9

Research and the Library Paper 325

10

Glossary of Usage (us glos) 361

Acknowledgments 381

Index 384

Preface

The Writer's Handbook is a guide and textbook for beginning writers, covering the major principles and techniques of rhetoric, grammar, and usage. Because each writing situation presents different possibilities and problems that require different choices and solutions, the *Handbook* focuses on the *process* of writing as a practical craft involving a unique writer-reader relationship. Numerous writing examples from a variety of nonfiction works and student papers help the student to understand the processes of writing and rewriting. Exercises are strategically located so that the student can practice the principles and mechanics of writing as they are introduced. Extensive end-of-chapter review exercises reinforce the student's understanding of the chapter's contents.

The Writer's Handbook has two major divisions: (1) rhetorical elements of writing (Chapters 1–5) and (2) grammar and conventions of writing (Chapters 6–10). However, the chapters have been designed to be used in or out of their present sequence in order to accommodate any one of many possible assignment plans and to facilitate use of the *Handbook* as a reference guide.

Each chapter begins with a headnote summarizing its content and objectives. Chapter 1 is an overview of all the elements a reader responds to in writing, and each subsequent chapter is an elaboration of one of those elements. Chapters 2-5 constitute the rhetoric portion of the *Handbook*. These chapters progress from the more generalized areas of rhetoric, such as focus and organization (Chapter 2), to such specific topics as the paragraph (Chapter 3), the sentence (Chapter 4), and diction (Chapter 5).

Chapters 6–10 concentrate on the conventions of writing. Chapter 6—covering manuscript form, capitalization, italics, abbreviation, spelling, and so on—includes conventions of documentation and footnoting. Discussing these two topics in the chapter on manuscript form allows the student to apply the principles of documentation and footnoting to a variety of writing assignments and not only to the library paper.

Chapter 7 examines punctuation in terms of particular writing situations. For example, the discussion of the series includes situations requiring the comma, semicolon, colon, and dash. This approach enables students to see punctuation as a process and not merely as a set of arbitrary rules.

Chapter 8 provides a succinct and comprehensive review of grammar. The glossary of terms and the list of common grammatical errors facilitate quick reference to key terms and common errors of grammar.

Chapter 9 discusses the techniques of library research, the availability and use of reference tools, and the preparation of the library paper. Library research is examined as an activity involving many of the writing principles, such as focus and organization, covered earlier in the *Handbook*. A sample library paper is included.

Chapter 10 is a glossary of usage concentrating on those questions of usage that have consistently caused students difficulty. Other, related high-frequency problems not listed in Chapter 10 are either referred to in the extensive topical index or included in the list of common grammatical errors in Chapter 8. Chapter 8 and Chapter 10 together comprise a full listing of guidelines for the most common grammar and usage problems.

The design of *The Writer's Handbook* is uncomplicated but sufficiently detailed to make the guidelines for writing and revision readily accessible both to students and instructors. The table of contents and index list all the major topics discussed in the *Handbook*. The numerical, alphabetized correction chart on the inside front cover is keyed to the text. The first number in all coded headings is the chapter number. The second number corresponds to the sequence of major topics or conventions within the chapter. Subtopics or conventions are labeled with the chapter number and major topic number and are lettered alphabetically. For example, *exactness*, as the sixth major topic in Chapter 5, "Diction," is coded 5.6. Under this major topic are the subtopics *accuracy, concreteness, appropriateness, economy,* and *variety,* coded 5.6a, 5.6b, 5.6c, 5.6d, and 5.6e, respectively.

Listed on the inside back cover are the major topics, keyed to the text; frequently used correction symbols, also keyed to the text; and proofreaders' marks, briefly illustrated. The topic listing pinpoints the major discussions to which instructors most often direct students. The correction symbols and proofreaders' marks commonly used for correcting and revising writing provide instructors and students with a clear and rapid method for communicating about writing.

For their assistance in reviewing *The Writer's Handbook* I want to thank James C. Raymond, University of Alabama; Ronald C. Fort, Tarrant County Junior College; and Janice E. Keller, State University of New York at Farmingdale. An appreciation for contributions to the *Handbook* is due to my students and colleagues at the United States Naval Academy and to the staff of the Book Project Division of Prentice-Hall, Inc. A special note of thanks must go to Philip K. Jason, who helped to prepare the Instructor's Manual, and to Richard Wohlschlaeger, who assisted in the preparation of Chapter 8. Finally, I want to express my appreciation to Louise Hockett, the editor, without whose assistance the *Handbook* could not and would not have been created.

The Writer's Handbook

The Writer and the Reader

1

Because the reader is the judge of whether a written communication has succeeded, the writer must be aware of audience level and audience expectations, among which are good organization, accurate use of conventions, and honest and logical use of evidence. None of these goals can be accomplished without rewriting. The awareness of what the reader expects is the first step in thinking like a professional writer.

THINKING LIKE A PROFESSIONAL WRITER

While few people are likely to become professional writers in the sense of earning a living only by their pens, everyone faces a variety of writing tasks in school and on the job. People have to write reports, papers, case studies, examinations, directions, summaries, job application letters, and a host of other assignments. Writing is not judged according to the specific standards of professional writing; it is judged on one standard only: Does it communicate to a reader? The minimum standards for successful communication are the same for everyone: to be effective, a piece of writing must be well organized, logical, and clearly expressed.

The way to achieve consistent results in writing is to approach the job as professionals do. They look upon writing as a craft whose techniques and strategies must be mastered in order to communicate effectively each time. Thinking like a professional helps the writer to achieve results that are really worth the effort—*professional* results.

The first step toward acquiring a professional attitude is to understand the unique nature of each writing situation. There is no single, miraculous formula that assures success in writing. Although all writing depends on basic skills, each situation is unique in the problems it poses for the writer. Each time out, the writer must identify his purpose in writing and find a way to communicate that purpose effectively.

The second step in thinking like a professional is to understand the role of the audience. The reader is the ultimate judge as to when something has been communicated. In most writing situations the writer and the reader perform tasks independent of the other. The reader is not going to call the writer and say, "Listen, I don't understand what you're getting at here in the first paragraph of your article. Explain it to me." Neither can the author follow the reader around earnestly explaining, "What I actually meant to say is this. . . ." From the largest patterns of thought and organization to the smallest details of spelling and margins, the writer must anticipate the needs and expectations of the audience.

The third step is to become a self-editor, to move away from one's own writing and look at it objectively. Since writers are also readers, they are used to seeing what succeeds or fails in the works of others. Self-editing enables writers to apply this awareness to their own work in order to avoid those shortcomings and oversights they notice when reading someone else's writing. In addition, self-editing helps writers see writing as a *process*, not simply a product, with a variety of options for communicating ideas.

The fourth step toward acquiring a professional attitude is to learn the value of constructive criticism. Most writers interpret a negative reaction to their writing as an assault not only upon their ability to write but also upon themselves personally. However, while writers may not eagerly look forward to an editor's or instructor's unfavorable comments, they can profit by viewing such criticism not as threats but as suggestions given in good faith for the improvement of the communication.

Acquiring a professional attitude ultimately means being constantly aware of how readers will react both to the whole and to the parts of a piece of writing. That the writer has given his work professional attention will be apparent to the reader as soon as he begins to read. And the professional quality that first captures the reader's attention will also keep him reading.

THE MEDIUM AND THE AUDIENCE

The audience the writer is attempting to reach determines a great many choices other than subject matter. Specifically, the type of audience determines:

1. the depth in which the subject is treated
2. the language and form in which the subject is cast

A writer for *Time* or *Newsweek* must discuss a new kidney transplant at a level and in terms that most readers can understand, but an audience of surgeons requires a much more technical discussion of the topic that few general readers would understand. A light or conversational tone may do nicely for general audiences, but a more scholarly tone is needed for special audiences.

3

For a clearer idea of the ways writers fashion their writing to fit the needs and tastes of their readers, take a look at the following passages, each of which comes from a review of a different musical recording. All were published in nationally circulated magazines, but in each review the writer has a different audience in mind. The first review comes from *The New Yorker,* a magazine geared toward a highly educated and sophisticated urban audience:

> Arnold Schoenberg is a debatable composer, but there is nothing obscure or unattractive about his Concerto for String Quartet and Orchestra (after Handel's Concerto Grosso, Opus 6, No. 7). It is middle-period Schoenberg (1933), composed when the famous atonalist had relaxed a bit. Being based on Handel, it is rather Handelian, but Schoenberg has added a great deal that has a Brahmsian or Regeresque flavor. The Lenox Quartet and the London Symphony Orchestra have, in Desto DC 7170 (two sides), given it what seems here and there a slightly harsh performance. Schoenberg's String Trio, Opus 45 (1946), is included. This is a completely twelve-tone work, and a raucous one.
>
> Winthrop Sargeant, "Concert Records"

The second review comes from *Stereo Review,* a magazine for people who want to learn about the latest in stereo equipment and about new classical, popular, and rock recordings:

> Why do I carry on about Diana Ross so? Because she gets to me, that's why. This time she's live (as if she was ever anything else) at Caesar's Palace in performances as shiny as her lip gloss. Her best efforts here are two medleys, one comprising her best-known works from her days with the Supremes, the other songs from *Lady Sings the Blues,* the film in which she portrayed Billie Holiday. The latter shows her real ability as an actress. She doesn't really sound like the great Lady Day at all, but somehow she is able to catch, by expressive means rather than by mere vocal imitation, the essence of that unique and tortured personality.
>
> The recorded sound is good enough to capture the glitter of Ross's electric effect on an audience, and the production is, as usual, just a slither away from being too much.
>
> Peter Reilly, "Diana Ross: Live at Caesar's Palace"

The last review comes from *Crawdaddy,* a hip magazine devoted to articles about rock music and singers:

> Downhome Dadaism in a cheap suit, but this time around it's a double-knit. Crumb becomes cartoonist-*cum*-crooner, ripe but two decades late for Spike Jones. The Serenaders are Allan Dodge, Paul Woltz, and Robert Armstrong (who does things with a hand saw that Black and Decker have no notion of). Even in the year of Moog Synthesizer Ragtime it is unlikely that this release will

capture the imagination of the greater public. But if the climate were any healthier—or becomes more desperate—these tunes should have all America singing and dancing.

George Arthur, "Capsule Reviews"

These passages illustrate three distinct styles of writing. The first is written in a rather formal style. The writer uses a fairly impersonal, objective tone in dealing with his subject. Furthermore, he assumes that his readers are well acquainted with both the history of classical music and the technical vocabulary used in music studies.

In the second passage the writer employs a general style appropriate for a wide reading audience. The writer assumes that the readers are familiar with Diana Ross's singing, but he does not become too technical in his discussion. Any reader having even a casual interest in and a limited knowledge of popular music could understand and appreciate this review.

The author of the third passage uses an informal style. He addresses his audience in a casual tone, peppering his language with slang. While this passage might not be appropriate for readers of *The New Yorker* or *Stereo Review,* it works fine in *Crawdaddy*.

Before putting his thoughts on paper, the writer must evaluate his audience in terms of their needs and expectations. The same reader who may enjoy the review in *Crawdaddy* may not appreciate the same style in a scientific report. The way to acquire the ability to judge the needs of an audience is through reading and analyzing a variety of writing styles, from general-circulation newspapers and magazines to more specialized publications, such as technical magazines and scholarly or professional journals. The more the writer reads and analyzes writing, the greater his awareness of which methods work for particular subjects and audiences.

Shaping Writing to the Audience

An awareness of the audience's needs and expectations does not mean the writer should change his ideas to suit his readers; doing so would only communicate the writer's unnecessary fear of displeasing the audience or show a lack of respect. On the one hand, the writer who avoids stating his own ideas will not communicate what he actually feels or observes. On the other hand, the writer who restricts his ideas to those he knows the readers are already familiar with will be unlikely to enlighten them or even to capture their interest.

The general principle for writing clear and efficient prose is to shape the expression to fit the thought. That is, the audience should

5

not have to struggle through language more complex than the situation requires. The writer who overcomplicates usually works from the best intentions; he wants to show the readers he is intelligent, well educated, and articulate. Unfortunately, an entirely different impression is created with such pretentious statements as:

> Having commenced my educational career at an institution of higher learning, I found my previous expectations remained unfulfilled.

What the writer meant was simply:

> College is very different from what I expected.

Pretentious, overcomplicated writing is likely to backfire; instead of being impressed, the reader is left confused or laughing.

Writing as simply as possible for the situation at hand does not mean writing down to the audience as if they were children. A general reading audience would resent oversimplified sentences like the following:

> The American Civil War was fought in the United States. This conflict occurred between the northern and southern states. The Civil War lasted from 1861 to 1865. As we can see, America was at war for four years.

As it stands, the paragraph merely treads water. Revised, however, it does more work just as clearly in less space.

> The American Civil War was fought between the North and the South from 1861 to 1865.

Oversimplified prose not only bores readers but also suggests to them that the writer may actually know very little about the subject under discussion.

Exercises

1. Which of the following two passages reflects professional-sounding prose? Identify the elements that indicate the writer has or has not clearly understood the purpose of his communication and the needs of his audience.

> **a.** It is easy to sail once you have learned the basic principles of balancing a boat in water. If you are a novice, you must first learn to keep the boat from jibbing, since this will make steering very difficult. Also, you must learn to tack so that you can sail smoothly into the wind. Practice these two techniques carefully and you will have little problem keeping afloat.

b. Just what actually is love? People are always talking about the topic of love. I will discuss love from the Walt Whitman point of view. He seemed to love everything in the world, simply for the fact that it was matter. Having no discrimination as to what this matter was, Whitman said he loved it because it was a part of everything, and everything worked together to keep this complex world going.

2. For each passage below write a brief description of the type of audience for whom it appears to be intended (general, technical, or professional). State specifically what aspects of the passage led you to your conclusions.

a. Although he was successful on television, in nightclubs, and even on the stage in "one-man shows," Jack Benny was perhaps the most enduring and astonishingly shrewd creation of radio. For anyone growing up in the nineteen thirties and forties, Sunday night at 7 o'clock meant Jack Benny and "the gang."

b. Native American oral literature ranges in form from riddle to folktale, in content from deeply religious emergence narratives to bawdy trickster tales, in function from healing chantways to satiric trials by poetry. Though their work with Native American oral literature was mainly a byproduct of ethnological studies, the quantity of material gathered by anthropologists and folklorists in the late nineteenth and early twentieth centuries from the more than two hundred North American Indian groups is unequaled in the history of folklore.

c. Absolute retardation in the time of emergence of universal cognitive competencies during infancy is not predictive of comparable deficits for memory, perceptual analysis, and inference during preadolescence. Infant retardation seems to be partially reversible and cognitive development during the early years more resilient than had been supposed.

d. Infants who are slow to develop normal behavior skills are not necessarily slow to develop them as they grow older. Children who were retarded as infants often show partial improvement, and they reach the normal rate of development fairly quickly.

MEETING THE READERS' EXPECTATIONS

The same reader may have different expectations about the depth and style in which a subject is handled in different circumstances. But no matter what the circumstance, the reader has a well-defined set of expectations about the writer's responsibility for (1) organizing the material, (2) following general grammatical conventions, and (3) presenting the subject reasonably and logically.

Formal Expectations

All readers begin reading with the assumption that the writer has shaped the material into an organized and meaningful whole. They do not expect to have to organize the order of sentences and paragraphs, to puzzle over the placement of a word or a sentence, to wonder about the meaning of a word or a phrase. Organizing is the writer's job; the readers' job is to follow along—to think, evaluate, understand, and enjoy. If the writer has not done the job of shaping, organizing, and structuring the writing, the readers' work becomes tedious.

Imagine the reaction of a reader who had purchased a new book and started to read the following:

> A visitor from another planet, or another century, would view the exercise as precisely lunatic behavior, but no one from outside would understand it. We must do things this way, these days. If there should be life on the moon, we must begin by fearing it. We must guard against it, lest we catch something.
>
> It is only after the long antiseptic ceremony has been completed that they are allowed out into the sun, for the ride up Broadway.
>
> There is ambiguity, and some symbolism, in the elaborate ritual observed by each returning expedition of astronauts from the moon. They walk briskly, arms up, untouching into a sterile box. They are levitated to another sealed box in Houston, to wait out their days in quarantine, while inoculated animals and tissues cultures are squinted at for omens. They celebrate first of all the inviolability of the earth, and they reenact, each time, in stereotyped choreography, our long anxiety about the nature of life. Instead, they wear surgical masks. They do not, as one might expect, fall to their knees and kiss the carrier's deck; this would violate, intrude upon, contaminate the deck, the vessel, the sea around, the whole earth. They wave enigmatically, gnotobiotically, to the President from behind glass panes, so as not to breathe moondust on him.

What has gone wrong in these three paragraphs? First, the opening paragraph refers to "the exercise." What exercise? So far the paragraph has not given the reader *any* concrete information, much less information about an exercise. Slightly puzzled, the reader continues. The second paragraph refers to "they" and their "ride up Broadway." But who are they, and why are they riding up Broadway? Still looking for answers, the reader moves to the third paragraph. Finally, he has a clue: astronauts returning from the moon. But in the second sentence of that paragraph, the reader again begins to lose the sense of the passage; it becomes impossible to trace a logical or chronological sequence of events or ideas. The reader realizes that there are some new and interesting thoughts here, but since the writing has not been ordered, whatever the writer had in mind stays right there. His message has not been communicated to the reader.

These three paragraphs are an extreme example of unintelligible writing, but they have been scrambled for a purpose. By contrast, examine the three paragraphs as they are actually written, by author Lewis Thomas in his book *The Lives of a Cell:*

> There is ambiguity, and some symbolism, in the elaborate ritual observed by each returning expedition of astronauts from the moon. They celebrate first of all the inviolability of the earth, and they reenact, each time, in stereotyped choreography, our long anxiety about the nature of life. They do not, as one might expect, fall to their knees and kiss the carrier's deck: this would violate, intrude upon, contaminate the deck, the vessel, the sea around, the whole earth. Instead, they wear surgical masks. They walk briskly, arms up, untouching into a sterile box. They wave enigmatically, gnotobiotically, to the President from behind glass panels, so as not to breathe moondust on him. They are levitated to another sealed box in Houston, to wait out their days in quarantine, while inoculated animals and tissues cultures are squinted at for omens.
>
> It is only after the long antiseptic ceremony has been completed that they are allowed out into the sun, for the ride up Broadway.
>
> A visitor from another planet, or another century, would view the exercise as precisely lunatic behavior, but no one from outside would understand it. We must do things this way, these days. If there should be life on the moon, we must begin by fearing it. We must guard against it, lest we catch something.
>
> Lewis Thomas, *The Lives of a Cell: Notes of a Biology Watcher*

How does the organized, structured version of the three paragraphs affect the reader? What do we gain here that we lost in the scrambled version?

The effectively written version begins with a generalization that introduces the reader to the subject. The second sentence, still on a general level, begins to clarify the observation made in the first sentence: the "elaborate ritual" is, specifically, a celebration of the "inviolability of the earth." The next five sentences go into even greater detail to describe exactly what it is the astronauts do on returning to earth. These five sentences are arranged in an exact order. They describe in chronological sequence what the astronauts do after they reach the carrier's deck. The order of these sentences is crucial; jumbling them would be as inefficient as jumbling a list of driving directions.

In the third paragraph, Thomas brings all his points together.

9

He evaluates the behavior he has described as "lunatic," and he indicates the underlying fears that motivate this behavior. The final paragraph is the culmination of the ideas presented in the entire passage. Without the third paragraph, the first two would be pointless; without the first two paragraphs, the last would appear to be senseless. Together, the sentences and paragraphs produce a unified, coherent, and meaningful whole.

Unity and coherence are both qualities found in well-organized, carefully structured writing. *Unity* refers to the observable fact that all the parts of the written work are about the same general subject. Both the scrambled and unscrambled versions of the astronaut piece above exhibit unity; they are both about what happens to returning astronauts and the author's ideas about these events. Coherence, however, is something different. *Coherence* refers to the flow, the continuity—ultimately, the *readability*—of a piece of writing. The scrambled version of the astronaut passage is not at all coherent, but the unscrambled version is.

Conventional Expectations

Conventions are behavior patterns that have been around for so long that we follow them out of habit. Eventually, we become so used to these conventions that we come to depend on them to organize the details of everyday living. Although the words *convention* and *conventional* have recently acquired some negative overtones— because many people associate these terms with stuffiness and needless formality—conventions serve some very useful functions.

In writing, certain conventions have developed because they make the work of the reader and the writer easier and more efficient. Conventions of writing include standard usage in grammar, punctuation, and presentation (spelling, capitalization, and so on).

Grammar refers to the "rules" used to describe how the language works. That the writer will generally follow the conventions of grammar is the most basic expectation a reader brings to any written communication. Readers expect the writer to follow grammatical conventions not because there is any special virtue in following "rules" but so that they can understand the writer. Consider these two sentences:

Our team **plays** a home game **last Thursday.**

On reaching nineteen, my **mother** let me move away from home.

10   In the first sentence, the verb is in the present tense, but the action described has occurred the preceding Thursday. Obviously, the writer meant to say "played" or "next Thursday" or just "on Thursday." By overlooking one convention of grammar (tense, the time of an action expressed by a verb), the writer confuses the reader. In the second sentence, the phrase "on reaching nineteen" appears to describe "mother," but it would be odd for a mother of nineteen to have a child old enough to move away from home. Clearly, this writer meant to say something like, "When I reached nineteen, my mother let me move away from home." In both sentences, the writer does not follow the usual conventions of English grammar, and, consequently, distracts the reader's attention from what the writer really wants to say. Because the reader must stop to puzzle through these ungrammatical sentences, he immediately loses the writer's flow of thought.

Punctuation marks, another convention, are not merely little dots and lines thrown into sentences at random spots; they are signals that join or separate the various parts of a sentence so that readers can read with accuracy and ease. Without punctuation, in fact, communication would be almost impossible. Reading a paragraph, for example, from which the punctuation marks have been omitted is very difficult:

> writers like anything else can be squeezed into two categories if you try hard enough some of them seem to have new books out every week no names you know who you are some are much less prolific and in consequence of their own meager output and the quality of what they have written the literary world hangs on their doings thomas pynchons gravitys rainbow only his third book in over a decade was last years most talked about novel it won the nba and would have won the pulitzer if more of the committees members had been able to read it truman capotes just finished answered prayers has been the subject of discussion and anticipation for almost six years joseph heller is definitely a member of this latter group

This unpunctuated paragraph requires the reader to stop repeatedly and try to figure out where one sentence ends and another begins, to determine which phrases go where in the sentences, to organize and make sense out of the words. If the writer does not assume the job of punctuating, then the reader must do so. Not only is this a difficult, if not impossible task for the reader, but it is an unfair demand on the writer's part.

Now look at the original paragraph. Notice how punctuation makes it easier to read and understand what the writer has written:

11

> Writers, like anything else, can be squeezed into two categories if you try hard enough. Some of them seem to have new books out every week. (No names; you know who you are.) Some are much less prolific, and in consequence of their own meager output (and the quality of what they have written), the literary world hangs on their doings. Thomas Pynchon's *Gravity's Rainbow,* only his third book in over a decade, was last year's most talked-about novel; it won the N.B.A. and would have won the Pulitzer if more of the Committee's members had been able to read it. Truman Capote's just-finished *Answered Prayers* has been the subject of discussion and anticipation for almost six years. Joseph Heller is definitely a member of this latter group.
>
> Ben Pesta, "Joseph Heller: Something Finally Happened,"
> *Changes: Journal of Arts and Entertainment*

Finally, the conventions or presentation—spelling, capitalization, footnoting, and the like—are not plagues inflicted upon writers in order to make their lives more difficult; these conventions facilitate communication. Since the reader is used to seeing such conventions observed in writing, the writer knows how they are interpreted by the reader and can use them accordingly. For example, the conventional ways of spelling words avoids confusion about what word a particular group of letters represents. Although readers can quickly figure out that by *thier* the writer really means *their,* they will become frustrated and confused after stopping a dozen times to adjust their expectation of what the word should look like to what it does look like. The writer who observes the conventions of spelling, grammar, punctuation, capitalization, and other elements that go into efficient and graceful communication helps the reader to understand, learn from, and enjoy what the writer has to say.

Content Expectations

Absolute truths are a great rarity in our world. Consequently, most of the writing we do is aimed not at establishing universal truths but at establishing one opinion about a particular issue. Because reasonable and intelligent people hold vastly different opinions on politics, sports, sex—and just about everything else—the writer's goal is not to prove to the reader the absolute truth of his conclusions but to get readers to hear out and seriously consider his arguments.

How does the writer engage readers as thinking companions and win the trust necessary to keep them reading? The only way is by being honest and straightforward in satisfying the readers' expectations about content—in other words, by playing fair with the readers.

Using Accurate and Sufficient Evidence

Even the most original or interesting conclusion is unconvincing if the grounds for accepting it are not reasonable and logical. An important fact to keep in mind is that readers have experience in the world and that they are going to use that experience in judging the accuracy of the author's statements. Suppose, for example, that a writer is trying to establish the thesis that America is suffering from moral decay. Part of the argument rests on the statement, "Most American teenagers are at present alcoholics." Even before the reader reaches the writer's conclusion, he is going to question the basic premise. It is unlikely that *most* American teenagers have become alcoholics. It is very possible, however, that teenagers are drinking more now than they did five years ago, or that alcoholism rates among teenagers have increased in the last few years.

The professional writer anticipates the reader's critical attitude and shapes his statements in a way that takes into account the reader's natural and justified skepticism. The following statement will do much more to convince the reader of the writer's argument concerning teenage alcoholism, because it is backed up with solid facts:

> Sociologists are studying the reasons for the 20 percent rise in alcoholism among thirteen- to nineteen-year-olds that has occurred in the last five years.

Because the reader may be familiar with the subject under discussion, imprecise, incomplete, or incorrect information will undermine the effectiveness of the communication by calling the writer's credibility into question.

It is easy to see that readers demand accuracy and precision from the facts that are being set before them in print. It is a little more difficult, however, to recognize that they expect the same qualities when reading a writer's personal reactions, judgments, and observations. Consider the following statements:

> What is good for General Motors is good for the country.
>
> Humanity will be destroyed when it runs out of oil.
>
> My whole life changed when I saw *Love Story*.

These statements provoke strong responses in the reader that may not have been intended by the writers. After reading the first sentence, the reader may wonder if the writer has analyzed his thoughts carefully. A reader of the second sentence knows very well that human beings were around long before oil was discovered, and that they are very likely to be around for years to come—even if they do eventually heat their homes and fuel their cars by means of nuclear or some other kind of energy. Anyone who reads the third statement will think that its writer is either very immature or very naive; a single movie rarely changes anyone's *entire* life.

These statements are just plain unbelievable; the reader's own experience tells him that. Professional writers recognize their own skepticism toward such statements and make sure that the content of their writing will strike the reader as thoroughly reasonable.

Acknowledging Other Sides of an Issue

One way the writer can convince readers that his argument is reasonable is to demonstrate that the issue has been examined from more than one side. Neglecting key facts and ignoring opposing sides of an issue will lead readers to suspect that the writer is not well informed about the subject or cannot account for the material left out. In either case, the reader will question the writer's conclusions.

Acknowledging other sides of an argument shows the reader that the writer is being fair and responsible. It also allows the writer to anticipate potential critics before they are able to object to his assertion. Consider, for example, the following excerpts from an article on minors and laws concerning sex-related medical treatment:

> "I don't think that teen-agers should have to ask their parents about contraceptives or abortions; these are their own concerns."

> Parents may disagree, but many teen-agers and a growing number of physicians concur with that statement by Leah Newman, 16, a member of a New York City high school group advocating freedom of sex information. Civil liberties groups are also leaning toward the concept that teen-agers should be able to get medical services where sex is concerned, without involving their parents.
>
> "Kids, Sex and Doctors," *Time*

The body of the article cites various state laws regulating medical care for people under eighteen who seek information, treatment, or medication for sex-related problems. The article also quotes doctors who do not think that minors should have to obtain parental consent before they can get medical help. The author seems to share this opinion but nonetheless acknowledges the other side of the argument in his conclusion:

> Some parents, feeling that their authority over their children will be further undercut, are dismayed by the trend. But there seems to be growing—if reluctant—acceptance of the fact that in a changing society, such measures are necessary.
>
> "Kids, Sex and Doctors," *Time*

In brief, anticipating and acknowledging other sides of an issue also helps to convince readers that the writer has studied the issue thoroughly and that his conclusions are therefore well informed.

Aiming for Accuracy

Professional writers take special care to make sure that the information used in formulating arguments is as accurate as possible. They know that the credibility of their writing depends on the fair and honest use of information.

When using the research of other people to support their own arguments, professional writers should make sure they understand the meaning of the original evidence. Suppose, for example, that a nutritionist reports on a study of food consumption in the United States:

> In 1944 one hundred tons of chocolate were consumed in the United States. However, chocolate consumption was very low that year because during World War II the government rationed chocolate.

A writer who researches chocolate consumption and does not take into account this qualifying information may write a report that comes to an erroneous conclusion:

> In 1944 U.S. chocolate consumption was 100 tons. In 1974 consumption of chocolate reached 900 tons. Over this period of thirty years, annual U.S. consumption of chocolate had increased by 900 percent.

Accuracy in formulating ideas and opinions is as important as using information accurately. Inaccurate statements are often made through *overgeneralization,* drawing a broader conclusion than the evidence at hand warrants. It is overgeneralization that leads to religious, ethnic, and sexist slurs:

> Catholics are superstitious.
>
> Germans are strict.
>
> Women are emotionally unstable.

These statements are easy to identify as prejudiced and nonsensical, but there are other loose generalizations that can be made meaningful only when qualified or explained more fully:

> Americans eat badly.
>
> Quakers believe strongly in their religion.
>
> Factory workers are underpaid.

15

In their present form these statements raise more questions than they answer. What, for example, does eating "badly" mean? Is this assertion true of *all* Americans? What do Quakers *do* to show they "believe" in their religion? Are *all* factory workers underpaid? Although these statements are not entirely clear or meaningful, the reader senses that a germ of truth lies behind them. An effective rewrite, in each case, can bring that germ of truth out into the open:

> Medical studies show that most Americans do not receive the minimum daily requirement of protein, minerals, and vitamins.

> Although it meant hardship for each of them, all the sons of the Quaker family that lived next door to us chose not to renounce their belief in pacifism when they were drafted.

> Even though the average factory worker makes $3.50 per hour, according to Department of Labor statistics, each of the people I worked with last summer in a Boston plastics factory had to work overtime to make ends meet.

Readers are more likely to give serious consideration to the revised statements because they are qualified and explained.

Overqualification, the opposite of overgeneralization, can also determine the reader's confidence in a piece of writing. Writers who anticipate an unfavorable response to their statements (or who perhaps are themselves not sure they are right) sometimes hedge and qualify their assertions until they say very little at all:

> Maybe the Vietnam War was immoral, **but** that is **only my opinion.**

> **It could be, perhaps,** that some people believe there is a God.

These statements, rather than communicating information, reveal the writer's insecurity about what he wants to say. They are so tentative that they say almost nothing about their subject matter.

Another kind of overqualification is made when writers end their remarks with statements like these:

> This essay has explained the importance of a neat appearance to a salesperson.

> I hope I have succeeded in interesting you in backpacking.

In the first example, the writer's statement of intentions is forced. In the second example, the writer's fear of failure is apparent.

Using Statistics and Examples Fairly

When statistics and examples are used in arguments, the figures must justify the conclusions. In our scientific age, statistics seem to have acquired an aura of authoritativeness for their own sake. People tend to think that numbers cannot lie. Professional writers, however, realize that statistics in and of themselves prove *nothing*. They are merely raw data that must be placed in a meaningful and appropriate context.

Read the following report, taken from a neighborhood newspaper, and decide whether its implied conclusion is acceptable:

> West Side police statistics for the first nine months of 1974 show increases in all major FBI crime categories except auto theft. The increases come after significant decreases in local crime during 1972 and 1973, a leveling-off period in the first quarter of 1974, and increased criminal activity after six months of 1974.
>
> "Crime Stats Show Increases in Most Major Categories,"
> *Wisdom's Child*

Before accepting the conclusion the statistics *seem* to point to (that the crime rate increased significantly in New York City during the summer of 1974), several questions must be asked. Is it possible that there were changes in the reporting of crime during this period? Was there a campaign to get citizens to report crimes they otherwise might not have reported? Is the crime rate usually higher in the summer than at other times of the year? The statistics alone do not answer these questions, and more information is needed to justify the conclusion indicated by the report.

The writer should also exercise caution when using examples to prove a point. For instance, a writer arguing that permissive child-rearing practices are better than strict ones would not prove this point if he wrote:

> My parents were very lenient with me; consequently, I grew up to be very well adjusted.

Examples should not be used just because they illustrate a point conveniently. A single example does not make a conclusive case. Most people know at least one well-adjusted person whose parents were very permissive. But this does not mean that all people raised this way grow up to be well adjusted, or that lenient child-rearing methods are better than strict ones.

1.1 Logical Conclusions and Logical Fallacies (log)

Being logical is sometimes confused with being correct. Logic is the *process* of reaching reasonable, legitimate conclusions based on principles or evidence. When the writer has been logical in building his arguments, readers accept the method of reasoning, even though they may disagree with the conclusions.

17

1.1 (log)

There are many methods of drawing conclusions that are false or deceptive. Such methods of reasoning about a subject may seem to be going in the right direction, but somewhere, sooner or later, they veer off the path and end in confusion. A discussion of the most common of these *logical fallacies* follows.

Ad Hominem. A writer who uses an *ad hominem* (Latin, meaning "to the man") argument shifts the entire content of the discussion away from the actual topic under consideration and mounts a personal attack. Suppose, for example, that a reporter is given the assignment of evaluating the President's plan to beat inflation and submits a report that includes these assertions:

> The President's program to beat inflation is entirely unrealistic, and this is not surprising. The President almost flunked economics in college—he was too busy playing football. He has chosen economic advisors who are so far behind the times that they do not know any more than he does. Obviously, the President's economic program cannot work.

Here the reporter has shifted gears entirely and enlisted the aid of prejudice in order to attack the person rather than the plan. Consequently, the argument will fail to convince readers that the writer's opinions are well thought out.

Appeal to Authority. Before citing an authority, it is important to be sure the citation is relevant to the argument at hand. Many beginning writers are intimidated by impressive names and feel they have no right to question the ideas and opinions of so-called experts. But before an authority can properly be used in an argument, he must pass several tests. After all, a person who is knowledgeable in one field may be totally ignorant in another. He may not have up-to-date information, may be prejudiced on a particular issue, or may just be wrong.

Suppose that a leading political figure has just read a new novel that contains passages dealing rather explicitly with sex. In response to the novel, the legislator makes the following statements to the press:

> This book will rot the moral fiber of our youth and make our great country vulnerable to the decadence that surrounds us. It should be banned from the stores, and on no account should it be let into our schools.

A writer would be mistaken to cite the legislator as an authority on the novel's literary worth. Although he may be well known and highly respected, he is not a literary critic. He has not evaluated the book as literature, and his own predispositions have made it impossible for him to find any merit in it. Quoting literary critics or established writers in the field would be far more convincing to readers.

Bandwagon. The aim of *bandwagon* appeal is to prove that something is true or right or good just because most people think it is. This method of arguing is psychologically effective, because it is natural for the reader to want to be in tune with everyone else. However, the value or truth of anything—from an idea to a new deodorant soap—is not established just because the majority of people believe in it or buy it. In addition, popular opinion is fickle; what may be generally accepted one year may be forgotten the next. Professional writers, therefore, avoid attempting to prove their arguments with statements like:

> Susan Gamage—having been endorsed by the Policemen's Benevolent Association, the local branch of the NAACP, the *Daily Times,* and 70 percent of the people polled—is clearly the candidate to vote for.
>
> The best way to save money is to deposit it in the Franklin National Bank. Franklin National has the largest number of depositors of any bank in the city.
>
> Drink wine with every meal. Sixty million French citizens can't be wrong.

While the writer may want to describe or comment on majority opinion, it is a fallacy to depend on it to prove a point.

Just as a majority opinion in favor of something does not establish its worth, neither does popularity establish worthlessness. Every issue must be evaluated on its merits, not according to the number of its supporters or detractors.

Begging the Question (The Complex-Question Fallacy). This method of arguing involves asking two questions in one. In answering the second question, readers find they have automatically answered the first. The classical example of this sort of argument is found in the old wife-beating question, Have you stopped beating your wife yet? If the man answers no, he is obviously a beast. If he answers yes, he is still a beast, because although he says he has stopped beating her, he admits that he *used* to beat her. There is no way out of this one. The phrasing of the question forces an answer that causes even the innocent person to sound guilty. The argument below, for example, will raise at least one question in the reader's mind:

1.1 (log)

> When are we going to stop wasting money on space exploration and put it into mass transportation instead? More and more cities are being overrun with cars. Our environment is being ruined by pollution. In large cities, mass transportation systems could be built with the money that is being wasted on space projects.

The first question that immediately comes to mind is, Is space exploration, in fact, a futile expenditure of money? Before the writer can legitimately ask the question in the first sentence, he must demonstrate the validity of the answer it implies. (Yes, space exploration *is* a waste of money.) Even though readers may not be able to spot the logical fallacy involved here, they will be vaguely dissatisfied with the argument—unless they agree with the implied answer to the writer's question.

Equivocation (Shifting Meaning). Writers who argue equivocally change the meaning of a term in the middle of an argument—always, of course, to their advantage:

> These superior-acting young liberals subvert the ideals on which our country was founded and on which the welfare of our country rests today: justice, freedom, and liberty. They have no regard for any of these ideals. I would pack them up and send them to Russia where they belong. Then you would see an example of justice in action.

In the beginning of this argument the writer appeals to the general definition of justice. However, three sentences later a rather different definition of justice is implied. Now the term refers to whatever punishment seems appropriate for a group of people the writer does not admire. In this case justice becomes a one-way trip to Russia. Ironically, the meaning of the term *justice,* which the writer claims to cherish so highly, has been reversed.

The equivocator enlists the audience's support of an ideal, such as justice, and then switches the meaning of the term and applies it in a much more limited fashion. Readers of the preceding passage, for example, are unlikely to believe that justice means sending people with liberal ideologies to Russia. Like the practitioners of the other logical fallacies, the equivocator tries to hoodwink readers into believing conclusions that they would ordinarily question if such conclusions were presented to them logically.

False Analogy. Writers often use *analogies*—likenesses drawn between two different objects or ideas—in order to make their prose more colorful and exciting. An analogy like "The wind howled through the canyon like a great angry beast" creates a more striking image than the simple statement "The wind blew through the canyon." However, while analogies can enliven one's writing style, inaccurate analogies used in an attempt to prove an argument may lead to an illogical conclusion. For example, a writer who has some proposals for reducing crime in the United States uses the following analogy:

> Just as crime rates are low in England, where policemen are not allowed to carry guns, so, too, could the United States lower its crime rate if policemen here were forbidden to carry firearms.

Although this analogy may sound reasonable, more proof is required if we are to accept the writer's conclusion. The writer would first have to prove that the types and causes of crime in the two countries are similar and that the policy forbidding policemen to carry guns, which worked in Britain, would work as well in the United States.

Non Sequitur. A *non sequitur* (Latin, meaning "it does not follow") is a statement that does not logically follow from the statement, used as evidence, that precedes it. For instance, an essay that advocates increased government spending for military purposes might begin with a discussion of nuclear disarmament:

> Many people think nuclear disarmament would solve all the world's problems. This belief is foolish. Where would America be today were it not the strongest country in the world?

There is no logical connection between the first sentence and the last sentence. The evidence the writer gives (the last sentence) to demonstrate that it is foolish to think nuclear disarmament would solve the world's problems does not, in fact, prove anything. Similarly, statements like, "Since she is from New York City, *she must be awfully snobbish*" and "He is over seven feet tall, *so he must be a great basketball player*" are *non sequiturs* because the italicized portions do not follow from the facts given.

Post Hoc, Ergo Propter Hoc. This kind of illogical argument (Latin, meaning "after this, therefore because of this") assumes a cause-and-effect relationship between two ideas because they are connected in time. Suppose a writer who is arguing against the legalization of marijuana writes the following statement:

> Drug addicts begin smoking marijuana and then go on to heroin. Therefore, marijuana causes heroin addiction.

This argument is like saying:

> All drug addicts drank milk when they were babies. Therefore, drinking milk leads to drug addiction.

Cause and effect is often a difficult and complex relationship to **21**

1.1 (log)

establish. That one event follows another in time does not necessarily mean the second event was *caused* by the first. Two events or ideas may merely bear an *associational* relationship and may not represent a real cause-and-effect relationship.

All the logical fallacies we have examined crop up in writing most often when there is no real evidence for the conclusions drawn, or when the writer has not supplied any evidence and tries instead to force readers into agreement. Even though this attempt to force agreement may be unconscious on the writer's part, readers are sure to notice it and may feel they are not being treated fairly by the writer.

Exercises

1. The following short paragraphs contain examples of the logical fallacies explained above. Identify the fallacy or fallacies in each paragraph and explain what is illogical about the argument.

a. Today, the novel is no longer a serious medium for the best writers. The most intelligent readers today are not reading novels but journalism in its various forms. Just as civilizations rise and fall, so do art forms. The Roman empire is dead, and so is the novel. Most people today, however, seem to care very little about either one.

b. My opponent claims that he will make a better governor than I have been. He issues many statements and makes many promises, but how can you trust a rich boy? He does not have to work and, therefore, he cannot possibly know the problems of the ordinary, hard-working person. He even has a servant whose only job is to get him dressed. Can a man who cannot even dress himself dare to claim he should be the governor of this glorious state?

c. I think it was when I first saw John with his family that I realized what a good executive he would make for the company. The sight of him with his wife and children was so touching.

d. Clyde J. Wingfield deserved to win the Baseball Manager of the Year Award. The Blue Sox were in third place when he took the helm in July, and they were in first place by the beginning of September. Senator E. Z. Winner is proud that Clyde has endorsed him for another term. But then it takes a winner to know a winner.

e. For some reason the twentieth century has been especially influenced by psychoanalysis. The fraudulent theories of that Viennese witch-doctor, Freud, have spread everywhere. More and more, however, mature and sensible men and women are coming to realize how badly they have been fooled.

f. The opponents of the new housing development in Greenwood Forest are the very same people who like to call themselves progressive. The progress of this country, however, has always depended on the opportunity for all people to own their own homes. The opponents say they are for conservation, but what about conserving the traditions that made this country great?

REVISION AND DRAFTING

Revision involves the writer in changing and refining his work until it meets both his own and his readers' expectations. This activity actually begins at the planning stage of a piece of writing and continues until the final copy has been prepared. However, the first major revision usually occurs when the first *draft*, or preliminary copy, of the whole communication has been completed.

Given the limitations of time (deadlines) and space, professional writers refine their work until it most nearly resembles the kind of communication they have in mind. Because writers often find out what they want to say during the very process of saying it, the first draft reflects the writer's uncertainties, hesitations, repetitions, fuzziness, unresolved contradictions, and other verbal confusions. After finishing the rough draft, the writer shifts into the role of reader, or editor, and begins to shape the rough clay of the preliminary copy into a finished sculpture.

Revision involves more than correcting such mechanical errors as misspellings, faulty punctuation, and incorrect grammar. Checking for such flaws, or *proofreading* the copy, is not at all the same activity as revision. Revision involves:

1. deleting ineffective or inappropriate material
2. adding words, phrases, sentences, paragraphs, explanations, and examples for more precision and clarity
3. reorganizing sentences, paragraphs, and entire sections for unity, coherence, and clarity

The goal of revision is to shape the final product to the writer's purpose. Sometimes a favorite example, sentence, or paragraph may have to be deleted if it does not fit appropriately in the context of the communication. Entire paragraphs or sections may have to be reorganized in order to increase clarity or coherence. Even the most experienced writers frequently revise their work half a dozen times before they feel confident it is ready to be read by others.

Every revision—even a minor one—has the potential to set off

23

a chain reaction in the rest of the work. Revise a key word, and the writer finds that others have to be changed, too; revise a sentence, and the sentence following has to be adjusted. The larger the unit changed (word, clause, sentence, paragraph, section, chapter), the greater the impact of that change on the rest of the communication. The time and effort involved in making these adjustments may be even greater than that invested in preparing the draft itself. However, the writer is repaid many times over for his efforts if the revision produces a polished, effective piece of writing that closely mirrors his intention.

RHETORIC AND THE ART OF CONVINCING

This chapter, by exploring the basic standards of effective communication, has provided an introduction to the techniques of professional writing. What we have seen is that successful writing is a *practical* craft. In order to be effective in their craft, professional writers follow certain conventions of spelling, punctuation, and grammar. These conventions govern the form of presentation and are flexible enough to allow for a good deal of variation in writing styles.

At the same time, professional writing is an art—the art of influencing, persuading, and delighting readers. Perhaps the most important element in the art of writing is *rhetoric*—the sum of those activities performed by writers that convince readers to keep reading. Rhetoric is a discipline that has played an important role in every educational system from classical Greece through the Middle Ages to the present day. In past eras, rhetoric was usually considered part of the oratorical arts—the task of convincing an audience through speech. Whether the speaker performed in the ancient Greek marketplace or the Roman senate, the conclusions reached by the audience measured precisely the speaker's effectiveness.

Without a live audience and its immediate feedback, writers face a somewhat more difficult rhetorical task. They must learn to anticipate the effectiveness their arguments will have on readers, and they must master strategies that produce logical and convincing arguments.

Readers are often more consciously aware of reading unsuccessful writing than successful writing. When the writer does not successfully communicate, the flaws in his presentation—in organization, logic, or mechanical detail—are highlighted in the reader's eye. However, when the writer communicates effectively, the reader is

24

more likely to be impressed by what the writer has to say than by the specific parts of the communication. Only when the writer has met basic professional standards through careful writing and revision will the reader's attention be focused on his message.

REVIEW EXERCISES

1. Each of the following passages was written for a different audience. Describe that audience as precisely as possible and support your description by analyzing specific choices and strategies the author has used in each case.

a. The Nonproliferation Treaty that went into force in 1970 was intended to limit permanently the size of the "nuclear club"—the countries with nuclear weapons. In essence, the nuclear countries signing and ratifying that agreement concurred on terms to keep the nonnuclear powers in a "virgin" state without nuclear weapons. But the treaty did not modify the behavior of the nuclear powers, although its terms included the "intention to achieve at the earliest possible date the cessation of the nuclear arms race."

Jack Ruina, *New York Times Magazine*

b. If you have two magnifying lenses, put one on top of the other. Things will look even bigger than they look with one lens. They will look twice as big. Sometimes even more than two lenses are used. A microscope has several lenses in it. Microscopes make tiny things look very big. There are some microscopes that can make things look a thousand times bigger than they really are.

Mae Freeman, *The Wonderful Looking-Through Glass*

c. Historically, women and the sea have not exactly been a twosome. In legends, woman's role was often downright unpleasant: the siren lured unwary sailors to their deaths; the mermaid collected drowned bodies. Though men named ships after their women, and carved female forms into figureheads, a woman aboard was considered unlucky, even as a passenger. It's taken a long time for the woman seafarer to be anything more than "the lady in stateroom B." Though they're still more likely to swim the channel than captain the ship, women are finally getting afloat, particularly in oceanography. The main occupational obstacle that limits dives and occasionally precludes research cruises is Victorian male prudery which insists on separate bathroom facilities.

Nancy Axelrad Comer, "Waterworks: Five Women in Oceanography," *Mademoiselle*

2. Each of the following three passages comes from a student paper. Assign a grade to each on the basis of the rhetorical principles discussed in this chapter. Identify any logical fallacies.

a. We have nothing to fear from communism. It is such an inherently weak doctrine that it is impossible for a movement to thrive without an ulterior force, such as unfulfilled nationalist desires. The fight against communism is an insane one, for communism will die a slow death if left to itself. Our military strategists believe there will be more wars like the Vietnamese War. They are right, but in the future let us fight on the people's side, not with the militarists and the privileged who form the ruling oligarchy. The principles on which this nation was founded are still revolutionary in most of Asia, Africa, and Latin America. I call for worldwide revolution led by the greatest nationalist-revolutionist nation of modern times, the United States of America. Communism will die only if we accept our revolutionary role in the century of nationalism.

b. Man, since the beginning of time, has fought to protect himself against the elements of his environment. As man progressed in technology—as well as in his ability to steal and murder—guns became the inevitable weapons for defense. America dictates the need for defense. In its cities, junkies rob and murder to support their habits, which sometimes reach one hundred dollars per day. The American city and its vastly growing twin, the suburbs, have been a common place for bank robberies, auto thefts, and murder. This has made America a dangerous place to live, thus forcing the people to protect their lives and property with guns. Gun control is a totally useless thing. It is the person, not the gun, that pulls the trigger. If America would get together and give the people what they need, the use of a gun in a detrimental way would stop.

c. It can be logically concluded that the divine within man, which is his salvation, is not only achieved through love but is love itself and that, consequently, love is man's most important obligation. The problem is that love and justice are often contradictory. For instance, the text of *Piers Plowman* says that love includes love of one's neighbors, which in the broadest sense is one's fellow man. Therefore on an absolute scale one should always give to a beggar, even if he does not deserve it, in order to ensure one's salvation. On the other hand, if one gives to an undeserving beggar, one contradicts the edicts of justice—give each his due—and thus undermines society and brings it further into the clutches of the anti-Christ. Thus societal and individual salvation seem to be in irreconcilable contradiction.

Focus and
Organization

2

The writer's responsibility is to organize each communication so that the reader can readily grasp his intention. To find the appropriate organization for the particular writing task, the writer must carefully think through the limits of his subject and thesis. This focusing process, which starts before the actual writing and continues throughout, reveals the most functional organization for ordering the material in a clear and interesting way.

THE SIGNIFICANCE OF FOCUS AND ORGANIZATION

Organizing a communication so that it adds up to a system the reader can grasp may be as simple as ordering the material for easy reference, as in a dictionary:

> origin
> original
> originality
> originally

or as in a government document like the U.S. Constitution:

> Article I
>
> Section 1. All legislative powers herein granted shall be vested in a Congress of the United States, which shall consist of a Senate and House of Representatives.
>
> Section 2. The House of Representatives shall be composed of members chosen every second year by the people of the several states, and the electors in each state shall have the qualifications requisite for electors of the most numerous branch of the state legislature.

The intent of the organization in a dictionary or constitution is straightforward and the order is clear: alphabetical on the one hand, by branches of government on the other. The reader is able to find the information sought only because each item is placed in its appropriate niche.

Whether organizing material for a reference work or for an essay, the writer must establish a pattern, almost a rhythm, so that each item placed on the paper will grow out of what has preceded and will lead logically to a new item. One of the writer's most creative activities is to discover the best way to organize the subject matter so as to communicate the intention to readers clearly and efficiently. Readers rightfully expect the writer to do this, and they cannot and will not accept a set of fragments to be put together at some later time.

Sometimes, even though a writer clearly states his purpose, the order of presentation is so confusing that he does not communicate to readers. For example, if the following instructions appeared on the back of a new car's sun visor, the prospective buyer would be justified in wondering what—if anything—lay beneath the hood.

How to Start Your Car

Release the pressure on the key once the engine has started.
Press the accelerator to the floor and release slowly.
Turn the key clockwise until the starter engages.
The ignition key is square-headed.
Insert the key into the ignition.

However, even if the *order* of a communication is clear, it is still possible for its *purpose* to be confusing:

President Starts Car

December 10
    At the White House this morning, the President started a car. He inserted the square-headed ignition key into the lock, turned the key clockwise until the starter engaged, pressed the accelerator, and then released pressure on the key once the motor had started.

If this were the whole report, the reader would be puzzled about its purpose. Although the information is clearly organized, why would anyone write it? But if, for example, the report explained that the President had been involved in a ceremony introducing a new gas-saving automobile, the reader would understand the intent.

The minimum responsibility of the writer, then, is to shape the material into a comprehensible system with a *purpose*. Occasionally this responsibility is easy to fulfill, as when the writer is given both topic and organization (filling out a job application, for example). In most situations, however, the writer will be told what to write about but will be given no system for ordering the material:

1. Write an essay describing the effects of inflation in various sections of the country.
2. Write an essay on how inflation affects educational institutions.

29

In each assignment, the writer has a clearly defined topic but must structure his material to convey a specific point. The *organization* —the necessary shape for communicating an intention—grows from the nature of the subject the writer is dealing with. In the first assignment above, several organizational patterns are possible, depending on the writer's purpose and his audience. One logical pattern is to present the information by sections of the country, listing all the appropriate statistics immediately after each section: inflation figures for the South, inflation figures for New England, and so forth.

In the second assignment, the writer must organize around the question "How?" In this case, a natural organization might be a presentation of the *results* of the facts: higher fuel costs lead to higher tuition, higher salaries lead to a reduction in teaching staff, and so on. In both assignments, any more detailed organization than those suggested would depend on what purpose the writer thinks would be served by presenting one discussion or set of facts before another.

Discovering the most appropriate organization for the writer's purpose can be as simple as recognizing that the material can be arranged alphabetically. Or it may be as complicated as finding a way to analyze and interpret events, facts, and opinions so that the reader can follow the presentation to a conclusion. Discovering the best system for communicating the purpose is the writer's job. And that job starts with clearly thinking through both subject and intention.

SUBJECT AND INTENTION

Every communication has a *subject* and an *intention*. *Subject* is relatively easy to define: it is the raw material on which the writer draws. Like the labels on the individual folders in file cabinets, the subject defines the category of the material:

1. Hamburger Recipes
2. Inflation
3. Sales Figures for 1976
4. The First Moon Landing
5. Oxides
6. Shakespeare's Comedies

In each of the categories above, the subject is all the raw data that would come under each heading. But *what* is being written about (the subject) is not *how* it is being written. What the reader usually is interested in is not the raw information itself but the writer's purpose in presenting it:

1. Hamburger recipes *are handy for preparing economical meals.*
2. Inflation *can be cured.*
3. Sales figures for 1976 *are down.*
4. The first moon landing *was a marvel of engineering.*
5. *Destructive* oxides *can be retarded.*
6. *Slapstick humor is evident in* Shakespeare's comedies.

What the writer intends in each case above is to demonstrate something about the subject: its value or importance; what can be done with it; how it came about; in short, something about the facts beyond merely naming them.

Although at times the writer may wish to present only the facts, the intention is usually to propose to the reader some position about the facts (their cause, result, importance). Such an intention is a *thesis.* The subject is the name we give to the category of facts; the thesis is the writer's promise to the reader of what will be said about the facts.

Exercises

Identify the subject of each paragraph below and then state its thesis or purpose.

1. *Fried Rice.* Wash quickly: $1\frac{1}{2}$ cups brown rice. Fry in: 3 tablespoons vegetable oil. Keep heat high, stir frequently, and cook until rice is well browned; add slowly: 2 cups soup stock or vegetable cooking water, $1\frac{1}{2}$ teaspoons salt. Simmer 30 minutes and add: $\frac{1}{4}$ to $\frac{1}{2}$ teaspoon crushed black peppercorns, 1 minced clove garlic, pinch each of basil and oregano. Cook until tender, allow about 45 minutes for the total cooking time. Just before serving, stir in: 1 cup diced American, Swiss, or Jack cheese.

Adelle Davis, *Let's Cook It Right*

2. All cultures, even the simplest, seem to be in a continuous state of change. The earlier anthropologists assumed that cultures with relatively simple technology and political structure represented only slightly modified survivals of the ancient conditions of our own ancestors and for that reason dubbed them primitive. Also, largely as a device for simplifying their own theoretical

31

studies, they assumed that such cultures were static or nearly so, persisting unchanged over long time periods. Actually, we have plenty of evidence that this is not the case. Not only do all archeological records, fragmentary as they are, show change through time, but wherever explorers have visited a "primitive" tribe at intervals of a generation or more, their reports show that changes have taken place. Since there is always the possibility that these changes may have been set in motion by the first explorer's visit or by contacts with other Europeans during the interval, the archeological evidence is more reliable. From this it appears that changes in technology, the only part of culture on which it provides conclusive evidence, were exceedingly slow during the first nine-tenths of human existence. Thousands of years seem to have gone by without the introduction of any new tool or appliance. However, during the last twenty-five or thirty thousand years, there has been a progressive speeding up of cultural change. Certain curious features of this speeding up process will be discussed later.

Ralph Linton, "Processes of Culture Change," *The Tree of Culture*

3. I am surely one of the few people pretending to intellectual respectability who can boast that he has read more comic books than attacks on comic books. I do not mean that I have consulted or studied the comics—I have read them, often with some pleasure. Nephews and nieces, my own children, and the children of neighbors have brought them to me to share their enjoyment. An old lady on a ferry boat in Puget Sound once dropped two in my lap in wordless sympathy; I was wearing at the time a sailor's uniform.

Leslie A. Fiedler, "The Middle Against Both Ends," *Encounter*

THE FOCUSING PROCESS

Focusing is the process of narrowing and shaping a subject and thesis. It is the means by which the writer locates or discovers what he wants to say. Bringing a topic into focus means finding a frame of reference for a subject and fixing one's attention on a clear, well-defined point within that frame.

A comparison with photography may clarify this concept. Given a 360-degree circumference, the photographer must choose some area within this circle to photograph. In the area he selects, he must decide which aspect to highlight. The aspect that he chooses, which will depend upon his purpose, becomes the *focus* of the photograph. Thus a snapshot whose purpose is to show a person's interesting

32

facial features will be effective only if taken at close range. If the face is not the central point of attention, or if the photo is taken from too far away, the "message" of the picture will be lost.

The same principles apply to focus in writing. Out of the vast subject area—the raw material—available, the writer must focus on a specific topic with a specific purpose. He must carve from his data a meaningful topic for discussion and decide what to demonstrate about that topic. To do this, the writer must begin by taking stock of his subject area, his interests, and his goals.

Consider, for example, the broad subject area "Shakespeare." The set of facts under this heading is enormous. Writers have spent a lifetime examining very specific aspects of Shakespeare's work. In attempting to limit and shape this subject for a paper, a writer might go through the following focusing process:

I. Shakespeare
  A. Shakespeare's dramatic works
    1. Shakespeare's tragedies
      a. *King Lear*
        (1) Lear's daughters
          (a) character of Cordelia

In a sense, focusing is a process of self-examination, of asking questions to determine one's interests and goals. Given the subject of Shakespeare, the writer first thinks, "What do I want to say about Shakespeare?" Depending on his knowledge or interests, he successively narrows the subject area: he is interested in Shakespeare's plays rather than in his poems; he prefers Shakespeare's tragedies; he has read and feels he understands *King Lear*. Now the writer asks "What do I have to say about *Lear?*" He is interested in Lear's daughters, especially the character of the youngest daughter, Cordelia.

Each successive narrowing of the subject brings the topic into sharper and sharper focus, until finally the writer has a *real* subject—a manageable topic around which he can formulate a discussion. In addition, focusing moves the writer closer and closer to discovering a thesis. For example, when the writer asks himself the next logical question, "What is Cordelia's character?", he is beginning to form a specific attitude toward his subject. The writer may make the following observations:

1. Cordelia is loyal to her father.
2. Cordelia refuses to be hypocritical.
3. Cordelia is the youngest yet the wisest daughter.
4. Cordelia is stubborn.

33

Once the writer begins investigating his subject at this level, he is entering the area of argument. He may wonder, "What are the reasons for Cordelia's loyalty?" or, "How is she wiser than her sisters?" or, "Why is she stubborn?" His answers to these questions can form the basis for a specific thesis about Cordelia's character.

The focusing process may also operate in the reverse direction, much like the zooming out of a movie camera to show a panorama. Sometimes the writer may focus so closely on a subject that he has to reverse the process slightly to get a grip on the material—a frame of reference in which to work. Suppose the writer has selected as a focused subject Cordelia's loyalty to her father. He may start writing down examples of Cordelia's loyalty and his thoughts about them. But this topic alone leads him no further, so he begins considering loyalty in a larger framework—the loyalty of Cordelia's counselor, Kent; the loyalty of Gloucester's son Edmund; even the loyalty of the Fool. In this reverse process, the writer may discover that loyalty takes many different forms in different characters and that it is a dominant theme in the play. That is, the writer finds himself intrigued by a narrow topic and then works his way back to find himself engaged in a broader concern: Shakespeare's attitude toward loyalty as demonstrated in *King Lear*.

Whatever direction the focusing process takes, it begins *before* the writer actually sets his thoughts on paper and continues during the writing process. In attempting to focus a topic, the writer continually changes his perspective on the subject matter. In so doing, he discovers what interests him about a subject, what the limits of the subject are, and how he can begin to talk about the subject with a specific purpose.

Why Focus?

Neither a subject nor an intention is an end in itself. Neither in itself leads to a communication with the reader. Even a well-defined subject needs a purpose, and a purpose must be shaped to the nature of the material available. The writer's task is to convert a loose set of ideas or beliefs—a generalized purpose—into a *meaningful* communication for the reader. The focusing process is the means by which the writer achieves this goal.

Focusing Shapes Writing to Its Context

Every writing task is both limited and shaped by a context. This context includes the nature of the assignment, the writer's knowledge of the subject, and the time and space available to him. The process of focusing helps the writer to fix on a topic and thesis within the constraints imposed by context.

Suppose, for example, that the writer is asked to write a five-hundred-word critical essay on some aspect of Shakespeare's work. Although the subject area of the assignment is very broad, the context is actually quite narrow. To begin with, the writer is limited by the nature of the assignment: a critical analysis of Shakespeare's works. The assignment excludes such items as a study of the man and his life, an examination of the Elizabethan background, or a survey of how Shakespeare was viewed by his contemporaries. It is to be a *literary* discussion of Shakespeare.

The writer is also limited by his knowledge and the time available to him. Although he might be interested in discussing certain rhetorical devices—for example, Shakespeare's use of oxymoron (a type of paradox)—he may not have sufficient knowledge of this topic or the time to do the in-depth research needed to acquire that knowledge. Focusing helps to narrow the writer's options and to find a topic that can be handled properly in the time available to him.

Finally, the writer is limited by the available space. The writer of the Shakespeare essay must find a topic that can be covered adequately and clearly within five-hundred words. The subject "Shakespeare's works" is far too broad, as are "Shakespeare's tragedies," "an analysis of *King Lear*," and even "the character of Lear's daughters." The writer must constantly narrow his subject to find a manageable topic that can be covered in the space limitations set.

Focusing Defines Needed Information

Another practical reason for focusing is to discover the depth and scope of information needed to cover a topic. Focusing on a narrow subject area sets limits on and defines the *types* of information a writer will need. Let us assume that in the assignment on Shakespeare the writer has chosen to discuss the reasons for Cordelia's loyalty to her father. To develop this idea, the writer will first need *overview information:* general expressions of loyalty in *Lear,* how loyalty is defined or evidenced in the play. In addition, the writer will need *specific information:* examples of Cordelia's loyalty in words or actions, observations by other characters, Lear's reactions to his daughter's behavior. Only after the writer has carefully focused his subject and thesis will he know the types of information he needs to discuss it fully.

35

Focusing Leads to Organization

A final reason for focusing is to help the writer shape his material into a comprehensible whole for the reader. A clearly focused subject and thesis can lead the writer to a specific pattern of organization for his topic. For example, the question "Why does Cordelia remain loyal to Lear?" suggests a possible organization for the writer's answer. The order could be a set of interconnected reasons explaining Cordelia's behavior and a discussion organized by cause and effect.

The process of thinking through and focusing on a subject and intention involves the writer in the processes of organizing—sorting out the facts, defining them, selecting and ordering them. Through the act of focusing, the writer comes to understand both the nature of his material and what he wants to say.

Exercises

1. Focus each of the following subject areas on a topic that would be appropriate for a five-hundred-word essay. Narrow each subject in four or five separate stages, as shown in the example in this section.

   a. Inflation
   b. Professional sports
   c. Travel in Europe
   d. American poetry
   e. Religious leaders

2. Write *three* specific essay titles for one of the general subjects listed below. What types of information would be needed to develop each essay fully?

   a. America's conversion to a volunteer army
   b. Changing sex roles in the 1970s
   c. The transition from high school to college
   d. The role of the Supreme Court in American government

3. Evaluate each of the following topics as an appropriate subject for a one-thousand-to-two-thousand-word essay. Is the topic clear and specific? Can it be covered adequately within the space limitations of the essay? Revise any topics that seem poorly focused.

   a. How I financed my new car
   b. The pros and cons of day-care centers
   c. Myths about food
   d. What were the Middle Ages like?

    e. The artificial surface in baseball: Has it changed the game?
    f. Comic relief in *Hamlet*
    g. Teenage crime
    h. The best equipment for hiking

2.1   Focusing a Subject

There are many approaches writers can use to focus a subject. They can divide a subject into parts; compare parts; combine parts into wholes; or analyze a subject in terms of its purpose, goals, or effects. All these processes—categorizing, comparing, contrasting, combining, analyzing—are natural patterns human beings use to think about and evaluate their experiences. Both writers and readers share these habits of mind; they are, therefore, natural ways to organize. For example, when a writer presents his subject through comparison and contrast—say, the memory of a computer compared with that of a human—the reader is automatically signaled about what to expect: a discussion of the similarities and differences between the two types of memory, and what each similarity and difference implies. This presentation is not arbitrary; it is the way the human mind typically organizes and clarifies experience. All the techniques used in focusing a subject are natural ways in which people think, argue, and decide.

2.1a   Classification

The simplest way to start limiting and defining a subject is to classify it—to divide it into parts according to some system. One such system is *classification by species,* dividing a subject into unique or natural subclasses. Consider the broad subject areas "private enterprise" and "advertising." Both subjects can be divided into logical subclasses:

   I. Private Enterprise
     A. Forms of private enterprise
       1. sole proprietorship
       2. partnership
       3. corporation

   I. Advertising
     A. Types of advertising
       1. media
       2. direct mail
       3. outdoor
       4. point-of-purchase
       5. word-of-mouth

37

2.1b Cause and Effect

Another way to classify a subject is to analyze its structure. How is an individual item put together? What are its parts? Such *classification by anatomy* is similar to dissecting a plant or animal in order to examine its structural elements. Structural classification can also be used to further subdivide a species or subclass, as shown in the first example below:

I. Private Enterprise
  A. Components of private enterprise
    1. private ownership of production
    2. private property
    3. free competition
    4. limited intervention of government
I. Advertising
  A. Elements of an advertising campaign
    1. capturing buyer's attention
    2. holding interest
    3. arousing desire to buy
    4. persuading buyer to buy
    5. reinforcing buyer's decision

However, classification does not in itself imply an intention. The writer who divides a subject into parts is not *proving* anything; he is limiting the subject by sorting out the facts. Nonetheless, classification is a useful first step in defining a subject. It can help the writer to see his subject clearly and to focus on a topic that may eventually suggest a thesis.

2.1b Cause and Effect

Cause-and-effect focusing limits a subject by concentrating on its development or history. When a writer asks any of the following questions about a subject, he becomes involved in seeking causes and effects:

1. How did it come to be as it is?
2. What happened to it?
3. What will it do to something else?

Like classification, cause-and-effect focusing is a natural method of inquiry, a basic means by which people come to know or understand facts. The two sample subject areas outlined above could also be focused by cause and effect in several ways:

I. Private Enterprise
  A. Origins of private enterprise in the United States
  B. The rise of the corporation
  C. Effects of corporate ownership on American business

    I. Advertising
      A. Steps in developing an advertising campaign
      B. How advertising costs affect retail prices
      C. Advertising as a means of increasing sales, improving product image, building good will

Cause-and-effect focusing can lead a writer to a broad topic within a subject area (the rise of the corporation) or to one that is more precise (advertising and higher sales). In the latter case, the focused subject may lead the writer to a possible thesis ("Advertising does— or does not—result in increased sales").

2.1c   Function

Focusing by function involves analyzing a subject in terms of its purpose and use. If focusing by cause and effect raises the question "Where did it come from?", focusing by function asks the question "What is its purpose?":

    I. Private Enterprise
      A. Goals of private enterprise
         1. maximum profit
         2. efficient supply of goods
         3. free and open competition

    I. Advertising
      A. Purposes of advertising
         1. to inform
         2. to persuade
         3. to remind

Focusing by function concentrates on purpose rather than on classes, structure, or development. Again, such an approach to a subject may begin to suggest a thesis to the writer ("Maximum profit is the major goal of private business").

2.1d   Evaluation

Focusing by evaluation limits a subject by concentrating on judgments or rankings. It involves a writer's assessments of effectiveness, appropriateness, correctness, or truth as related to a given topic:

    I. Private Enterprise
      A. The degree to which free competition is maintained in a private enterprise system
      B. The best form of ownership for a new business venture

    I. Advertising
      A. Ethical practices in modern advertising
      B. The degree to which advertising is successful in building good will

2.1e Relationships

In each of these cases, the writer's opinion or assessment of the topic could form the basis for a specific thesis ("The recent advertising campaigns of oil companies have improved—or worsened—their image").

2.1e Relationships

Focusing by relationships concentrates on the connections that exist among various sets of facts. The connections may be either within a specific class or among classes:

I. Private Enterprise
   A. The separation of ownership and management in a corporation
   B. Private enterprise versus government as a means of efficiently distributing goods and services
II. Advertising
   A. Advantages of point-of-purchase advertising over media advertising
   B. The relationship between advertising and politics

Note that in the second example in each category above, focusing by relationships actually involves broadening a subject to include a larger set of facts. Although the subject "private enterprise" has been narrowed to its function in distributing resources, focusing by relationships has broadened the scope of discussion to include this function in another topic area (government).

2.1f Combined Types of Focusing

Although we have discussed the various types of focusing as separate activities, all these processes are interrelated. In practice, most writers will use a combination of approaches to define and focus a subject.

Almost every type of subject focusing involves some preliminary classification. For example, in order to determine the best form of ownership for a new business venture, the writer must first distinguish different forms of private enterprise. Before discussing relationships among different types of advertising, the writer must define the classes. Similarly, focusing by evaluation usually involves the consideration of relationships or function. To discuss the effectiveness of advertising in increasing sales, for example, the writer must first establish a relationship between advertising and sales or identify increased sales as a goal (function) of advertising.

The possibilities for combining different types of focusing are almost endless. The challenge to the writer is to examine various approaches and test different combinations until he finds the most suitable method. As the next section will show, the best method is determined not only by the subject but by the writer's purpose in dealing with his material.

Exercises

1. Focus two of the following subject areas in at least three different ways (classification, cause and effect, function, evaluation, relationships).

Example Subject: The U.S. government
Classification: the executive, legislative, and judicial branches
Function: The role of the legislative branch in government
Evaluation: the degree to which the legislative branch serves the interest of the people

a. Narcotics laws in the United States
b. American movies
c. The English language
d. College grading practices

2. Each of the following passages indicates the direction and scope of a much longer piece. Define the subject of each piece and discuss the method by which each author has focused his subject. More than one type of focusing may be found in each.

a. The index of a book points out the page or pages on which certain information can be found. The card catalog, which is made up of individual catalog cards, is an *index* to the materials in a library. Each catalog card indicates, by means of a call number, the location of a book or other kind of material. The catalog card may give the pages on which certain material can be found in a given book; for example, the card may have the notation *Bibliography: pp. 210–212.*

Jean Key Gates, *Guide to the Use of Books and Libraries*

b. It seems proper that I should prefix to the following biographical sketch, some mention of the reasons which have made me think it desirable that I should leave behind me such a memorial of so uneventful a life as mine. I do not for a moment imagine that any part of what I have to relate can be interesting to the public as a narrative, or as being connected with myself. But I have thought that in an age in which education, with its improvements, is the subject of more, if not of profounder study than at any former

41

period of English history, it may be useful that there should be some record of an education which was unusual and remarkable, and which, whatever else it may have done, has proved how much more than is commonly supposed may be taught, and well taught, in those early years which, in the common modes of what is called instruction, are little better than wasted. It has also seemed to me that in an age of transition in opinions, there may be somewhat both of interest and of benefit in noting the successive phases of any mind which was always pressing forward, equally ready to learn and to unlearn either from its own thoughts or from those of others.

John Stuart Mill, *Autobiography*

c. To examine, as light-heartedly as possible, the relationship between murder and metaphysics I am going to look into the work of two writers who stand at opposite poles—Mickey Spillane and Georges Simenon—but who have one arresting thing in common. Mickey Spillane is the author of super-tough whodunits which belong, intellectually, to approximately the same world as the comic strip. Georges Simenon, who has published a raft of detective novels featuring Inspector Maigret and also a great deal of serious fiction, has been mentioned as a candidate for the Nobel Prize. The common denominator between Spillane and Simenon is that both are phenomenally popular. Spillane, during the past three years, has become the fastest-selling writer in America; Simenon, over the past twenty years, has been probably the fastest-selling writer in Europe.

Charles J. Rolo, "Simenon and Spillane: The Metaphysics of Murder for the Millions," *Town and Country*

Subject and Thesis Work Together

Although the discussion up to now has treated subject focusing as a separate activity from thesis focusing, the two processes usually work together. As noted in the preceding section, the focusing of a subject will often lead to the establishment of a thesis. As a topic becomes more and more precise, the possibilities for discussing it become well defined. By the same token, a preliminary decision about intention will often refine and shape a topic by delineating clearly the depth and scope of the subject area.

For example, through subject focusing, the topic of pollution might be narrowed as follows:

I. Pollution
   A. Industrial pollution

1. industrial pollution of rivers and oceans
   a. effects of industrial pollution of rivers and oceans on human life

Narrowing the subject to the *effects* of water pollution begins to suggest a purpose: to demonstrate how a cause (pollution) leads to a certain result. But it is still necessary to focus on a specific effect. From his knowledge and experience, the writer may decide that one evident effect of water pollution is that it threatens the world's food supply: it upsets the ecological balance of the oceans; it kills or contaminates various forms of marine life. Note that in the process of specifying a thesis the writer has also expanded the subject area (pollution *plus* food resources), although in each case he has focused on a narrow area within the particular subject.

Focusing is directed by the writer's intention and leads both to the real subject and to possible thesis statements. It is in the context of narrowing a subject and defining an intention that the writer discovers what he is going to write about.

2.2 Focusing a Thesis

A writer begins to focus a thesis by deciding on a general purpose for a given writing task. At the simplest level, the writer's purpose may be to *relate* the facts about a subject in a way that interests readers. Or the writer may seek to *explain* a subject to convince readers of its importance, relevance, or value. At a more complex level, the writer may seek to *argue* the merits of a topic to convince readers of the justness, correctness, or appropriateness of his point of view.

Sometimes, particularly in simple or short writing assignments, the decision about purpose may be all that is needed in thesis focusing, and organization will follow directly. For example, if the writer is seeking to describe an experience or explain a set of facts, his task may be to organize the material very simply: to alphabetize it, discuss it in categories, explain what it does. However, if the writer's purpose is to present an argument—to take a position on the facts—then focusing involves the additional step of framing a specific thesis. The writer must focus on a clear and workable thesis statement before he can fully define his subject or organize his material.

What elements produce a well-focused thesis? In a sense, a good thesis is one that leads to a successful argument. That is, the writer

43

knows that it works only after he has tried it. Having framed a specific thesis, he sketches the broad areas of argument and evaluates their effectiveness. It is possible to suggest specific guidelines for recognizing potentially unsuccessful thesis statements and for finding workable topics for discussion.

2.2a Find a Thesis Worth Arguing

Clearly, no thesis will succeed unless it is worth arguing—worth the writer's effort to demonstrate it and the reader's effort to understand. Inexperienced writers often devote a great deal of time and effort trying to prove an obvious thesis. Consider the following statements:

> *Huckleberry Finn* is a novel.
>
> India is suffering from a food shortage.
>
> There are biological differences between men and women.

In each of these cases, the writer is asserting as an argument a set of facts no reader would dispute. *Huckleberry Finn* is by definition a novel; it is so categorized by convention. Few people would question the assertion or be interested in an argument that makes it an issue. The same is true of the other two statements. Both assert facts as they are currently viewed. Although they are clearly provable, they are not worth arguing about.

Such statements are better treated as points of departure rather than as points to be proved. That is, the writer should focus his thesis further and ask: "What are the *implications* of such a state of affairs?" or "Given this fact, what else is true?" By asking such questions the writer might arrive at the following focused thesis:

> *Huckleberry Finn* is a racist novel.

Such a thesis is clearly open to argument and immediately calls to mind certain facts the writer will need for proof: some knowledge of racial concepts when *Huckleberry Finn* was published and specific examples of how racial stereotypes are used in the book.

Similarly, the writer might argue the causes of India's food shortage or propose various solutions. He might discuss the social consequences of biological differences between men and women or argue that such differences are a false basis for social distinctions between the sexes. In each case, the writer has a topic of interest worth arguing about and a thesis that suggests the areas of information he will need to prove his point.

Furthermore, such a thesis begins to suggest further extensions.

For example, the fact of India's food shortage could support the contention that the country's government and social systems need to be changed. The fact of discrimination against women based on biological differences could suggest the need for a new educational policy or changes in the law.

Although at times it may be necessary and interesting simply to establish a fact, ultimately the reader is interested in the results or consequences of the fact. Proving the world is round may be interesting; the ideas suggested by the fact are still more interesting.

2.2b Base the Thesis on a Realistic Premise

An effective argument is one that makes a realistic and reasonable point to readers. What is realistic and reasonable varies among people, to be sure, but the basis of an argument—its premise—must be within the bounds of possibility, and its point, once reached, should not be meaningless or trivial, as it is in the following:

> Noah's ark could have held all the animals in biblical times because Darwin's theory shows that there were fewer species in Noah's day.

The problem with such a thesis is that the writer attempts to compare two incompatible sets of beliefs—one based on religious faith, the other on scientific evidence. Moreover, the premise does not take into account a key point in both Darwin's central hypothesis (species evolve slowly over thousands of years) and in the religious tradition (the belief that all species were created at once). The average reader will immediately be aware of these omissions. And even if the thesis could be reasonably argued, what would it add up to except that the story of Noah's Ark *might* be true?

A more common type of trivial or unrealistic thesis is the artificial question, as illustrated in the following statements:

> The Great Gatsby would have been a different novel if Hemingway had written it instead of Fitzgerald.
>
> The English political system would have been different if the Norman Conquest had not occurred.

In both of these examples, the projected arguments have little practical value for readers. They are, at best, futile intellectual exercises—self-evident yet difficult to demonstrate, and pointless even if provable. The writer must reassess his objectives and focus on a thesis of interest or practical value to readers:

> Fitzgerald's treatment of the romantic ideal in The Great Gatsby is similar to that of Hemingway in The Sun Also Rises.

45

> The Norman Conquest had a significant effect on the political structure of Great Britain by changing the relationship between land owners and land tillers.

In these thesis statements, the writer proposes a realistic evaluation of his material rather than a theoretical discussion with no clear purpose or point.

A realistic thesis must also be a reasonable interpretation of the facts—that is, readers must find the thesis logically acceptable so that they are willing to listen to it. A thesis that attempts too sweeping a connection—the farfetched thesis—will alienate readers and be difficult to prove satisfactorily:

> Gun control will force every man, woman, and child into slavery.

Since gun control is a controversial issue, it is a potentially fruitful subject for a thesis. Many points of view can be taken on it. However, the writer of the thesis statement above has chosen to argue for a remote, tenuous connection—gun control and slavery. Few people view slavery as a realistic problem posed by gun control. It is doubtful that readers would accept the writer's premise, and unlikely that they would be willing to invest their time and energy in hearing the writer out. In view of the facts, the argument calls for too great an emotional commitment by readers. The writer would have done better to restrict his thesis to one that asserts a plausible and demonstratable connection:

> A restriction on private ownership of handguns will not only limit our freedom as individuals but also our constitutional right to bear arms.

Such a thesis statement offers the writer a clear line of reasoning and a foundation that supports argument. The writer could define personal freedom so as to argue legitimately that any government interference with individual rights is potentially tyrannical. The writer could also argue that Article II of the Bill of Rights was added to the Constitution precisely to assure that people would have the means to revolt against the government if necessary. To support the argument, evidence from feudal law, which limited to the nobility the right to own arms, could be cited as evidence that the people need weapons to remove their rulers. Although the readers may disagree with the argument and the interpretation of the facts, they must be able to accept the premise as reasonable and agree that it is worth listening to.

2.2c   Restrict the Thesis to a Workable Topic

A thesis must be appropriate to its context—the context of the writer's audience, his subject, and the time and space available to him. Often, inexperienced writers attempt to take on too large an argument, one that exceeds the bounds of their knowledge and the time and space they have to accomplish their task. Such an *over-ambitious thesis* will either overwhelm the writer or result in an empty, superficial argument:

> Pollution in America can be controlled.

The area of argument projected by this thesis is enormous. It cannot possibly be covered in a short essay. Nor does the writer have the time to sort out the vast quantities of information available on the subject and reach meaningful or practical conclusions. The argument is unsuited to the context of the writing assignment. Such a thesis must be restricted to a workable topic. The writer could, for example, suggest specific ways in which a specific type of pollution could be avoided:

> Air pollution from cars can be reduced by giving people incentives to use public transportation.
>
> Noise pollution in urban areas can be controlled by constructing truck routes around the cities.
>
> Water pollution by industry can be reduced by forcing companies to recycle their wastes.

These thesis statements begin to define a manageable area for argument in an essay. They can be covered meaningfully with a limited amount of information seeking and within the constraints of the time and space imposed on the writer.

2.2d   Avoid a Circular Thesis

Beginning writers often argue in a circular fashion, either by using an argument that assumes the very issue to be proved or by using the premise of an argument as proof.

Suppose that a writer is puzzling over the following question: "What did the Japanese hope to gain in their 1941 bombing of Pearl Harbor, which destroyed over a dozen battleships and crippled the American fleet?" The writer might begin to answer the question in the following manner:

> Japan bombed Pearl Harbor in 1941 in order to destroy the American fleet. Although America was not yet at war, the Japanese destroyed many American ships and sought to cripple U.S. naval power.

47

In this response, the writer uses the premise of the argument, as stated in the original question, as his answer. The thesis is circular: the writer is saying, in effect, that Japan destroyed the American fleet in order to destroy the American fleet. On another level, the writer has simply not dealt with the question; he has avoided it.

Had the writer read more closely, he would have understood the specific question: *What* did Japan hope to gain by bombing Pearl Harbor (or by destroying the American fleet)? The writer might conclude:

> Japan bombed Pearl Harbor in order to gain time to complete its conquest of the Pacific.

> Japan bombed Pearl Harbor in order to gain allies among neutral nations by demonstrating its naval superiority.

Here, clear definition of the writing task leads to a logical and appropriate argument, one that uses the premise as its point of departure rather than as a point of proof.

Exercises

1. Each of the following passages has a specific thesis, either stated or implied. Read the passage carefully, and state its thesis in a brief sentence.

> **a.** If you're feeling slightly more optimistic these days about personal safety in the city of New York, you're not entirely out of your mind. The statistics alone should make you feel better: last year, our rank among the 25 largest cities for overall crime dipped down to eighteenth. Now we are informed by a recent statistical study that New York is safer by far than twelve other selected big cities. None of these announcements should be taken, of course, as encouragement to go streaking along empty streets in the wee hours of the morning. But the statistics do—it seems to a growing number of people one talks with these days—indicate that progress, however modest, has been made in the war on crime.
>
> Thomas Plate, "Ups and Downers," *New York*

> **b.** The log house was a large and sturdy structure and would have been a comfortable place had it not been very drafty. One of the Long girls remembers it as the "biggest, coldest house" she ever saw. Built of split logs, it had a center hall twelve feet wide, with two rooms on either side and an L-shaped back wing, containing a kitchen and a dining room. Three more Long children were born

in this house, two girls, Olive and Clara, and on August 30, 1893, a boy who was given the name of his father. Huey P. Long, Jr., could legitimately utter the politician's stock boast, that he had been born in a log cabin.

T. Harry Williams, *Huey Long*

c. The most obviously upsetting force likely to strike the family in the decades immediately ahead will be the impact of the new birth technology. The ability to preset the sex of one's baby, or even to "program" its IQ, looks, and personality traits, must now be regarded as a real possibility. Embryo implants, babies grown *in vitro*, the ability to swallow a pill and guarantee oneself twins or triplets, or, even more, the ability to walk into a "babytorium" and actually purchase embryos—all this reaches so far beyond any previous human experience that one needs to look at the future through the eyes of the poet or painter, rather than those of the sociologist or conventional philosopher.

Alvin Toffler, *Future Shock*

2. Evaluate each of the following thesis statements as an appropriate topic for a four- or five-page essay. What principle of effective thesis writing does it violate? Revise *three* of the statements so that they focus on a workable thesis.

a. Inflation is a worldwide problem.
b. We would have been better off if the American Revolution had never occurred.
c. The telephone is a form of mass communication.
d. French cooking is better than Italian cooking.
e. Lowering the voting age to eighteen will destroy democracy as we know it.
f. Benedict Arnold was a traitor because he gave American military secrets to the British.
g. All the great Russian novelists treat war as a major theme.

2.3   Subject and Thesis: A Contract with the Reader

The writer's statement of his subject and thesis is an implicit contract with the reader. In undertaking discussion of a topic, the writer is asking the reader to become engaged in his material, to accept or listen to his argument. In return, the writer makes certain promises to the reader: to stay within the limits of his subject, to develop the subject clearly and adequately, and to communicate his intentions in full to the reader. The writer's fulfillment of this

49

contract involves more than a carefully focused subject and intention; it also requires a focused *presentation* of the topic. The writer can focus his presentation only through a careful sifting and selection of facts and clear, logical development of ideas.

2.3a Keep in Focus

The writer's first obligation to the reader is to keep his writing in focus. Fulfilling this part of the contract requires distinguishing between material that is relevant to the topic and material that is irrelevant. It also means selecting facts that convey and support the writer's intention. A misplaced or irrelevant fact can interrupt the flow of the material and confuse the reader.

Failure to keep in focus can take two distinct forms: wandering away from the subject and wandering away from the thesis. Both of these problems are illustrated in the paragraph below:

Anatomy of Saturn 5

Everything about the Saturn 5 rocket was big and splendid. When topped with the Apollo spacecraft, the three-stage rocket stood 363 feet tall—more than twice the height of the Statue of Liberty. **The statue, which resides in New York harbor, was presented by France to the American government in 1886.** The Saturn's first, or booster, stage was the biggest aluminum cylinder ever machined. Its valves were as big as barrels; its fuel pumps (for feeding engines at the rate of 700 tons of fuel a minute) were bigger than refrigerators. Its pipes were big enough for a man to crawl through, and its engines were the size of trucks. **Nonetheless, microminiaturized circuits in the third stage could not be distinguished by the unaided eye.**

The intention of this paragraph is implicit in the opening sentence: to demonstrate how everything about the Saturn rocket was big. However, the two boldfaced sentences weaken the focus of the discussion and obscure the writer's point. The first intrusive sentence—an "explanation" of the Statue of Liberty—is unrelated to the subject and unnecessary to clarify the writer's comparison. Contrast this statement with the writer's parenthetical explanation of the Saturn's fuel pumps in the fifth sentence. There the explanation is useful both in clarifying part of the subject and in enhancing the writer's point about bigness.

The second intrusive sentence, at the end of the paragraph, violates the writer's thesis. Rather than amplifying the theme of bigness, it is actually a new thesis (that parts of the Saturn were also very small). This seemingly minor addition—while still on the subject—confuses the writer's point. To avoid such confusion, both sentences should be eliminated.

2.3b Cover the Topic Adequately

Another obligation of writer to reader is to cover the topic adequately. The writer must make sure he has drawn sufficiently upon his data (subject matter)—to clarify every aspect of the topic and to justify his purpose. At the most basic level, covering the topic adequately means including *all* the pertinent facts. Note how this aspect of the reader-writer contract is violated in the following passage:

> Instructions for Hamburger Grill
>
> Assembling the outdoor hamburger grill is extremely easy. All you need are the five basic parts of our new model: two wheels, a base, the detachable grill, and the center grill support. First, screw the grill support into the hole in the center of the grill. Then slide the attached support into the slot in the base. You are now ready to roll the assembled grill anywhere in your backyard.

The problem with these instructions is that they fail to mention what is to be done with the unassembled wheels. If the sentence "Attach the wheels to the special inserts at the bottom of the base" were added after the next-to-last sentence, the directions would make perfect sense. The omission of this key point violates the implicit intention of the paragraph: to show purchasers how they can assemble a *working* hamburger grill from the parts mentioned. That this intention is not expressly stated is beside the point. The writer has failed to cover his topic adequately—to provide readers with the information they need to understand his point.

At a more complex level, adequate topic coverage means proper utilization or *treatment* of the facts. The writer who undertakes a comparison must spell out the comparison rather than list two separate sets of facts side by side. The writer who seeks to demonstrate a causal connection between two ideas must prove the connection rather than state or assume it. An illustration must be truly illustrative; a definition must truly define. In all these cases, the writer has a specific obligation to use his material to convey his intentions fully.

2.3c Present a Meaningful Arrangement of Ideas

A final aspect of the writer's contract with the reader is to present the facts in meaningful order—that is, the order the reader needs to understand the material. In an argument, a meaningful arrangement is one that shows how the evidence *proves* the point; in a comparison, it is one that shows how two ideas are truly comparable. In an explanation, it is a set of facts that draws logically to a conclusion. Suppose, for example, that the hamburger grill instructions were presented as follows:

51

> Assembling the outdoor hamburger grill is extremely easy. All you need are the five basic parts of our new model: two wheels, a base, the detachable grill, and the center grill support. Slide the center grill support into the slot in the base. Attach the wheels to the special inserts at the bottom of the base. You are now ready to roll the assembled grill anywhere in your backyard. Important: it is necessary to screw the center support into the grill before attaching it to the base, as it will be impossible to do this after the support is in place.

In this version of the directions, the topic is covered adequately (all parts are mentioned) but in illogical order. If the reader followed the instructions in sequence, he would have to take the grill apart after the second step in order to complete the assembly. Again, a basic part of the reader-writer contract—the meaningful ordering of ideas—has been violated.

Exercises

Read the following short essay. Does it violate the reader-writer contract? If so, identify the ways in which this is done. What happens when the reader-writer contract is broken? How might the essay be revised to fulfill the contract—the writer's promise to the reader?

Movie Ratings Are Nonsense

> Movie ratings are a topic of serious discussion among today's youth. The common consensus of the young appears to be that movie ratings are nonsense. The reasoning behind this opinion is easily supported by the common observation that the proper audiences are not geared to the proper films, that ratings are erroneous and inexplicit, and that ratings lack consistent structure.
>
> The lack of an agreed upon standard for evaluation of film matter is highly evident. Certainly it is not the type or amount of sex involved. One movie that contains prostitution, "The French Connection," is rated GP. But the deeply emotional love in "The Summer of Forty-two" draws an R rating. A movie based entirely upon the pleasure of sex and containing almost total nudity, "Barbarella," is rated only R, while "A Clockwork Orange," a film intertwined with nudity and projecting the take over of the world in the future by gangs of teenagers is rated X.
>
> Supposedly, violence intermixed with profane language plays an important role in determining film ratings. Again, the films themselves repudiate this theory. It appears as though "The Summer of Forty-two" was also "overrated" in this area. It contained no more violence or undesireable language than encountered in everyday life, but it was rated R. Yet, a movie receiving a parallel rating, "The Godfather," is based entirely upon the corruption and

violence of the underworld, and contains a great deal of profane language. Although "The Godfather" may deserve an R rating by the present system, "The French Connection"—which is based upon the same type of underworld theme, with a supporting role of profanity and violence displayed by the main character—received a GP rating. It is therefore hard to decide upon what these ratings are based.

As a direct result of this somewhat erroneous rating system, one finds that he cannot predict the subject matter of the film from its rating. From the title and rating of "Paint Your Wagon," GP, one would never suspect it dealt with the lack of women in a mining camp and the camp's corresponding problems, results, and solutions. I expected to see a calm, relaxing film, because I had had a particularly rough day. Needless to say, I was somewhat surprised to find violence, drunkenness, and numerous scenes within brothels contained in the film. One looking for sex and violence in an R movie would be greeted with a comedy intermixed with limited sex in both "Hospital" and "Where Does it Hurt?"

Should the movie rating system be changed? The evidence of the necessity for a change has been presented. Only the future holds an answer to this seemingly minor, but pressing, problem.

2.4 ORGANIZATION

Once the writer has determined a subject and purpose, he must organize the development of his topic to convey his intentions clearly to the reader. Organization—the necessary shape for communicating an intention—grows out of the very nature of the writer's subject and his purpose in dealing with it.

Generally, if the writer has focused carefully on a subject and thesis, the organization of his writing will follow naturally. That is, a clearly defined subject and purpose will invite a particular pattern of organization. The sections below, demonstrating how this process works, examine several patterns of organization that typically emerge with certain types of intention. Note that the system used to organize a communication is often the same one used to focus the subject and thesis.

2.4a Chronological and Spatial Order

Most descriptive writing tasks are controlled by some concept of time or space. The writer seeks to describe events and experiences as they occurred or as he viewed them. Chronological or spatial order is a natural organizational pattern for this type of writing.

53

2.4a Chronological and Spatial Order

Chronological order—the ordering of events in time—is the basis for most histories, biographies, news stories, and fictional or non-fictional narratives (descriptions of the rise, growth, development, or decline of a particular subject).

Chronological order is also used in explanatory writing tasks when the steps involved in a particular procedure are controlled by time. Suppose, for example, that a writer wants to explain to readers the major steps in the development of the computer:

I. History of the Computer
  A. First mechanical adding machines (1650–1700)
  B. First typewriter (1867)
  C. Use of punched cards for data tabulation (1920)
  D. First stored-program electromechanical computer—the Mark I (1944)
  E. First electronic computer—the ENIAC (1946)
  F. First computer installed for business data processing—the UNIVAC (1954)

In this case, chronological ordering of the facts is the logical pattern for the writer's intention. To discuss the stages in computer development in random order or in the order that seems significant to the writer (for example, "The invention of a stored program was the greatest hurdle to overcome in computer technology") would defeat his purpose. Only chronological order shows computer development as an *evolutionary* process, in which each new stage depends on those that have preceded.

Closely allied with chronological order is *spatial organization*—ordering a subject in terms of the physical relationship among its parts. Spatial ordering is commonly used in physical descriptions, explanations, and instructions and often follows a logical physical pattern—front to back, left to right, top to bottom, up to down. Spatial order is useful in stating relationships (as in geographical directions) and in describing how a subject is organized.

Assume, for example, that a writer wants to inform readers of the safety features to look for in new cars:

I. Safety Features in New Cars
  A. Outside the car: flexible bumpers, unit body construction, tinted windows, laminated windshield, radial tires
  B. Inside the car: shoulder harness, head supports, collapsible steering assembly, modular seats
  C. Under the hood: power brakes, power steering, automatic fire control, safety brake device

Here the writer's spatial ordering of the topic (outside to inside) is a logical and natural way of explaining the subject. Instead of listing each feature—say, in alphabetical order—the writer follows a pattern the reader might follow if he were actually examining the car. In this sense, spatial ordering is closely related to chronology—it follows a "theoretical" sequence in time. Spatial ordering also satisfies the reader's need for a way of perceiving the topic; it gives the reader a visual frame to follow the writer's discussion.

2.4b   Ordering by Classification

Ordering by classification is commonly used when the writer's basic intent is to present the facts in a way that is agreeable to or convenient for readers. Classification—the arrangement of a subject into classes or groups—is a natural and simple way of organizing and is useful in a variety of writing tasks.

How a writer divides a subject will be shaped both by the subject matter itself and by the writer's purpose. For example, a cookbook writer who wishes to present a series of recipes could classify them in three different ways:

Classes of food—meats, vegetables, desserts
Types of cuisines—French, Italian, Spanish
Types of meals—breakfast, lunch, dinner

The specific pattern the writer chooses will depend on the nature of the information available—that is, whether the recipes lend themselves to a particular classification. The pattern chosen will also depend on the writer's purpose. If he wishes to appeal to a gourmet audience, he may organize the recipes by cuisines. If his appeal is to a family audience, he may decide that the meal-planning classification is best.

Although classification is a simple and useful system for organizing, it is not an arbitrary one. The writer must evaluate his subject matter and purpose clearly to determine the classification that best suits his subject and intention.

2.4c   Ordering by Importance or Complexity

Ordering by importance is often used when the writer's goal is to evaluate or explain a subject: to tell why it is valuable, how it is useful, the reasons for it. Rather than listing or classifying the facts, the writer imposes an interpretation on them—for example,

55

arguing that one fact is more important than another or instructing the reader, one step at a time, about complex material.

The decision to organize by importance is controlled by the writer's thesis or view of his subject. For example, the cookbook writer may view cooking as a learning process and believe that the mastery of simple skills is essential to perform more complex cooking tasks. In this case, instead of classifying recipes, the writer may evaluate the recipes in terms of their difficulty and present them in that order—simplest (boiling, baking, frying) to most complex (the preparation of an eight-course meal).

Similarly, the writer who is discussing the safety features of new cars may believe that some features are especially critical to highway safety. He would then evaluate the various features in terms of importance, discussing the less significant ones first and those he deems critical last in order to heighten their importance for the reader.

2.4d   Ordering by Cause and Effect

Cause-and-effect ordering is used primarily when the writer's thesis is an argument about "process" and the subject is the beginning or end result of that process. Ordering by cause and effect implies a direct causal connection between two or more ideas, and the writer's goal is usually to *prove* that connection. The writer may argue from cause to effect or from effect to cause. He may argue for several causes leading to a single effect or several effects traceable to one cause.

The exact form of the writer's presentation will be governed by his thesis, or controlling idea about the subject. Suppose, for example, that a writer wants to explain the causes of the War of 1812. He may see five basic causes, all contributing equally, and thus present them as a cluster:

I. Five major causes of the War of 1812
   A. British impressment of American seamen
   B. The *Chesapeake* affair
   C. Violations of neutral shipping rights
   D. Economic blockades and counterblockades
   E. America's desire for territorial gain

Alternatively, the writer may see several causes as interconnected, with one leading directly to another, in a domino effect. He may then combine cause-and-effect ordering with chronological order, presenting several causes in sequence:

A. The *Chesapeake* affair
B. Leads to intensified economic blockage
C. Results in further violations of shipping rights
D. Leads to America's ultimatum and war declaration

Finally, the writer's thesis may be that the war had one overriding cause and that all other causes were actually subordinate to it, were only apparent rather than real causes. The logical organization for such an intention would be cause and effect combined with order of importance:

A. Apparent or immediate causes
 1. freedom of seas
 2. neutrality violations
 3. economic blockades
 4. impressment of seamen
B. Real cause (most important)
 1. U.S. desire for territorial gain: Canada, Florida, West Indies.
  a. Other causes only pretext to get into war

Thus, within the area of cause-and-effect ordering that has been determined by the writer's subject (a discussion of process), the writer will often select another organizational pattern, depending on his specific intent.

2.4e Ordering by Comparison and Contrast

Another common organizational pattern is comparison and contrast. Comparison points out the similarities between things; contrast highlights their differences. Organization by comparison and contrast closely parallels the way the human mind works in sorting out experiences. When faced with an unfamiliar idea or event, we instinctively compare it with other, familiar things in order to "know" it. Through its similarities with and differences from the familiar, we come to categorize, compartmentalize, and understand it.

Because comparison and contrast is such a natural way of organizing experience, it is effective in many types of writing tasks. Organization by comparison and contrast is often used for description ("Except for facial resemblances, the two brothers were entirely different"); explanation ("Swinging a golf club requires the same skills as swinging a baseball bat"); and argument ("Both Britain and France entered the war against Germany, but they did so for very different reasons"). In addition, comparisons and contrasts are frequently developed in conjunction with other organizational patterns. For example, sorting out the similarities and differences among certain facts is a form of classification. And moving from superficial similarities to deeper, more fundamental similarities is a way of ordering by importance.

For the beginning writer, it is especially important to understand the mechanics of comparison. To be effective, comparisons must be made between truly comparable items or ideas; contrasts must truly contrast:

> The chief comparison between Oedipus and Hamlet is that they were both royalty. However, Oedipus was a king and Hamlet was only a prince. This situation led to the chief difference between them: Oedipus was decisive and Hamlet was not. This difference was probably caused by Hamlet's extreme attachment to his mother. Oedipus, on the other hand, had to fend for himself from an early age.

Although the fact that both Oedipus and Hamlet belong to royalty may be of some significance, it is not the chief similarity between the two characters. If it were, then the differences the writer cites are so great that the comparison is made meaningless. A truer basis for comparison and contrast would be the fact that both are tragic heroes in literature whose suffering is caused by their different faults.

Not only must comparisons be guided by a unifying idea; they must also be developed clearly and explicitly. The art of comparison consists of skillfully interweaving the facts to *demonstrate* similarities and differences. For example, a writer who sought to compare Italian and Jewish immigrants in Boston in the early twentieth century might mistakenly proceed as follows:

> The West End Italians emigrated to Boston at the turn of the century and found jobs as unskilled laborers. They placed a strong emphasis on family ties and on keeping the family a closely knit unit. Children were discouraged from leaving the neighborhood or from leaving the family circle, even after marriage. In contrast, the Jewish immigrants in Boston came from Poland and Russia. They sought to improve their social conditions and worked hard to give their children a good education. Jewish parents took great pride in the accomplishments of their offspring.

The trouble with this comparison is that it neither compares the two groups in similar terms nor establishes clear relationships. The writer describes when the Italians emigrated, what jobs they held, and their feelings about family ties. For the Jews, he discusses where they emigrated from, their attitudes toward education, and their pride in their children's success. Nowhere does the writer indicate comparable relationships or establish a controlling idea. Although there are potential comparisons to be made (children, family, work), they remain hidden. The reader is left to do all the work and to draw conclusions, if there are any to be drawn.

Now examine how a writer successfully uses comparison and contrast to bring out the essential characteristics of these two immigrant groups:

> Finally, the West Enders may be contrasted to the Jews, an ethnic group which came to America at about the same time as the Italians, but with a different occupational history. The Jews who emigrated from Poland and Russia around the turn of the century were neither laborers nor peasants, but peddlers, shopkeepers, and artisans with a more middle-class occupational tradition. They also differed from their fellow immigrants in their belief in education, partly for reasons related to this tradition. Although they worked initially as unskilled and semiskilled laborers in America, they reacted differently to their environment than did the ethnic groups from peasant and farm labor origins.
>
> Superficially, the Jewish family structure resembled the Italian one, with a nuclear household surrounded by a large family circle. Because of the high value placed on education, however, the immigrants did not restrain their children from contact with the outside world. As already noted, they encouraged the children to use the schools and settlement houses to prepare themselves for white-collar and professional occupations. Thus, the Jewish young people pursued careers that drew them apart from the parental generation at the same time that their Italian neighbors rejected such careers as "lonely ventures" that could only break up the cohesion of the family circle. Although the Jewish immigrants did bemoan the children's acculturation into styles of life congruent with their higher occupational level, they also took pride in the successful mobility of their offspring.
>
> Herbert Gans, *The Urban Villagers*

Here a series of comparisons and contrasts are drawn between the two groups along parallel lines—time, occupation, family structure, education, goals. The writer uses words like *same, different, resembled, differed* to make the similarities and differences explicit. He also focuses his ideas to make the comparison more than a mechanical exercise. Instead of listing two separate sets of facts or summarizing the history of each group, he integrates the facts around a central purpose—a sociological description of the two immigrant groups. That is, he uses the techniques of comparison and contrast to help the reader understand the characteristics of each group.

59

Exercises

1. Choose *two* of the following statements and suggest an appropriate organizational pattern for a paper developing each topic. Sketch the main blocks of thought that the paper would include. Keep in mind that some types of intention call for a combination of organizational patterns.

> Example   How to Stock an Aquarium
> [Organization: classification; chronological order]
> 1. The tank
> 2. Gravel and plants
> 3. Fish
> 4. Food and feeding
> 5. Cleaning and maintenance
>
> **a.** Uses of the dictionary.
> **b.** Why the United States withdrew from Vietnam.
> **c.** Benefits of the four-day work week.
> **d.** Living in a fraternity or sorority house versus living in a dorm.
> **e.** College—the first day on campus.
> **f.** Tips on purchasing a new stereo.

2. Examine the following passages and state the ways in which they use ordering by chronology or space, ordering by classification, ordering by importance or complexity, ordering by cause and effect, or ordering by comparison and contrast. Identify the type (or types) of organization most evident in each passage. Remember that patterns of organization often work together.

> **a.** Every sound has three characteristic properties. Let us take an everyday example. When walking along the street we hear several sounds at the same time; cars, motorbikes, aeroplanes, radios, people walking and talking, simultaneously produce sounds of higher and lower, louder and softer degrees. With our ear we automatically distinguish between the highness of a child's voice and the lowness of a man's, the loudness of a passing plane and the hum of traffic, and we know whether the tune coming from somebody's radio is played on a trumpet or a violin. In doing this, we are unconsciously selecting the three characteristics of a sound: *pitch, volume,* and *quality.*
>
> Otto Károlyi, *Introducing Music*
>
> **b.** The immediate cause of World War I was the spread of nationalism in the Balkans, as shown by the assassination at Sarajevo and the determination of the Austrians to destroy the Serbian "hornets'

nest." More fundamental reasons for this conflict lie further back. Among them was the division of Europe into rival camps by a system of alliances, originally defensive in character but made dangerous through a lessening of international trust by successive crises—Morocco in 1905, Bosnia in 1908–1909, Agadir in 1911. Anglo-German relations had worsened because of naval rivalry and, to a much lesser extent, trade competition.

Adapted from A. W. Palmer, A Dictionary of Modern History

c. Most mornings at home when the weather was good, Whistler would go out from seven to eight for a row on the river with the Greaves brothers, then join his mother for breakfast or—taking advantage of the tide upstream—visit Howell in Putney for an even later breakfast. Afterwards, in Chelsea, he painted or sketched through the day, stopping for a meal only if someone were sitting for him, and then only reluctantly and late. Sometimes after seven he would join his mother for dinner, and two or three evenings a week he would remain with her for the evening, reading or sketching, until she retired, which was always early enough for Whistler to go out again.

Stanley Weintraub, Whistler: A Biography

2.5 THE INFORMAL OUTLINE

In organizing the development of a subject and thesis, most experienced writers use some type of outline to guide them in their work. The degree of detail included in an outline will depend on the writer's purpose and the nature of his task. For most shorter writing tasks, such as class papers and examination questions, an *informal outline* is usually sufficient to guide the writer toward his goals. An informal outline is a brief, preliminary sketch of the writer's thoughts, ideas, and intentions. It is not a formal blueprint for writing but a set of guidelines to aid the writer in organizing and developing his material. Such an outline is often called a *scratch outline,* a term that reflects the casual, tentative nature of the undertaking. In more complex writing assignments, such as library papers, the writer may find it necessary to prepare a *formal outline,* in which sections of the paper are worked out more completely before writing. (See p. 62 for an illustration of a formal outline.) A formal outline gives a detailed structural breakdown of the finished work. (Preparation of the library paper is discussed in Chapter 9.)

What to Include in an Informal Outline

The informal outline represents the writer's thoughts and objectives before he actually starts to write. The informal outline should contain the writer's thesis, a list of the main divisions of the topic, and brief notations of items to be discussed, key words or facts, and illustrations or supportive evidence. For example, the following might be a scratch outline for the first two sections of this chapter:

> (how to)
> Thesis: Why {focus and organize writing?
> I. Define "focus"
>   A. narrowing and shaping (like photography)
>   B. Why focus?
>   1. shapes writing to context
>   2. limits info. seeking   3. helps to organize
>   C. Focusing — an ongoing process } Stress
> II. Importance of focusing and organizing
>   (mention different writing tasks) } Intro.

In the outline above, the writer states his thesis and then lists the main divisions of the two chapter sections in outline form. The outline is an informal statement of the writer's main ideas and approaches to his subject. It includes a loose set of facts and key points, finally rearranged in logical order of presentation.

Such an outline is clearly an informal, preliminary statement of the writer's projected work. Although it will probably be most understandable to the writer himself, it is adequate as a guide to assist him in beginning his task. Because the scratch outline is a tentative, open-ended statement, it is a perfect vehicle for including odd thoughts and ideas that cannot be used immediately, and for keeping in mind various facts that may later be developed fully, rearranged, or even discarded.

2.6 WRITING THE FIRST DRAFT

Many writers waste a great deal of time and effort trying to perfect the first draft of their work. They do not recognize that the first draft need not be perfect, and that most of the smoothing and polishing occurs in revision. Even most experienced writers do not compose a flawless draft on the first try. They are aware that the first draft is only a preliminary version of their work and that, at this point, establishing the overall shape and organization of their writing is far more important than polishing and revision.

2.6a Beginning to Write

One of the biggest problems inexperienced writers have is starting the assignment. All writers have at some time or another, struggled with "first-sentencitis." Unable to devise an opening, they become frustrated and wonder: "How can I write this communication when I can't even get the first sentence right?" The answer is that it is practically impossible to find the best opening for a piece until the process of writing is well underway. Often, it is only then that the writer fully understands his purpose and that the best direction for an opening becomes clear. Instead of worrying about getting a "perfect" opening statement, the writer should set down a tentative opening—even a summary of his thesis or intention—to get himself started. Then he can proceed with the body of the paper. Usually, once he has become immersed in the assignment, the best way of introducing the topic becomes clear.

2.6b Developing the Paper

Having written an opening statement, however preliminary or incomplete, the writer concentrates next on developing his thesis in broad sections. The writer's goal in writing the first draft is to get all his ideas on paper, to give general shape to his work. He sets out his main ideas, as directed by his informal outline. Then he tries to compose a topic sentence for each main idea and to work out the supportive details and illustrations. As the writer composes, he lets his ideas flow. If his writing begins to take another direction, he continues; he need not follow the outline exactly. Later, in revision, the writer can review, reevaluate, and polish his thoughts.

63

In developing the body of the paper, the writer must concentrate above all on arranging his ideas clearly and logically. At this point he need not worry about every detail of grammar, punctuation, or spelling. Often, if he cannot make a sentence as smooth as he wishes or recall the exact word he wants, he will leave the problem for revision and move on to avoid interrupting his flow of thought.

2.6c   Taking a Break

Unless the assignment is a very short one, it will probably not be possible to complete the first draft in one session. Taking a break helps the writer to relax, to get a fresh perspective, and to revitalize his thoughts. It is important, however, that the writer prepare himself to get back into the assignment *before* he takes his break.

One useful technique is for the writer to leave a written reminder of what he intends to do next, so that he will have some direction in which to proceed when he returns to his task. Instead of relying on memory, the writer should write down as precisely as possible his intentions. He can also devise certain incentives to get himself back into the flow of writing. Some writers deliberately stop before they run out of ideas so that the "pump is primed" for the next session. Others stop in the middle of a sentence so they will have something concrete and specific to do when they begin again. Still other writers purposely leave the easy tasks for last. All of these devices can aid the writer in starting up again.

2.6d   Reviewing the First Draft

Once the first draft has been completed and all the writer's ideas have been written out, it is necessary to review the draft carefully before proceeding with revision and polishing. There are several points the writer should check for in the reviewing stage. Specifically, he should ask the following questions:

1. Do I have a satisfactory thesis? Is the thesis clearly focused, manageable, unified?
2. Have I used enough evidence to support my thesis? Have I drawn upon my raw material fully and accurately?
3. Is all the material relevant to my thesis? Do I have undeveloped or irrelevant ideas? Should these ideas be expanded or eliminated?

4. Is each major point developed fully? Have I provided sufficient details, examples, and illustrations to clarify and support each point?
5. Are all the ideas presented logically? Does one idea move smoothly into the next according to some organizational pattern? Do the ideas flow naturally to a conclusion?

Once these review questions have been satisfactorily answered, the writer can proceed with the final draft—revising by filling in fine details and smoothing arguments, proofing by checking spelling and grammar.

REVIEW EXERCISES

1. The following passage begins a twelve-page essay by Hollywood screenwriter Dudley Nichols:

> Ours is the age of the specialist. In older times, before the Machine, men did specialize of course in the various arts and crafts—but those arts and crafts were not themselves subdivided into specialized functions. The man who painted did the whole job himself: he was a painter. So with the silversmith and the shoemaker and the sculptor. But the Machine changed all that. The painter today has his materials prepared by other people, by specialized craftsmen or tradesmen, and only wields those materials in the final function of creating pictures. The etcher buys his copper plates already prepared and seldom pulls his own prints. The sculptor models in clay and leaves to others the pouring of the mold or the work of the pointing machine. The writer no longer turns out beautiful manuscripts that may be passed from hand to hand: he pounds out a script on the typing machine and passes it on to his publisher's printing factories. In science and art we have become specialized, narrowing our fields of study and work, because those fields have grown too enormous for the single mind to embrace.

What is the subject of this passage (its raw material)? What seems to be its thesis (what the writer is trying to prove with the raw materials)?

Notice the lack of focus in the passage as it stands. It is difficult to determine what Nichols is going to do with his apparent topic in the space of a short essay. Now read carefully the last two sentences of this same introductory paragraph:

65

> We are all specialized, for better or worse, and it is only natural that the one new art form which the Machine has produced should be the most highly specialized of all. For the motion picture *is* an art form, whether it be so regarded or not.
>
> Dudley Nichols, "The Writer and the Film," in John Gassner and Dudley Nichols, eds., *Great Film Plays*

Compare the paragraph with and without these final sentences. How has the subject of the piece of writing changed? How has the thesis been changed? Discuss *why* it is necessary for the author to focus the ideas developed in the first, incomplete passage. Finally, try to identify the specific ways in which the subject receives focus in these last two sentences. (See Sections **2.1** and **2.2** for techniques of focusing.)

2. The following two passages are also opening paragraphs which express a topic that can later be developed at length. First identify the subject and thesis of each passage. Then identify the most important way (or ways) in which the subject of each has been focused. To what extent do the subject and thesis go together in each passage?

a. When an acquaintance greets me on the street by lifting his hat, what I see from a formal point of view is nothing but the change of certain details within a configuration forming part of the general pattern of color, lines and volumes which constitutes my world of vision. When I identify, as I automatically do, this configuration as an object (gentleman), and the change of detail as an event (hat-lifting), I have already overstepped the limits of purely formal perception and entered a first sphere of subject matter or meaning. The meaning thus perceived is of an elementary and easily understandable nature, and we shall call it the factual meaning; it is apprehended by simply identifying certain visible forms with certain objects known to me from practical experience, and by identifying the change in their relations with certain actions or events.

Erwin Panofsky, *Meaning in the Visual Arts*

b. If we look at the supporters of the three major positions in most democratic countries, we find a fairly logical relationship between ideology and social base. The Socialist left derives its strength from manual workers and the upper rural strata; the conservative right is backed by the rather well-to-do elements—owners of large industry and farms, the managerial and free professional strata—and those segments of the less privileged groups who have remained involved in traditionalist institutions, particularly the Church. The democratic center is backed by the middle classes, especially small businessmen, white-collar workers, and the anticlerical sections of the professional classes.

Seymour Martin Lipset, *Political Man: Essays on the Sociology of Democracy*

3. Carefully read the following short essay. First try to state its subject and its thesis. Also discuss whether or not the subject and thesis work together. Is the thesis realistic? Has the information available for proving the thesis been used sufficiently? Does the topic seem to be covered adequately? Are irrelevant elements excluded, as they should be?

In your discussion of the essay, try to specify the kinds of logical organization used. (See Section **2.4** for types of organization.) Which is the most important in terms of the *overall* structure of the piece? What other means of organization are used to develop this primary pattern?

The motion picture is a unique art form. It is *not* television, and it is *not* theater. The motion picture is as distinct from these art forms as music is from painting, as poetry is from architecture.

The visual requirements of television are dictated by the fact that the finished work is projected onto a very small screen and is usually viewed by the audience at home, in a semi-darkened room, subject to a variety of distractions. Thus long shots, medium shots, and compositional subtleties are largely lost, just as the details of a fine painting are lost when rendered onto a postage stamp. Only close-ups have impact. Lighting details are also minimized, and what remains is a simple frame that is either bright or dark. Regardless of the creative effort applied to the visual image, the final telecast is a small picture totally devoid of the subtle detail that comprises the visual image as created for motion picture projection.

When the art of the motion picture is compared with that of the stage, the factors that make film unique are even more striking. The key element in the creation of the image is the filmmaker's ability to *control the eye of the audience at all times*. The stage director can utilize a variety of tricks to command the audience's attention; but in the final analysis, the boundaries of the stage remain fixed and the attention of the audience vagrant.

Derek Golby, a talented young English stage director, effectively staged Tom Stoppard's play *Rosencrantz and Guildenstern Are Dead*. In the closing scene, the two leading characters stand on either side of the stage for their final speeches. It is essential that the audience give full attention to their words and to the questioning, uncomprehending expressions on their faces. Golby darkens the entire stage and places a strong white spotlight on each of their faces. Rosencrantz completes his speech, and as his life is snuffed out, so is his spotlight. Now the audience is left in darkness, save for the single white light illuminating the face of Guildenstern.

It would be hard to imagine a more effective means (in the theater) of riveting the audience's attention on the face of a protagonist. Yet, unless one is sitting in the center of the first few rows, one still sees the boundaries of the dark stage, with a small head illuminated in the foreground. And if the actor is not superb, the attention of the audience will stray.

The filmmaker, however, deals with an image in which all is motion. The boundaries of the frame change, contracting and expanding at the command of the director. When it is important to focus attention on the face of an actor, the director simply provides a close-up—and the audience cannot look elsewhere.

It is this factor of multiple motion—the movement of the frame in the scene itself and the action within the scene—that imparts to film a quality not present in the theater. It is this ceaseless flow of motion, the ability to view significant acts and action from many vantage points, that makes the art of film unique.

Lee R. Bobker, *Elements of Film*

4. Draft an informal outline for the essay printed above. Be sure to include the thesis statement and a list of the items discussed. Also fill in some of the key words and facts that are used in the body of the essay to prove the thesis.

3

Paragraphs

The first paragraph of a communication establishes for the reader the writer's intention as to subject and thesis. Each new paragraph not only grows from the one preceding it but also contributes information necessary for grasping the writer's overall intention. Every paragraph is organized around a topic sentence, stated or implied, which provides the paragraph with a controlling central idea and links it to the writer's overall intention. An effective paragraph stays in focus (unity), develops the topic in detail (completeness), and is arranged in a logical order (coherence). The particular organization of a paragraph depends upon its function in the total communication.

PARAGRAPHS AND THE WRITER'S INTENTION

Although a written communication is a unified whole from beginning to end, the writer has a formal device available for breaking up each page—the paragraph. Sometimes the division into paragraphs serves a practical purpose—as in newspaper stories, where long passages are often divided to avoid column after column of unbroken prose. The paragraph breaks give the reader's eye a resting place.

In most writing situations, of course, the paragraph is more than a convention. Each paragraph serves to express a specific part of the writer's overall intention as to his subject and thesis; it communicates an appropriate bit of information. Paragraph breaks signal to the reader that a new aspect of the writer's intention is about to be discussed.

In most written communications, two or more paragraphs are usually required to convey the writer's total meaning. Each new paragraph is related to the entire communication in two ways: (1) it is an extension of the preceding paragraph, and (2) it contributes additional information important to the writer's goal. The interrelationships among paragraphs can be seen in the following example, taken from a book on motion picture production:

One of the most significant developments in motion pictures in the past decade has been the revolution in the technology of filmmaking. For almost forty years the equipment with which films were made remained essentially the same. Although the art of film made slow but steady progress, the equipment and techniques of motion picture production did not keep pace—with the exception of some minor streamlining of bulky equipment and, of course, the advent of sound. From the Hollywood production of a Cecil B. DeMille epic in the 1920s to the production of a John Huston classic in the 1950s or even a Doris Day film in the early 1960s, the basic procedures by which films were made remained unchanged: the production was rooted to the studio, the equipment was heavy and relatively immobile, and hordes of technicians stood about doing very little.

These conditions made it very difficult for new talent to break into filmmaking. The expense and rigidity of the equipment, the viselike hold of the craft guilds on the filmmaking organizations, and the mystique with which those in film guarded their secrets all served to discourage the aspiring filmmaker. To be sure, some dedicated and committed filmmakers like Stanley Kubrick surmounted these difficulties, but they were the exception rather than the rule.

Fortunately, dramatic changes began to take place in the 1960s, and they continue into the 1970s. The technology of film has begun to catch up. Technological advances have led to the development of lighter, more mobile, and considerably less expensive equipment. Production has broken free of the studios and has moved outward onto locations. Films like *Knife in the Water, David and Lisa,* and *Easy Rider* heralded the era of the small production unit. Filmmaking is no longer rooted in Hollywood and New York. Editing equipment has become more flexible and easier to use. The iron grip of the industry's unions has been broken by a variety of factors, not the least of which has been the demonstration by small groups of unknown and relatively inexperienced artists that one could make a film and make it well, even without the advantages of an established name and impressive financial resources. All these changes have combined to encourage many young men and women to move into filmmaking as a life's career.

Lee R. Bobker, *Making Movies*

The writer's intention in this passage is implicit in the opening sentence: to explain why he believes technological developments have changed modern filmmaking. Each paragraph in the passage conveys a separate idea that is related to the writer's overall point. In the first paragraph the writer describes the old pattern of studio production that dominated film for forty years. In the second paragraph he explains the results of this situation: that it prevented independent filmmakers from entering the industry. In the third paragraph the writer describes recent changes in film—the advent of on-location photography and the small production unit—and shows how this paved the way for independent film production.

Each of these paragraphs conveys a separate unit of the writer's thought. At the same time, each builds on the information that has preceded it and advances the writer's overall intention. Only after reading all three paragraphs does the reader understand why, in the writer's opinion, recent technological developments have changed the art of film.

3.1 PARAGRAPHS AND THE TOPIC SENTENCE

Every paragraph is organized around a controlling central idea, often expressed in a *topic sentence.* The topic sentence must clearly define the main purpose of the paragraph and must connect the information presented in the paragraph to the writer's overall intention. The topic sentence (in bold type) in the following paragraph, from a *Reader's Digest* article on the Great Pyramid of Giza in Egypt, satisfies these requirements:

> **The Great Pyramid embodies extraordinary architectural skills.** So accurately were the facing stones cut and fitted, for example, that a sheet of paper can scarcely be inserted in the joints between. The southeast corner stands only half an inch higher than the northwest corner, and the difference between the longest and shortest sides is less than eight inches, a discrepancy of less than .09 percent.
>
> Ronald Schiller, "Unsolved Mysteries of the Great Pyramid," *Reader's Digest*

The writer states his central idea in the opening, topic sentence: that the Great Pyramid is an exceptional architectural achievement. He then cites specific details to demonstrate its careful and accurate design: the close fitting of the stones, the almost perfect symmetry of the sides. Through example, this information supports the general statement made in the topic sentence. In addition, the paragraph advances the writer's overall intention in the article: to demonstrate the skill of Egyptian pyramid builders, despite the primitive construction methods available to them.

When writing, it is a good idea to reread the topic sentence in each paragraph of the communication after the first draft is finished. The sentences should follow one another in logical order and together spell out a clear pattern of thought. Similarly, before beginning to write, it is often helpful to jot down a series of topic sentences that cover, in logical order, the major ideas to be discussed. The sentences will serve as a rough outline from which to begin writing. For example, the following topic sentences provide a chronological framework for a paper on the public life of the late President Lyndon B. Johnson. The topic sentences alone—even without the supporting information—give a clear idea of how the essay might look:

1. The long public career of Lyndon Baines Johnson included moments of glory and moments of defeat. [Introductory paragraph.]
2. Johnson first became a national figure during his years as Senate majority leader.
3. In 1960, after a disappointing campaign for the Democratic presidential nomination, Johnson was elected vice-president.
4. Johnson became president of the United States in November 1963, after the tragic assassination of John F. Kennedy.
5. In his early years as president, Johnson actively fought for civil-rights and social-welfare legislation.
6. The escalation of the Vietnam War weakened Johnson's popularity with the American people.
7. After a poor showing in the 1968 presidential primaries, Johnson stunned the nation by announcing that he would not run for reelection.
8. Johnson retired to his ranch in Texas and lived there until his death in 1973.
9. Historians may remember Johnson as one of the most powerful and complex men ever to run the American government. [Concluding paragraph.]

As this sample illustrates, once a writer has a well-organized set of topic sentences, the direction of the paper is clear. Each paragraph in this essay would cover an important period or series of events in Johnson's career.

Although the topic sentence usually begins a paragraph, writers sometimes vary the placement of the topic sentence to create more interesting prose, as in the following description of the street life of alcoholics:

Sometimes all this repressed emotion breaks out into a fist fight on the Bowery. If they were not so tragic, they might be funny. The violence is a ballet of mistakes, of drunken, sweeping impossible punches. The men cannot really hurt each other with any calculation. The real danger is that a man will throw himself off balance when one of his roundhouse blows miscarries. **The weakness and ineffectualness of the Bowery are summed up in these fights.**

Michael Harrington, The Other America

In this paragraph the writer provides supporting evidence first and then presents his conclusion in the topic sentence at the end (in bold type).

Occasionally, a topic sentence will not appear at all in a paragraph. Instead, it will be *implied* in the text. This technique is illustrated in the following paragraph on Susan B. Anthony, one of the first women's-rights leaders in the United States:

She started out on Christmas Day, 1854, with a bag full of literature, petitions, and $50 loaned to her by Wendell Phillips. In each town she had to make all arrangements for her meeting, engage the hall, see to the lights and ushers, and get throwaways printed and distributed announcing the meeting. Sometimes audiences were friendly and openhanded, coming from miles around despite bitter weather, and she was able to pay not only her expenses but make a small surplus, which would be promptly swallowed up at the next stop, where the audience might be negligible, or where perhaps she could find no proper meeting place.

Eleanor Flexner, Century of Struggle: The Woman's Rights
Movement in America

This paragraph gives a general description of Susan B. Anthony's activities as a feminist. None of its three sentences establishes a controlling idea. Yet each follows from and supports a basic underlying premise: Susan B. Anthony faced a very difficult struggle in her campaign for women's rights. This unstated theme is the implied topic sentence of the paragraph.

Exercises

1. Identify the topic sentence in each of the following paragraphs.

a. Given a choice between supporting the teachers or the students, most school officials have no difficulty recognizing their natural allies. Among the school administrators we interviewed, one told us candidly he would never support a student in a dispute with a teacher, but would only try to convey an impression of fairness "to prevent parents from getting involved."

Craig Haney and Philip G. Zimbardo, "Stimulus/Response:
The Blackboard Penitentiary—It's Tough to Tell a High
School from a Prison," Psychology Today

b. Caught in a rip tide of the consumer movement, the television industry justifiably maintains the right to shape its own product. Listening to too many kooks can spoil even TV's froth. But being responsive to legitimate minority concerns is an obligation that comes with the franchise. The irony is that there is no organized protest against the most tyrannical minority of all. Who really owns television? Nielsen's 12,000 families—which comprise a staggering .000018 per cent of the video audience.

"TV: Do Minorities Rule?" Newsweek

c. Since nonverbal messages are frequently unconscious and almost always taken for granted, we may be unaware of just how important they are in communication. A mother's soft touch may reassure her child when he is hurt; a teacher's frown can be a warning to a misbehaving student; and the frequent eye contact of two people in friendly conversation may show that they like each other very much. A great deal of meaning shared by mother and child, teacher and student, boyfriend and girlfriend, husband and wife, salesman and customer, traffic policeman and motorist, train passenger and conductor, is the result of their nonverbal behavior.

Ralph Webb, Jr., *Interpersonal Speech Communication: Principles and Practice*

2. Review pages 72–74 and write individual topic sentences for five or six paragraphs that could be used to develop the following topics:

a. The advantages of a college education today
b. A profile of an historical figure
c. The increased popularity of tennis
d. The advantages (or disadvantages) of having a child

PRINCIPLES OF PARAGRAPH ORGANIZATION

Every paragraph needs a clear topic sentence—either stated or implied. But even the best topic sentence, by itself, cannot make a paragraph work. A well-written paragraph must meet three basic requirements: it must be *unified;* it must be *complete;* and it must be *coherent.*

75

3.2 (¶un)

3.2 Unity (¶un)

One of the crucial elements of a good paragraph is *unity:* every sentence should fit into the central idea of the paragraph (as stated in the topic sentence). The following excerpt from *The Autobiography of Malcolm X* is an example of a unified paragraph:

> **I learned early that crying out in protest could accomplish things.** My older brothers and sister had started to school when, sometimes, they would come in and ask for a butter biscuit or something and my mother, impatiently, would tell them no. But I would cry out and make a fuss until I got what I wanted. I remember well how my mother asked me why I couldn't be a nice boy like Wilfred; but I would think to myself that Wilfred, for being so nice and quiet, often stayed hungry. So early in life, I had learned that if you want something, you had better make some noise.
>
> Alex Haley and Malcolm X, *The Autobiography of Malcolm X*

The topic sentence of this paragraph (in bold type) states a specific premise: protest can be effective. The writer backs up this thesis with an illustration from his childhood. He then concludes by restating his theme. The paragraph has unity because it makes a single point, concentrates on that point, and clearly illustrates it.

Unity is achieved by organizing a paragraph around a central topic or theme and sticking to it. Sometimes beginning writers weaken the unity of a paragraph by trying to include too many topics:

> There were several reasons for the destruction of the English religious houses. Moral, political, and financial considerations forced Henry to evict the monks. When he did, the people rebelled and organized pilgrims' groups to save the monasteries. Their efforts failed, and many religious houses were sold or dismantled. Beautiful churches were destroyed. Many great medieval manuscripts were lost forever.

The first two sentences of the paragraph suggest that the writer is going to discuss *why* the English monasteries were destroyed. But then the writer lapses into a description of *the people's response* to Henry's action and the *consequences* of that response. These topics are totally unrelated to the stated theme. If the writer had concentrated on the topic of the opening sentence, and so kept the focus, the paragraph could have been expanded:

> There were several reasons for the destruction of the English religious houses. The official reason given by King Henry was mo-

rality: the monks, he claimed, were acting immorally by accumulating wealth at the expense of the poor. However, there were political reasons as well. Thomas Cromwell, the new vicar-general, was opposed to pilgrimages and the worship of relics, and Henry did not wish to see his new government split into factions. But the chief reason for the action was financial. The resources of the Crown were no longer sufficient to meet the costs of government and the expenses of Henry's overseas campaigns.

Another way in which paragraph unity can be weakened is by tacking on irrelevant or extraneous ideas in the middle or at the end. Inexperienced writers often start a paragraph with a clear idea but then go off on a tangent (out of focus), as in the example below:

> "Marcus Welby, M.D.," creates a ridiculous picture of a doctor's life. Dr. Welby has few patients and always seems to have hours—if not days—to spend with a patient individually. Much of his time is spent advising people about personal rather than medical problems. But even real doctors behave as if they were kings. Not only are their prices outrageous, but they treat their patients as mere objects with no feelings. Being an M.D. doesn't mean they know everything.

The writer's opening sentence suggests that the paragraph will be a critique of a popular television program. The reader expects the rest of the paragraph to defend and illustrate this critique. But in the last three sentences the writer goes off the track, launching into a tirade against the high prices and arrogance of doctors. However, neither high prices nor arrogant doctors has anything to do with the fictional character of Marcus Welby. To improve and unify this paragraph, the writer would have to eliminate the irrelevant ideas and instead add details that clarify the topic sentence:

> "Marcus Welby, M.D.," creates a ridiculous idea of a doctor's life. Dr. Welby has few patients and always seems to have hours—if not days—to spend with a patient individually. Much of his time is spent advising people about personal rather than medical problems. And Welby always seems to make everything come out right in the end. Such continuous miracles are possible only on television, not in real life.

Now the writer has a more unified paragraph that sticks to the central point: the unrealistic image of doctors put forth on "Marcus Welby, M.D." The criticism is made in the first sentence, supported with additional details, and clarified at the conclusion.

The importance of unity in paragraphs cannot be overstated. Every element in a paragraph must be directly and *clearly* tied into the central theme, just as each paragraph must be linked to the overall intention of the communication. Going off on tangents, minor points, or irrelevant personal judgments about minor points causes the paragraph to go out of focus.

3.3 Completeness

An effective paragraph must be unified and *complete*. The writer should present enough detailed information so that the reader understands the central theme. How much elaboration of the content is necessary for effectiveness is determined by the particular writing situation. The following paragraph, in which George Orwell discusses his experiences fighting in the Spanish Civil War, provides the kind of detail that makes a paragraph complete:

> All of us were lousy by this time; though still cold it was warm enough for that. I have had a big experience of body vermin of various kinds, and for sheer beastliness the louse beats everything I have encountered. Other insects, mosquitoes at least, make you suffer more, but at least they aren't *resident* vermin. The human louse somewhat resembles a tiny lobster, and he lives chiefly in your trousers. Short of burning all your clothes, there is no known way of getting rid of him. Down the seams of your trousers he lays his glittering white eggs, like tiny grains of rice, which hatch out and breed families of their own at horrible speed. I think the pacifists might find it helpful to illustrate their pamphlets with enlarged photographs of lice. Glory of war, indeed! In war *all* soldiers are lousy, at least when it is warm enough. The men who fought at Verdun, at Waterloo, at Flodden, at Senlac, at Thermopylae—every one of them had lice crawling down his testicles. We kept the brutes down to some extent by burning out the eggs and by bathing as often as we could face it. Nothing short of lice could have driven me into that ice-cold river.
>
> George Orwell, *Homage to Catalonia*

This vivid and detailed description of lice illustrates the power of completeness in writing. Orwell does not merely *tell* readers that lice are horrible. He makes them *feel* his inner revulsion and disgust. Sentences like "The human louse somewhat resembles a tiny lobster . . ." and "Down the seams of your trousers he lays his glittering white eggs, like tiny grains of rice . . ." jolt and shock readers. The idea of insects crawling all over one's body, living in one's clothes, becomes almost unbearable—and so does the idea of war. Orwell accomplishes his intention—to convey his distaste of war to readers—by detailing one of the gruesome features of wartime existence.

An effective paragraph must be clear and specific enough to convey the writer's point. Vague and overly general paragraphs that do not extend the topic sentence through detail, analysis, and example leave the reader dissatisfied, asking questions the writer should have answered. The following paragraph about basketball star Connie Hawkins is incomplete because it lacks necessary detail:

> In 1961, Connie Hawkins went to Iowa to go to college. Iowa City seemed strange to him. It wasn't anything like the black neighborhood he grew up in. The white students were difficult to mix with, and classes were intimidating and demanding. People were friendly, but Hawkins was lonely nevertheless.

The writer tries to show how Hawkins felt out of place in Iowa, but the paragraph leaves many questions unanswered. In what ways was Iowa City different from Hawkins' black neighborhood? Why were the white students difficult to mix with? Why were classes so intimidating? Why was Hawkins lonely if people were friendly to him? The writer should have anticipated these questions and expanded his statements with more specific information.

With detail, the same information communicates more effectively, as illustrated in the following passage from a biography of Connie Hawkins:

> In September of 1961, Connie Hawkins packed his sneakers and his comic books and went off to be Joe College. An apprehensive eighteen-year-old, alone for the first time, he arrived in Iowa City to find an alien world, more indifferent than hostile. He was another in the endless succession of black athletes pulled from the urban core, plopped into a midwestern campus, and told to make themselves at home. But Iowa wasn't anything like home. Hawkins had nothing in common with the flaxen-haired farm boys who populated his dorm. Once they finished discussing the basketball team and the football team, there was nothing to talk about. Connie's classes—which the recruiters told him he could handle—were more overwhelming and humiliating than his worst experiences at Boy's High. Unfamiliar words buzzed about his ears like angry mosquitoes, and reading assignments for a month totalled more pages than he had read in his life. People were not unfriendly; they smiled and said how happy they were he had come to Iowa. But Hawkins soon found life on the college campus dull, lonely, and sexually frustrating.
>
> David Wolf, *Foul: The Connie Hawkins Story*

This description of Hawkins' introduction to college contains many rich and clarifying details: Hawkins' sneakers and comic books; his youth and apprehensiveness; the image of the "flaxen-haired farm boys"; and the magnitude of the reading assignments. These details answer many questions left by the first paragraph. They help the reader understand why Hawkins found it so difficult to adjust to college life.

Another common writing error occurs when the writer asserts a specific viewpoint in a topic sentence but does not give readers enough solid reasoning and data to support his position. The following paragraph, for example, adapted from Robert Sherrill's book on the workings of the American government, makes a strong but undefended assertion:

> It is not surprising to see Congress most energetic in those matters which mean profits, because to a great many men in Congress making legislation and making profits mean the same thing. Many of the people in Congress are rich and are anxious to become more wealthy. They care more about their own pocketbooks than they do about the welfare of constituents.

This paragraph makes a serious charge: the political workings of Congress may be significantly affected by the business of its members. But the paragraph does not pin down for the reader what those ties are. How many rich people are there in Congress, and what positions do they hold? A damaging assertion is made, but without supporting data only those who are already convinced will agree. The reader who wants supporting evidence will be disappointed and skeptical.

Now compare the adapted paragraph with the original version, in which Sherrill supports his assertion with concrete information:

> It is not surprising to see Congress most energetic in those matters that mean profits, because to a great many men in Congress making legislation and making profits mean the same thing. There are ninety-seven bankers in the House, and at least a dozen of them are on the House Banking Committee, which of course writes legislation relating to these members' investments and outside livelihood. (How many banking executives sit on the Senate Banking Committee is uncertain because senators have so far successfully fought off all efforts to make them publicly acknowledge their business ties.)
>
> Robert Sherrill, *Why They Call It Politics: A Guide to America's Government*

Sherrill backs up his strong charges against Congress with some startling data: there are almost a hundred bankers in the House of Representatives and more than a dozen are on the influential House Banking Committee. Sherrill further informs the reader that senators have prevented disclosure of their financial ties. This information gives weight to his assertions about Congress.

(¶coh) 3.4

Paragraphs and essays that effectively persuade readers to accept or listen to a line of reasoning are filled with solid analysis and evidence. The writer must convince readers that he has thought the matter out seriously and fairly.

3.4 Coherence (¶coh)

A writer establishes unity by sticking to the topic in a paragraph and completeness by including necessary detail. In addition, he must be sure that the paragraph is *coherent*. Coherence refers to the tight organization and logical structure of a paragraph. Sentences must be arranged so that the reader understands the flow of thought and the relationships among ideas. In the following passage, for example, taken from a magazine article by singer Helen Reddy, the writer presents her ideas in a clear and organized form:

> When I began looking for material for my first album, I wanted songs that reflected the feminist consciousness, that would express what was happening in my head. I really wanted an I-am-woman kind of song. But all the songs I found were "I am woman, you are man. I am weak so you can be stronger than . . ." or "I am woman, W-O-M-A-N, I can cook a mess of grits in three minutes . . ."—all those dreadful songs. So I thought I should write a kind of I-am-woman protest song against all that junk. One night I was just sitting in bed and the lines "I am strong, I am invincible, I am woman" kept going over and over in my head. The whole song came from that.
>
> Helen Reddy, "To Be a Woman," *Redbook*

This paragraph could be broken down into four parts:

1. Reddy explains the kinds of songs she wanted to find for her first album.
2. She discovers that existing songs included demeaning stereotypes about women.
3. She decides to write a song in protest against existing songs about women.
4. One night the basic idea of the song comes to her.

This thought process is easy to follow. Reddy shows us how her feminist consciousness and disappointment with the existing music led to a new song about women. She backs up her assertions with details (the parodied song lyrics) that exemplify the stereotyped songs about women. The paragraph is coherent, because the writer moves from sentence to sentence in a clear and logical manner.

To establish coherence, think of the paragraph as a unit rather

81

than as a collection of individual, unrelated sentences. Thinking of a paragraph as a unit helps the writer avoid choppy writing and broken-up thought patterns, like those in the following examples, adapted from an introductory psychology textbook:

> The most powerful tool of psychology is the experiment. This study method is also used in all other sciences. For example, the chemist can conduct experiments to show that combining hydrogen and oxygen will produce water. The psychologist usually works in his laboratory. He makes a careful and rigidly controlled examination of cause and effect. He can determine that certain conditions will result in certain measurable changes in the behavior of his subjects. The psychologist works with humans and with animals.

In this paragraph, the writer's ideas are not organized around a central theme. The writer seems to be thinking about what to say, composing a sentence, thinking about what to say next, and so on—without giving any thought to how ideas should work together. Now examine the original paragraph, with the same ideas organized to express a central point:

> The most powerful tool of psychology, as of other sciences, is the study method known as the experiment—in which the psychologist, usually in his laboratory, makes a careful and rigidly controlled examination of cause and effect. Just as the chemist can determine that combining hydrogen and oxygen will produce water, so the psychologist can determine that certain conditions will result in certain measurable changes in his subjects, either human or animal.
>
> Jerome Kagan and Ernest Havemann, *Psychology: An Introduction*

This paragraph is much more cohesive. The sentences have been structured to focus on and define a single idea: the nature of the psychological experiment. Other ideas—methods used in other sciences, where the psychologist works, the psychologist's subjects—have been subordinated to this central theme. The paragraph presents a series of logically related ideas rather than a list of unconnected statements.

There are many other elements that contribute to the coherence of a paragraph. These include placing sentences in logical order, clarifying the relationships among sentences, and including all the crucial points needed to clarify a discussion. Writers should carefully build their paragraphs so that each idea flows logically from the preceding one and so that sentences work together to create a convincing point.

Writers use a number of techniques to keep their paragraphs coherent. Among them are precise references, parallelism, repetition of key phrases and terms, and the use of transition words.

3.4a Precise References (ref)

Precise references avoid confusion; they keep the reader focused on the subject being discussed. The most common reference markers used by writers are pronouns—words that take the place of nouns. Pronouns allow writers to avoid repeating names and subjects over and over again. But pronouns must be used carefully or the reader will become lost. In the following example, the use of imprecise pronouns produces an incoherent and nonsensical paragraph. The "problem" pronouns are shown in bold type:

> People today yearn to unload their problems on "experts" and let **them** tell **them** what to do. Experts can help. But what **they** really need is a good dose of reason and common sense. **He** must try to figure out why his problems exist and why he undergoes personal trauma, **which** is the only healthy way to live.

The careless use of pronouns in this paragraph creates confusion and ambiguity. For example, in the first and third sentences, it is unclear whether the pronouns *them* and *they* refer to *people* or to *experts*. In the fourth sentence, there is no earlier referent for the pronoun *he*. The placement of "which" in the closing sentence is confusing because it appears to modify "trauma." But is the writer really suggesting that trauma is the only way to live?

The pronoun problems in this paragraph could be solved in one of two ways: by substituting nouns ("people" or "experts") for pronouns, or by changing one of the groups to a singular noun. The ambiguous "which" can be avoided by starting a new sentence with a precise referent. Here are two possible rewrites:

> People today yearn to unload their problems on "experts" and let these experts tell them what to do. Experts can help. But what people really need is a good dose of reason and common sense. They must try to figure out why their problems exist and why they undergo personal trauma. This introspective approach is the only healthy way to live.

> The average person today yearns to unload his problems on "experts" and let them tell him what to do. Experts can help. But what the average person really needs is a good dose of reason and common sense. He must try to figure out why his problems exist and why he undergoes personal trauma. This introspective approach is the only healthy way to live.

83

3.4b (¶//)

In each of these versions, specific references have been substituted for confusing pronouns. The subject of each sentence is clear, and the paragraph is a coherent whole.

3.4b Parallelism (¶//)

Writers can also improve and clarify their writing through the technique of parallelism. Parallelism in a paragraph means using similar grammatical structures in a number or successive sentences to establish coherence, as illustrated in the following:

> In time living fragments became cells. Cells became tissue. Tissues were formed into creatures. Countless trillions of different individuals were born into a million species, and died. Some, like the dinosaur, perished forever. Others, like man, endured and became more complex.
>
> Benjamin A. Kogan, *Health: Man in a Changing Environment*

Note the close parallel structure of the first four sentences. In each case, something became or was changed into something else. In addition, each sentence uses a word or concept from the preceding one to link ideas and move the paragraph forward. The last two sentences illustrate another type of parallelism. The same grammatical structure is used to express opposite ideas—the fate of the dinosaur as opposed to that of man. The repeated use of a similar phrase structure ties these sentences closer. In this way parallelism creates cohesion and a paragraph.

3.4c Repetition

Repetition is a technique similar to parallelism in that it uses the same elements a number of times in a paragraph. The difference is that parallelism involves the repeated use of grammatical structures, whereas repetition involves the use of key words or phrases. In the paragraph below, for example, a key phrase is repeated:

> **Every President** has to establish with the various sectors of the country what I call "the right to govern." Just being elected to the office does not guarantee him that right. **Every President** has to inspire the confidence of the people. **Every President** must become a leader, and to be a leader he must attract people who are willing to follow him. **Every President** has to develop a moral underpinning to his power, or he soon discovers that he has no power at all.
>
> Lyndon B. Johnson, *The Vantage Point: Perspectives of the Presidency*

The repetition of the expression "every President" in this paragraph captures and holds the reader's attention. It also serves to strengthen and reinforce the writer's point: that "the right to govern" must be won anew by each new President; it is not an inherent part of the presidency itself. Substitution of pronouns or synonyms for the repeated phrase would have weakened the effect.

3.4d Transition Words and Phrases

Transition words and phrases build coherence by connecting sentences. Transition markers appear in virtually every paragraph of an essay. Their job is to help readers move easily through the writing.

Transition markers serve a variety of functions in writing:

1. *Additions.* To indicate an addition to what has been said: *and, also, moreover, in addition, furthermore, first, second, next, then, last, finally.*
2. *Specification.* To indicate a specific example or instance: *for example, for instance, specifically, that is, in particular.*
3. *Qualification.* To qualify or contradict a previous statement: *but, nevertheless, however, yet, still, in spite of, if . . . then.*
4. *Comparison.* To indicate a similar or contrasting relationship: *similarly, in the same manner, by the same token, by contrast, on the other hand, conversely.*
5. *Emphasis.* To set off or emphasize a point: *indeed, in fact, as a matter of fact, clearly, of course, no doubt.*
6. *Conclusion.* To indicate a conclusion to be drawn from a previous statement or statements: *therefore, consequently, as a result, thus, then, to conclude, in sum.*

The following paragraph contains examples of three types of transition markers (shown in bold type):

> Existentialism is not a philosophy **but** a label for several widely different revolts against traditional philosophy. Most of the living "existentialists" have repudiated this label, **and** a bewildered outsider might well conclude that the only thing they have in common is a marked aversion for each other. **To add to** the confusion, many writers of the past have frequently been hailed as members of this movement, **and** it is extremely doubtful whether they would have appreciated the company to which they are consigned. **In view of this,** it might be argued that the label "existentialism" ought to be abandoned altogether.
>
> Walter Kaufmann, *Existentialism from Dostoevsky to Sartre*

This paragraph shows how transition markers serve as mental signals to readers, alerting them to a shift in the writer's thought. The transition word *but* in the first sentence is a *qualification.* The writer shows that he wishes to contradict a popularly held view of existentialism: it is a label, not a philosophy. The word *and* and the phrase "To add to" in the second and third sentences indicate *additions.* They notify the reader that the writer is offering further evidence in support of his argument. In the last sentence the transition phrase "In view of this" signals the reader that the writer is presenting a *conclusion.* The writer claims that, in view of the arguments he has presented, *existentialism* even as a label is not satisfactory.

It is vital to use the appropriate transition marker when indicating a shift in thought. If two parts of a sentence involve an addition of some sort, be sure to choose a transition that suggests addition. If the two parts contain a qualification, the transition must qualify. If a conclusion is implied, then the transition must signal a conclusion. Also, be sure when using a transition term that there is, in fact, a shift in thought. Using a transition unnecessarily can confuse the reader, as in the following example:

> There are many ways in which people can satisfy their need to be creative. **Nevertheless,** some people find creative expression in dancing or playing the piano. **Moreover,** other people satisfy their creative urges by cooking or writing letters.

The terms *nevertheless* and *moreover* make no sense when used this way. In the second sentence, *nevertheless* implies a qualification or contradiction, but there is nothing in the first sentence that it contradicts. Rather, the second sentence serves as an example of the first. *Moreover* suggests an addition to the second sentence, but it is actually a contrast rather than an extension of the earlier idea. Such inappropriate use of transition markers will mystify the reader.

Transitions used precisely build coherent paragraphs. Transitions used imprecisely create doubt and misunderstanding in the reader's mind. Thus, these "little" words are, in reality, very important.

Exercises

1. Read the three paragraphs below. Are they unified, complete, and coherent? Why or why not? Specifically, how could they be improved?

> **a.** What does it really take to stimulate someone's imagination? Most imaginations can be tapped by presenting someone with a familiar topic but one that he knows very little about. For instance,

a question that has always intrigued me is, "If a large tree is struck down by lightning and there is no one around, is any noise produced?" Now, everyone can imagine what a large tree would sound like falling in the woods, but no one could prove whether any sound was produced if no one was present to hear the crash.

b. All known human populations yield males and females who differ in primary sex characteristics, and in many secondary sex characteristics. Males typically are of greater height, strength, and hairiness, and possess a higher muscle-to-fat ratio, more massive skeleton, and so on. This poses the question regarding the extent to which anatomic-structural differences in the sexes restrict the range of possible behaviors that the child may be taught. In short, to what extent is there a natural, intrinsic relation between the physiological sex of the individual and the realm of behaviors which may be patterned?

B. G. Rosenberg and Brian Sutton-Smith, *Sex and Identity*

c. Some people in America today have lost their spirit of Christmas, but it is to their good fortune that most Americans have not. Christmas still has a way of bringing people together. It is common to hear complaints about having to visit Aunt Helen or Uncle Fred, but these same people would be hurt if they were not invited. Strangely enough, good old Dad, who was giving everyone such a hard time about getting dressed up to go out, always ends up being the life of the party. Even though some people get carried away with buying gifts, the spirit of Christmas is far from lost. Material values are of little importance when the holiday arrives.

2. List the elements of coherence (precise references, parallelism, repetition, and transition words and phrases) in each of the following paragraphs.

a. In both the Egyptian and Mesopotamian kingdoms, the will of the ruler was enforced through a standing army, which was also the instrument of royal ambition. Military conquest, leading to the establishment of the first empires, was accompanied by commerce. The combined demands of government and of widening trade led in turn to the invention of writing—first ideograms, in which signs represented some idea or object, then syllabic writing, and finally the earliest alphabet. Here was one of the most precious of all human inventions, making possible not only the preservation of records and documents, both public and private—on papyrus, baked clay, or stone—but the growth of literature and science.

Thomas H. Greer, *A Brief History of Western Man*

b. The basic difference between downhill, or alpine, skiing and cross-country skiing is the terrain on which the skier travels. Downhill skiers literally ski down hills (or mountains, to be more accurate), while cross-country skiers travel on relatively level ground (although they must negotiate some tricky, if not sheer, terrain). These differences in terrain require different kinds of equipment and techniques. For example, the downhill skier uses alpine skis, in which the entire foot is secured to the ski itself with bindings, but the cross-country skier has only the toe secured to the ski, with the ankle left free of bindings.

3.5 PARAGRAPH LENGTH

There are no fixed rules for how long a paragraph should be. A good paragraph may be only a few short sentences, or it may run to nearly a page. The crucial consideration is whether the paragraph conveys a unified, complete, and coherent idea.

Generally, a paragraph should be long enough to fully develop its topic sentence, and a new paragraph should begin with a new topic sentence. In the following article, about life in Cuba under the Castro government, three separate topic sentences are run together without a paragraph:

Regimentation begins at the age of 5, when boys and girls start school. It is then that most of them join the first of many mass organizations they will belong to in the course of their lives, the *pioneros,* the Communist scout movement. They are given blue and white scarves and responsibilities—one *pionero* is in charge of the first-aid kit, a second keeps the flowers watered, a third wipes the blackboard clean, and a fourth, a political commissar in short pants, keeps a daily diary of *pionero* activities. ¶ Becoming a *pionero* is a useful thing to do. Between two students with equal grades, seeking admission to the same high school, the *pionero* will have the edge. As he grows up he will learn that, along with more duties, there are advantages to joining, and he may progress from the *pioneros* to the Communist party when he is 27, if he makes the grade, for the party, with 200,000 members, is an élitist rather than a mass organization. ¶ Those children who do not join the *pioneros* are considered members of *non-integrado* families— they are not fully integrated into the regime; they are not on the bus. About 80 percent of all Cuban schoolchildren up to the age of 14 are *pioneros.* They receive an illustrated weekly, an odd mixture of ideology and sports—on one page there will be a biography of Carlos Marx or Federico Engels, and on the next an article on how to pitch, describing *la rapida* (the fast ball), *la lenta* (the slow ball), and *la curva.*

Ted Morgan, "Cuba," *The New York Times Magazine*

Two possible breaks are indicated by ¶. Paragraphing at those points would group off the writer's ideas and make them easier for the reader to grasp.

Paragraphs that are too short can also be troublesome to readers. Short paragraphs may distract readers and make them lose the thread of the discussion, particularly when a single topic is being discussed. Often, short paragraphs have no topic sentences—or they have topic sentences that are poorly developed. Either way, the reader is left dissatisfied. The following passage, from an essay on automobile safety, illustrates the difficulty of using short paragraphs:

> Automobile tires have been made safer in recent years as a result of the Federal Tire Safety Act, which requires tire manufacturers to meet a number of safety standards.
>
> The government now requires that certain information be printed on the sidewalls of tires to assist consumers.
>
> These measures are helpful, but they are not enough. The consumer is still faced with choosing from over one thousand tire brands, which vary considerably in quality and in construction. Moreover, the federal government still has not developed a uniform grading system for tires.
>
> The consumer is left at the mercy of the tire companies, whose own labeling systems invariably inflate the quality of the tires. Manufacturers' labels range from "Champion" (for the *lowest* grade of tire) to "Deluxe" (for the highest).

The paragraphing in this passage is choppy as journalistic paragraphing often is. The first two paragraphs appear to be topic sentences for longer discussions, but they are never developed. They leave the reader wondering what kinds of safety standards and printed information are now required by law. The last two paragraphs relate to the same topic (why existing legislation is inadequate) and could easily be combined into one smooth discussion. Abrupt paragraphs such as these make it difficult to follow the flow of the writer's thoughts.

3.6 BEGINNING PARAGRAPHS

To be complete, a communication must have a beginning, middle, and end. The point at which the writer states his subject, orients the reader to it, and establishes his intention, or thesis, constitutes the beginning.

The length of a beginning paragraph depends on the nature of   **89** the assignment. Obviously, if a writer's task is to prepare a one-thousand-word essay, his opening should be limited to three or four sentences. Otherwise, there would be little room left to develop the initial ideas. In general, it is best to keep introductions short and concise. After all, the job of an opening is to *introduce* the subject matter of the communication.

In short communications a brief, well-stated opening is particularly important. An overelaborate beginning will interfere with rather than aid the reader. This problem is evident in the following example, from an essay on the legend of King Arthur:

> It was the beginning of the fifth century and the Roman Empire was slowly losing its power. Its grasp over Roman Britain was weakening. Then the Saxons started invading England, murdering people, plundering villages, and burning everything in sight. Rome refused to send aid, so all the British subjects who did not want to live under Saxon rule fled to a kingdom in the western part of the country. The kingdom was called Dumbrosia, and it was ruled by the powerful Ambrosius.
>
> Ambrosius was a valiant warrior, but at the end of the fifth century he died and the people needed a new leader. This new leader, legend has it, was King Arthur. The story of Arthur's exploits is one of England's greatest sagas. But historians are still wondering whether Arthur really existed and where, if at all, he fought his battles.

This introduction becomes lost in a maze of historical incidents. The writer seems more interested in recounting the history of the Dark Ages than in introducing his topic. The thesis of the paper is not brought in until the middle of the second paragraph. By this time the reader may have lost interest in the essay because the writer has failed to come to the point. Through revision, a more effective opening is possible:

> The story of King Arthur is England's most celebrated tale of knighthood. Over the centuries, however, many questions have been raised about its accuracy. Did King Arthur really exist? If he did, was he a king or just a warrior? Where was Arthur's castle, and where did he fight his battles? These are questions that historians are just now beginning to answer.

This introductory paragraph is simple and direct. It provokes the reader's interest by raising questions and promising answers, and *it defines the subject area of the essay.* In subsequent paragraphs the writer might explain the historical background of the legend before presenting the evidence. But the opening paragraph has let the reader know what direction the essay will take.

The beginning paragraph sets the tone for an entire communication. The opening must attract the reader's attention and orient the reader to the subject matter of the communication. It is in the opening that a pattern of unity, completeness, and coherence must be established. In the paragraph below, note how these principles have been observed:

> The background of the Pearl Harbor assault reads like a cloak-and-dagger mystery. Late in 1940, a year or so before the fatal attack, ingenious American experts had succeeded in "cracking" the main Japanese diplomatic code. During the succeeding months, the State Department was privy to the secret messages exchanged between Tokyo and its representatives in the United States. Official Washington knew, shortly before Pearl Harbor, that the Japanese were going to strike somewhere, for one decoded dispatch read that after the deadline date in late November "things are automatically going to happen." Then why the gigantic surprise party at Pearl Harbor?
>
> Thomas A. Bailey, *A Diplomatic History of the American People*

This opening paragraph is lively and provocative. The writer succeeds in arousing the reader's interest in the topic by presenting Pearl Harbor as an unsolved mystery rather than a closed historical case. Such a beginning makes the reader curious and eager to learn more.

In many situations, the final sentence of a beginning paragraph functions as a key lead-in to the supporting paragraphs that follow. In the following example, from an article on one of President Ford's speeches to the United Nations, the opening paragraph serves as a lead-in to the supporting paragraphs:

> **President Gerald Ford, appearing to deliver "the first of my addresses to the representatives of the world," agreed that "the economy of the world is under unprecedented stress."**
>
> In his first formal venture into international diplomacy, Ford offered the delegates the same thing he had given the American people in his Inaugural Address, "a little straight talk among friends." The delegates who heard him agreed afterward that the President had been uncommonly blunt. "Developing and developed countries, market and nonmarket economies—we are all part of one interdependent economic system," he said. Ford went on to imply that some countries—namely the oil-producing nations—appeared to be acting less interdependently than they had a right to.
>
> "The World 'Straight Talk Among Friends,'" *Time*

91

The last sentence of the article's opening paragraph (in bold type) focuses on Ford's statement to the UN General Assembly about the critical situation of the world economy. The paragraph that follows begins to elaborate on Ford's remarks. Subsequent supporting paragraphs in the article (not shown) continue to explore in depth the remarks made by the President.

As in the example above, the lead-in sentence works as a kind of traffic sign to show readers what direction the communication will take. This task is vital to the coherence of the writing.

Typical Patterns of Beginning Paragraphs

There are many types of opening paragraphs. In this section several models frequently used by writers will be examined.

Beginning paragraphs are sometimes panoramic in their approach. The following sample shows such an opening for a paper on the long-range effects of thermal pollution:

> From the age of Noah's flood to the age of nuclear warfare, prophets of doom have been predicting the demise of the human race. The most recent doomsters, however, do not expect that humanity will end with a bang, but with a whimper—shivering in the cold of an ice age brought on by thermal pollution. Those predicting our final extinction in an ice age base their conclusions on imperceptible but measurable changes in the environment.

The introduction above begins with a broad view of predictions about the end of the human race. It then shifts from the general to the specific, to forecasts of an ice age resulting from thermal pollution. The last sentence says, generally, that evidence exists to support this gloomy outlook. The supporting paragraphs will have the job of documenting and analyzing this evidence.

In many cases, the function of the opening is to state a subject or problem briefly and clearly:

> Some have called the United States an "affluent society." But the most recent poverty statistics indicate that 20 percent of American families are—in one way or another—disadvantaged.

This introduction gets right to the point. The writer states the problem directly, without elaborate introductions or flourishes. Such an opening suggests to readers that solid evidence and factual data will be provided to support the writer's argument.

While some beginning paragraphs state that a problem exists, others discuss the results of a particular problem:

> For years, American history textbooks have ignored the contributions of blacks, women, and other disadvantaged groups to the development of our nation. This failure has been a major cause of the poor public image and self-image of these groups.

The writer's opening presents a thesis: that a specific practice (omission of certain groups in textbooks) has led to a certain result (ignorance about the contributions of these people to American life). Supporting paragraphs will have to show that the problem does in fact exist, that the problem has led to the stated effects, and that these effects have had a certain impact in our society.

Sometimes, an opening paragraph begins with a commonly held belief that the writer wishes to disprove:

> Most people have a vision of welfare as a refuge for cheats and scoundrels. But a fair investigation of surveys made of welfare recipients shows that the overwhelming majority are honest and truly in need of assistance.

This introduction presents a widely accepted belief about the welfare system. It is the writer's intention to disprove such stereotypes about welfare recipients. Subsequent paragraphs will explain who welfare recipients are, why they need government aid, and what kinds of programs serve the recipients. As supporting evidence, the writer will include results of surveys conducted among welfare clients.

A writer may begin an article with an obvious value judgment:

> *The Exorcist* is the major American film of the last twenty-five years. It will be remembered long after *On the Waterfront, Bonnie and Clyde,* and *The Graduate* have been forgotten.

Here the writer starts off with a clearly stated bias. Often, this approach is a deliberate attempt to provoke controversy and thereby arouse the reader's interest. Such a thesis will have to be defended with logical, persuasive arguments or readers will not be convinced.

Occasionally, a writer will suggest a change of opinion or concession in an opening paragraph:

> In the past, I always believed that hiking was a tremendous waste of time and energy. But a few recent trips outdoors with friends have led me to change my mind.

The writer begins this essay with a shift of opinion. Such a concession wins the reader over because it demonstrates the writer's open-mindedness and arouses the reader's curiosity about why the writer's position has changed. Supporting paragraphs will explain the writer's change in viewpoint and what his present feelings on hiking are.

Here is another type of concession opening, from an article on Indian Prime Minister Indira Gandhi:

> A few years ago, people used to speak of Mrs. Gandhi admiringly as "a Joan of Arc" and "a modern mind," but now they speak of her disparagingly as "the Empress," "the Lady," "Madame," or simply "she." They say things like "She is a sort of doll presiding over a dolls' tea party while cutthroat politicians line their pockets behind her back and exploit their supporters for their own selfish ends and use their power to crush dissent."
>
> Ved Mehta, "Letter from New Delhi," *The New Yorker*

This opening describes a shift in public opinion rather than in the writer's own views. The examples are carefully chosen to convey the extremeness of the change. This type of opening is dramatic and involves the reader immediately in controversy; the reader is curious to learn why the change has occurred and what supporting evidence the writer will offer.

Sometimes, a writer introduces the subject matter of an essay with a crucial event:

> My introduction to the problems of owning a car really began when I received the insurance bill. Only then did I realize that having a car might not be all fun and games.

In the paragraph above, the writer tells of a jarring event: the arrival of the first insurance bill for his car. Such an opening is used to capture the reader's attention at the outset. Subsequent paragraphs will describe the writer's having a car, what happened when the insurance bill came, and how the writer's attitudes toward owning a car changed.

There are, of course, many other kinds of introductory paragraphs. But all introductions are governed by the same rules: Be simple, clear, and direct—no matter what style of opening is used. Decide how the entire task should be organized. Then determine the kind of opening paragraph that will fit in best with the larger framework of the essay.

Exercises

1. Choose one of the following topics and write three different opening paragraphs for it (panorama, statement of a subject or problem, belief, value judgment, concession, crucial event). Phrase the openings so that each will lead to a different development of the topic.

a. Why the popularity of football has increased so sharply in the last decade.

b. The importance (or unimportance) of space exploration.

c. A particularly pleasant (or unpleasant) childhood memory.

d. Citizens' fears of street crime in urban America.

2. The following introductory paragraphs need improvement. Rewrite each, keeping in mind the guidelines for opening paragraphs: An effective opening attracts the reader and defines the topic of the essay clearly and concisely.

a. Task: A short essay on hitchhiking.

> Nothing is worse than being lost on the road in a strange place. Especially when it's raining. It makes you feel like you never want to hitch a ride again. Also, sometimes you meet really wonderful people when you're on the road.

The paper goes on to discuss some of the writer's most enjoyable and difficult experiences as a hitchhiker.

b. Task: A short essay on the advantages of owning one's own business.

> When you own a business you are your own boss and can't be fired. Most important, you have an opportunity to share in the profits of the business rather than just taking home a salary. Some friends of mine who own a sporting goods store say that what they like best is being able to use their own creative ideas. You get to do a little of everything—purchasing, managing, selling, accounting. If you aren't good at numbers you might have to hire an accountant, and this could be a problem. Also, you could go bankrupt. Nonetheless, you have a chance to be independent and to make money in proportion to the amount of time and effort you put into the business.

The paper goes on to explain and illustrate each advantage of being self-employed.

3.7 SUPPORTING PARAGRAPHS

The opening paragraph of a communication lays the groundwork. It establishes the basic subject matter and the writer's intention or thesis. The supporting, or developing, paragraphs must fit into the framework created by the opening. They give evidence and arguments to back up the writer's thesis and supply convincing detail. Supporting paragraphs should contain useful data, relevant quotations from authorities, specific evidence to confirm general statements, and solid reasoning to back up theories and opinions.

Beginning writers sometimes restate a thesis many times in supporting paragraphs. That is, they tend to rewrite the first paragraph in different ways so that the essay stays in one place. Supporting paragraphs should echo the basic thesis, but they should also carry along the flow of the argument. Presenting the thesis at the beginning will suffice—as long as the middle paragraphs offer supportive detail. Without sufficient detail, the reader will be unconvinced, no matter how many times the thesis is repeated.

Types of Supporting Paragraphs

A writer can choose from many different patterns of supporting paragraphs, but the selection process is not arbitrary. The writer should not just choose a pattern and try to fit his material to it. Instead, before attempting to develop an idea, he must ask himself the following questions:

1. What material do I need at this point in my writing to develop my paragraph further?
2. How does this material relate to the preceding material and to my overall thesis?
3. How can I express this relationship clearly and efficiently?

Only after answering these questions can the writer decide what kinds of supporting paragraphs to use. For example, suppose the assigned topic of a paper is the merits of primitive and modern art. The structure of the paper could be based on comparison and contrast. The paper might begin with brief descriptions of primitive and modern art and follow with a few paragraphs about the differences between them. The conclusion could analyze the ways in which modern art shows more advanced thinking than primitive art and the ways in which some might consider it less satisfying. Of course, within this structure there is room for different techniques. The overall method will be to compare the two periods, but individual paragraphs may be used for analysis, for exemplification, or for elaboration of specific points.

There are five principal types of developing paragraphs:

1. Definition
2. Exemplification

3. Cause and effect
4. Analysis
5. Comparison and contrast

3.7a Definition

Certain paragraphs within a communication define a particular term, object, or concept. Defining paragraphs must be especially clear and concise. If a crucial term is poorly defined (or not defined at all), the reader will have difficulty with the material that follows.

In the following paragraph from a scientific article on the "primary events" of photosynthesis, the authors clearly and concisely define this unfamiliar term early in the essay in order to clarify the discussion to readers:

> In this article, we are concerned mainly with the first steps in photosynthesis: the absorption of light by a specific molecule and the transfer of that energy from one molecule to another, as in a bucket brigade, until it is eventually conveyed to those few molecules that participate in chemical reactions. These initial processes are called the "primary events" of photosynthesis. They are physical in nature, and they must be completed before the chemical activities of photosynthesis can begin.
>
> "The Absorption of Light in Photosynthesis," *Scientific American*

This definition makes the "primary events" of photosynthesis a clear concept to the average reader as well as to the scientist. The comparison to a bucket brigade is an important part of the definition, since it enables the reader to relate an unfamiliar idea to a common, well-known phenomenon.

It is important to avoid unnecessary or pointless definitions—ones that do nothing to develop the writer's intent. The following passage, from an essay on science-fiction writer Isaac Asimov, is weakened by an unnecessary definition:

> Isaac Asimov has written hundreds of science-fiction stories. Among my favorites are the stories in his collection *I, Robot*. A robot is a sort of man-made being, made of metal. Some robots can speak and carry out mechanical tasks. Asimov's writing is interesting because he raises fascinating questions about the relationship between people and technology. Some of the interactions between the robots and their "masters" are surprising.

There is no need to define the term "robot," since it is a familiar word and is not being used in any special way by the writer. It is not a word that might confuse or mislead readers. Unnecessary definitions talk down to readers and interrupt the flow of a discussion.

97

3.7a Definition

Just as writers should avoid unnecessary definitions, so they must guard against imprecise definitions, which misinform or confuse the reader. The following is a case in point:

> The Communist Bloc is a group that usually follows the lead of the Soviet Union in opposing the United States. Although the Soviet Union sometimes gives aid to the Communist Bloc, often the only link between the two is a shared opposition to the United States.

This definition of the Communist Bloc is inadequate because it is imprecise. The first sentence tells the reader that the Communist Bloc is a group, but he is not told what countries it is composed of. The second sentence tells the reader that the Soviet Union and the Communist Bloc share an opposition to the United States, but this information does not clarify the definition; the reader is still not given enough information to understand the meaning of the term as the writer is using it.

When defining newly coined words, specialized words, or words being used in a new or different way, providing complete information may not be enough. Sometimes, for example, the definition has to be generated rather than stated directly, as in the following example from Alvin Toffler's book *Future Shock:*

> The parallel term "culture shock" has already begun to creep into the popular vocabulary. Culture shock is the effect that immersion in a strange culture has on the unprepared visitor. Peace Corps volunteers suffer from it in Borneo or Brazil. Marco Polo probably suffered from it in Cathay. Culture shock is what happens when a traveler suddenly finds himself in a place where yes may mean no, where a "fixed price" is negotiable, where to be kept waiting in an outer office is no cause for insult, where laughter may signify anger. It is what happens when the familiar psychological cues that help an individual function are suddenly withdrawn and replaced by new ones that are strange or incomprehensible.
>
> Alvin Toffler, *Future Shock*

Toffler builds a definition of the term "culture shock" through a series of statements and examples. He begins with a general description that all readers will understand and cites familiar, well-known examples. Then he moves to more specific examples and to a precise definition of "culture shock" in psychological terms. The earlier description and examples help to clarify this "technical" meaning to readers.

In order to be effective, defining paragraphs must be complete, precise, and understandable. Do not leave any questions in the reader's mind about a definition, or the effectiveness of the entire essay will suffer.

3.7b Exemplification

A good supporting paragraph provides specific examples of general points made in the opening, as in the following passage, also taken from *Future Shock:*

> A look at the "help wanted" pages of any major newspaper brings home the fact that new occupations are increasing at a mind-dazzling rate. Systems analyst, console operator, coder, tape librarian, tape handler are only a few of those connected with computer operations. Information retrieval, optical scanning, thin-film technology all require new kinds of expertise, while old occupations lose importance or vanish altogether. When *Fortune* magazine in the mid-1960's surveyed 1,003 young executives employed by major American corporations, it found that fully one out of three held a job that simply had not existed until he stepped into it. Another large group held positions that had been filled by only one incumbent before them. Even when the name of the occupation stays the same, the content of the work is frequently transformed, and the people filling the jobs change.
>
> Alvin Toffler, *Future Shock*

The paragraph above is intended to illustrate Toffler's premise that American occupations are changing at an accelerating rate. Toffler begins by giving examples that are familiar to all readers—the help wanted listings in newspapers. He then cites a research study on job patterns conducted by *Fortune* magazine. The combined use of evidence plus statistical data makes the generalization convincing.

Paragraphs of exemplification often use quotations to support a writer's thesis. When quoting, the writer should be sure to spell out the meaning he wishes the reader to draw from the material. It is not enough to copy a quotation and hope that the reader agrees with the writer's interpretation. The following paragraph, from an essay on Arthur Miller's play *Death of a Salesman*, describes the movement of the play after its hero, Willy Loman, has died. The paragraph is effective because the writer not only uses quotations but also explains how they illustrate his points:

> Willy Loman is a victim of his own flashy rhetoric. But the deception and the sacrifice do not stop with him. They are endemic in his family. The tragic irony of the play is explicit in the final speech of the play. When his wife asks for forgiveness because she cannot cry—"It seems to me that you're just on another trip"—she sounds the note of unreality which the flute has played

as background music throughout the play. It makes little difference whether Willy is dead or alive; his world is an illusory one. Linda Loman's last sobs are because the house is free and clear—"I made the last payment today. . . . And there'll be nobody home. We're free and clear. We're free. We're free. . . . We're free. . . ." The family is free, or at least is capable of making itself free, free of Willy's kind of deception, free of illusion.

Barry Ulanov, Makers of the Modern Theater

Quotations, like examples, must serve the writer's purpose. They should never be used as a substitute for the writer's own thoughts and analyses. Thus, in the paragraph above, the writer uses quotations from the play together with his own interpretations, guiding the reader to the meaning he wishes to convey.

3.7c Cause and Effect

Some supporting paragraphs use causal reasoning to indicate a relationship between two or more events. That is, they show how certain events either caused or were caused by other events. This type of reasoning may take several forms: the writer may describe a single cause leading to a single effect, a single factor resulting in several effects, and so on. The following paragraph is an example of cause-and-effect reasoning in which the writer shows how a certain factor—the massive public health program undertaken in the early twentieth century—led to a certain effect, namely, increased life expectancy in the population. The writer cites specific examples and relevant statistics to support his argument:

At the turn of this century, infectious diseases were the primary health menace to this nation. Acute respiratory conditions such as pneumonia and influenza were the major killers. Tuberculosis, too, drained the nation's vitality. Gastrointestinal infections decimated the child population. A great era of environmental control helped change all this. Water and milk supplies were made safe. Engineers constructed systems to handle and treat perilous human wastes and to render them safe. Food sanitation and personal hygiene became a way of life. Continual labors of public health workers diminished death rates of mothers and their infants. Countless children were vaccinated. Tuberculosis was brought under control. True, new environmental hazards replaced the old. But people survived to suffer them. In 1900, the average person in the United States barely eked out fifty years of life. Some twenty years have since been added to this life expectancy.

Benjamin A. Kogan, Health: Man in a Changing Environment

In establishing a cause-and-effect relationship, the writer may move from cause to effect, as in the preceding paragraph, or from effect to cause:

> Experts say several factors contribute to the rising tide of volunteers: shorter workweeks, earlier retirement, growing numbers of young people who aren't forced—or aren't able—to find paying jobs. Those in the movement say that its biggest impetus comes from individuals who need personal involvement in an age seemingly dominated by computers, television, hermetically sealed homes, and far-flung suburbs.
>
> "50,000,000 Helping Hands," *Reader's Digest*

In this paragraph the writer explains how one event—the recent growth in the number of volunteers in the United States—can be attributed to several possible causes.

Cause-and-effect paragraphs always involve accounting for a specific set of circumstances or events. However, a particular explanation may not be the most likely reason for the effects, as the following example demonstrates:

> Many people have wondered why it was that James Bond novels and movies became such a rage in the last fifteen years. My own belief is that the Bond mania was due to the fact that Bond was British. Lots of people in America have an overblown respect for anyone with a British accent.

The writer attributes the immense popularity of the character James Bond to his British accent. The question that the writer needs to ask is the same one that readers will be asking: Is this explanation the most likely reason for James Bond's popularity? The answer seems at best uncertain. There are many other possible causes for "the Bond mania"—the sex and violence in the Bond stories, the traditional American love of detective heroes, the boost given Bond novels when President John F. Kennedy revealed that he was an avid reader of them. The "British accent" theory is far from convincing.

Because it is often difficult to show that a certain factor has caused a specific effect or set of effects, the writer must be prepared to use solid reasoning, detailed evidence, and convincing counterarguments to other theories of causation.

3.7d   Analysis

Paragraphs of analysis support the theme of an essay by helping the reader to look at various aspects of a subject one at a time. Analytical schemes organize a topic in some systematic way in order to promote logical and informative discussion. The specific scheme chosen will depend on the nature of the subject.

Often, a paragraph of analysis will break a topic down into convenient categories or types; subsequent paragraphs then elaborate on each of these types. The paragraph below, from an article on mountain climbing, illustrates this process:

> Expert mountaineers classify one another as rock men and snow men: rock climbing requires more agility; snow climbing needs more subtle skills. On most high slopes a climber must be well versed in both techniques.
>
> Sir John Hunt, "Mountaineering," MD

The writer divides the topic—the techniques of mountain climbing—into two major categories: rock climbing and snow climbing. This device provides a useful framework for subsequent discussion. In the next few paragraphs the writer will explain, contrast, and illustrate the two climbing techniques.

Many times, a writer will analyze a subject by dividing it into chronological time periods. This is done in the paragraph below, which discusses the rise of the SDS (Students for a Democratic Society) in the 1960s:

> This book is a story of that decade. It is a story roughly divided into four periods: the first, a period of Reorganization from 1960 to 1962 when SDS takes a new name and lays the basis for the shape it was to assume; the second, the period of Reform from 1962 to 1965 when SDS tries to make American institutions live up to American ideals; the third, the period of Resistance from 1965 to 1968 when SDS spreads out from coast to coast with open confrontations against these institutions; and the last, the period of Revolution from 1968 to 1970 when SDS sets itself consciously for a thorough—and, for some, a violent—overthrow of the American system.
>
> Kirkpatrick Sale, SDS: Ten Years Toward a Revolution

In this selection, the writer explains his intention to divide the history of SDS into four key time periods. The entire book is structured on this basis. The writer will return to this breakdown in his discussion of each major period and explain why that period was different from the others.

Not all subjects, of course, can be divided conveniently into categories or assigned specific labels. Sometimes, an analytical scheme is an overview of a subject, examining various aspects of its organization:

> One might go on, scoring a litany of instances in which the federal intelligence and investigative machinery seems to have been penetrated by, or come under the undue influence of, special interests. More helpful than such a list, however, would be to understand how a private intelligence apparatus actually works, how it came to exist, and who its clients and employees are. With that knowledge it may be possible to do more than take note of past abuses.
>
> Jim Hougan, "A Surfeit of Spies," *Harper's*

Here, instead of describing specific practices and abuses associated with private-intelligence work, the writer approaches the topic through a step-by-step examination of how a private-intelligence agency operates.

Dividing a subject into analytical schemes is a useful tool for the writer, especially in handling a broad subject. But it is important not to make arbitrary divisions in the name of analysis. An essay on how people spend their leisure time would serve little purpose if classified according to days of the week. A more sensible classification scheme would be an analysis of different types of leisure activities—reading, movies, hobbies, sports, and so on.

Analytical schemes, when used properly, make a subject easier to organize. The writer's task is simplified and, eventually, so is the reader's task of understanding the material.

3.7e   Comparison and Contrast (comp)

Effective comparisons and contrasts provide a *perspective* on the subject under discussion. For example, saying that a nursery-school teacher earns seven thousand dollars a year gives readers a bit of information to reflect on. But putting that figure in a comparative framework by stating that an electrician earns nineteen thousand dollars a year opens up a whole new way of evaluating the teacher's salary. The following paragraph illustrates this principle more specifically. The writer defines two terms by comparing and contrasting examples of each:

> There is a basic principle that distinguishes a hot medium like radio from a cool one like the telephone, or a hot medium like the movie from a cool one like TV. A hot medium is one that extends one single sense in "high definition." High definition is that state of being well-filled with data. A photograph is, visually, "high definition." A cartoon is "low definition," simply because very little visual information is provided. Telephone is a cool medium, and one of low definition, because the ear is given a meager

103

amount of information. And speech is a cool medium, or one of low definition, because so little is given and so much has to be filled in by the listener. On the other hand, hot media do not leave so much to be filled in or completed by the audience. Hot media are, therefore, low in participation, and cool media are high in participation or completion by the audience.

Marshall McLuhan, *Understanding Media*

The writer points out two key features that distinguish "hot" media from "cool" media. Hot media have a high degree of informational content and low audience participation. In contrast, cool media are low in information but high in audience involvement. The writer illustrates this contrast with several specific examples to clarify for the reader the concepts of hot and cool media. In effect, comparison and contrast provides the reader with another way of grasping the writer's intention.

Exercises

1. For each of the examples listed below, identify the kind of developing paragraph used (definition, exemplification, cause and effect, analysis, or comparison and contrast) and explain why it fits into that particular category.

a. Task: A profile of Edward Kennedy, Jr., son of Senator Edward Kennedy of Massachusetts.

This love for the outdoors and sports is something he shares with most of the 28 grandchildren of Rose and the late Joseph P. Kennedy. But otherwise, he is very different in temperament and behavior from most of his cousins. In fact, all three of the Edward Kennedy children are different from the other, more rambunctious Kennedys.

Lester David, "Teddy, Jr., Bravest of the Kennedys," *Good Housekeeping*

b. Task: An article on relationships between children and fathers.

Because of the absence of old traditions and often because of the lack of grandparents nearby, Americans have been particularly receptive to psychoanalysis and child psychology, which have focused a lot of attention on the mixture of loving and hating feelings that co-exist in the relationships of most families. Bringing negative feelings into the open has made conscientious parents guilty about them, has made them anxious to hold antagonism to a minimum and to try to be predominantly friends with their children.

Benjamin Spock, M.D., "A Father's Companionship," *Redbook*

c. Task: A story about a woman's experiences learning martial arts and self-defense.

> The principle of *yin* and *yang* is at the heart of kung-fu. As a "soft" martial art, its premise is the defeat of the opponent by yielding to him, then using his strength against him. When an opponent attacks with force, one becomes pliant and soft like a reed in the wind, leading the opponent to one's own strength. Similarly, if the opponent becomes soft, kung-fu allows its follower to be aggressively hard. There are over 200 different styles of schools of kung-fu—a bewildering choice for the new student—but I am content with the type taught by my teacher which I came to so casually.
>
> Kate Coleman, "Kung-fu," Women Sports

2. Write a brief supporting paragraph for each of the following subjects showing definition, exemplification, cause and effect, analysis, or comparison and contrast. Illustrate each type of supporting paragraph at least once.

  a. Living in the country (or city).

  b. The style of a well-known musical group.

  c. Bureaucracy in the United States.

  d. The meaning of the word *freedom*.

  e. Society's attitude toward the elderly.

3. Each of the following paragraphs is meant to illustrate one of the methods of paragraph development. Do the paragraphs fit the method indicated? Why or why not?

  a. Analysis.

> Personal conflicts fall into two general groups. One group includes conflicts between a person's desires and his ideals—between what he wants to do and what he feels he should do. A person in conflict feels torn, distressed, and uncertain. These feelings are what make conflict such an unpleasant part of life and a threat to normal behavior. A person cannot act normally when he has two conflicting desires—goals that are incompatible. You can't have your cake and eat it too.

  b. Definition.

> Mere novelty isn't enough. Some people come up with new and unusual ideas, but they are totally inappropriate to the problem at hand. Other people devise gimmicks and fads that serve no useful purpose; these things just divert our attention from what is really needed. And some people just spend all their time thinking up ideas that are totally impractical—that could never be carried out. None of these things are innovations.

105

c. Comparison and contrast.

> The two major forms of mass entertainment—the film and the theatrical play—offer very different advantages to the viewer. A film can range widely in time, depicting past, present, and future in rapid succession. Also, a film can quickly shift location, showing scenes from any part of the world. Films give actors an opportunity to correct their mistakes. If an actor misses his lines, the scene can be reshot. Finally, films sometimes let the audience see stunt men perform instead of the actors themselves. By contrast, in the live theater, where real actors are performing a few feet from the audience, none of these things are possible.

d. Exemplification.

> An argument has gone on in American families for years about which kind of music is more popular—rock music or classical. The consensus seems to be that people prefer rock music. For example, in some colleges even the drama club draws more people than the orchestra. And so does the swimming team. Also, almost all college students prefer rock music. The only ones who like classical music are those whose parents forced them to learn instruments.

3.8   CONCLUDING PARAGRAPHS

Just as opening and supporting paragraphs are shaped to fit the entire communication, so are concluding paragraphs. If the basic structure of an essay is analytical, the concluding paragraph should show where the analysis has led. The writer should draw conclusions and then sum up, as illustrated in the following paragraph from an essay on the dangers of pollution:

> It seems, then, that air and water pollution are becoming an increasing menace to the health and well-being of millions of Americans. Hard evidence shows that more people are dying every year as a result of pollution. And current antipollution legislation is clearly weak and unenforceable. A few citizens' groups are desperately trying to alert Americans to this silent danger, but they need help—before it is too late.

The writer briefly states a conclusion, interprets the evidence presented, and ends with a dire warning about the need for citizen action to fight pollution.

In many communications a comparison-and-contrast, analytical, or cause-and-effect structure may have been used to point out a problem. In such cases a reasonable conclusion may propose solutions or the need for solutions. The following paragraph, for example, ends with concrete suggestions:

> It seems clear that citizens' action is the only answer to fighting the growing problem of pollution. The work that must be done includes: educational campaigns to increase knowledge of the problem and dangers; lobbying in Congress and state legislatures for tougher anti-pollution laws; pressure on Government agencies to enforce all legislation with a maximum effort; campaigns within large corporations to elect "public interest" trustees committed to ending pollution and waste; and formation of local citizens' groups in every city and town of the country to build a nationwide movement against pollution. The task seems monumental, but these efforts *can* work and citizens *can* prevent pollution disaster—if we act now.

This paragraph is another possible ending for a paper on pollution. Instead of drawing a conclusion on the basis of the evidence, as in the previous example, the writer offers specific alternatives to help solve the problem.

An effective conclusion can be a brief restatement of the major points made in an essay. This technique is often used when the purpose of a communication is to instruct the reader:

> Extent, Originality, and Value. These are the main tests to apply to a piece of work under consideration. All of the questions that arise when we apply the tests will not have sharp and specific answers; if we knew the results before doing the work, the project would hardly seem worthwhile. When we oblige ourselves to face these questions intelligently, however, we do a great deal—perhaps as much as we can do—toward establishing natural limits and disciplining our efforts.
>
> James Thorpe, *Literary Scholarship*

The entire essay describes the criteria a reader should use in evaluating a work of literature. The writer defines the terms *extent, originality, and value* and explains how these criteria can help the reader gain insight into a literary work. In this concluding paragraph the writer reemphasizes the major points the essay has made.

Types of Conclusions to Avoid

The purpose of a concluding paragraph is not simply to have an end to go with a beginning and a middle. The conclusion must clearly and coherently wrap up the communication, leaving the

107

reader with a summary statement, a final analysis, or a set of conclusions or solutions to a problem. A communication should not abruptly end:

> Other court decisions on both sides have established the effectiveness of BBB arbitration.
>
> Sylvia Porter, "A Leap Forward," *New York Post*

This sentence is the concluding paragraph of a news article on how consumers can use the Better Business Bureau (BBB) to help resolve their complaints. The reader expects some elaborating detail on these "other court decisions" and may think that perhaps the writer ran out of space or time.

On the other hand, a conclusion should not be added on to a paper just to fit the formula "Every essay has to have a beginning, middle, and end":

> In concluding let me say that this paper has shown how the music of Chuck Berry was a major influence on the rock-music styles of the 1960s, including country rock, hard rock, and blues.

Such conclusions are mechanical restatements of the writer's original purpose. Rather than convincing readers that the writer has fulfilled his intention, they suggest only that the essay has been going in circles instead of leading to a point.

Concluding paragraphs that are oversimplified or that finger-point should also be avoided:

> The drug problem in America, as the statistics I have presented show, is at a shocking level. Only one solution can solve this problem: religion. If people turn back to religion, all the crime and violence and addiction connected with drugs will disappear.

This conclusion seems naive and simplistic. A problem as widespread and complex as drug addiction will not be solved so easily—or by any single method. Religious education may be part of the answer, but it certainly will not be enough in itself. Furthermore, this type of conclusion creates a problem because the proposed solution is introduced without any preparation in the body of the paper. A solution should be a logical outgrowth of the issues raised in an essay. It should be appropriate and convincing and should follow realistically from the nature of the evidence presented.

Conclusions are also ineffective when they suddenly jump into new issues:

> It seems clear that Eastern gurus like the Maharaj Ji and the Reverend Moon have won the hearts and minds of many young Americans. Some people think that these spiritual leaders should

> be prevented from entering the country. But that would be a denial of civil rights—particularly the right of free speech. Free speech is one of the cornerstones of American democracy—and of democracy throughout the world. Revolutions and wars have been fought to uphold it. Future wars may well be fought on its behalf. Free speech is one of the fundamental issues of our time.

The writer of this paragraph becomes completely lost at the end. The essay has discussed the rise of Eastern religious cults among American youth. The writer begins the conclusion logically but jumps off the topic into a discourse on free speech.

REVIEW EXERCISES

1. Analyze two of the paragraphs below by performing the following tasks:

Underline the topic sentence.
Point out key transitions used.
Evaluate the *unity* of the paragraph.
Evaluate the *completeness* of the paragraph.
Evaluate the *coherence* of the paragraph.
Suggest any necessary or helpful improvements.

a. Back in the 1950s, Italian Movie Belle Gina Lollobrigida spent idle time on the set sharpening her own photographic skills with a still camera. At 47, la Lollo has now turned her hobby into a second career. On assignment for a magazine series on "the most interesting men in the world," she has already shot Statesman Henry Kissinger, Astronaut Neil Armstrong, and Ship-owner Aristotle Onassis. Most recently she has been in Havana, cameras and notebooks at the ready, interviewing Premier Fidel Castro.

"People," *Time*

b. For almost a year now, Sly Stone has been talking about making changes in the way he lives. There will be more and better music, Sly promises, no more drugs, and now people who expect to see him in concert "better believe" that he will show.

Robert DeLeon, "Sly Stone Talks About New Family," *Jet*

c. Something else—a sense of unreality, some persistent note of recognition of difference—stayed with me after all of my visits to the Mets' clubhouse this year. Only in the end did I realize what it was. Instead of resembling a real ball team, the new Mets reminded me most of a Hollywood cast assembled to play in still

109

another unlikely baseball movie. They seemed smaller and younger and more theatrical than a real team, and their drama was hopelessly overwritten. Certainly the cast was right—Harrelson and Boswell (Bud and Ken), the eager, sharp-faced infielders; Wayne Garrett, the freckle-faced rookie with the sweet smile; Jerry Grote, the broken-nosed, scrappy catcher; Agee and Jones, the silent, brooding big busters; Jerry Koosman, the cheerful hayseed; Ed Charles, the philosophical black elder; Art Shamsky, the Jewish character actor with persistent back pains; Hodges and Berra, the seamy-faced, famous old-timers (neither, unfortunately, called Pop); and Tom Seaver, of course, the hero. And who can say that the Mets didn't sense this, too—that they didn't know all along that this year at Shea life was imitating not just art but a United Artists production?

Roger Angell, *The Summer Game*

2. Do the paragraphs below adequately serve as conclusions for the assignments indicated? Why or why not? Rewrite the paragraphs that seem to need improvement, keeping in mind the principles of concluding paragraphs discussed on pp. 106–109.

a. Task: An essay on cancer.

Cancer has become one of the most serious killers of American people. Yet government funding for cancer research is still inadequate. I think it is all the fault of the American Medical Association. What we should do is get rid of the doctors.

b. Task: An essay on becoming a parent.

The day Susie was born was the happiest day of my life. After all the months of waiting and preparing, her arrival was even more wonderful than I could have imagined. Now Susie is three years old, and she is just beginning to read simple words. Her grandmother marvels at how fast she is learning to read. But children today do things that children never did before.

c. Task: A biography of comedian Bob Hope.

All in all, the seventies have been a difficult decade for Bob Hope. The Vietnam War—which he defended ardently for years—became unpopular with just about everyone. Then his two good friends, President Richard Nixon and Vice President Spiro Agnew, both left office amidst scandal and disgrace. Ah, life is difficult; the seasons come and go; the first ones now will later be last; when the going gets tough, the tough get going.

Sentences

"THE MOST IMPORTANT PLAY OF THE SEASON AND PERHAPS OF ANY SEASON IN RECENT MEMORY." Pat Collins, WCBS-TV

"THIS IS A VERY FINE AND ENTHRALLING PLAY. It has all of Mr. Shaffer's masterly command of the theatre. The direction holds all the elements of the play together with consummate skill. The performances blaze with theatrical life." Clive Barnes, New York Times

"A SIMPLY DEVASTATING EXPERIENCE. Begins with a power drive that does not let up until intermission, gives you a quick break to catch your breath and then it goes like a shot the rest of the way. Breathtaking." Martin Gottfried, New York Post

> The various methods for shaping sentences enable the writer to construct each sentence so that it is both clear in itself and moves the reader forward. The writer should become practiced in these methods as well as aware of the many sentence structures that confuse readers rather than communicate to them.

THE TASK OF THE SENTENCE

Because the reader sits at a distance from the writer, he can grasp the writer's intention only through what is actually on the page: words shaped into sentences. Translating the "what-I-mean-to-say" (intention) into sentences that accurately reflect the author's perceptions, interests, and organization involves the laborious and often frustrating task of shaping and reshaping sentences, carving away at words until they form for the reader an exact picture of what was in the writer's mind. While the reader may end up with the impression that the words flowed easily from the writer, this impression is the result of the writer's efforts to mold sentences that communicate ideas accurately and efficiently and with as much style as possible. Moreover, translating intention into meaningful sentences requires that the writer not only make each sentence clear, effective, and graceful in itself, but also that each sentence fit appropriately into its context (the written environment in which it occurs).

Sentences in Context

Beginning writers sometimes have difficulty understanding that a sentence can be correct grammatically but ineffective rhetorically—that is, unsuccessful in communicating its point clearly and accurately to readers:

> With fuel still scarce, the risk of carbon monoxide poisoning may increase this winter, warns Dr. Frank Lisella of the Center for Disease Control in Atlanta. To keep warm some people may insulate their homes without providing for adequate ventilation.
>
> *Woman's Day*, December 1974

Although the first sentence is grammatical, the reader might wonder for a moment what the fuel shortage has to do with carbon monoxide poisoning. In the second sentence the connection is made, but the two pieces of information necessary for making the connection are rather widely separated. This separation may momentarily create difficulty for the reader. With minor revision, however, the reader's task is made easier:

> The risk of carbon monoxide poisoning may increase this winter, warns Dr. Frank Lisella of the Center for Disease Control in Atlanta. With fuel still scarce, some people, in order to keep warm, may insulate their homes without providing for adequate ventilation.

In extreme cases poor sentence management can cause the writer to communicate an entirely different impression or meaning from the one intended:

> When I went to New York City, I saw the Empire State Building walking down Fifth Avenue.
> Over one hundred people were injured in a crash between Chicago and Detroit.

In these classic cases the reader, after a pause or two, would mentally adjust the meaning and arrive at the writer's true intention. But in many other cases such mental adjustments may not be so easy to make. For example, responding to the claim that Americans have lost the true spirit of Christmas, the writer writes:

> Many people think that Christmas is for the purpose of exchanging gifts. These people are wrong, unfortunately, because the sole purpose of Christmas is to celebrate the birth of Christ.

It takes a moment to figure out that the writer did *not* mean to say it is unfortunate that the purpose of Christmas is to celebrate the birth of Christ rather than to exchange gifts. The author could easily have avoided the confusion by beginning the first sentence with *unfortunately* rather than placing it where it is in the second.

Even when sentences are clear in context, each one may be so similar in structure to the one before it that the sum is boring to the reader:

> A calculator is a very handy tool for anyone doing math. A calculator increases the speed and accuracy of computations. Many different models of calculators are on the market today. Only a few calculators have advanced functions. The better calculators have these advanced functions.

113

In addition to its other faults, the paragraph above consists of sentences that clack along like a line of boxcars until their similarity slowly hypnotizes the reader into inattention.

Why do writers write sentences that confuse or bore the reader? There are three principal reasons:

1. They are unaware of their reader's needs.
2. They have not fully thought out their subject or theme.
3. They lack experience or familiarity with the devices available for constructing rhetorically effective sentences.

The first and second reasons are problems either of attitude or of concentration. Generally, most writers are able to avoid both failings as they gain experience and maturity in writing. The third reason, however, raises a practical question: How does a writer acquire the techniques for constructing rhetorically effective sentences? The remainder of the chapter is devoted to answering this question.

VARIED SENTENCE PATTERNS (var)

Just as people have become accustomed to a wide variety of dress styles, so are they willing to accept—within reasonable limits—a wide variety of sentence patterns for transmitting information, ideas, and attitudes:

> A few months ago my wife and I went to the wedding of a friend's daughter. The bride was a lovely girl—charming, witty, talented. By comparison her young man seemed, so far as surface impressions go, totally unprepossessing. As the couple exchanged vows my wife leaned over and whispered to me, "I wonder what she sees in *him*?"
>
> Norman M. Lobsenz, "What Do They See in Each Other?" *Woman's Day*

> We, therefore, the Representatives of the United States of America, in General Congress, Assembled, appealing to the Supreme Judge of the world for the rectitude of our intentions, do, in the Name, and by the Authority of the good People of these Colonies, solemnly publish and declare, that these United Colonies are, and of Right ought to be Free and Independent States; that they are Absolved from all Allegiance to the British Crown, and that all political connection between them and the State of Great Britain, is and ought to be totally dissolved; and that as Free and Independent States, they have full Power to levy War, conclude Peace,

> contract Alliances, establish Commerce, and to do all other Acts and Things which Independent States may of right do.
>
> Declaration of Independence
>
> To believe is very dull. To doubt is intensely engrossing. To be on the alert is to live; to be lulled into security is to die.
>
> Oscar Wilde
>
> Beauty is truth.

One sentence above is longer than most paragraphs; another is only three words long. One group of sentences tells a little anecdote; another gives a philosophy of life. Whether sentences are long or short, simple or complex, the reader is familiar with and used to receiving information from each type.

Furthermore, it is interesting to note that sentences with the simplest structure do not necessarily contain the simplest thought. Beginning writers often make the mistake of equating profound thought with sentences that are long, complex, and difficult to form; or they equate simple thought with sentences that have a short, simple structure. Actually, the simplest as well as the most complex sentences above are the result of careful crafting. In fact, some of the simplest sentences—the Oscar Wilde one, for example—contain highly complex thought.

4.1   Sentence Length and Complexity

In each communication, the length or complexity of individual sentences or of sentences as a group is determined by three factors:

1. The writer's intention.
2. The relationship of a sentence to other sentences.
3. The audience addressed.

Since each writing situation requires a different combination of these factors, it is impossible to set rules for sentence length or complexity. Still, some helpful guidelines do exist based on how a reader usually reacts to sentence structure and length.

It is useful to think of the possible varieties of sentence structures in terms of a spectrum from the simplest to the most complex. At one end are those sentences based on a single subject-verb-object (I–saw–the-book) pattern. Such sentences contain a single thought or action for the reader to grasp:

> Good news these days is rare.
> Do not carry cash when you travel.

115

> Each student should write an essay.
> We are celebrating the bicentennial.

At the other end of the spectrum are those sentences with multiple subjects, verbs, objects, qualifying clauses, and modifiers, all woven together within one structure:

> As you listen at every turn to those countless accents and vocabularies that color the voice of Uncle Sam; as each morning brings a new landscape as easily before your Pullman window as a fresh backdrop is lowered on the stage; as elms turn into palms and palms into oranges; as wheat changes into cotton and race horses into cattle; as the snow by the Northern lakes melts in a few hours into spring in Texas; or as you leave behind you the East's cool, manicured green to cross the great muddy inland rivers and traverse the granaries, and the Rockies suddenly rise from the plains, you cannot help sensing the differences in race, class, and religion of those *millions who have either become or are becoming* that new people, the Americans, and marveling at the miracle which is their country.
>
> John Mason Brown, *Jubilee: One Hundred Years of the Atlantic*

Stripped of its six introductory clauses and the qualifying detail, this sentence asks the reader to grasp two ideas at once: (1) you cannot help sensing the differences between Americans; and (2) you cannot help marveling at the miracle of their country. Of course, this pared-down version of the sentence is far less effective than the original, which communicates through a single complex structure a series of impressions about the unity within the variety of America. The thought is not especially difficult to grasp, but along the way the reader receives the detail that makes the thought convincing or at least reasonable. This sentence is not inherently "better" than another writer might have written. It simply serves his purposes in a particular place within a particular communication. In another context shorter sentences might have served his purposes better.

Although the length and complexity of individual sentences depend on the writer's purposes, the writer must also consider the effect a *pattern* of sentences will have on the reader. Short, simple sentences are read more quickly than long, complex sentences. The former are often used for instructions or reports; the latter in analyses, arguments, and comparisons—that is, on occasions when the writer needs to make elaborate qualifications and subtle evaluations. But whether his sentences are long or short or in between, the professional writer avoids piling sentences having the exact same pattern on top of one another—as in the example on the bottom of page 113 and in the two that follow. In the first of these two, a student is explaining why education has increased her doubts about the meaning and purpose of life:

> I have come to see myself in a different light. I have changed many of my opinions. I now have a somewhat better view of what life is about. But where does that put me? I am still in the same position. I have much to say. Few are willing to listen. Those in a position to help me are lost in idealism. They will lead society to eventual destruction. But who is to determine the best methods of salvation? Who can look into the future? Who can see if life is worth the effort? Should I revert and pursue happiness? Life was much simpler when I was younger. I was ignorant. Education brought me to this state.

The writer of the second example is attacking the tendency of young people to think they have discovered everything:

> While astrology has become popular in recent years, especially among young people and even more particularly in the so-called counterculture, in reality this science is as ancient as the history of humanity itself. Sometimes recent enthusiasts, who sadly lack any sense of history, fail to understand this obvious truth and act instead as if they were the first generation to have discovered astrology, and as if their parents' and grandparents' generations knew nothing of this field—or any other branch of human knowledge. This antihistorical sense, American as it is, is upsetting to older people, who quite rightly do not wish to be treated in such a patronizing manner, no matter what the reason, no matter how alienated the young generation claims it is.

In the first example, the series of short sentences is likely to impress the reader as immature, while in the second example the series of complex sentences about a relatively simple subject sounds pretentious.

For any particular writing task there is a wide variety of sentence patterns available to the writer. By using a combination of sentence patterns that fit well together, the writer will interest his readers.

Exercises

Revise the sentences in the two sample paragraphs above to clarify the writers' intentions, to provide variety, and to fit the subject more appropriately. The order of the sentences may be changed.

SHAPING EFFECTIVE SENTENCES (ef)

The ability to manipulate sentences to increase their clarity begins with the realization that sentences can be shaped after they have been written for the first time. The two basic methods for shaping sentences are *coordination* and *subordination.* Any sentence, beyond the simplest "Jane-saw-Dick" (subject-verb-object) sentence, uses these two devices.

4.2   Coordination

Coordination is the act of combining and relating words, phrases, and clauses by means of *and, but, for, or, nor, yet,* and other coordinating words:

> The use of music by the military has ancient origins **and** was first employed to encourage one's own troops, dismay the enemy, **and** transmit orders across the battlefield. Perhaps the earliest recorded **and** most effective display of encouragement was provided by Joshua at the siege of Jericho, when on the seventh day priests led by armed men circled seven times around the city sounding seven trumpets, at the last blast of which, **and** aided by a mighty shout from the army **and** the people, the walls came tumbling down.
>
> Patrick Ryan, "Rev up the Jeeps, Let's Hear the Music!" *Smithsonian*

> Compared to the lifetime of an individual, **or** even of a nation **or** a culture, half of history may seem a long time, **but** it is only a small fraction of the total span of man's sojourn on earth to date.
>
> William W. Hallo and William Kelly Simpson, *The Ancient Near East*

> We warrant each unit to be free from defects in material **and** workmanship under normal use **and** service, **and** in accordance with the conditions set forth below.

It is possible to coordinate whole sentences, clauses, subjects, verbs, modifiers—in short, any language element. The reader accepts the combinations as long as the elements are truly related or truly opposed. To the reader, the second of the two examples below makes just as much sense as the first, if not more:

| Uncoordinate | His commitment as a congressman is not apparent from the record books. His leadership is not apparent from the records. |

| Coordinate | **Neither** his commitment as a congressman **nor** his leadership is apparent from the record books. |

However, the reader is only confused if the combinations are either contradictory or unparallel:

| Unparallel | Many spiritual concepts are contained in T. S. Eliot's critical writing **and** included a sense of evil or fear. |
| Unparallel | Each student who walks off the platform on graduation day leaves with a college degree **but** also a great future. |

In the first sentence *and* appears to link writing with the rest of the sentence, but the linking makes no immediate sense. The reader does not know whether the writer meant:

| | T. S. Eliot's critical writing contained **both** spiritual concepts **and** a sense of evil and fear. |

or:

| | Many spiritual concepts, **including** a sense of evil and fear, are contained in T. S. Eliot's critical writing. |

In the second sentence, the reader has difficulty in understanding how a college degree and a successful future are opposed and wonders if the writer has left something out. The writer may have meant:

| | Each student who walks off the platform on graduation day leaves **not only** with a college degree **but also** with a great future. |

In both of the original sentences the coordination of the elements is incomplete and is therefore inefficient in communicating meaning to the reader. When the coordination is completed, however, the sentences are more efficient, meaningful, and graceful.

4.3   Subordination (sub)

Subordination involves taking a piece of information that could stand as an independent sentence and making it a dependent element of another sentence. The dependent element may be a word (an adjective or adverb), a phrase (a group of words expressing an incomplete action, usually beginning with a preposition or a verb), or a clause (a group of words expressing a complete action, containing both a subject and a verb). Subordinate clauses generally begin with subordinating conjunctions (*when, after, before, because, if,* and so on) or a relative pronoun (*who, which, that*).

119

4.3 (sub)

In the following examples, two sentences are combined into one through the process of subordination (the dependent elements are in bold type). Note how subordination smooths out choppy sentences, gives emphasis to important points, and clarifies the relationships among ideas:

Ineffective	Few consumers have taken advantage of the new truth-in-lending laws. This is unfortunate.
Revised	**Unfortunately,** few consumers have taken advantage of the new truth-in-lending laws. (adverbial modifier)
Ineffective	The meeting is scheduled for Monday. It will start at eight o'clock.
Revised	The meeting is scheduled for Monday **at eight o'clock.** (prepositional phrase)
Ineffective	Six thousand workers were laid off without notice. The union called a strike.
Revised	**When six thousand workers were laid off without notice,** the union called a strike. (subordinate clause)
Ineffective	My uncle is sixty-three. He has decided to retire.
Revised	My uncle, **who is sixty-three,** has decided to retire. (relative clause)
Ineffective	Several people were sitting to my right. They began to protest the committee's decision.
Revised	Several people **sitting to my right** began to protest the committee's decision. (verb phrase)

Through the same process of subordination, the sentences in the following paragraph can be reshaped into a single sentence:

Unsubordinate	It was the early sixties. I quit my jobs. I quit three of them. This happened in less than two years. Finally I found a good spot.
Subordinate	In the early sixties, I quit three different jobs in less than two years before I found a good spot.

The single longer sentence is actually easier to understand than the series of short sentences, because the writer has already put together for the reader the relationships among the events. All the time elements in the first group of sentences are made into clauses that become dependent portions of the basic sentence, *I quit jobs.* This process does not make the subordinated elements less important in the sense of being less meaningful; it simply shows more clearly the relationships among the pieces of information.

The writer can rely on the reader to understand the relationships among coordinated or subordinated elements in a sentence as long as the process is carefully completed. In fact, the reader may actually begin mentally to edit a piece of writing if the writer has not coordinated and subordinated:

> Only one aspect of the course leaves a sour taste in my mouth. This is the daily quizzes. It is understandable that there must be grounds to base grades on. There should be an indication that students have completed the assigned readings. It seems unnecessary, however, to prove that each assignment has been completed at a specific time. The students are in the class of their own free will. They want to learn. The teacher should acknowledge the students' motivation. The time of completing an assignment should be left up to them.

The reader of these sentences may mentally reshape them to look like this:

> Only one aspect of the course leaves a sour taste in my mouth—the daily quizzes. Although there should be some means of evaluating students' work, it seems unnecessary to prove that each assignment has been completed at a specific time. Since the students are in class of their own free will, they must want to learn. The teacher should acknowledge the students' motivation by leaving the time of completing an assignment up to them.

It should be obvious by now that coordination and subordination allow the writer not only to communicate more clearly the intended relationships among events, facts, and ideas but also to do so more efficiently. In the following groups of sentences, the writer wastes the reader's energy by making him wade through unnecessary words:

> A calculator is a very handy tool for anyone doing math. A calculator increases the speed and accuracy of computation.

> The beginning of good theater is the written play. The written play contains almost all of the message that the playwright is trying to transmit.

> I have very little experience in writing subjective essays. Being a nurse, I have much experience in writing objective reports. The kind of writing with which I am most familiar is laboratory reports.

Such wheel-spinning sentences carry the reader through a great many words, but very little distance is covered. Subordination and coordination would increase the writer's mileage:

> Calculators are handy tools for increasing the speed and accuracy of mathematical computations.

> The beginning of good theater is the written play, which contains almost all the playwright's message.
>
> As a nurse, I have a good deal of experience in writing laboratory reports but little experience writing subjective essays.

Some of the increased efficiency is the result of coordination and some the result of subordination. At times a coordinated sentence can be made even more efficient by subordination, as is demonstrated in the third sentence above.

Of course, coordination and subordination are already familiar to everyone because of their constant use in everyday speech. In writing, however, the frequency and care with which these devices are used must increase if the writer wishes his communications to tell the reader precisely what he means.

4.4 Inversion and Transposition

English sentences are most frequently written in the subject-verb-object structure:

> The man who lives under a good government is fortunate.
>
> The viewer of films is sometimes overwhelmed by the number of experiences he is bombarded with because films can express many ideas and emotions simultaneously.

The writer, however, can change this basic order and the order of other elements in the sentence so as to increase clarity, change the emphasis, or provide variety.

> Fortunate is the man who lives under a good government.
>
> Because films can express many ideas and emotions simultaneously, the viewer of films is sometimes overwhelmed by the number of experiences he is bombarded with.

The use of *inversion* and *transposition* depends, of course, on the context. To change the order of a sentence simply for the sake of variety may be inappropriate. For example, the following sentence is structured inappropriately for the context of a cookbook:

> Until they stand in firm peaks, beat egg whites.

Moreover, if writers are not careful, they may make adjoining sentences or clauses unclear by transposing elements in one:

> From the French word *chambre* (room) comes the English word *chamber*. This in turn is derived from the Latin *camera* (vault).
>
> *Hue* is one feature determined by the length of a light wave—a scientific term commonly referred to as color.

In both of these examples, the inverted word order creates confusion and ambiguity. As a consequence, the information is not efficiently communicated to the reader. The sentences can be clarified by using regular word order:

> The English word *chamber* comes from the French word *chambre* (room). This in turn is derived from the Latin *camera* (vault).

> One feature determined by the length of a light wave is *hue*—a scientific term commonly referred to as color.

Whether transposing the elements of a sentence or inverting its structure works can be determined only in the context of other sentences. For a sentence that stands alone, many patterns are possible:

> I found myself in emotional and mental limbo for about two months following the rift in our relationship.

> For about two months I found myself in emotional and mental limbo following the rift in our relationship.

> Following the rift in our relationship, I found myself in emotional and mental limbo for about two months.

> Disintegrating forces were at work beneath the surface of political serenity.

> Beneath the surface of political serenity, disintegrating forces were at work.

> At work beneath the surface of political serenity were disintegrating forces.

In isolation, it is impossible to say which of the three sentences in each group works best. However, inversion and transposition give writers more flexibility in shaping sentences that are best suited to a particular writing situation.

4.5 Condensation

We have already discussed how coordination and subordination can help the writer to shape more efficient prose. The guiding principle behind those two devices is that sentences should be *condensed;* that is, they should contain only those words or phrases that do some work by adding information, qualifications, ideas, or structural elements that clarify the author's intention. Each of the following sentences, for example, contains excess verbal baggage:

> **There are** a great many people who question the value of higher education.

123

> The Oakland Athletics is the team **that** won the game **that** I watched.
>
> The name **of** the author **of** the book is Budd Schulberg.

The structure of these sentences can be condensed with no loss of clarity:

> Many people question the value of higher education.
>
> The Oakland Athletics won the game I watched.
>
> The author of the book is Budd Schulberg.

Condensing the original sentences becomes relatively easy once we recognize that such structural elements as *there is, there are, that* clauses, and phrases containing *of* can often be eliminated without jeopardizing the clarity of the sentences.

Other common examples of excess verbal baggage are *the use of, the utilization of,* and *use* (as a verb):

> Her **use of** logic is impressive.
>
> **The utilization of** vitamins as supplements to a good diet is probably not necessary.
>
> Sometimes I **use** sleeping as a way to avoid difficult problems.

Writers may resort to such structures to make their prose sound more weighty. In fact, the structures put unnecessary words between the reader and the meaning and can easily be eliminated:

> Her logic is impressive.
>
> In a balanced diet, supplementary vitamins are probably not necessary.
>
> Sometimes I sleep to avoid difficult problems.

A bit of revision in each case highlights the key information instead of burying it. The professional writer is always on the lookout for ways to save a few words, especially when condensing a sentence increases its precision and impact.

4.6 Repetition

Repetition used deliberately to build suspense, to drive home a point, or to provide unity and balance in a sentence or group of sentences can be rhetorically effective:

> As a teacher, he lacked **care** in research, **care** in preparation of class lectures, **care** in grading student papers, and **care** about the personal needs of his students.

When not overdone, such repetition can create emphasis necessary for grasping the writer's intent. In this case, the repetition of *care* drives home the writer's disappointment in the teacher.

A writer may also choose to repeat sentence patterns for extra rhetorical force. For example, the writer of the following passage chose the same sentence structure four times:

> Does the theater change my way of thinking? No. Does the theater change my social views? No. Does the theater make me more liberal or more conservative? No. Does the theater expand my mind? No. The theater transforms me from an anonymous college student with class rank and identification number into a person who thinks and responds as an individual.

The repeated use of a question-and-answer format creates suspense and anticipation, building still another question in the reader's mind ("What does the theater do?"). The writer's final explanation becomes the focus of the paragraph, since it breaks the pattern set for the reader. That is, the writer uses repetition followed by a break in the repetition to drive home his point.

This example demonstrates the close relationship between repetition and parallel structure. Effective repetition is often a matter of building parallel sentences—of using similar grammatical patterns to express similar ideas. The rhythm of the parallel pattern emphasizes the relationships among ideas and unifies separate sentences into a coherent, logical whole. In certain situations, however, repetition may clutter up a communication and cause *redundancy:*

> Eugene O'Neill's *Long Day's Journey into Night,* about his doomed family, contains the ultimate tragic theme. This play is the epitome of failure and tragedy. The play presents no optimistic message. This ominous pessimism is the problem addressed by the play.

Although the writer of this paragraph repeatedly refers to the theme in O'Neill's play, he never really says anything about the theme. As a consequence, the paragraph stagnates in a series of redundant statements. To grasp the writer's meaning most readily, the reader should have to wade through as few words as possible.

4.7 Balance and Antithesis

In some contexts, the devices of coordination, subordination, condensation, and repetition can be used to create a particularly lively sentence that the reader can enjoy for itself:

> When we cannot act as we wish, we must act as we can.
>
> My sister never votes for Republican candidates, and my brother-in-law never votes for anyone.

The punch in such sentences comes from two elements: (1) the similarity of the grammatical structures on each side of the punctuation (*balance*); (2) the contrast between ideas expressed in some of the same words (*antithesis*). The meaning of the words in such sentences often differs slightly in the contrasted parts. In the second sentence above, for example, "never votes" has two meanings: to vote against something as opposed to not voting at all.

Such sentences take a great deal of crafting, but the writer is rewarded with colorful prose. The following paragraph, a statement by Franklin D. Roosevelt, illustrates this point nicely:

> The issue of government has always been whether individual men and women will have to serve some system of government or economics, or whether a system of government or economics exists to serve individual men and women.

The same idea expressed differently loses the conciseness and rhetorical power of the original:

> One point of view about governments and economic systems holds that the people's duty is to follow what the system thinks is right. The other point of view is that governments exist to service the needs of individuals.

The conflict between two ideas about government, heightened by the antithesis in the first presentation, is lost in the second.

4.8   Active and Passive Constructions

Many sentences can be structured so that they appear in either the *active* or the *passive* form:

> Active   Shakespeare **wrote** *Hamlet.*
>
> Passive   *Hamlet* **was written** by Shakespeare.

In either case, it is clear to the reader who wrote *Hamlet.* The difference lies in the order and corresponding stress of the elements. In the active construction, the actor (*Shakespeare*) precedes the action (*wrote*) and receives the stress. In the passive construction the order is reversed. The receiver (*Hamlet*) of the action (*was written*) comes before the actor and, therefore, becomes the element stressed.

Although passive sentences can solve some problems and tasks the writer may meet, active constructions are generally stronger, livelier, and more efficient. They put the actor before the action:

Passive	It **is believed** by many people that all politicians are corrupt. This opinion **was** also **held** by the author of this piece, until there **was provided** an opportunity for him to work on a political campaign.
Active	Many people **believe** that all politicians are corrupt. I shared this belief—until **I had** an opportunity to work on a political campaign.
Passive	South America **was viewed** by the Spanish *conquistadors* as El Dorado, the land of gold.
Active	The Spanish *conquistadors* **viewed** South America as El Dorado, the land of gold.

The passive form of the examples above are more static and slow the reader down because they tell who the actor was indirectly and employ such awkward phrases as *was also held, until there was provided,* and *was viewed by.*

Although active constructions generally turn out to be more effective than passive, in some situations a passive construction may be preferable. For example, a writer may wish to stress the receiver of the action rather than the actor.

> Andrew Johnson **was impeached** by Congress on the grounds that he had violated the Tenure of Office Act. Johnson's assertion, however, that the law was unconstitutional **was** later **upheld** by the Supreme Court.

The writer uses a passive form to keep the focus on Andrew Johnson. An entirely different emphasis is created if the sentences are rewritten in active form:

> Congress **impeached** Andrew Johnson on the grounds that he had violated the Tenure of Office Act. The Supreme Court, however, later **upheld** Johnson's assertion that the law was unconstitutional.

The active version shifts the emphasis in the sentences from Johnson to the actions of Congress and the Supreme Court. This version would be acceptable—and preferable—if the writer's purpose were to compare the two federal bodies. But in a paper on Andrew Johnson the passive form is more effective, since it keeps the focus on the subject.

Passive constructions are widely used in scientific, military, and academic writing to establish a more impersonal or objective tone than can be achieved with the active first-person form (*I found, I believe*). Yet scholarly writing can become bogged down in passive constructions. One way to create an objective tone without awkwardness is to substitute the action or results of the action for the

127

I subject, instead of falling back on passive forms:

First-Person Account	**I found** that many of Pope's ideas on criticism were drawn from the works of John Dryden. In my research **I discovered** many similarities, for example, between passages in Pope's "Essay on Criticism" and Dryden's "Essay of Dramatic Poesy."
Passive Voice and Third Person	Many of Pope's **ideas** on criticism **were drawn** from the works of John Dryden. **There are** many **similarities,** for example, between passages in Pope's "Essay on Criticism" and Dryden's "Essay of Dramatic Poesy."
Active Voice and Third Person	**Pope drew** many of his ideas on criticism from the works of John Dryden. For example, several **passages** in the "Essay on Criticism" **bear** a strong similarity to Dryden's "Essay of Dramatic Poesy."

Each successive rewriting of this passage expresses the writer's ideas more sharply and succinctly. The subject under discussion comes into focus with no loss of clarity or meaning. Note too that the elimination of the first-person subject does not weaken the writer's credibility as a critic—indeed, it draws more attention to the perceptiveness of the analysis. Credibility is obtained not through using the *I* subject but through providing specific examples to support a point.

Passive constructions and third-person forms do not, of course, prove objectivity. They merely establish the appearance of it. To avoid saying "I" in order to sound intellectual sometimes results only in sounding stuffy. This is particularly true when the writer's role in the subject is part of the meaning he wishes to convey:

Awkward	Attendance by this writer at the Kennedy Center production of *Jumpers* proved a disappointing experience.
Improved	I was disappointed by the Kennedy Center production of *Jumpers.*

The writer's determination to avoid an *I* subject results in an awkward, pretentious statement. The revised sentence is smoother and simpler—and says what the writer means.

4.9   Interrupted Movement

Interrupted movement—the insertion of a phrase or clause between subject and verb or between verb and object—is another device avaiiable to writers for managing their prose style. Interrupted sentences add variety and emphasis to writing and create a more informal tone:

> The tapes were, **if accurately transcribed,** highly incriminating.
>
> The director, **desperately trying to improve the show's Neilsen ratings,** fired two of the leading actors and hired some fresh faces.

Interrupted movement is a form of subordination. It involves condensing the thought of one sentence into a clause or phrase and embedding that clause or phrase within another sentence:

> Political candidates are eager to win public approval and votes. They spend many months on the campaign trail.
>
> Political candidates, **eager to win public approval and votes,** spend many months on the campaign trail.

The second sentence above is actually a condensation of the two simple sentences in the example that precedes it.

Writers sometimes use interrupted sentences to demonstrate hesitancy or fairmindedness:

> The actor, **realizing perhaps that he was losing control of the audience,** began to speak louder and louder.
>
> Critics of Pope, **understandably enraged by his attack on literary scholarship,** condemned the "Essay on Criticism" as a "poetic tantrum" and "meaningless act of spite."

Interrupted movement can add liveliness and interest to writing. But it must be handled carefully or the meaning of a sentence will be lost. Inexperienced writers sometimes try to manipulate clauses and phrases for effect, believing that the placement of a clause or phrase in an unexpected position adds professionalism and sophistication to their prose. More often than not, however, the result is an awkward, incoherent construction that leaves a subject or verb hanging in midair:

Awkward	Very little of Donne's poetry was, **except for the *Anniversary*** poems, published during his lifetime.
Improved	**Except for the *Anniversary* poems,** very little of Donne's poetry was published during his lifetime.
Awkward	The leading character, **every time he said it,** mispronounced the name *Desdemona*.
Improved	The leading character mispronounced the name *Desdemona* **every time he said it.**

Both of these sentences are made incoherent by interrupted movement and are more effective without the distraction in the middle.

Exercises

1. Rewrite the following passages to make them more effective structurally and stylistically by employing one or more of the devices for sentence management discussed in the preceding section:

Coordination
Subordination
Inversion and transposition
Condensation
Repetition
Balance and antithesis
Active and passive constructions
Interrupted movement

Next to each rewritten version, state which device you used.

a. Representative Bella Abzug gave the speech that attacked the pardon of Nixon that President Ford gave the former chief executive.

b. *A Connecticut Yankee in King Arthur's Court* is a satire. It was written by Mark Twain. It describes the adventures of a New England man. The Yankee falls asleep and suddenly wakes up in a medieval court.

c. To the Mideast flew Secretary of State Kissinger to talk with Arab and Israeli leaders. But unsuccessful was his visit.

d. The downfall of the Puritans in England occurred in 1660. There dawned in Britain a new era with the restoration of King Charles II.

e. In the early Christian era many people believed that the universe was controlled by two antagonistic forces: one was light, which represented goodness and was identified with God; the devil was the embodiment of the other force, darkness, and this stood for evil.

f. I believe that *Ulysses* should be judged by critics on its literary merits, not on its autobiographical implications.

g. I am frightened of people who find it necessary to utilize drugs in order to achieve happiness.

2. The following paragraphs are correct grammatically but they do not communicate smoothly and efficiently to readers. Rewrite each paragraph, using the techniques indicated, to shape it into a smooth, coherent, and unified whole.

130   **a.** Condensation (Coordination and Subordination)

John Dos Passos is a novelist and poet. He was born in America. He is best known for his structural innovations in the novel. He is also acclaimed for his stylistic experiments. Many of his techniques suggest the influence of James Joyce. Dos Passos's style is best exemplified in his trilogy *USA* (1938). The three-part work consists of *The Forty-second Parallel, 1919,* and *The Big Money.* These three novels were written in 1930, 1932, and 1936, respectively.

b. Active Constructions

Neoclassicism was a movement in European literature during the late seventeenth and early eighteenth centuries. Its main characteristic was a revival of the style of Greek and Roman classics. It was believed by neoclassical writers that the techniques of ancient drama and poetry were purer, more dignified, and loftier in purpose than modern techniques.

c. Balance and Repetition

The autonomic nervous system mobilizes the body's resources in times of emergency. It stimulates the adrenal glands, increasing the level of blood sugar. The spleen, which stores red corpuscles, releases more of them into the blood. It enlarges the blood vessels of the heart to speed up circulation. The liver is activated, and an emergency sugar supply is rushed into the bloodstream. The body obtains more oxygen because the lungs are stimulated to breathe harder. In a matter of seconds, every part of the body is ready to go into action.

BASIC SENTENCE FAULTS (sen flt)

This section will present types of mismanaged sentences that confuse readers or cause them to lose interest in the communication. An ineffective sentence is usually caused by (1) lack of unity, (2) lack of coherence, or (3) lack of emphasis.

Effective sentences are *unified.* The main thought must be clear and comprehensible, and supporting details, evidence, quotations, or data must be relevant to the main thought.

Effective sentences are *coherent.* That is, the reader must understand how all elements in the sentence fit together. A sentence should be a meaningful unit in itself, not a collection of diverse phrases and clauses.

Finally, effective sentences are *emphatic.* Major ideas must be

131

written forcefully and placed in strategic parts of the sentence. They should not be obscured by unimportant detail or verbiage.

In this section sentences that do not meet these three criteria will be examined. The deficiences of the ineffective sentences will be explained, and each sentence will be corrected to demonstrate a more satisfactory model.

4.10   Lack of Unity (sen un)

A unified sentence states a single major idea, focuses on that idea, and develops it fully. Often a sentence does not express a point clearly or loses track of its point (lack of unity) when a writer puts down whatever comes to mind or does not include a connecting thought that is crucial to the meaning of the sentence.

Lack of unity is most often caused by confusing coordination, confusing subordination, and excessive detail.

4.10a   Confusing Coordination

Effective coordination requires joining two ideas that are *equal or similar in importance*. When two parts of a sentence are not equal in value, coordinating them will confuse the reader:

Confusing	Words are symbols for objects, and we can express our desire for an object without it being physically present.
Clear	Because words are symbols for objects, we can express our desire for an object without its being physically present.

In the first sentence, the writer coordinates two ideas that are not logically equal; *and* implies addition, but the writer uses it to imply *results*. Consequently, the reader may wonder what the first part of the sentence has to do with the second. As the revised sentence shows, one idea is actually dependent on the other and should be subordinated to it.

In the following example, the omission of a crucial connecting thought creates a confusing, poorly unified sentence:

Confusing	I am basically a happy person, and I believe I can make nursing a rewarding career.
Clear	Because I am generally cheerful and not easily depressed by the sight of suffering and pain, I believe I can make nursing a rewarding career.

The original sentence makes no clear connection between a happy disposition and nursing. Subordination and the insertion of a clarifying clause unify the writer's thoughts.

The omission of a key element in a cause-and-effect statement can also lead to lack of unity:

Confusing	I come from a dairy farm and I hate milk. I use it only in my coffee.
Clear	After growing up on a dairy farm, where I had to milk cows every morning, I came to hate milk. Now I use it only in my coffee.

The *and* in the first statement serves as an implied (and illogical) *therefore:* there is no reason to assume that living on a dairy farm would make a person dislike milk. The revised version unifies the sentence by supplying the missing cause.

Excessive coordination, like faulty coordination, produces confusing and poorly unified sentences. Inexperienced writers often attempt to string many ideas together, in an effort to smooth out sentences and give flow to short, choppy writing. In most cases, however, this only emphasizes the writer's patchwork pattern. Excessive coordination creates long, awkward sentences that are difficult to follow:

> The computer is a machine created by humans to serve their purposes, and it can sift through data, organize it, and perform various mathematical computations on it, but a computer can never produce a creative concept or an incomprehensible concept—an idea that is anything more than the information brought to it or an idea that is beyond the range of human knowledge and the limits of human intelligence.

The writer has strung together so many ideas about the computer that there is no clear point to the sentence. Nor is there any place for the reader to stop and absorb the information. To unify the passage, the writer should sort out the major ideas and express each one in a separate sentence:

> The computer is a machine created by humans to serve their purposes. It can sift through data, organize it, and perform various mathematical computations on it. But a computer can never produce a creative concept—an idea that is anything more than the information brought to the machine. Nor can it produce an incomprehensible concept—an idea that is beyond the range of human knowledge or the limits of human intelligence.

133

4.10b   Confusing Subordination

Effective subordination requires establishing clear relationships among the various elements of a sentence. Failure to place clauses in logical order or to clarify relationships among them produces confusion and poorly unified sentences.

In the following example, the writer attempts to condense ideas by combining two sentences into one:

> A course in accounting is helpful for understanding the complexities of business, preparing students for law school.

The result, however, is confusing. The phrase *preparing students for law school* seems to come out of nowhere and bears no relationship to the rest of the sentence. The writer should subordinate more effectively:

> A course in accounting is helpful in preparing students for law school because it introduces them to the complexities of business.

Faulty placement of modifying clauses distracts the reader and breaks down the unity of a sentence:

Confusing	Hawthorne examines the character of Hester Prynne in *The Scarlet Letter,* who is a type of feminist.
Clear	In *The Scarlet Letter* Hawthorne examines the character of Hester Prynne, who is a type of feminist.

The clause *who is a type of feminist* refers to Hester Prynne, not to Hawthorne or to *The Scarlet Letter.* A simple transposition straightens out the confusion. The revised sentence is coherent and unified, with the modifying clause placed directly after the word it modifies.

While subordination is an effective technique for condensing and smoothing out a writer's prose, excessive subordination can lead to confusion and lack of unity. Trying to include every fact or qualifying statement in a single sentence will result in writing like the following:

> The American dream of each man making a success of his own life is being increasingly criticized because of the growth of monopolies, which have great capital resources that can be used to undersell small businesses, which do not have the resources of capital that can enable them to stand long periods of small margins of profit, which are necessary for the purchase of new stocks of goods or machinery necessary for up-to-date production and distribution.

134   The sentence is actually a long and complex paragraph. Because readers will be lost within its many twists and turns, it must be divided into sentences:

> The American dream of each man making a success of his own life is being increasingly criticized because of the growth of monopolies. Large corporations with great capital resources are consistently underselling small businesses. The small enterprise lacks the capital to survive long periods of small profit margins. Yet such capital is essential if the small business is to purchase new stocks, goods, or machinery and maintain up-to-date production and distribution.

The revised paragraph has four sentences instead of one. The material is easier to follow since the reader can pause after each sentence and absorb the material.

4.10c   Excessive Detail

Excessive detail can detract from the coherence in writing by obscuring relationships between ideas and by distracting the reader from the writer's main points. In the following example, the writer overwhelms the reader with so many details in each sentence that the main thrust of the passage is lost:

> At the federal level, government regulation of industry is carried out by commissions whose members are appointed by the president. **Also, under the requirements of our Constitution, they must be** approved by **a majority vote** of the Senate. Among the most important federal agencies are the Interstate Commerce Commission, the Federal Communications Commission, the Civil Aeronautics Board, the Atomic Energy Commission, and the Securities and Exchange Commission **(which has received a great deal of public criticism in recent years).** These commissions supervise the prices charged by the regulated businesses—**such as the costs of a telephone call or, in recent years, the price of cable TV**—the quality of the service provided, and the maximum profits the business may obtain. Regulatory decisions **of federal agencies** are determined by a majority vote of commission members and may be reviewed, **again under the requirements of federal law,** by federal courts.

Eliminating irrelevant details and unnecessary or excessive examples (shown in bold type) unifies the sentences and creates coherence.

> At the federal level, government regulation of industry is carried out by commissions whose members are appointed by the president and approved by the Senate. Among the most important federal agencies are the Interstate Commerce Commission, the Federal Communications Commission, the Civil Aeronautics Board,

135

the Atomic Energy Commission, and the Securities and Exchange Commission. These agencies supervise the prices charged by regulated businesses, the quality of service provided, and the maximum profits the businesses may obtain. Regulatory decisions are determined by a majority vote of commission members and may be reviewed by federal courts.

4.11 Lack of Coherence (sen coh)

An effective sentence must not only be unified; it must also be coherent. Coherence depends on arranging the elements of a sentence clearly so that the reader understands the relationships among them. Failure to establish clear relationships results in confusing, ambiguous, and illogical sentences.

Lack of coherence is most often caused by dangling modifiers, misplaced modifiers, lack of parallelism, faulty pronoun reference, needless shifts, and mixed constructions.

4.11a Dangling Modifiers (dgl)

A common cause of incoherent sentences is a *dangling modifier,* a word or phrase that does not modify or bear any other logical relationship to any other element in the sentence.

One frequently encountered type of dangling modifier is the misused *participial phrase*—a phrase that begins with an *-ing* verb form:

Dangling	Watching *Our Town,* the spareness of the dialogue and simple movements of the actors intrigued me.
Revised	Watching *Our Town,* **I was intrigued by** the spareness of the dialogue and simple movements of the actors.

In the first sentence above, the phrase *watching Our Town* is a dangling modifier—there is no element in the rest of the sentence to which it logically relates. Although such a phrase is not a complete action, it does have an *implied* subject: *someone* was watching *Our Town.* This implied subject must become the stated subject of the main part of the sentence to avoid a dangling construction. In the revised version, a logical subject (*I*) is found to connect the participial phrase to the rest of the sentence.

A dangling participial phrase may also be avoided by expanding it to form a subordinate clause:

As I watched *Our Town,* I was intrigued by the spareness of the dialogue and the simple movements of the actors.

In this revision, the subject of the subordinate clause, *I*, becomes the subject of the main part of the sentence.

Infinitive phrases—phrases that begin with the infinitive verb form—are also frequently made to dangle:

Dangling   **To understand the Middle Ages,** examination of the Christian concept of afterlife must be our first task.

Revised   **To understand the Middle Ages,** we must first examine the Christian concept of afterlife.

Like participial phrases, infinitive phrases must have a stated subject that they modify elsewhere in the sentence. In the original version of the sentence above, the subject, "examination" is illogically related to the infinitive phrase: an examination cannot "understand." In the revised sentence, the addition of "we" creates a logical connection between the main part of the sentence and the opening infinitive phrase.

4.11b   Misplaced Parts (mis pt)

Coherence depends not only on all the necessary elements being in a sentence but on their being placed in logical order. A misplaced word, phrase, or clause can create ambiguity and confusion. Modifiers should always be placed as close as possible to the words they modify:

Illogical   We **nearly read** every play by Shakespeare this semester.

Clear   We **read nearly** every play by Shakespeare this semester.

In the first sentence above, the adverb *nearly* has been misplaced: there is no such thing as "nearly reading." The revised sentence shows what the writer actually means.

In the example below, the writer has misplaced the modifying clause "which has only two characters," creating an obscure sentence. The revised version places the clause directly after the noun it modifies (*Two for the Seesaw*) and so clarifies the sentence:

Illogical   I saw *Two for the Seesaw* at the Shubert Theater, **which has only two characters.**

Clear   I saw *Two for the Seesaw,* **which has only two characters,** at the Shubert Theater.

Another type of misplaced modifier is the *squinting modifier.* Such a modifier is confusing because it can refer either to the word before it or to the word after it:

Ambiguous   The man who was running down the street **frantically yelled** for help.

137

4.11c (sen //)

Clear	The man who was running down the street **yelled frantically** for help.
Ambiguous	The professor said **after the lecture** he was flying to France.
Clear	**After the lecture,** the professor said he was flying to France.

The modifiers *frantically* and *after the lecture* are ambiguous because it is unclear whether they refer to the preceding or following elements of the sentences. Was the man yelling frantically or running frantically? Did the professor make his announcement after the lecture or did he fly to France after the lecture? In each example, the sentence is clarified by moving the squinting modifier to an unambiguous position.

The *split infinitive*—an infinitive that is separated by an adverb or adverbial phrase—is also a type of misplaced modifier. Generally (though not always), splitting infinitives leads to awkward structures that break up the rhythm of a sentence:

Awkward	The Constitution guarantees every American the right **to** *freely* **think** and act.
Improved	The Constitution guarantees every American the right **to think** and act *freely*.
Awkward	Every language has a set of rules **to** *meaningfully* **combine** words into sentences.
Improved	Every language has a set of rules **to combine** words *meaningfully* into sentences.
Awkward	The writer's task is **to** *not only* **instruct** but to entertain.
Improved	The writer's task is *not only* **to instruct** but to entertain.

In each of these cases the sentence is improved by rejoining the infinitive.

4.11c Lack of Parallelism (sen //)

Parallel ideas in a sentence should be expressed in similar grammatical form. For example, if one element of a series begins with an infinitive form (*to go*), others should follow suit to maintain coherence. If one phrase includes a participial form (*going*), succeeding phrases should contain the same form. There is no such thing as a half-parallel sentence.

Lack of parallelism is inefficient because it breaks up the pattern of a sentence and disrupts the reader's train of thought. The reader must stop, retreat, and try to straighten out the confusion:

Faulty	China is attempting **to wipe out** hunger, **to establish** a universal health program, and **develop** worker control of industries.
Revised	China is attempting **to wipe out** hunger, **to establish** a universal health program, and **to develop** worker control of industries.
Faulty	I love **camping** in the woods, **hiking, cooking** outdoors, and **to swim** in mountain streams.
Revised	I love **camping** in the woods, **hiking, cooking** outdoors, and **swimming** in mountain streams.

The first sentence begins with an infinitive but then changes its pattern; the second begins with a gerund and then switches to an infinitive. Each sentence should be made consistent to avoid confusing the reader.

4.11d   Faulty Pronoun Reference (ref)

Pronouns can be valuable tools for a writer in providing connections between ideas and avoiding needless repetition. However, they must be selected and used with care. Every pronoun depends for its meaning on an antecedent—a preceding noun or pronoun. If a pronoun is placed too far away from its antecedent, or if the antecedent is unclear, the sentences will lose their coherence.

Pronouns like *this, they, which,* and *it* do not have meaning in themselves. They take on meaning only when placed in a precise context. Sentences with vague pronoun references will confuse the reader and should be rewritten so that the meaning or antecedent of the pronoun is clear:

Vague	Sports and movies are means of relieving depression and violent emotions. **This** is why they are necessary in a society.
Clear	Sports and movies are necessary in a society in order to relieve depression and violent emotions.
Vague	Leaders of the Women's Liberation movement have criticized American doctors severely. **They** are angry—and justifiably so.
Clear	Leaders of the women's liberation movement have criticized the medical profession severely. They are angry—and justifiably so.
Vague	In the Royal Shakespeare production of *Othello,* Frank Finlay played Iago and was well suited to **it.**
Clear	In the Royal Shakespeare production of *Othello,* Frank Finlay played Iago and was well suited to the role.

139

4.11e (pv)

The revised sentences are clearer because they have been restructured to eliminate the pronoun or to supply an unambiguous antecedent.

4.11e   Needless Shifts (pv)

A sentence should be consistent to be coherent. Sudden shifts from active to passive voice (or vice versa), from one subject to another, from one person or number to another, or from one tense to another interrupt the flow of the sentence, forcing the reader to make an adjustment he should not have to make.

In the example below, the writer shifts from passive to active voice. Consistent use of passive makes the sentence more coherent:

Faulty	Once the new admissions policy **was approved** by the college administrators, **they adjourned** the meeting.
Revised	Once the new admissions policy **was approved by** the college administrators **the meeting was adjourned.**

In the following example, the writer changes his subject unnecessarily, forcing the reader to shift gears:

Faulty	**Hemingway** knew a great deal about hunting and fishing, and **his stories** incorporated this knowledge.
Revised	Hemingway knew a great deal about hunting and fishing and incorporated this knowledge into his stories.

The shift of subject in the first sentence abruptly changes the direction of the reader's thoughts. The reader is unprepared for *his stories* as a subject and is momentarily distracted from the writer's point. The revised sentence, with a single subject, conveys the same information more smoothly and clearly.

A shift from one person to another also distracts and confuses the reader:

Faulty	When in a foreign country, always carry **your** passport. **One** can get into a lot of trouble if **he** loses it.
Revised	When in a foreign country, always carry **your** passport. **You** can get into a lot of trouble if **you** lose it.

The writer shifts from second person ("your") to third person ("one"; "he"). The passage is more unified and coherent when the second person is maintained.

In the following example, the writer shifts number from singular to plural, first from one sentence to the next and then within a sentence:

Faulty	**The Mexican Tourist Bureau** has launched an extensive advertising campaign to attract American visitors. **They**

hope to increase tourist income by 50 percent this year. If **a traveler** wants information on visiting Mexico, **they** should consult the tourist bureau.

Revised   **The Mexican Tourist Bureau** has launched an extensive advertising campaign to attract American visitors. **It** hopes to increase tourist income by 50 percent. If **a traveler** wants information on visiting Mexico, **he** should consult the tourist bureau.

In the second sentence above, the use of *they* to refer to the tourist bureau creates confusion, since the pronoun appears to refer back to American visitors. In the third sentence, the shift to *they* is equally confusing, since there is no plural antecedent for this pronoun. Consistent use of singular number, in the revised paragraph, avoids ambiguity and makes the writer's meaning clear.

Needless shifts in tense are a common writing error, particularly in literary discussions. Beginning writers often alternate between past and present tense in describing the action of a literary work or the techniques employed by an author. References to literary action and to stylistic techniques should be handled consistently and, usually, in the present tense:

Faulty   Alceste, the hero of *The Misanthrope,* **is** rejected by the woman he loves and cast out by society. Yet, in many ways, he **brought** about his own downfall.

Revised   Alceste, the hero of *The Misanthrope,* **is** rejected by the woman he loves and cast out by society. Yet, in many ways, he **brings** about his own downfall.

Faulty   In the third act, after Hamlet **has killed** Polonius, he **sees** the ghost for a second time

Revised   In the third act, after Hamlet **kills** Polonius, he **sees** the ghost for a second time.

Faulty   The poem **is divided** into four parts. In the first part Yeats **described** his sadness at the loss of beautiful things.

Revised   The poem **is divided** into four parts. In the first part Yeats **describes** his sadness at the loss of beautiful things.

Indirect quotations—paraphrases of what a speaker has actually said—are another frequent source of trouble for inexperienced writers. In general, the tense of a paraphrase should follow the tense used in the sentence as a whole. If the writer wishes to maintain the tense of the original quotation, he should quote directly:

Faulty   In a speech to Parliament at the outbreak of World War II, Winston Churchill **said** that he **has** nothing to offer but blood, sweat, and tears.

4.11f (mix)

Revised	In a speech to Parliament at the outbreak of World War II, Winston Churchill **said** that he **had** nothing to offer but blood, sweat, and tears.
Revised	In a speech to Parliament at the outbreak of World War II, Winston Churchill **said:** "I **have** nothing to offer but blood, toil, tears, and sweat."

4.11f Mixed Constructions (mix)

A mixed construction is a needless shift in the *grammatical structure* of a sentence: the mixed sentence begins with one pattern of expression and then switches to another, creating an ungrammatical or incoherent sentence. Like shifts in subject or person, mixed constructions cause confusion. They force the reader to make a mental adjustment, to correct the sentences in his mind in order to make them coherent.

Mixed constructions are most commonly caused by hasty writing or by trying to combine simple sentences into complex thoughts. In writing complex sentences, the writer should check to see that the overall sentence has a single main thought (subject-verb-object) and that all other elements are subordinate to it.

Mixed	**While society continues to insist on conformity,** only strengthens the individual's desire for self-expression.
Revised	Society's continued insistence on conformity only strengthens the individual's desire for self-expression.
Mixed	**In every system of republicanism** requires a balancing of states' rights against the rights of the federal government.
Revised	Every system of republicanism requires a balancing of states' rights against the rights of the federal government.
Mixed	I was especially struck by the play's carefully interwoven subplots, **which they made an effective counterpoint to the main action.**
Revised	I was especially struck by the play's carefully interwoven subplots, which made an effective counterpoint to the main action.

In the first example, the writer has inadvertently made the subordinate clause (*While society continues to insist on conformity*) the subject of the sentence. In the second example, the same is true of the prepositional phrase (*In every system of republicanism*). In the third example, the writer has made the subordinate clause (*which made an effective counterpoint to the main action*) take on an extraneous subject (*they*).

One frequent type of mixed construction is the awkward or incomplete comparison. All comparisons should involve similar terms and grammatical structures, and they should be precise and direct:

| Incomplete | There are many similarities between Willie Loman in *Death of A Salesman* and Blanche DuBois in *A Streetcar Named Desire*. Just as Willie is deluded by the fantasy that he will succeed as a salesman, so Blanche clings to illusion. |
| Complete | There are many similarities between Willie Loman in *Death of A Salesman* and Blanche DuBois in *A Streetcar Named Desire*. Just as Willie is deluded by the fantasy that he will succeed as a salesman, so Blanche clings to the illusion that she can regain her beauty and youth. |

The first passage above is incomplete because the writer explains *how* Willie Loman is deluded but fails to make a similar explanation for Blanche DuBois.

Comparisons that contain the word *than* are those most often open to ambiguity, since the reader cannot be sure what aspect of the comparison *than* refers to:

| Ambiguous | The president of the United States is more powerful than in Great Britain. |
| Clear | The president of the United States is more powerful than the prime minister of Great Britain. |

In this sentence, the first version is ambiguous because the writer makes a comparison between a person and a country when a person-to-person comparison is called for.

4.12 Lack of Emphasis (emp)

One of the most important aspects of effective writing is *emphasis*—the arrangement of words or sentences so that key points stand out in the reader's mind. Sentences that are structured for emphasis have rhythm, focus, and flow. In contrast, unemphatic sequences, anticlimactic order, unnecessary repetition, and wordiness weaken writing and destroy the rhythm that leads the reader clearly from point to point.

4.12a Unemphatic Sequences

The order in which words are arranged in a sentence plays an important role in their impact on the reader. Generally, the middle of a sentence is the position of least emphasis, the beginning and

143

end of the sentence the positions of most emphasis. The writer should place important words or ideas in these emphatic positions.

| Unemphatic | By 1985 about a billion more people will be added to the earth, **barring a catastrophic disaster.** |
| Emphatic | By 1985, **barring a catastrophic disaster,** about a billion more people will be added to the earth. |

The first version of this sentence is unemphatic because the least important idea (the phrase *barring a catastrophic disaster*) is erroneously placed in an emphatic position. The revised version is more effective than the original because the writer's major points (the date and the prediction) appear at the beginning and the end of the sentence. The least important phrase is placed in the unemphatic middle position.

| Unemphatic | People react to anxiety by seeking some form of escape, **in many cases.** |
| Emphatic | **People often** react to anxiety by seeking some form of escape. |

The phrase *in many cases* is a weak tag line. The sentence is made more emphatic by eliminating the phrase and incorporating the idea in the body of the statement.

| Unemphatic | My fondest dream was to visit Scandinavia **throughout my adolescence.** |
| Emphatic | **Throughout my adolescence,** my fondest dream was to visit Scandinavia. |

The first version of this sentence is both unemphatic and ambiguous. Transposing the final phrase to the beginning of the sentence eliminates the ambiguity and gives emphasis to the writer's main thought.

4.12b Anticlimactic and Illogical Order

Parallel items in a sentence should be arranged in an order that has meaning and impact for the reader. This order may be the natural or logical sequence of thought, the chronological order of events, or the climactic order of ideas—the order that builds drama or suspense. No matter which method of order is followed, the main thrust of the sentence comes at the end; all previous clauses lead up to the conclusion.

Anticlimactic order results in dull, unemphatic prose and blurring of key points:

Anticlimactic	He burst into the darkened room after moving slowly up the stairs, looking cautiously to his left and right, and turning the door handle.
Climactic	He moved slowly up the creaking stairs, looked cautiously to his left and right, turned the door handle, and burst into the darkened room.
Anticlimactic	Throughout the long desert march, she thought, above all, of the next waterhole; she also thought of her childhood, of her college years, and of her medical career.
Climactic	Throughout the long desert march, she thought of her childhood, of her college years, and of her medical career; but, above all, she thought of the next waterhole.

In the first and third examples, the climactic idea is presented first, eliminating the chance for tension or suspense to develop gradually. The revised versions *build* to a climax, involving the reader and giving emphasis to the final point.

Sentences written in illogical order seem to jump back and forth, so that the connections between ideas are difficult for the reader to follow.

Illogical	Modern industrial techniques can transform a dying city into a dynamic urban center, an impoverished nation into a prosperous industrial power, and a quiet village into a bustling metropolis.
Logical	Modern industrial techniques can transform a quiet village into a bustling metropolis, a dying city into a dynamic urban center, and an impoverished nation into a prosperous industrial power.
Illogical	Like Oedipus, King Lear is blinded by pride, but, unlike Oedipus, he comes to understand the reasons for his folly; like Oedipus, Lear's pride leads to his downfall.
Logical	Like Oedipus, King Lear is blinded by pride and, like Oedipus, pride leads to his downfall; but, unlike Oedipus, Lear comes to understand the reasons for his folly.

In each of these examples, there is a logical *underlying* pattern of ideas that the writer fails to bring out in the original statement. In the first case the pattern is "small-to-large"; in the second case, "similarities-versus-differences." The revised versions are more emphatic than the originals because they stress this logical sequence of thought.

145

4.12d (W)

4.12c Repetitive Constructions

Repetition of unimportant words or ideas can weaken the force of a sentence, distracting the reader from the writer's main point:

Repetitious	**The average** American family spends **an average** of $60 a week on food.
Improved	The average American family spends $60 a week on food.
Repetitious	All the farmers agreed they could not recall having as much **rain** as the **rain** they had the previous summer.
Improved	All the farmers agreed they could not recall having as much rain as they had the previous summer.

Because repetition attracts the reader's eye, it is an important method of building emphasis. However, the writer must be sure that repetition enhances rather than detracts from the intended meaning. (See also Section **4.6**.)

4.12d Wordy Constructions (W)

Sentences that convey meaning effectively do not necessarily contain a great number of words. However, they do contain carefully chosen words that communicate ideas clearly and concisely. Wordy constructions bog writing down and complicate the reader's task of understanding what the writer is trying to say:

Wordy	The Soviet army is one of the strongest armed forces in the world.
Concise	The Soviet army is one of the strongest in the world.
Wordy	I could not decide whether to go to the rock concert or whether to go to the sculpture exhibit.
Concise	I could not decide whether to go to the rock concert or the sculpture exhibit.

Eliminating inessential phrases also adds emphasis and focus to writing:

Wordy	In addition to my previous remarks, I wish to discuss the decline of organized religion.
Concise	I also wish to discuss the decline of organized religion.

In the examples above, the writer eliminates such phrases as *armed forces* and *to go to* from the wordy sentences in order to shape concise sentences that are unified and emphatic and focus on a single major point. (See also Section **5.9**.)

REVIEW EXERCISES

1. Read each of the following paragraphs carefully. Select and rewrite individual sentences that need improvement in unity, coherence, or emphasis.

a. Gary and Richard got into and out of enough scrapes to keep them in conversation pieces the rest of their lives—but they all weren't that grim or frightening. Buddies for years ("that sounds funny when you're only 22, but we met in the *first grade*"), by the time they were in the fourth grade, they were cocky beyond belief—and probably more sure of themselves than they are today! Gary reveals that they'd already decided they were going to be "very heavy in show business. Richard had said, 'You and I are *bound* to be behind footlights!'" Gary laughs about it today. But it turned out to be more prophetic than they could have guessed.

Motion Picture, November 1974

b. Back in my youth I had a comic book collection which would make any enthusiast proud. Weekly my Dad would furnish me with some change, and I would head down to the corner store and pick up a few comics. My sister's favorite was *Archie*. My Dad casually would suggest that I pick up a few *Superman* comics for him to read. I was happy with anything from war comics and ghost stories to *Donald Duck*. When I first started reading comics I was too lazy to read the captions. I could tell most of the story through the pictures, and I was always in a hurry to see how the story would come out. After a while my Dad started picking up a few Classic comics for me. These were a little too sophisticated to follow by looking at the pictures only, but the inconvenience of reading the entire comic book was more than offset by the great stories.

Kim Mosley, "Superman Lives!" *Autochton* '77

c. Down to the store I went to order a new pair of shoes to buy. Suddenly I notice that my money was gone. So I ran to the nearest phone booth and began to start calling all of my friends. One sure finds out who his friends are at a moment like this. The first person I called was my friend John I knew from high school. John just laughed at it and then told me that he has no money. I certainly wasn't sure that he was really telling the truth, but what can you do? Suddenly, out of nowhere, I saw two of my best friends, Richie and Stan, walking down the street. I ran out and caught them, and he was nice enough to loan me fifteen dollars. Asking nothing in return, it sure was nice of him to do.

d. This hidden paradise is without a doubt one of the more scenic landscapes restricted to the eyes of the midshipmen and their   **147**

officers. The large variety of things to do and see in this wonderland is almost without end. For example the music lover is exposed to a wide selection of musical pieces ranging from the theme song of *Patton* to the latest song on the top ten in hard rock, provided that he can isolate their melody from those of anywhere from five to fifteen others, all playing at the same time and at full volume.

2. Rewrite each of the sentences or paragraphs below to demonstrate effective use of one or more of the following techniques. Demonstrate each technique at least once.

Coordination
Subordination
Inversion and transposition
Condensation
Repetition
Balance and antithesis
Active and passive constructions
Interrupted movement

a. Until I took a course in music theory, I never understood the concept of harmony. "Major" and "minor" keys were beyond my understanding, and it was a mystery to me that the human voice could be a musical instrument.

b. An anonymous poet wrote *Sir Gawain and the Green Knight* in the middle of the fourteenth century.

c. A director should select crew members for their skills, not their reputations. A director should select members of the cast on the same basis.

d. The lawyer hoped to make a million dollars before he was thirty. He invested all his money in the stock market.

e. Just as we should organize our thoughts before we speak, so in writing.

f. The college student who does not have to work hard to get good grades is lucky.

g. A word can acquire a less respectable or less positive meaning over time. This process is the definition of the term *pejoration*. Consider, as an example, the word *criticize*. *Criticize* used to mean "to judge or analyze." Now *criticize* often means "to judge negatively" or "to find fault."

h. The name of the man who conducts the New York Philharmonic is Pierre Boulez.

i. We learn best by doing. Student teaching is a valuable technique.

j. Wood has beauty and texture, but it is not durable; metal is more durable, but it rusts. The problem with stone is that it is heavy, even though it will not rust.

3. Each of the following sentences needs revision. Identify the problem (dangling modifier, split infinitive, shift of tense, faulty pronoun reference, and so on), and rework the sentence.

a. The poem that I like best is "Ozymandias" by Shelley, because it makes me feel that the writer understands that civilization is a very fragile thing that can fall apart easily.

b. The audience gave Betty Friedan a standing ovation after she finished her talk on the "feminine mystique" and the oppression of women.

c. I firmly believe that the utilization of mass transit is the only solution to our urban problems.

d. At the end of *Who's Afraid of Virginia Woolf?*, in the scene between George and Martha, demonstrates Albee's skill in dramatic irony.

e. Nineteenth-century critics condemned the *nocturnes* of Whistler, who felt that such abstract paintings were not true art.

f. The class was given a lecture on the dangers of smoking by the professor.

g. Hoping to avoid a bad grade, a revision of my paper was essential.

h. The supply of fertilizer was cut drastically by the oil shortage, and the wheat crop in India was much smaller last year.

i. The first disaster in Keats's life happens in April 1804, when his father is killed by a horse; his mother remarried two months later, and the children go to live with their grandparents.

j. Many psychiatrists believe that bodily changes trigger emotions rather than that we undergo changes in our bodies because we experience emotions. In other words, we do not cry because we feel sad; our sadness is caused by the fact that we are crying.

k. In junior high I thought of poems as sentences that rhymed; in college I came to appreciate the symbolic value of poetry, whereas in high school I began to appreciate poems for their literal meaning.

l. Conservation is a method of conserving the future for future generations of people.

m. *Waiting for Godot* is a study of the absurdity of life and the futility of hope, in the final analysis.

n. In his junior year he switched to a liberal arts major, and teaching was his chosen career.

149

o. The careful reader will appreciate Donne's satire of the Petrarchan love sonnet. He is a master of the conventions of traditional love poetry and exaggerates them to the point of absurdity.

p. There are many different approaches to helping people with emotional problems—psychoanalysis, transactional analysis, behavioral therapy, group therapy. Any form of therapy has value if they work.

q. When Thomas Edison was asked to define genius, he said: "It was 99 percent perspiration and 1 percent inspiration."

r. In *The Ambassadors* Henry James seems more interested in analyzing the character of Lambert Strether than the plot development.

s. In one of his last architectural achievements, the Solomon R. Guggenheim Museum, completed in 1959 and named after a member of a prominent American industrial family, which was noted for such philanthropic endeavors as annual fellowships to scientists, artists, and writers, Frank Lloyd Wright demonstrated the use of reinforced concrete for decorative effect and structural innovation.

t. In the sixteenth century there developed a strong reaction to Roman Catholic doctrine in the form of the Protestant Reformation. The movement was given leadership by such men as John Calvin and Martin Luther.

5

Diction

Effective diction involves choosing words that are appropriate for the particular writing context at hand so that the writer can communicate his message to the reader accurately, concretely, economically, and with variety. Through understanding. how readers react to individual words and combinations of words the writer learns how to achieve these qualities and how to improve his diction.

WHAT IS EFFECTIVE DICTION?

Despite a good organization and effectively structured sentences, a written work may be rhetorically dull, lifeless, vague, and even confusing if the words chosen are limp and lame. However, "effective word choice" (effective diction) is difficult to define:

Ineffective Diction	After **a few months of difficult talks,** the mine workers and the coal-mine operators may be close to getting together on a new agreement. But despite the **terrible things that could happen** if there were a strike, the **large membership** of the United Mine Workers Union, who **take care of a large percent** of the country's coal, were ready for a strike that would take at least two weeks and maybe even longer.
Effective Diction	After **two months** of **dogged negotiations,** the mine workers and the coal-mine operators appeared close to agreement on a new contract. But despite the **perilous consequences** of a strike, the **120,000** members of the United Mine Workers Union who **dig 70 percent** of the nation's coal were poised for a nationwide walkout that seemed almost certain to last at least two weeks and perhaps longer.

"The Mines: Striking a Bargain," *Newsweek*

What makes the second paragraph more effective than the first and enables the reader to grasp not only what is going on but also what a strike would mean? The writer uses diction that is appropriate for the context (a news magazine), accurate, concrete, economical, and rich in variety. Although "difficult talks," for example, may generally convey the information required, "dogged negotiations" communicates the same idea more vigorously. "Dogged" suggests that the talks have been both difficult and determined; "negotiations" is the precise word for meetings that are intended to settle contract disagreements. "A few months" is vague; "two months" is precise. Miners "dig" coal rather than "take care of" coal. In short, the diction in the first paragraph is ineffective because it lacks substance, the by-product of detail and precision.

Making suitable diction choices involves the writer in selecting words that reveal his message to the reader. To choose words effectively, the writer should (1) be familiar with the nature and the extent of word resources, (2) know when one word or group of words will serve better than another, and (3) be aware of the diction habits to avoid.

THE NATURE OF WORDS

The English language is a rich storehouse for writers, who have some one million words at their disposal. Yet most writers are familiar with only a small percentage of these words. The average working vocabulary is close to two thousand words, and the average reading vocabulary is about twenty thousand words. Part of the writer's education involves both an expansion of his vocabulary and an increased understanding of the impact of words.

The English vocabulary is composed of two types of words: native and borrowed. A *native* English word is a word derived from Old English or its predecessors, Anglo-Saxon and other Germanic languages. A *borrowed* word is a word taken from other languages, primarily Latin, Greek, and French. Borrowed words constitute a large percentage of the English word pool. For example, of the one thousand most commonly used English words, over one-third are borrowed. Many of these borrowed words have native equivalents. The Latinate word *maternal,* for example, is a synonym for the Germanic word *motherly.* Other borrowed words and their native equivalents are listed below:

Native	*Borrowed*
belly	abdomen
building	edifice

153

earthly	terrestrial
end	terminate
fat	corpulent
forecast	prognosticate
friendly	affable
house	domicile
lie	perjure
lively	vivacious
murder	homicide
understand	apprehend
undertake	endeavor

It is more important for the writer to have a sense of the great variety of words in the English language than to have a precise knowledge of the history of individual words. This variety enables the writer to create the precise tone and to convey the exact meaning he intends. The writer can make consistently appropriate diction choices if he is aware of the meanings that words communicate to readers and of the corresponding feelings they evoke.

5.1 Denotation and Connotation

Effective writing depends on an awareness of the different levels of meaning that words convey. Words do not only have literal meaning, they also evoke emotional responses—ideas or feelings about them. These two aspects of meaning are known as *denotation* and *connotation.*

The denotation of a word is its literal, or dictionary, meaning—the meaning most speakers of a language agree upon. For example, the denotation of *criticism* is "evaluation." The denotation of *silviculture* is "forestry." The denotation of *library* is "a place where books may be read or borrowed."

In addition to denotation, most words have mild or strong connotations, positive or negative responses which they evoke in the reader or listener. These responses are based on one's personal experience with the object or idea represented by that word. The connotations of a word may be quite different from its denotative meaning. For example, to most people *criticism* suggests a negative, offensive act. This association has even become part of its denotative meaning, despite the fact that *criticism* originally meant (and still does) an evaluation or judgment—whether positive or negative. Although connotations involve personal reactions that are often shared by many people, the reactions may not always be the same for everyone. For example, to some people, *library* has favorable connotations—peace, quiet, knowledge. To others, the word has unfavorable connotations—confinement, stuffiness. The writer must therefore be aware that words have different connotations for different readers.

Although words themselves have denotations and connotations, the writer is primarily concerned with these qualities in a context—the written environment in which a word occurs:

> The **library** is the storehouse of human knowledge and aspirations.
>
> He was a boring person because all he had was **library** knowledge.

What a word actively denotes and connotes, then, depends upon its context. In fact, some words have more than one possible denotation and become clear to readers only in a particular context. For example, *game* can denote a diverting amusement, the quality of readiness, or something one hunts:

> For some investors, the stockmarket is merely a **game.**
>
> She was quite **game** to continue the tennis match even after injuring her ankle.
>
> Richard Connell's "The Most Dangerous Game" is a short story about a man who is hunted as **game.**

The connotations of a word may also depend on the particular context. *Mother,* for example, usually has favorable connotations, as in the sentence "She *mothered* me during my illness." But in the sentence "I resent being *mothered,*" the writer is evoking the less typical, negative connotations of mother—overprotectiveness, possessiveness, smothering. Similarly, the word *ego,* which usually has negative connotations (self-centered, selfish, conceited) can in some contexts have positive overtones: "Most psychologists believe that a strong **ego** is beneficial to one's mental health." Some words, of course, have such deeply rooted positive or negative connotations that the feelings associated with them rarely change: *sick, peace, happy.*

That many words do acquire new or additional denotations and connotations is not particularly surprising. They are, after all, symbols that are manipulated for communication. For example, the word *Watergate* denotes an expensive apartment complex in Washington, D.C. Its connotations include *rich* and *luxurious*. Recently, however, the word has come to connote political corruption. Indeed, this recently acquired connotation is so firmly linked to the word that *Watergate* now has the additional denotation of corruption.

155

Effective word choice depends on an awareness of these different aspects of meaning and their effect on readers. In each writing situation the writer needs to determine whether the overtones, as well as the literal meanings, of the words he uses suit his purpose and audience. (See also Section **5.14.**)

5.2 Idiomatic Expressions

Idioms are words and phrases that are characteristic of or peculiar to a language. For example, the phrases *catch a train* and *take a plane* do not make sense literally; they are intended in a figurative sense. Although they may violate logic or grammar, such expressions are clearly understandable to anyone whose native language is English. They make sense to native speakers because idioms are part of the conventions and usage of the language learned through experience.

Idiomatic expression refers to the way the speaker or writer uses the idioms of the language. Often it is the ability to use these idioms accurately that distinguishes native from foreign speakers and writers. The French speaker, for example, who says, "How do you call yourself?" or "I have hunger" is using the literal translations of the French idioms *"Comment vous appelez-vous?"* and *"J'ai faim."*

It is possible, however, for even native speakers to slip into unidiomatic expressions in speech or writing either through haste or oversight:

Unidiomatic	*Idiomatic*
Having pets was **consolation to** other disappointments.	Having pets was **consolation for** other disappointments.
Don Quixote's life is **fraught with** illusion.	Don Quixote's life is **filled with** illusion.

Exactly why it is unidiomatic to write "consolation to" or "fraught with" is sometimes difficult to understand, especially since it would be perfectly idiomatic to use the same combination of words in other situations:

My pets were a **consolation to** me in times of disappointment.

Don Quixote lives a life **fraught with** danger.

The writer's ability to use idiomatic expressions with precision is, in part, what creates a sense in the reader that the writer is using diction effectively.

Writers sometimes have difficulty using idioms effectively because they confuse idiomatic expressions with *clichés*—flat, worn-out expressions that have ceased to be effective:

as luck would have it
better late than never
it goes without saying
set the world on fire
cream of the crop
easier said than done
this day and age
one and the same

Writing that is full of clichés appears dull, insincere, and trite. Readers sense that instead of searching for the most exact expression to communicate a specific feeling, observation, or thought, the writer has used the first handy expression that came to mind. Clichés lack the natural, lively quality of idiomatic expression, and they are often so overused that they become imprecise or meaningless. (See also Section **5.8.**)

5.3   Multiple Vocabularies

We each own several vocabularies—or will come to own several during the course of our lives. For example, we have a basic vocabulary—consisting of such everyday words as *run, red, school, father,* and *please*—whose denotations and connotations are generally shared by all speakers of the language. In addition, we have sets of *dialectical words* (words associated with a particular geographic location) and *jargon* (words associated with a particular profession or group). For example, a native of Great Britain has an *accumulator* in his *lorry,* not a *battery* in his *truck.* A New Yorker orders a *soda,* but a Texan orders a *pop.* To the botanist, the *rose* by another name is *Rosaceae.*

A word with a general meaning may also have a special denotation within a particular group or when used to discuss a special activity: *run* (baseball); *transference* (psychology); *bear* and *bull* (stock market); *bug* (spying); *score* (music, sports). To a printer, *makeup, points,* and *justify* have meanings different from those generally associated with these words. And the wine connoisseur uses *bouquet* and *body* when discussing vintages to denote special meanings that differ from the way these words are commonly used.

The ongoing formal and informal education of any individual is largely a matter of acquiring new vocabulary. New locations, groups of people, courses of study, or professions make it necessary

157

to learn new words or the special denotations of words that are already familiar.

The writer must know not only the vocabulary of the field he is writing about but also whether the audience he is addressing is familiar with the vocabulary. Although the reader may be expected to look up the meanings of a few unfamiliar words, a work made up entirely of technical terms and familiar words used in a special sense places an excessive demand on the reader's knowledge of vocabulary. For example, given a specialized audience of physicians and psychiatrists, the writer uses *dissociative neurosis;* given a general audience, the writer uses *split personality.* Unnecessary use of specialized or technical words makes the writer seem pompous (especially if the words are used in an inappropriate audience context) or illiterate (if the words are used incorrectly).

Finally, the writer must be aware of the extent to which his own vocabulary is composed of words with special denotations or connotations. One person's vocabulary—developed through living, studying, working—may not communicate effectively to audiences who do not share that person's particular language experience.

5.4   Formal and Informal Diction

One way writers adjust their vocabularies to various audiences is by making diction choices either from words and expressions considered to be formal or from those considered to be informal. *Formal diction* is associated with Latinate words, technical terms, and scholarly prose. It is the consistent choice of words considered suitable for professional subjects, state occasions, and other structured situations. *Informal diction* is associated with less obviously Latinate words, contractions, abbreviations (such as *auto* for *automobile* and *phone* for *telephone*), and even *slang* (colorful words and expressions that do not follow the conventions of grammar and usage). Informal diction is used for communication in everyday situations. The following list illustrates the distinction between words and expressions considered to be informal or formal:

Informal	*Formal*
suspicious about everyone	paranoid
pass a law at the same time	legislate concurrently
worthless facts	meretricious data
flunk a course	fail a course
workable	feasible
pay back	recompense

native people	autochthonous population
most of the time	in the majority of circumstances
by the book	in accordance with established procedures

The difference between formal and informal diction does not entail merely substituting a fancier word or expression for one more common or direct. When used accurately and appropriately, formal diction can be more precise and efficient than informal diction:

> Informal   The person who is suspicious about everyone believes that people are out to get him.

> Formal   The paranoid operates under the delusion that he is being persecuted.

As a definition, not only does the second sentence make its point more concisely than the first (eleven versus fifteen words) but also the words used to limit the concept are more precise denotatively. For example, *delusion* is a more specific term than *believes* in that a *delusion* is a false belief whereas a *belief* can be either true or false.

5.5   Tone and Distance

An individual instance of using a formal or informal word or expression in a communication is not, of course, what creates a formal or informal *tone*—the writer's attitude (humorous, serious, emotional, objective) toward his audience as reflected in the language he uses. Tone is created by the sum of diction choices. These choices also determine the *distance* between writer and reader—that is, the degree of closeness or aloofness the writer establishes with the reader. Consider, for example, the following paragraph on William Faulkner's *The Hamlet*, taken from a scholarly literary journal:

> The poetic quality here—derived chiefly from parallelisms, repetitions, periods, and assonances—establishes the emotional rhythm of the entire idyll. The primordial quality of the moment before dawn is conveyed chiefly through evocations of darkness, lethargy, and enriching decay. The classical and medieval allusions especially suggest the permanence and fecundity of nature until, after the carefully wrought, richly detailed transition, they give way to the sun and bucolic reality. The implications of fertility are then made explicit, so that the progress is from slumbering potency to inchoate and, finally, aroused desire.
>
> T. Y. Greet, "The Theme and Structure of Faulkner's *The Hamlet*," *Publication of the Modern Language Association*

159

Part of what creates the objective and dignified tone and aloofness in this example is the consistent choice of formal diction. The writer uses Latinate words (*primordial, fecundity, bucolic, inchoate*) as well as specialized terms that are part of the vocabulary of literary analysis (*assonances, idyll, allusions*). The tone (formal) and distance (impersonal) created by such diction choices is appropriate for the intended audience—scholars.

These same readers, however, out of their professional context, would find the diction choices in the following garden column perfectly appropriate:

> It's possible to have a lovely flower garden all summer long by planting annuals. They can provide masses of color outdoors and cut flowers for bouquets indoors.
>
> Annuals are plants which complete their life cycle in one year. They start from seed, grow, bloom, produce seed and die. Zinnias, snapdragons, scarlet sage and marigolds are annuals.
>
> Tom Stevenson, "Why Not Plant Some Annuals?"
> *Washington Post*

In this passage, there's no evidence of Latinate diction or of specialized vocabulary. The contraction *it's,* the general modifiers (*lovely, several kinds*), the popular names (*zinnias, snapdragons*), and informal expressions (*all summer long, start from seed*) create a casual, familiar tone and diminish the distance between writer and reader, as if the two were engaged in direct conversation.

Although informal and formal diction patterns may be found throughout personal or professional writing, the trend in much of modern writing is to combine elements of both. This type of writing—found in such publications as newspapers and general-interest books and magazines—employs a vocabulary accessible to most educated readers but avoids both slang and technical terms (unless they are defined).

> While sentimentalists prattle about the supposedly unfettered freedom of the primitive, evidence collected by anthropologists and historians contradicts them. . . . As an Australian social scientist was told by a Temme tribesman in Sierra Leone: "When Temme people choose a thing, we must all agree with the decision—this is what we call cooperation."
>
> This is, of course, what we call conformity. The reason for the crushing conformity required of preindustrial man, the reason the Temme tribesman has to "go along" with his fellows, is precisely that he has nowhere else to go. His society is monolithic, not yet broken into a liberating multiplicity of components. It is what sociologists call "undifferentiated."
>
> Alvin Toffler, *Future Shock*

Here the writer uses informal expressions (*prattle, get along with*) and direct, active sentences. He joins forces explicitly with the reader ("This is, of course, what *we* call conformity") to create a familiar, subjective tone and distance. At the same time, he uses Latinate words understandable to most educated readers (*unfettered, preindustrial, multiplicity*) and less familiar, technical terms of sociology (*monolithic, undifferentiated*), which he defines and clarifies.

The pattern of diction choices the writer makes—whether formal, informal, or somewhere in between—is ultimately determined by his intentions and the context within which he works. The writer must judge whether the words and expressions may be inappropriate for one audience, too technical for another, insufficiently technical for another, and so on. These decisions depend on the writer's acquiring both a sense of audience and English idiom as well as an understanding of denotation and connotation.

Exercises

1. For each of the following sets of synonyms (or near synonyms), list as many different *connotations* as you can.

   a. begin, commence, initiate
   b. amateur, novice, beginner
   c. person, human being, individual
   d. advertising, propaganda, publicity
   e. enemy, opponent, antagonist
   f. proof, evidence, goods

2. Analyze the diction in the following paragraphs in terms of word choice, idiomatic expression, specialized vocabulary, and formal versus informal diction. Make any revisions that would improve the writing.

   a. Pope's "Essay on Criticism" was his key to fame; it recognized him as an accomplished poet. The poem was an aesthetics of poetry for his age. It provided his contemporaries an insight into the purpose of literary criticisms and showed them what they should be on the lookout for in critical reviews. The "Essay" conforms exactly along the definitions of Neoclassical poetry. It is an ideal Neoclassical poem.

   b. Scat Man, a regular cast member of the *Chico and The Man* series, said he doesn't see anything wrong with a clean-headed guy joining a bald-headed men's club. Offhand, he couldn't recommend anyone to join the club, but when his memory was jogged

161

he thought of bald-pated composer Isaac Hayes, dancer Geoffrey Holder, and actor Yaphet Kotto as prime candidates.

"Scat-Man Agrees: Bald is Beautiful," *Jet*

3. In the two preceding paragraphs find as many idiomatic expressions as you can.

4. In the following sentences rewrite the words or expressions used unidiomatically.

a. The fact that rich and poor are not alike would tend to negate the Declaration of Independence.

b. In contrast to what most people believe, it is possible to be happy at work and at home without having society status.

c. There is no formula for success, but hard work and determination have rewarding achievements.

d. Life is not a set of rules to follow, but a freedom to expose one's own creativity.

e. It is normal for a person to reach a goal, quickly become bored with it, and strive to attain a harder goal.

f. Man either spends his time conquering other people or throwing off the yoke that governs him.

g. The author also offers a description of Huck Finn.

h. Arthur Miller portrays Willy Loman as a locker-room personality, which makes this character well-liked and funny.

5. The following paragraphs deal with the same subject (English usage) and have the same purpose (to instruct readers). Yet each writer expresses his message in a different way. How would you characterize each paragraph as to type of language used, tone, and distance? Cite specific word choices to support your answers.

a. This difference of degrees [in English usage] is usually thought of in terms of higher and lower, of upper levels of speech appropriate to certain occasions of more formal character, or lower levels existing, if not necessarily appropriate, among less elevated circumstances. These popular distinctions of level may be accepted without weighting them too heavily with significance in respect of good, better, and best. A disputatious person might very well raise the question whether literary English, ordinarily regarded as being on a high level, is really any better than the spoken word—is really as good as the spoken word, warm with the breath of the living moment.

George Phillip Krapp, *The Knowledge of English*

b. In short, the entire structure of our notions about "correctness" and "right" vs. "wrong" in language is not only inaccurate, erroneous, and useless; it is definitely harmful, and we would do well to outgrow it. When purists tell us that we are using "bad" or "incorrect" or "ungrammatical" language, they are simply telling us that what we say would not be acceptable in the upper social levels; sometimes they are right as to the facts of the case, and sometimes they are just talking through their hats. What our purists give us in the way of rules and laws to observe has no authority, no validity aside from their own preference.

Robert A. Hall, Jr., *Linguistics and Your Language*

STYLE AND DICTION

All speakers and writers have a particular *style*—a characteristic way of expressing themselves. A writer's style is the result of his habitual choice of sentence patterns and diction. Diction habits, however, are the most noticeable aspect of a writer's style, and it is usually these habits that readers and writers have in mind when they speak of a lively versus a dull, light versus heavy, or exact versus vague style.

5.6 Exactness (ex)

The writer's first step toward making diction choices that result in a consistently effective style is to develop an increased awareness of words and audiences. This awareness leads to *conscious* word choice from among the available alternatives. The second step is to understand what qualities in diction produce exactness in writing by creating for the reader a clear and precise picture of what the writer wishes to communicate. The basic qualities that contribute to exact diction are:

1. Accuracy
2. Concreteness
3. Appropriateness
4. Economy
5. Variety

By choosing words and expressions that possess these qualities, the writer can communicate his message to the reader clearly and effectively.

163

5.6a **Accuracy**

Using accurate diction means selecting a word or expression whose denotative meaning is closest to the writer's intended meaning. The word or expression should describe the particular object, quality, action, or idea as precisely as possible:

> Ernest Hemingway's "The Killers" is an interesting **article.**
>
> Detente will mean we need to train more students to speak **fluid** Chinese.

Article does not accurately describe "The Killers," a short story, and *fluent,* not *fluid,* is the precise word for describing proficiency in speaking a foreign language. Although the reader often may be able to figure out the intended word or expression, having to do so detracts from the effectiveness of the communication. Additionally, the reader may consciously or unconsciously judge inexact diction as a reflection of imprecise thinking.

Among the most obvious cases of inaccurate diction are those caused by misspelling or by confusing words that are similar in form but that have different meanings:

> Union leaders often **disuse** their bargaining power.
>
> The arbitration board for a labor-management dispute should be composed of **uninterested** parties.
>
> The woman's broad shoulders and six-foot height gave her a regal **status.**

In the first sentence the accurate verb is *misuse,* which means "to use incorrectly or improperly." *Disuse* means "to stop using." In the second example the correct word is *disinterested,* which denotes fairness or impartiality. An arbitration board should be fair and impartial but not *uninterested*—indifferent and apathetic. Finally, *stature,* not *status* is the noun that accurately describes the woman's regality. The writer is referring to the woman's physical height (*stature*), not to her social position (*status*).

Another cause of inaccurate diction is the misuse of *homonyms*—words that have the same or similar pronunciation but different meanings:

> Public ownership of the means of production is a basic **principal** of socialism.

The accurate word is *principle,* a noun that denotes a rule of fundamental truth. *Principal* refers to a person in authority.

The following list of word pairs are frequently confused because they are similar in either form or sound. (See also Section **6.5d.**):

adapt, adopt
affect, effect
all ready, already
amoral, immoral
confidant, confident
deduce, deduct
definite, definitive
device, devise
emerge, immerge
faint, feint
fatal, fateful
faze, phase
formally, formerly
forward, foreword

human, humane
imminent, eminent
insure, ensure
local, locale
meat, meet, mete
pedal, peddle
perpetrate, perpetuate
persecute, prosecute
perspective, prospective
proceed, precede
prophecy, prophesy
respectable, respectful
sleight, slight

Accurate diction is not simply a matter of using words that are denotatively precise; they must also be idiomatically accurate. Two words or expressions may have similar denotations, yet each may convey a slightly different meaning and so be more appropriate in some contexts than in others. For example, the words *empty* and *vacant* are synonymous in many circumstances. We speak of "an empty room" or a "vacant room"; "an empty lot" or "a vacant lot." But "a vacant bucket" is an inaccurate idiomatic use of the word *vacant*. *Empty* is the opposite of *full* or *occupied; vacant* can be opposed only to *occupied*. Similarly, we may refer to "a vivacious person" or "a lively person"; but "a vivacious argument" is not quite precise. Vivacity is a quality associated more with persons than with abstract ideas.

When the writer expresses himself unidiomatically, the reader may recognize the accurate word or expression within the distortion but will be confused nonetheless. Compare, for example, the first and second versions of the following pairs of sentences:

Unidiomatic	Peanuts **leans toward the obsession** with baseball.
Revised	Peanuts is **obsessed** with baseball.
Unidiomatic	The actors smoothly and humorously **carried out** the play.
Revised	The actors smoothly and humorously **performed** the play.
Unidiomatic	Part of the irony is that the character's dream is not **accomplished**
Revised	Part of the irony is that the character's dream is not **realized.**

Unidiomatic	Laughter **infested** the audience.
Revised	Laughter **infected** the audience.
Unidiomatic	Because she is slightly paranoid, she **has a suspicion** of other people.
Revised	Because she is slightly paranoid, she **is suspicious** of other people.

As illustrated by these examples, imprecise diction distorts the writer's message. Such inaccuracies often result from oversight or an attempt to use a word for its impressive sound rather than for its meaning:

> Aaron Burr **disillusioned** himself about his success because he could not admit that he had failed in life.

> The doctrines of Martin Luther were a threat to the **firmament** of the Catholic religion.

In the first sentence, the intended word is *deceived*, not *disillusioned.* The intended message is that Aaron Burr became disillusioned about the need for success in life. In the second sentence, the writer probably means "foundation," not "firmament," a more impressive, sophisticated word that is, nonetheless, inaccurate in this context. The effect of such word choices almost always creates confusion for the reader, who can only guess at the writer's intended meanings. When the writer chooses words by feel or sound alone and does not consider meaning, the result is usually inaccurate diction.

5.6b Concreteness

When a word is said to be concrete, two meanings are implied:

1. The word refers to a *specific* object, quality, or action rather than to a *class* of objects, qualities, or actions. "The crowd **ran** to the scene" is more concrete and specific than "The crowd **went** to the scene."
2. The word is the most specific referent possible to describe the particular object, quality, or action. "**Five** summer houses were burned" is more specific than "**A few** summer houses were burned."

Accurate diction communicates precisely what the writer intends his words to mean; concrete diction communicates precise information. The more specific a word, the more specific an idea the reader receives:

> I met a **writer** who is **related to** a **politician.**
> I met a **newspaper writer** who is **related to** a **senator.**

> I met a **columnist** who is **related to** a **senator from New York.**
>
> I met the **columnist William F. Buckley, Jr.,** who is **related to Senator James L. Buckley of New York.**
>
> I met the **columnist William F. Buckley, Jr.,** who is **the brother of Senator James L. Buckley of New York.**

This series of sentences moves from a very broad statement to the most precise referents possible for the idea described. The progression is from general to specific, from abstract to concrete. For example, there are thousands of politicians, one hundred senators, and two senators from New York; but there is only one Senator James L. Buckley. Each new sentence narrows the reader's conception until there is only one possible association in his mind.

The concreteness of a word or words is determined in part by the audience. For example, scientific and technical writing often involves abstract statements of laws or rules. To a mathematician, such abstractions are clear, precise, and economical. For example, the axiom *any number minus itself is zero* contains a thought that might be difficult to grasp for some readers, and it would be totally incomprehensible to a second-grader. To the mathematician, however, the words make concrete references that produce a clear picture.

Like so many other writing qualities, concreteness depends upon context. In any context, however, the writer should provide the reader with words that produce the necessary detail to clarify or explain the writer's ideas. Suppose, for example, that a music critic submitted the following review for publication:

> Frank Sinatra is still unique. Everything he sang at Carnegie Hall, despite signs of aging and problems with the orchestra, was wonderful.

The diction in the statement does not communicate a clear picture. Exactly what does the critic mean by "unique" and "wonderful"? And, specifically, what were the "signs of aging" and "the problems with the orchestra"? Additional detail and a more concrete choice of words answers these questions:

> Sinatra does remain unique for the vividness and intensity of his response to song. Everything he sang at Carnegie Hall, even with the wavering voice, the lapses of memory, and the overstuffed arrangements in the outsized backup orchestra, became a song a little larger than life and a lot better than it really was.
>
> Alan Rich, "Return to Sunnybrook Farm"
> *New York Magazine*

This version gives the reader a clearer picture of why, in the writer's

167

5.6b Concreteness

opinion, the performance was "unique" and "wonderful." The reader has an image of Sinatra fighting against an aging voice and an overpowering orchestra to deliver a song to his audience. Words like *unique* and *wonderful* are so vague, so broad in denotation, that they are empty of meaning in most contexts. Similarly, words like *great, nice, situation, large, interesting, unusual, regular, business, thing, matter, funny, element*—often called *utility words* or *all-purpose words*—are so inclusive in meaning that they remain vague and imprecise in most contexts. (See also Chapter 10, "Glossary of Usage."):

> Mark Twain's brilliant use of description is **interesting** and **unusual.** It enables him to get across the **funny** aspects of his stories in a way that is **great.** He even **handles nicely things** that have **rather humorless elements.**

The writer of this passage is using words but is not communicating meaning. Words like *funny* and *element* do have precise meanings ("He told a *funny* joke"; "hydrogen is an *element* that can explode"), but in contexts like those above, such words are vague and do not communicate ideas of any real value. Substitution of concrete words and elaboration with concrete detail clarifies the writer's meaning:

> Mark Twain uses his precise descriptions of household items both to keep the reader's interest and to reflect satirically on the characters. We laugh at Huckleberry Finn's puzzled reaction to the artificial fruit in the bowl on the Grangerford's table. However, we also note that the chipped fruit is a serious comment on the family's false gentility.

In this revision, instead of describing his general response to Mark Twain, the writer evokes a specific, concrete experience in the reader's mind. The precise experience and the general impression are simultaneously communicated. Listed below are several other examples of how concrete diction linked to precise detail creates a clear picture for the reader:

Vague	**Trees** surrounded the **water** near our summer **place.**
Concrete	**Old elms** surrounded the **lake** near our summer **cabin.**
Vague	*The Godfather* is a **relevant** movie.
Concrete	*The Godfather* is a movie about **corruption in America.**
Vague	*Moby Dick* has a **philosophical** theme.
Concrete	The theme of *Moby Dick* is the **battle between human will and the natural forces of evil.**
Vague	**Certain people in my family** disagree with my **attitudes** toward grades.

> Concrete **My mother and father** disagree with my view that **acquiring knowledge is more important than getting good grades.**

5.6c Appropriateness

The writer must choose diction that is not only accurate and concrete but also suitable for the audience, the subject, and his own purposes. For example, whether the writer uses formal or informal language depends on the audience. While slang and clichés may be appropriate in a letter to a close friend, such diction would be out of place in a business letter to a stranger. The formal language called for in the latter situation (e.g., "I would appreciate hearing from you at your convenience") would seem ridiculous and inappropriate in a letter to a friend.

The writer's choice of technical or everyday words also depends on the audience. For example, the writer may use the word *bunny* in a children's book, *rabbit* in general writing situations, and *Oryctolagus cuniculus* in a scientific paper. Each term is appropriate for its specific audience. Depending on the audience, the writer may seek a useful middle ground:

> A rabbit, or *Oryctolagus cuniculus,* is a member of the hare family but is smaller and has different physical characteristics.

This style is appropriate for a general audience who would profit from learning the scientific name for *rabbit.*

At the same time, the writer must make diction choices appropriate to the subject. If the subject is serious—a death or an accident—the writer is likely to use formal diction. For example, "I was sorry to hear about your brother's death" is more appropriate than "Too bad about your brother"—even in a letter to a friend. "Too bad" is inappropriately informal and frivolous in this context. Considering the somberness of the subject, the expression sounds almost flippant. In the following sentence, the diction is also unsuitable for the subject and context, an essay intended to be a scholarly analysis:

> **Craziness** is a theme that is evident in many of Shakespeare's plays.

In this sentence, the subject and context call for a more formal, sophisticated term than *craziness,* such as *madness, insanity,* or *lunacy.* Although *craziness* would be appropriate in a more casual context ("The children were especially taken with the comic *craziness* of the clowns"), it is too informal a word for the sample sentence above.

Finally, appropriate diction depends on the writer's purpose in establishing a certain tone through the connotation of his words.

169

He must decide whether he wishes to evoke positive or negative associations toward his subject and whether he wishes to establish a tone that is "formal," "informal," "literary," "popular," or "old-fashioned." Given two words with the same denotative meaning—such as *car* and *automobile*—the writer must select the word with the most appropriate connotations for his purpose. He would use *car* for an informal tone, *automobile* for a formal tone. It is impractical, however, to try to categorize diction according to audience, subject, and purpose. All three are equally important in choosing appropriate diction.

5.6d Economy

Economy in word choice also contributes toward effective diction. Every communication should include all the words necessary for the reader to understand completely the writer's intended message. However, excess words—those not needed for clear, concrete expression—only weigh down the communication. Not only do unnecessary words obscure those that *are* essential for meaning, but they also reduce the total impact and effectiveness of the prose.

Economy in diction is achieved by choosing accurate words, by avoiding unnecessary repetition (*redundancy*), and by revising sentences to eliminate nonessential words whenever possible:

Wordy	Out of all the plays Tennessee Williams **has written,** *The Glass Menagerie* is the most poetic **play.**
Economical	*The Glass Menagerie* is the most poetic of Williams's plays.
Wordy	After **he had finished** his speech, the president **boarded a plane headed for** San Francisco.
Economical	After his speech, the president flew to San Francisco.
Wordy	**There are many instances in which** students have difficulty adjusting to the demands of academic life.
Economical	Many students have difficulty adjusting to the demands of academic life.

By reorganizing and condensing, each of these sentences has been revised to eliminate useless words and phrases so that the writer's meaning can be isolated and stated directly. As a result, the economical sentences are more efficient and more emphatic.

Although in practice all the methods for achieving economy work together, each can be discussed separately. The most obvious way to achieve economy is to avoid needless repetition (*redundancy*):

Redundant	The team has never been a success by any **standard of measurement.**

Economical	The team has never been a success by any standard.
Redundant	To understand **how** photosynthesis **works,** we must **classify** the process **and break it down into stages.**
Economical	To understand photosynthesis we must classify its various stages.
Redundant	**Unwarranted and unjustified** hostility toward immigrants is often the result of **fear and apprehension.**
Economical	Unwarranted hostility toward immigrants is often the result of fear.
Redundant	In F. Scott Fitzgerald's *The Great Gatsby,* Daisy Buchanan is **vain, conceited, egotistical, and thinks a great deal of herself.**
Economical	In F. Scott Fitzgerald's *The Great Gatsby,* Daisy Buchanan is egotistical.
Redundant	**The subject of physics** is my most difficult subject.
Economical	Physics is my most difficult subject.

The revised, economical sentences are identical in meaning to the redundant versions, but they use fewer words. For example, since "classify" and "break down into parts" are synonymous, there is no need to include both expressions. Similarly, because "physics" is, in fact, a "subject," the former word alone sufficiently communicates the writer's meaning.

Sometimes economy can be achieved by substituting one word that means exactly what the writer has said in several words:

Wordy	Oliver even lacked the **ways and means** to buy food.
Economical	Oliver even lacked the **money** to buy food.
Wordy	The birth of his son **gave Shelley the inspiration to put together the words and ideas he had been working on and to create** the poem "Ode to the West Wind."
Economical	The birth of his son **inspired Shelley to write** the poem "Ode to the West Wind."

In both examples, the word substituted in the economical version basically communicates the same message contained in the wordy one.

Economy can also be achieved by reordering and condensing the elements of a sentence or sentences:

In his **novel** *The Stranger,* Albert Camus bases the **book** on the philosophy of existentialism.

171

By shortening and rearranging its parts, this sentence can be made economical and still remain clear enough for a reader unfamiliar with the novel:

> Albert Camus's novel *The Stranger* is based on the philosophy of existentialism.

For an audience familiar with Camus's work and with philosophy, the writer could produce an even more economical sentence:

> Albert Camus's *The Stranger* is based on existentialism.

Choosing diction for economy means being selective but not sparse or oversimplified. Eliminating words does not improve writing when done at the expense of clarity or accuracy. Exact descriptions need vivid, precise explanations. Without them, writing is bland or vague:

Sparse	I love Van Gogh's paintings.
Wordy	I love Van Gogh's paintings because their vivid colors and desperate brush strokes are always moving to me.
Economical	I am always moved by the vivid colors and desperate brush strokes of Van Gogh's paintings.
Sparse	Other elements of a play are just as important as the acting.
Wordy	Other elements of a play—in particular, lighting, costumes, and set design—are just as important as the acting.
Economical	The lighting, costumes, and set design of a play are just as important as the acting.
Sparse	The term *undergraduate* is better than *undergraduate student.*
Wordy	The term *undergraduate* is better than *undergraduate student* since it is more concise.
Economical	The term *undergraduate* is more concise than *undergraduate student.*

(See also Section **5.9.**)

5.6e Variety

The purpose of using variety in diction is to maintain the reader's interest by eliminating boring, needless repetition. Variety is achieved by using synonyms and pronoun substitutes effectively and by varying the grammatical patterns in a communication. Writing that lacks variety often results in heavy, awkward prose that can interfere with reading ease:

> **Shakespeare's** plays are notable for their moral neutrality. For example, in *Julius Caesar* **Shakespeare** is not wholly **sympathetic** to Caesar. **Shakespeare** does not **sympathize** with **Brutus, Antony,** or **Octavius.** Caesar is killed in the middle of *Julius Caesar.* Then **Shakespeare** directs the audience's attention to **Brutus, Antony, and Octavius.** As a result, **Shakespeare** gives *Julius Caesar* no single hero. **Shakespeare** gives an objective view of the characters throughout *Julius Caesar* by alternating between **favorable and unfavorable assessments. Shakespeare** does not give final approval to the **favorable assessment** or **unfavorable assessment.**

The monotony in this paragraph is caused by redundancy (Shakespeare; sympathetic, sympathize; *Julius Caesar;* Brutus, Antony, Octavius; favorable assessment, unfavorable assessment). Moreover, the sentences are choppy and similar in grammatical pattern. One way to give the paragraph greater variety would be to substitute synonyms and pronouns for some of the proper nouns:

> Shakespeare's plays are notable for their moral neutrality. For example, in *Julius Caesar* Shakespeare is not wholly sympathetic to Caesar. **He** does not sympathize with Brutus, Antony, or Octavius. Caesar is killed in the middle of **the play.** Then Shakespeare directs the audience's attention to the **other main characters.** As a result, the **playwright** gives *Julius Caesar* no single hero. **He maintains** an objective view of the characters throughout **the play** by alternating between favorable and unfavorable assessments. Shakespeare does not give final approval to **either** assessment.

This version eliminates much of the repetition. But choppy sentences and a monotonous grammatical pattern remain—that is, almost every sentence begins with a subject (Shakespeare) that performs a direct action. The paragraph can be further improved by grammatical refinements, including shifts in voice (elimination of unnecessary "actors"), inversion, coordination, and subordination:

> Shakespeare's plays are notable for their moral neutrality. For example, in *Julius Caesar* Shakespeare is not wholly sympathetic to Caesar, Brutus, Antony, or Octavius. Caesar is killed in the middle of the play and the audience's attention is then directed to the other main characters. As a result, *Julius Caesar* has no single hero. Throughout the play Shakespeare maintains an objective view of the characters by alternating between favorable and unfavorable assessments, without giving final approval to either.

173

This revision is more concise, more emphatic, and more to the point. The elimination of repetitious words and unnecessary actors removes a block between the reader and the meaning. The use of coordination and subordination makes the sentences smoother and more concise and demonstrates clearly the relationships among ideas.

Nevertheless, variety in writing is not an end in itself. Variety at the expense of other writing goals—clarity, accuracy, and appropriateness—defeats the purpose of a communication. In some situations effective repetition may be needed to create emphasis or to establish unity. Pronouns must be used carefully to avoid confusion or ambiguity, and substitution of synonyms must also be handled carefully and in moderation. Excessive variation in synonyms calls attention to itself and weakens the focus of writing. Suppose a writer had revised the original paragraph above to avoid repeating the name *Shakespeare* at all costs:

> Shakespeare's plays are notable for their moral neutrality. For example, in *Julius Caesar,* **the playwright** is not wholly sympathetic to Caesar. **The great bard** does not sympathize with Brutus, Antony, or Octavius. Caesar is killed in the middle of the play. Then the **"swan of Avon"** directs the audience's attention to the other main characters. As a result, **the master of dramatic poetry** gives *Julius Caesar* no single hero. . . .

This type of writing seeks variety at the expense of appropriateness and clarity. The trade is not a good one. Phrases like *the great bard* and *master of dramatic poetry* are vague and out of place in this context. The expression *swan of Avon* is a poetic reference to Shakespeare that some readers may not be familiar with. In a sense, the writer goes off on a tangent, devising different names for Shakespeare instead of concentrating on the message. Actually, repetition of the name *Shakespeare* occasionally helps the reader touch base and adds unity to the paragraph. Forced variation is inappropriate and pretentious. Essentially, it is self-conscious writing rather than natural writing.

Exercises

1. The following sentences lack one or more of the basic qualities that contribute to effective diction and good writing—accuracy, appropriatness, concreteness, economy, and variety. Revise the sentences to improve the diction:

> **a.** In the show *On the Waterfront* Marlon Brando says he has been given a one-way ticket to "Palookaville." I thought this was a funny term, until I realized that it meant "nowhere."

b. My professor made a statement saying that she had occasion to be less than satisfied with my work.

c. Sir Laurence Olivier, the imminent British actor, is reported to be the greatest living interpreter of Shakespeare.

d. Some people are the masters of their emotions, but in the majority of instances they are not.

e. In one study, a patient subject to frequent migraine attacks was given two milligrams of the test drug daily. On this regimen, he began losing scalp hair by the bushel, although the migraine attacks subsided.

f. First the President decided to raise taxes. Then the President decided against his original decision and asked Congress to lower taxes.

g. *Romeo and Juliet* is a charming play.

h. In the first stanza of "The Cloud," Shelley uses concrete, sensory verbiage to make his experience more alive to readers.

i. Genuine, unforced, spontaneous inspiration is what distinguishes the great writer from the good writer.

j. The play precedes uneventfully until the appearance of the ghost.

2. Evaluate the diction in each of the following paragraphs. Point out both strong points and weak points. Make any revisions that would improve the writing.

a. In times of psychic despair, it has been a great comfort to me to read of an ordinary man (often a "failure") who was transformed into a superman by a literal *deus ex machina* (what else can you call an alien in a flying saucer?). There I was, dissolved in time, flying across the universe at many times the speed of light in a ten-mile-long fire and steel body, capable of vaporizing entire planetary systems at my slightest whim. With my razor-sharp mind and my body an unequaled fighting machine, I would single-handedly destroy planets, battle titans, and seduce Amazonian superwomen who lusted after my perfect maleness. I traveled into the past and changed history. I traveled into the future and rekindled a dying human race.

b. Of all of the countries that I visited in Europe, my favorite was without the slightest doubt Denmark. I spent a few days in the city of Copenhagen, and it is without a doubt one of the most charming cities on the continent. There's a wonderful zoo. The Tivoli amusement park is very lively during the summer, and there are lots of places to go at night to hear music and dance. There are also many nice shopping areas. I would greatly recommend Denmark to anyone who is able to travel to Europe.

3. To produce an effective style, sentence structure and accurate diction must work together. As if you were an editor, analyze one of the following paragraphs. Write an evaluation, making specific recommendations for stylistic improvements.

a. *Subject:* A course evaluation written by a student for a college dean.

English 387 classes were generally pretty interesting. The instructor projected the attitude of interest in whatever idea someone would come up with. I think this factor is what opened up communications in class. The instructor's idea was to hit on a subject that was of interest to all the students and then to let the students give their responses. In my opinion, the class was just too large to really get into the idea. I myself was hesitant about opening up in such a big group simply because I had no idea of what type of people were in the group. I see the worthiness of communication; however, not one-sided communication or communication in an atmosphere where the person communicating does not at least have some kind of idea of how the people will take it. In short, I was inhibited.

b. *Subject:* An article written for a sports magazine.

Even though I have not played individual sports as much as team sports, I have observed enough to safely say that team sports are more demanding overall than individual sports. On the coordinated side of things, when one plays a team sport, one has to coordinate himself with the rest of the team or the whole idea of a team is reduced to individualism. How many times have we seen a great basketball player or one of the major athletes not be able to identify himself or herself with a team and thus have to be traded? On the other hand, with individual sports one has only to coordinate his own mind and his own body, which in itself is a very hard task to do when compared with the addition of coinciding with a whole team. Things can become extremely difficult.

From the physical point of view, team sports involve having more physical contact. Therefore, the chance of being injured increases immensely as more individuals get involved.

Most important is the mental attitude of the players between the two different kinds of sport. The team player has to think about the team first before he thinks of himself. He has to think about what is good for the team rather than about his own individual accomplishment. When one makes a play that greatly benefits the team, he also benefits as well. On the other hand, in individual sports, one has to do things just for oneself. Thus, individual sports are easier on the player mentally, because he is free to do what he wishes. In individual sports, only the player himself can be injured.

c. *Subject:* A humorous editorial on losing weight, written for a general-circulation newspaper.

A lot of people would give anything to lose weight. They go on diets, do exercise, use sauna baths, watch Jack LaLanne, and try just about anything they can think of to lose weight, but they don't seem to lose too much. However, the ultimate form of weight control has been found, and that is basic training in the military.

During basic training one is exposed to sure-fire ways of losing weight. In the morning, before the rooster crows, one goes through a pep routine. This pep routine is the means by which the marines wake up the recruits. One does a little running, does a few exercises, sweats some, and just generally burns up a few calories. During the day there are a number of activities that burn off a few calories off of anyone. There are swimming classes, boxing classes, and wrestling classes that just make one's day. When one wants to go anywhere, all one has to do is to run to wherever one is going. Every once in a while there are "uniform races." These races are guaranteed methods of losing a few pounds.

The best part of the day comes at meals. If one is forgetful enough to try to eat something, one is likely to get a "whamo." Whamming discourages big bites and convinces one to eat less. Oh, I almost forgot about the two hours of marching in the hot sun with one's rifle. This little outing is designed to help one lose eleven pounds in one outing—if one doesn't pass out cold. These methods are some of the military's way of producing the skinnier man.

IMPROVING DICTION

Writers often make errors in diction because their idea of effective diction is inaccurate. Most writers learn the qualities of good diction through experience, and practice gives them the opportunity to polish their diction. To improve one's diction, however, it is also necessary to become aware of the most common diction errors inexperienced writers make. The following section can be used as a review glossary of the most frequent lapses in diction.

5.7 Pretentiousness

Inexperienced writers often feel that the more complex a word or sentence, the better the writing style—that is, the more impressed readers will be. Actually, pretentious writing often creates exactly the opposite effect. Readers are generally puzzled at high-flown language used in ordinary situations (e.g., "waste receptacle" for "trash can") or at the inexact denotation or connotation conveyed (e.g., "divulge" for "publish"). Pretentious writing is vague, inappropriate, and uneconomical. The writer invests too much stylistic energy in a simple message:

> **Pretentious** Of all the multitudinously diverse spheres of endeavor in which the offspring of our educational institutions choose to participate, the field of endeavor that provides this writer with the most continual degree of satisfaction is influencing the behavioral patterns of youthful members of our society.

> **Clear** Of the many professions open to college graduates, I have found working with young children to be the most satisfying.

The pseudo-sophisticated language of the first version is unsuited to the context. The reader must work hard to understand the message and receives little reward. The second version says all that the writer wishes to say and says it simply, concretely, and meaningfully to the reader.

High-flown language is often used to glorify a subject or to deceive readers. The employer who advertises for a "sanitary engineer" rather than a "janitor" is misleading potential employees. The company that labels its new drug "acetylsalicylic acid" without mentioning the more familiar term *aspirin* is also guilty of deception. When pretentious language is used to mask the truth, a basic professional principle of writing has been violated. Words should reveal rather than hide meaning; and writers who attempt to mislead readers will find their ethics as well as their credibility called into question.

Jargon—the specialized vocabulary of a particular profession or social group—is also pretentious when used out of context. Within a professional journal, jargon may be acceptable and even essential, but in a communication intended for the general reader it is confusing, inappropriate, and imprecise:

> Upon entering the academic community, I discovered a need to cope with the simultaneous arousal of incompatible motives. On the one hand, I sought to attain mastery in intellectual tasks. On the other hand, I had a need for affiliation and interaction with my peers.

The writer makes a commonplace, concrete experience abstract and inaccessible to readers by using psychological jargon. The "simultaneous arousal of incompatible motives" is a *conflict*. The "attainment of mastery in intellectual tasks" is "doing well in one's studies;" "affiliation and interaction with peers" means "making friends and socializing." These are terms that a general-reading audience can recognize and relate to. The use of psychological jargon does not give greater credibility or significance to the writer's experience. Instead, such jargon obscures the message by weighing down the reader with needlessly heavy or unfamiliar prose.

5.8   Clichés

Ineffective writing is often characterized by an abundance of *clichés*—trite, worn-out expressions that have lost their meaning or effect. These include stock phrases such as "nerve-tingling" and "we must tighten our belts" and faddish expressions such as "tell it like it is" and "the silent majority." A few more examples of clichés are listed below:

add insult to injury	leave much to be desired
after all is said and done	method in one's madness
at a loss for words	momentous decision
beginning of the end	nipped in the bud
benefit of the doubt	none the worse for wear
by leaps and bounds	path of least resistance
cut a long story short	point with pride
depths of despair	sadder but wiser
due consideration	see the light of day
eminently successful	sweat of one's brow
finer things in life	time of one's life
food for thought	too numerous to mention
goes without saying	trials and tribulations
heart of the matter	view with alarm
in no uncertain terms	viselike grip
last but not least	walk of life

Clichés are poor substitutes for clear thinking and creative expression, and writing that contains such worn-out, trite expressions is likely to be judged as unimaginative:

> I came home after jogging and had a cold beer, which really **hit the spot.** Suddenly I heard a noise that nearly **scared the life out of me.** I ran upstairs and discovered that my bookcase had collapsed and my record player had been smashed. I knew it would be **curtains for me** when my parents saw the damage. It would just be **the end of the world.**

179

5.9 (W)

The overworked expressions in this paragraph result in boring, dead prose. They tell the reader nothing new about the writer's experience. Phrases like "hit the spot" and "curtains for me" have no literal meaning and have lost all their connotations—except, perhaps, for the connotation "trite."

Inexperienced writers are often unaware that phrases which seem clever or original to them have become meaningless expressions to most readers. In general, the pleasing phrase that comes too easily to mind should be avoided—unless the reader can inject new life into it with an unusual twist:

> The movie was so nerve-tingling that my foot went to sleep.
>
> Economists need a little belt-tightening of the mind when they argue that the larger investor has been hurt most by inflation.
>
> When an Englishman talks about "football," Americans must be on their bilingual toes to realize that he means "rugby."

In the first sentence, the writer revitalizes the cliché "nerve-tingling" by using it to coincide with the phrase "my foot went to sleep." The cliché "belt-tightening" works well in the second sentence because it refers to the *mind* rather than to the purse, its usual referent. The third sentence contains a form of the cliché "to be on one's toes," but the writer has used the expression creatively by applying it to "bilingual." (See also p. 156.)

5.9   Wordiness (W)

Two words are not necessarily better than one. Wordiness slows down writing, distracts the reader, and obscures the writer's message. (See also Section **5.6d**.)

5.9a   Loose Synonyms

A writer should not use loose or inexact synonyms when one word expresses an idea precisely:

Wordy	The theory is **outdated and no longer relevant.**
Improved	The theory is **obsolete.**
Wordy	There are many **connections and relationships** between the two poems.
Improved	There are many **similarities** between the two poems.
Wordy	Sherlock Holmes is a **highly regarded and skillful** detective.
Improved	Sherlock Holmes is a **master** detective.

5.9b   Deadwood

Deadwood consists of words or phrases that take up space but do no work. Deadwood often occurs in introductory phrases but can appear anywhere in a sentence:

Wordy	**In the matter of coed dormitories,** I am in favor of men and women sharing dormitories.
Improved	I am in favor of coed dormitories.
Wordy	**There are claims by many historians** that King Arthur did not exist.
Improved	Many historians claim that King Arthur did not exist.
Wordy	James Joyce was **known to be** an experimental writer.
Improved	James Joyce was an experimental writer.
Wordy	Norman Borlaug's **work along the lines of** experimentation with different strains of wheat earned him a Nobel prize.
Improved	Norman Borlaug's experimentation with different strains of wheat earned him a Nobel prize.

5.9c   Redundancy

Redundancy is the use of a word or phrase that duplicates part of the meaning of another word. Redundant writing is circular and awkward. In the following examples, the bold words and phrases are redundant and should be eliminated:

This journal is written in chronological order **according to the sequence in which the events occurred.**

As a **general** rule, a college education is a **necessary** requisite for teaching.

A major theme among modern dramatists **of today** is the futility of human existence **in this world.**

One cause of pollution is **on account of** the reluctance of industry to recycle waste products.

The Boston Celtics are **complete** masters of **the important fundamentals of** basketball.

5.9d   Circumlocution

Circumlocution refers to writing that talks around a subject rather than coming to the point. Circumlocutions are often imprecise and pretentious, as well as wordy:

Wordy	**I had occasion to be present at** the opening of *The Glass Menagerie* at Kennedy Center.

181

Improved	**I attended** the opening of *The Glass Menagerie* at Kennedy Center.
Wordy	Hollywood is **somewhere in the vicinity of** Los Angeles.
Improved	Hollywood is **near** Los Angeles.
Wordy	The sparse set decoration in *Waiting for Godot* was **effective from a dramatic standpoint.**
Improved	The sparse set decoration in *Waiting for Godot* was **dramatically effective.**
Wordy	**During the time that I was a freshman,** I was interested **to a greater degree** in sports than in my studies.
Improved	**As a freshman,** I was **more** interested in sports than in my studies.

5.10 Overuse of Intensives and Qualifiers

Intensives—words like *very, a lot, definitely, certainly, rather, really, somewhat, myself*—are often used by writers to add emphasis to a statement. Actually, such words are so vague and overworked that they have little impact on readers and usually result in wordiness rather than emphasis. It is best to eliminate them or to substitute stronger modifiers:

Weak	The third act is **very** important.
Improved	The third act is **the most** important in the play.
Weak	I **myself definitely** enjoy going to the theater.
Improved	I enjoy going to the theater.
Weak	The critics **really** liked Al Pacino's performance in *The Godfather.*
Improved	The critics **praised** Al Pacino's performance in *The Godfather.*
Weak	I am **somewhat** apprehensive about another fuel shortage this winter.
Improved	I am apprehensive about another fuel shortage this winter.

(See also Chapter 10, Glossary of Usage.)

Beginning writers often try to tone down their opinions or to appear more objective by using *qualifiers*—words and phrases like *probably, maybe, could be, seems, I think, I believe, kind of, so-called,* and *is said to.* In most cases, such qualifiers are unnecessary. They weaken writing and make the writer seem uncertain or indecisive. (See also p. 16.):

Weak	**It seems** that the economy is in a period of inflation.
Improved	The economy is in a period of inflation.
Weak	*Everyman* is **said to be a kind of** morality play.
Improved	*Everyman* is a morality play.
Weak	**I think** that Elton John is **probably** my favorite musician.
Improved	Elton John is my favorite musician.
Weak	The **so-called** First Folio edition of Shakespeare's plays appeared in 1623.
Improved	The First Folio edition of Shakespeare's plays appeared in 1623.

5.11   Euphemisms

Euphemism (literally, "good sounding") is the substitution of a delicate, imprecise expression for an unpleasant but more natural (and accurate) term. Usually, a euphemism attempts to avoid words with unpleasant or negative connotations, especially those relating to death, sex, crime, body functions, and profanity. For example, there are many euphemisms in American English for the word *toilet,* ranging from *bathroom* to *powder room, lounge,* and, most recently, *comfort station.*

Like circumlocutions, euphemisms are wordy and often pretentious. They talk around a subject rather than describing it directly and call attention to the writer's attempt at delicacy rather than to his message. In most cases, euphemisms sound prudish or cowardly to the reader rather than careful:

Weak	Fortinbras filled the political void created by the **untimely and unfortunate departure** of Hamlet.
Improved	Fortinbras filled the political void created by Hamlet's **death.**
Weak	The movie *Love and Anarchy* depicts the lives of **ladies of the evening** in a **house of ill repute.**
Improved	The movie *Love and Anarchy* depicts the lives of **prostitutes** in a **brothel.**
Weak	The man was stopped by a **custodian of the law** and found to be in a **state of intoxication.**
Improved	The man was stopped by a **police officer** and found to be **drunk.**

183

5.12   Ineffectively Mixed Vocabulary

It is important to maintain a consistent tone in writing and to keep the goal of a communication in mind. Shifts from formal to informal diction or from technical to everyday language—unless intended for a specific effect—suit no purpose and are acceptable neither to special nor general audiences:

Mixed	The dislocation caused by reliance on the automobile for mass transit has resulted in **one big headache for the cities.**
Improved (formal)	The dislocation caused by reliance on the automobile for mass transit has resulted in **a variety of urban problems.**
Mixed	She ran down to the store **to purchase the nourishment necessary** for dinner.
Improved (informal)	She ran down to the store **to buy food** for dinner.
Mixed	Robert Dahl's book *Who Governs?* is a seminal work in the development of pluralist theory. It is **a real mind-expander** for **all those who are zeroed in on political science.**
Improved (formal)	Robert Dahl's book *Who Governs?* is a seminal work in the development of pluralist theory. **Every serious student of political science** should be familiar with this **exceptional study** of decision making.

5.13   Mixed Metaphors

A *mixed metaphor* is an attempt to combine two or more images that are not logically related. Mixed metaphors, like mixed vocabulary, send the reader off in two different directions, confusing rather than clarifying the writer's thought. The result is a bewildering, often amusing, jumble of ideas:

Mixed	Shakespeare's "Sonnet 130" points out that people should not treat love like a **sugar-coated crutch.**
Improved	Shakespeare's "Sonnet 130" points out that people should not use love as a **crutch.**
Mixed	Writing is a lot like **gardening:** you have to **prune out** the bad ideas to give the good ones **some meat.**

Improved	Writing is a lot like **gardening:** you have to **prune out** the bad ideas so the good ones will **flourish.**
Mixed	Current news stories suggest that the nation has developed **an addiction to** political scandals and has to be **fed a steady diet** of them every day.
Improved	Current news stories suggest that the nation has acquired **an appetite** for political scandals and has to be **fed a steady diet** of them every day.

A metaphor should not only be consistent internally; it should also be appropriate in context. To say "The children scampered like birds in a storm" is inappropriate, since birds do not scamper. A better choice of words is *scattered,* since it can be applied both to children and to birds. Similarly, the sentence "The theater is no stranger to me" is an awkward inversion. "I am no stranger to the theater" makes more sense. Writers should always work out metaphors carefully to make sure that they are consistent, logical, and exact.

5.14 Inappropriate Connotation

Words that are similar in denotative meaning often have very different connotations, or take on unexpected connotations in context. Readers may be amused or puzzled by an inappropriate choice of words, or they may take offense. Here, for example, is a well-known newswriter's apology for using a word with an unintended and inappropriate connotation:

> In this space the other day, I asked: "Who are the friends of Israel? . . . Those who urge her to give up territory occupied by aggression or those who urge her to hold on to everything she has?" The use of the word "aggression" instead of "force" implied that Israel was responsible for starting the 1967 war which I did not intend and which was a mistake.
>
> James Reston, *The New York Times*

Beginning writers often consult a dictionary or thesaurus for synonyms that will add variety and sophistication to their prose. But dictionaries rarely list the connotations of words; nor can they predict their effect on readers in context. Writers must understand the full meaning of unfamiliar words and choose all words carefully, with an awareness of their potential impact on the reader:

> This course has **indoctrinated** me in the techniques of modern painting.

185

> The skillful writer **warps** the mirror of reality to reflect the reader's experience.
>
> My aunt is a generous and charitable woman; she is very **pious** in her desire to help others.

In each of these examples the writer's choice of words calls up an unwanted, negative association in the reader's mind. *Indoctrinate* means "teach" or "instruct," but it has unfavorable overtones—propaganda, forced instruction, and so on. *Warp* means "bend," but with negative connotations—distorted, sick, prejudiced. *Pious* can have favorable associations when used to describe earnestness or devotion in religion. Outside of religious contexts, however, *pious* has negative connotations. It suggests self-righteousness, or the pretense of religious devotion. (See also Section **5.1**.)

5.15   Fine Writing

Fine writing refers to stilted, artificial diction. Often it results from a writer's misconception that effective writing should not sound like speech because it is a different "language" from speaking. However, effective writing is *not* another language; it is natural, idiomatic English used appropriately in context:

Artificial	In my own humble opinion, one of the ultimate satisfactions in life is the opportunity to delve into a skilled work of literature.
Natural	Reading a good book is one of the great pleasures in life.
Artificial	Gerald Ford succeeded to the presidency on the eve of Richard Nixon's taking leave of the office.
Natural	Gerald Ford became president after Richard Nixon resigned.
Artificial	Having had frequent encounters with Hemingway's writing, I recognized the passage immediately.
Natural	I was familiar with Hemingway's writing and thus recognized the passage immediately.

Another characteristic of fine writing is the use of ornate or flowery diction in an attempt to create "poetic" prose. This self-conscious style is often marked by excessive repetition of similar sounds (excessive *alliteration*):

Ornate	The pulsating pace of these poetic lines underscores the poet's sense of confusion and limitless loss.

Natural   The broken rhythm of the stanza reinforces the poet's sense of confusion and loss.

Ornate   The continual commotion outside the confines of the theater alienated actors and audience alike.

Natural   The commotion outside the theater disturbed the actors and audience.

Fine writing is inappropriate because it calls attention to itself rather than to the writer's message. Readers often feel that the writer is more interested in creating an effect than in communicating a clear idea.

Exercises

The following sentences violate basic principles of good writing. Describe the fault in each sentence (pretentiousness, wordiness, euphemisms, mixed vocabulary, clichés, fine writing, and so on) and rewrite it to improve the diction.

1. I was amazed and surprised to learn that my brother had joined the army.

2. *King Lear* is a play about the hypocrisy of the power structure and the helplessness of the disenfranchised.

3. My mother is always elated to receive a written communication from a member of our family.

4. The lawyer carried a briefcase that was rectangular in shape and blue in color.

5. I know that the landlord certainly evicts tenants whenever he gets the chance.

6. The doctor arrived just in the nick of time.

7. The survivors clung to the last glimmer of hope—a ship appearing in the distance.

8. I think that honesty is probably the best policy.

9. Never again will I set these sad eyes on the sunny sands and shimmering surfs of southern California.

10. Of the many poems that it has been my privilege to encounter during a long and productive existence, surely one of the most gratifying and unforgettable has been the magnificent "Ozymandias" by Shelley.

11. It looked like the end of the line for my chances of getting a job at the department store.

187

5.16 DICTIONARY USE

To check diction, spelling, word division, and the like, the writer needs an up-to-date dictionary that is portable but extensive. Four college-edition dictionaries that are adequate for use in most writing situations are *Webster's New World Dictionary of the American Language, Webster's New Collegiate Dictionary, The Random House College Dictionary,* and *The American Heritage Dictionary of the English Language.* No matter what dictionary is used, however, it is good practice to examine the table of contents, read the introduction, and become familiar with the key to the abbreviations used in the entries.

The dictionary is consulted most frequently on the following points. The sample dictionary entry on the opposite page illustrates each kind of information.

Spelling, Syllabication, Pronunciation. Each entry word is spelled, with its preferred spelling given first when there are two or more possible spellings. The word is divided into syllables by dots that show where the word can be correctly divided at the end of a line. If the word consists of more than one syllable, an accent mark (´) is used to indicate how each syllable is stressed when the word is pronounced.

Parts of Speech and Inflected Forms. Each meaning of the entry word is followed by an abbreviation showing its part of speech (for example, *n.* for *noun; v.t.* for *verb, transitive*). The inflected forms of the word follow the parts of speech.

Definitions. The order of definitions (for example, historical, frequency of use) varies among dictionaries. The arrangement of meanings is explained in the introductory section of the dictionary.

Synonyms and Antonyms. The location in the entry of synonyms (words with similar meanings) and antonyms (words with opposite meanings) varies with the particular dictionary used. The arrangement of synonyms and antonyms is explained in the front of the dictionary.

Usage Labels. Usage labels specify level (*Colloquial, Slang, Formal*), region (*Brit.*), and specialization (*Math., Law*). General-usage words, like *prefer,* are not labeled.

Etymology. The origin of a word is usually given in brackets. The sample entry below, for example, shows that "prefer" is derived from (<) Latin (L.) via Middle French (MFr.).

In addition to the kinds of information listed above, the dictionary contains such useful information as a directory of colleges and universities; a style guide for punctuation, capitalization, and so on; and guidelines for manuscript preparation and business-letter format.

SAMPLE DICTIONARY ENTRY

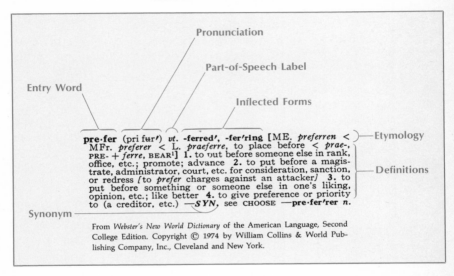

Pronunciation

Part-of-Speech Label

Entry Word

Inflected Forms

pre·fer (pri fur′) *vt.* **-ferred′, -fer′ring** [ME. *preferren* < ──Etymology
MFr. *preferer* < L. *praeferre*, to place before < *prae-*,
PRE- + *ferre*, BEAR¹] **1.** to put before someone else in rank,
office, etc.; promote; advance **2.** to put before a magis-
trate, administrator, court, etc. for consideration, sanction, ──Definitions
or redress [to *prefer* charges against an attacker] **3.** to
put before something or someone else in one's liking,
opinion, etc.; like better **4.** to give preference or priority
to (a creditor, etc.) —*SYN*, see CHOOSE —**pre·fer′rer** *n.*

Synonym ──

From *Webster's New World Dictionary* of the American Language, Second
College Edition. Copyright © 1974 by William Collins & World Publishing Company, Inc., Cleveland and New York.

REVIEW EXERCISES

1. For each of the following topics, write a brief, descriptive paragraph. Use diction that is precise, accurate, and concrete as possible.

a. A first meeting with someone who later became a close friend

b. A vacation in an unfamiliar city or town

c. A conflict with a person in authority

d. A humorous childhood experience

e. A literary work that has influenced you

189

2. Evaluate the diction in the following paragraphs in terms of (1) accuracy, (2) concreteness, and (3) appropriateness. Make any revisions that would improve the writing.

a. So far we have discussed television in the broadest sense—the sort of thing we experience in our living room—broadcast television. From our central transmitter it balloons out over an area of approximately 50 miles, or is ricochetted from microwave tower to microwave tower, pours through the walls of our houses, streams through our bodies, and a part of it is picked up by antenna and becomes a pattern of dots on a screen, moving so fast they appear, to us, to be a picture.

Don Fabun, *The Dynamics of Change*

b. It was a pitch-black night in Chicago. Somehow the fall nights seem darker than at any other time of the year. The darkness camouflages many things. It is perfect, this night, for recrowned world heavyweight boxing champion Muhammed Ali to cram a station wagon driven by his bodyguard with his devilishly cute twin daughters, Jamillah and Reeshemah; his brother, Rahman; an interpreter from Kinshasa; and a couple of friends, and creep through the streets unnoticed.

Ronald E. Kisner, "Ali Looks Ahead after Regaining His Boxing Title," *Jet*

c. As a matter of fact, the educated man uses at least three languages. With his family and his close friends, on the ordinary, unimportant occasions of daily life, he speaks, much of the time, a monosyllabic sort of shorthand. On more important occasions and when dealing with strangers in his official or business relations, he has a more formal speech, more complete, less allusive, politely qualified, wisely reserved. In addition, he has some acquaintance with the literary speech of his language. He understands this when he reads it, and often enjoys it, but he hesitates to use it. In times of emotional stress hot fragments of it may come out of him like lava, and in times of feigned emotion, as when giving a commencement address, cold, greasy gobbets of it will ooze forth.

Bergen Evans, "Grammar for Today," in Elizabeth M. Kerr and Ralph M. Aderman, eds., *Aspects of American English*

3. Analyze the diction in each of the following passages. Describe the type of language used (formal or informal) and evaluate the tone and distance, precision, economy, and variety.

a. One day in February we saw a Fascist aeroplane approaching. As usual, a machine gun was dragged into the open and its barrel cocked up, and everyone lay on his back to get a good aim. Our isolated positions were not worth bombing, and as a rule the Fascist aeroplanes that passed our way circled round to avoid machine gun fire. This time the aeroplane came straight over, too high up to be worth shooting at, and out of it came tumbling not bombs but white glittering things that turned over and over in the air. A few fluttered down deep into the position. They were copies of a Fascist newspaper, the *Heraldo de Aragon,* announcing the fall of Malaga.

George Orwell, *Homage to Catalonia*

b. The problem of motivation is talked about endlessly in Boston, and the point has been made repeatedly in the writings of Miss Sullivan and others that the motivational difficulty has its origins in the children and in their backgrounds, rather than in the teachers or the schools. I think the opposite is true. But the predictability with which this wrong assertion has been restated suggests the nervousness which the school administration of this city must experience in regard to its own failure.

Jonathan Kozol, *Death at an Early Age*

c. Of all the areas in which men fail women, this is the one that cuts the deepest and, ultimately, evokes the most contempt. Nothing contrasts more sharply with the masculine image of self-confidence, rationality, and control than men's sulky, obtuse, and, often virtually total dependence on their wives to articulate and deal with their own unhappy feelings, and their own insensitivity, fear, and passivity in helping their wives to deal with theirs. This, more than anything else, disillusions women about their men. Bromides like "Men are just overgrown little boys" are both a description of this phenomenon and an attempt, by labeling it innocuously, to ease the pain of disillusionment: disillusionment at having subordinated yourself to a person who isn't, it turns out, special enough to justify the sacrifice, who is probably not much smarter than you are in most ways and in some important ways, is a lot less perceptive, more dependent, and more childlike.

Mark Feigen Fasteau, *The Male Machine*

d. The shocking passing of Peter Lorre has left a wide gap in horror-fantasy films that will be impossible to fill.

Unlike Karloff and Lugosi, his screen career did not always center around the macabre; it was, rather, his unusual appearance and extraordinary acting ability that added a strange fascination even to his more fatuous roles. His large, pale, moon-faced head, emphasized by a pair of heavy-lidded, bull-frog eyes, on his short five-foot-three, squat frame, and his chilling childlike accented speech and mannerisms helped to create his personal brand of menace and terror.

Richard Bojarski, "Lorre: 1904–1964," *Castle of Frankenstein*

e. I have an idea that he met his match in Stalin. The Georgian Asiatic, as squat as a toad, found Churchill formidable, but, from all I've read and heard, also amusing. After having made Churchill mad with rage in accusing the British of cowardice for not opening the second front in 1942, Stalin laughed at him. I would have given a great deal to be present at that famous meeting: the scion of the only remaining aristocracy in the world against the drunken cobbler's son. In this corner, Winston Spencer Churchill fighting out of England and centuries of "breeding" and in this corner Joseph Dzygashvili, alias Stalin, fighting out of Gori, Georgia, U.S.S.R., and centuries of serfdom. May the greatest force win.

Richard Burton, "Memories of Winston Churchill,"
TV Guide

f. Yet, for a while, it seemed as though there were no limits to what Stein could win. A stagestruck kid from the Lower East Side (he lives on Park Avenue now), he established the first suburban rock beachhead at Port Chester's Capitol Theater in 1970. A year later, the way opened by Bill Graham's departure for points west, he set up shop at the Academy of Music, grossing more than a million dollars. In 1972, he began expanding into other cities, and the gross (from which he admits to taking 15 per cent, "on average") was up to 2.5 million. Last year, with five branch offices scattered around the country, Howard Stein Enterprises, Inc., produced more than 300 concerts in 17 cities, and his average 15 per cent came to a gross of $4.5 million.

Geoffrey Stokes, "Rock Feels the Pinch," *Village Voice*

4. Using your dictionary, trace the etymology of each of the following words:

barbarian	myriad
control	scapegoat
droll	talent
lunacy	urchin

5. Using your dictionary, list synonyms for each of the following words:

blaze	grand
change	happy
decide	old
different	small

6. Identify the parts of speech for each of the following words:

associate	kind
compound	mystical
eloquent	perjure
guard	systematic

Conventions of Writing

6

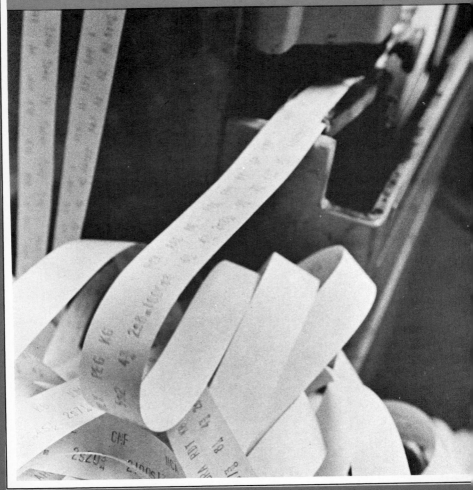

Whatever is seen on the page should be presented in a manner that does not interfere with the reader's concentration on the meaning. The very look of the manuscript—the degree to which the conventions of format, spelling, punctuation, grammar, capitalization, and the like have been followed—communicates to the reader how much care the writer has taken. Any distraction interferes with the communication.

THE FUNCTION OF WRITING CONVENTIONS

Writers are often not fully aware of exactly how much an unconventional presentation—uneven margins, improper capitalization, poor spelling, careless punctuation, or any other such failure—can interfere with a reader's acceptance or understanding of a manuscript. Readers themselves may not be conscious of just how much they expect from a writer in terms of the mechanics, or conventions, of writing. But every professional writer knows that readers *do* expect maximum perfection of detail.

Two changes in expectation occur when we move from speaking to writing. First, the demand for conventional ordering of words and sentences is greater, as we shall see in Chapter 8, "Grammar." Second, written communication acquires additional conventions simply not found in conversation. These standard ways of presenting the written word can be and are modified from generation to generation, and even from writer to writer, to simplify them or to make them more up to date. But, as a general rule, the reader expects the writer to follow the existing conventions of format, capitalization, spelling, footnoting, quotation, and punctuation.

Readers expect traditional presentation in writing for one simple reason: they are used to it. A writer's only good reason for not following the conventions is the wish to create a special effect. The one good reason for following the conventions is to keep the reader's attention on what the writing means, not on how the writing looks.

In sum, care in conventional presentation and mechanics is a sign that the writer is thinking professionally about the communication and wants nothing to interfere with the reader's acceptance of its content. In this chapter and the two that follow, these conventions are discussed in detail. Keep them in perspective, of course. A letter-perfect manuscript may still be weak or unacceptable because it is poorly thought out or expressed. Nevertheless, beginning writers who do not know the details of writing conventions or who do not follow them consistently will benefit from studying the conventions and learning to follow them out of habit.

CONVENTIONS OF FORMAT

Before reading a single word of a written communication, the reader will see how that communication looks and react accordingly. The conventions governing the look, or *format,* of a piece of writing are of two kinds: (1) those that make the material easy for the reader to see, (2) those that make it easy for the reader to understand.

Assisting the Reader to Read

One way to make it physically easy to read a communication is to follow the conventions of format consistently. Often forgotten in a writer's haste to finish the job is this list of dos and don'ts:

Dos	*Don'ts*
White bond paper, $8\frac{1}{2}$ by 11 inches.	Onionskin paper.
	Yellow or legal-sized paper.
Unlined paper for typed material.	Sheets torn from a notebook.
One-inch margins on all sides.	Crowded margins.
Double-spacing for typed papers.	Single-spaced typing.
Fresh ribbon in typewriter and clean keys.	
Blue, blue-black, or black ink only for written material.	Red, green, or other odd-colored inks.
Paper clip to fasten pages.	Stapled or folded pages.

In addition to taking care in presenting conventional copy, professional writers also keep a carbon or photocopy of their work. Employers, editors, and teachers have been known to misplace originals. Unless specifically requested to do so, professional writers

195

also avoid putting in the way of their reader such obstacles as blank pages, bindings, and folders. These items make it difficult for the reader to turn the pages and to make comments on them. Blank sheets not only waste paper (save trees!), they can also be interpreted by the reader as padding.

Assisting the Reader to Understand

The second group of format conventions guarantees that the following important information will be in the communication:

1. name of author
2. correct sequence of pages
3. title

The first two are obvious needs, and the writer should supply the information needed in a standard form: name and other information (address, course number, job number) in a block in the upper left-hand corner of the first page; pages numbered consecutively throughout in Arabic numerals usually placed in the upper right-hand corner of each page. (See Chapter 9, "Research and the Library Paper," for a visual example of the correct format.)

Effective Titles

A title is an important part of any written communication, for it eases the readers into the material and quickly identifies the topic for them. Although, as we shall see, good titles involve a measure of creativity, the format for them is also rather simple. Either capitalize the title fully or capitalize the first letter of each word—except articles, prepositions, and coordinate conjunctions, unless they are the first or last word in the title:

> Popular Music in America: 1955 to 1975
>
> Whatever Happened to Rock-and-Roll?
>
> An Analysis of Prospero in Shakespeare's *The Tempest*
>
> American Foreign Policy under Harry S Truman
>
> The Art of Macramé
>
> My Life as an Eldest Child

Note that the writer's own title is not underlined or placed in quotation marks. However, if a published work or a direct quotation appears in a title, it is placed in quotation marks or underlined. No period is used at the end of a title, but a title that asks a question does require a question mark. The title is usually placed two or three inches from the top of the first page and is not repeated. (For titles of long compositions, such as library papers, see Chapter 9, pp. 351–352.)

Perhaps the simplest kind of title is one that tells what the paper is about:

| Hemlines in America since 1955

In addition, the title may indicate the writer's approach to the topic or the special emphasis it is being given:

| Rock-and-Roll Is Here to Stay: Popular Music in America since 1955
| The Rock Revolution: 1955–1975

A title does not have to be clever or profound. It should identify the topic clearly and indicate the writer's approach and personal attitude toward it. The reader regards a good title as one sign that the writer is in control of the subject.

CONVENTIONS OF MECHANICS

Mechanics refers to such technical conventions of writing as capitalization, italics, abbreviation, numerical form, spelling, and hyphenation. From the beginning of written English to the end of the eighteenth century, when our modern conventions were set in the form we use by and large today, mechanical conventions were often a matter of personal taste. Now, because printers have standardized mechanics more and more, readers expect everything—from business and personal correspondence to whole manuscripts—to follow the conventions closely. With the exception of spelling, the mechanical conventions professional writers use in final copy are relatively few. And if writers do not remember the exact convention, they look it up in a dictionary or handbook of English usage.

6.1   Capitalization (cap)

When capitalization was invented, late in the ninth century, a capital letter indicated the beginning of a sentence. Soon thereafter capitals were used to show other words the writer thought particularly important. Originally, the convention was rhetorical. That is,   **197** by showing which words the author thought important, capitals told the reader how to react to the writing. Capital letters are used for the same reasons today. But writers usually limit their use of internal capitals to one class of words: proper nouns and their derivatives—words that name the specific and the particular:

> **Thomas Edison** was the first person to record sound.
>
> It is difficult to decide whether I prefer **New York,** with its magnificent skyscrapers, or **San Francisco,** with its **Golden Gate Bridge.**
>
> We associate **Jeffersonian** democracy with **Thomas Jefferson,** third president of the **United States.**

Other conventional situations for using capitals (or for not using them when it seems we should) simply must be memorized.

6.1a Capitals with Punctuation

Capital letters are used to show the beginnings of certain word groups.

Capitalize the first word of a sentence:

> **The** best driver I know is Clyde Ferrari.

Capitalize the first word after a colon when it begins a complete sentence:

> When you shop for your own car, the basic rule is simple: **Check** out all mechanical defects, test-drive each candidate, and then buy the car you really like.

Do not capitalize the first word of a sentence enclosed in parentheses or dashes when it is part of a larger sentence:

> Drivers chasing the land speed record (**record** is 617.287 mph) will have to catch Gary Gabelich and his Blue Flame. (**I** sometimes wonder why anyone would want to move that rapidly.)

Note: Be sure to capitalize the first word of a sentence enclosed in parentheses when it is *not* part of another sentence.

Capitalize the first word after quotation marks showing direct speech:

> I asked, "**Do** you think I need a Hurst shift?"
> Ferrari explained, "**All** you need is a four-barrel carburetor."

Do not capitalize the first word in speech that has been interrupted:

> "Maybe you should use two carburetors," Clyde suggested, "**and** a supercharger, too."

Capitalize the first word of quoted material from the work of another writer when it is introduced by a colon or a comma:

> According to the *Guinness Book of World Records:* "**The** highest terminal velocity recorded by a piston-engined dragster is 307.689 mph."

Do not capitalize the first word of quoted material when the quotation is used as part of your own sentence and not separated by punctuation:

> The Blue Flame, powered by a "**liquid** natural-gas–hydrogen-peroxide rocket engine," can travel almost twice as fast as a piston-engined car.

6.1b Proper Nouns

Proper nouns, their derivatives, and their abbreviations are always capitalized.

Capitalize the names of persons, nationalities, and races:

> Amerigo Vespucci
>
> Latin
>
> Caucasian

Do not capitalize the words *black, red, yellow,* or *white* when they are used to refer to races:

> "The Third World" is a term used to refer to nations whose inhabitants are predominantly **black, red,** or **yellow.**

Capitalize the adjectives derived from proper nouns:

> Italian
>
> Puerto Rican
>
> Oriental
>
> Jewish

Capitalize the names of religious denominations and their derivatives, and religious services, events, concepts, and writings:

> Catholic
>
> Episcopalian
>
> Holy Communion
>
> the Resurrection
>
> the Ten Commandments

199

6.1c Common Nouns

Capitalize common nouns (*first, lady, statue, liberty*) when they are used as proper nouns (*First Lady, Statue of Liberty*).

Capitalize the names of specific organizations and movements and their abbreviations:

> The Know-Nothing party
> Democrat
> Women's Liberation movement
> Y.W.C.A.

Do not capitalize the names of academic classes, subjects, and course titles unless they are derived from proper nouns or are followed by numbers or letters that give them a specific reference:

> junior class
> geometry

But

> French
> Math 9-B

Capitalize forms of address that precede a person's name:

> Prime Minister Harold Wilson
> President Ford
> Senator Kennedy

Do not capitalize titles when they stand alone:

> four senators
> the president of the bank

Do not capitalize the names of relatives unless they precede a person's name or are used in place of a person's name:

> My **sister** introduced **Dad** and **Uncle Ned** to her fiancé, Willard ("Bombs") Bombella.

Capitalize the names of historical events and documents:

> the Battle of Lexington
> the Second Continental Congress
> the Declaration of Independence

Capitalize each word in the titles of books and other published works except articles, coordinating conjunctions, and prepositions, unless these words begin or end the title:

From Here to Eternity
Gone with the Wind
The Reader's Digest
A Manual of Home Repairs for the Beginner

Capitalize specific brand names and trade names:

Coca-Cola
Vaseline
Bayer Aspirin

But

ginger ale
petroleum jelly
aspirin

Capitalize the names of places, including streets, counties, cities, states, regions, countries, and continents:

104 Elliman Place, Syosset, New York
Cook County
the industrial Northeast
the United States
North America

Do not capitalize common nouns like *street, avenue, lake,* or *river* unless they are an essential part of a place name.

She lived on a dead-end **street** near an extremely polluted **river.** Her house was only ten minutes away from the **Lake Street Community College,** and the rent was quite low.

Do not capitalize *street, avenue, lake,* or *river* when they are applied to two or more preceding place names:

The Hudson and Mississippi **rivers**
Jackson and Mulberry **streets**

Do not capitalize the directions of the compass (*north, northern*) unless they refer to a specific geographical area:

the Deep South
the West Coast

But

the southern route
the western coastline

201

Capitalize the days of the week, months of the year, holidays, and days of religious observances:

Tuesday

December

New Year's Day

Christmas

Yom Kippur

Do not capitalize the seasons of the year:

the winter holidays

an early spring thaw

Exercises

Correct the capitalization errors in the following paragraphs.

1. "The New England Governments are in a State of Rebellion," king George III confided to lord north in 1774. "Blows," the king continued, "Must decide whether they are to be subject to this Country or independent." After the skirmishes at Lexington and concord, the Assault on breed's hill (often called The Battle Of Bunker Hill) proved his highness was right.

2. The rt. hon. Sir Winston leonard spencer Churchill was given 211 lines in the 1965 edition of the british who's who. But the most titled person in the world is the eighteenth duchess of Alba. She is eighteen times a duchess, fifteen times a Marchioness, twenty-one times a Countess, and nineteen times a spanish Grandee.

3. Despite lukewarm reviews and box-office returns, *dr. dolittle* garnered nine Academy award Nominations, including one for best Picture. In the final balloting, the film, produced by Twentieth-Century Fox, won two oscars: for best song ("Talk To the Animals") and for best special Visual Effects.

4. Thornton Wilder has won the Pulitzer prize for *the bridge of San Louis Rey,* a best-seller that has been filmed three times. "His description of peru," said Critic Edmund Wilson, "Is solid, incandescent, and distinct." wilder won pulitzer prizes in the thirties for his Play, *our Town,* and in the forties for *The Skin Of Our Teeth.* Many admirers predict he will win the nobel prize for literature as well.

5. The Chicago Gangster Alphonse ("scarface") Capone had an estimated gross income of 105 million dollars in the year 1927 alone. Capone's business card gave his title as Second-Hand Furniture

Dealer. The highest annual salary currently paid in the u.s. is to Henry Ford II, the Chairman of the Ford motor company, who earned nearly 875 thousand dollars in salary and bonuses in 1971. In japan, the national Tax Administration agency identified the "number one man" as Heima Seki, President of the seikhei seibaku company. seki grossed 10.6 million dollars in 1972.

6.2   Italics (ital)

In printed copy, italics are typefaces that *slant toward the right*. In typewritten or handwritten copy, italics are shown by <u>underlining</u>. All the conventions that govern the use of italics have the same purpose: to give emphasis by making the word or words stand out from the text.

Italicize the titles of books, magazines, newspapers, and pamphlets:

I never paid much attention to reports about visitors from other planets. But then I read Erich Von Däniken's book, **Chariots of the Gods,** and the historical findings in it made me reconsider my doubts.

The couple next door read **The New York Times** every Sunday morning. He starts with **The New York Times Magazine,** and she starts with **The New York Times Book Review.**

Do not italicize the titles of chapters in a book, magazine articles, or short poems:

The second chapter of Bill Talbert's *Weekend Tennis* is the best part of the book. The title of the chapter is **"The Things Weekend Players Do Wrong."**

On October 1, 1972, there was a provocative article in *The Washington Post* by David S. Broder called **"The President's Shield."**

(See Section **7.12b** for the conventions of punctuating these items.)

Do not italicize titles of legal documents, the Bible, and parts of the Bible:

The **Civil Rights Act of 1964** made it illegal to discriminate according to race, color, religion, or national origin. A separate **Civil Rights Act for American Indians,** introduced in 1969, provided Indian tribal law with a **Bill of Rights.**

In the **Bible,** the opening chapters of **Ephesians** contain Paul's famous sermon on love.

203

6.2 (ital)

Italicize titles of motion pictures, plays, and works of art:

> George Bernard Shaw's play *Pygmalion,* written in 1913, was the source for the Broadway hit *My Fair Lady* and the movie of the same name.

> Most of us are familiar with Van Gogh's *The Starry Night,* although we might not recognize the title.

Italicize the names of ships, aircraft, and spacecraft:

> The most accurate recovery from space was the splashdown of the *Gemini IX.* The capsule landed only 769 yards from U.S.S. *Wasp* in the western Atlantic.

Italicize letters, words, and numbers used as letters, words, and numbers:

> The numbers *2–5* on the map indicate our campgrounds. We will follow the routes shown by the letters *A* or *B,* depending on the weather. With luck we will reach the cache (the word *cache* means "hidden storehouse") and find it undisturbed.

Italicize foreign words and phrases:

> John's baked Alaska was, by far, the *pièce de résistance* of the lavish dinner.

Foreign words and phrases that have become familiar enough to be accepted as part of the English language are not italicized:

> Joyce graduated **magna cum laude** in political science, with an expert knowledge of revolution and the **coup d'état.**

Italicize a word or phrase to give it special emphasis, but use this convention sparingly. A more effective, professional way to call the reader's attention to a certain word or phrase is by organizing and wording the sentence carefully so that the word or phrase in question is emphasized.

Unnecessary italics	The Johnsons have *two* sets of twins.
Improved	The Johnsons have not one but two sets of twins.
Unnecessary italics	When he approached the stand, the boy looked embarrassed and nervous. During cross-examination, the jury learned he had been arrested *five times in the past year.*
Improved	When he approached the stand, the boy looked embarrassed and nervous. During cross-examination, the jury learned he had been arrested no fewer than five times in the past year.

Exercises

Correct the following paragraphs for errors in italics.

1. Harold was not a slow reader. He finished The Wall Street Journal and the Christian Science Monitor every morning during breakfast. Although he enjoyed his reading, Harold often explained that a picture like the Last Supper was worth a thousand words.

2. In her *last will and testament,* Hannah left the house and the *deed* to the country property to Harold, the son whom she had not seen for thirty years. Harold explained his good fortune in terms of the *Bible.* "I love the *New Testament,*" he said, "especially the story about *the prodigal son.*"

3. Yesterday appears in many collections of modern song lyrics, and the Yellow Submarine is still shown from time to time on television. But you can be sure that the poems in John Lennon's book, In His Own Write, will never appear in the *Oxford Book of English Verse.*

4. For many fourth graders in Greenville Elementary School, Mississippi is a difficult word to spell. They seem to have trouble remembering how many i's, s's, and p's are in the word.

5. The museum spared no expense for its exhibits. Ten-foot replicas of the Merrimac and the Monitor were constructed against a realistic background of the Atlantic Ocean; and an amazing model of Tom Thumb, Robert Fulton's steamship, was given a river of its own.

6. As anyone with any savoir faire knows, it is a *faux pas* for a dinner guest to begin eating before the host or hostess has started.

7. The most powerful rocket that has yet been publicized is the Saturn V, used for the Project Apollo three-man lunar-exploration mission. The most powerful conventional aircrafts are the Boeing 747B and the North American XB-70A Valkyrie.

8. The French expression hors d'oeuvres simply means "appetizers." But many people are so intimidated by a menu that includes a foreign phrase that they order something they do not like or something they know how to pronounce. Many a *specialité de la maison,* such as *boeuf bourguignon,* has gone untasted.

9. A recent issue of the American Civil Liberties Union's publication, the Civil Liberties Review, includes an article by Stephen Gillers entitled *Secret Government and What to Do About It.*

10. Marlon Brando made his acting debut as Stanley Kowalski in the Tennessee Williams play "A Streetcar Named Desire" and played the same role in the subsequent film version.

6.3 Abbreviations (ab)

When writing footnotes, charts or tables, addresses, or other material in which space is at a premium, abbreviations save space, and if they are used consistently, they save time and effort for the writer and the reader alike. In formal prose, however, abbreviations are generally avoided. When in doubt, it is best not to abbreviate.

6.3a When Not to Abbreviate

Do not abbreviate the names of people, cities, or countries:

> Benjamin Franklin [*not* **B. Franklin**] traveled frequently from Philadelphia [*not* **Philly**] to Paris, France [*not* **Fr.**], and London, England [*not* **Eng.**], where he visited the Court of George III.

Do not abbreviate the words *avenue, street,* or other words used in addresses:

> She rang the bell at 26 Baltimore Street [*not* **St.**] five minutes before she saw the little note directing her around the corner to Pacific Avenue [*not* **Ave.**]. But she turned the wrong corner and found herself on Park Place [*not* **Pl.**]. "Visiting you is like playing Monopoly," she told me later. "If you give me two hundred dollars, I'll be ready to start over again."

Do not abbreviate the word *company* or *corporation* or a company name:

> She worked for years as a writing consultant for the Norden Division of the United Aircraft Corporation [*not* **Corp.**].

Do not use the ampersand (&) as the abbreviation for *and* unless the abbreviation is part of an official title:

> Jack was proud to serve as president of Simon **and** Schuster, but he was delighted when he was elected to the board of directors at Harper **&** Row.

Do not abbreviate the name of a subject or the words *volume, chapter,* and *page* in a published work:

> Beginning on **page** [*not* **p.**] 109, **Chapter** [*not* **Ch.**] 7 explains technical writing. Read the explanation and refer to **Volume** [*not* **Vol.**] 3 of the *Natural Sciences Handbook* for more detailed examples. The preface and the introduction to **Part** [*not* **Pt.**] Two give the reasons why technical writing is so important today.

Do not abbreviate days of the week or months of the year:

Independence was declared on **Tuesday** [*not* **Tues.**], April [*not* **Apr.**] 17, 1858.

6.3b   Abbreviations of Titles

Always abbreviate the titles *Mr., Mrs., Ms., Jr.,* and *Sr.* The abbreviations *Jr.* and *Sr.* are used only after a person's full name:

Mr. Wallace Franklin, **Jr.,** is survived by **Mrs.** Franklin and his daughter, **Ms.** Angela Franklin Jones.

Military, political, professional, and ecclesiastical titles are often abbreviated before the full name of a person. When a title stands alone, it should not be abbreviated:

Lt. Col. John Herschel Glenn, Jr., was given the largest ticker-tape parade in the city's history. New Yorkers threw over 3,474 tons of paper to celebrate the **colonel's** tri-orbital flight on March 1, 1962.

Rev. I. H. McIntyre delivered the sermon in place of **Rt. Rev. Msgr.** Richard O. Carlsen, who was in the hospital that Sunday.

6.3c   Abbreviations of Proper Nouns

Abbreviate (without periods) the names of well-known government agencies:

The **FBI,** the **FCC,** and hundreds of similar organizations have made Washington, D.C., the bureaucratic center of the world.

The full name of the Soviet Union is often abbreviated *USSR* (without periods). United States is often abbreviated *U.S.* when used as an adjective:

They traveled extensively in the **USSR** to discuss the coming export of **U.S.** agricultural commodities.

6.3d   Abbreviations of Common Latin Terms

Abbreviate expressions of time: A.D., B.C., A.M., P.M. Notice that A.D. is conventionally written before the date:

Successive appearances of Halley's Comet have been traced back to 466 **B.C.** Its next appearance should be at 9:30 **P.M.,** Greenwich Mean Time, on February 9, **A.D.** 1986.

The abbreviations *i.e.* (that is), *e.g.* (for example), *et al.* (and others), and *etc.* (and the rest) are used in general writing. The abbreviation *etc.* should be used only when the ideas it refers to are obvious to the reader:

Minnesota, home of the headwaters of the Mississippi, is one of the most scenic states in the nation. The topography (**e.g.,** the rolling prairie, fertile valleys, high bluffs, deep pine woods, and more than 11,000 lakes) makes tourism a major revenue producer for the state.

All the items necessary for a child's birthday party—cake, ice cream, party hats, **etc.**—had been ordered well in advance. But when the ice cream arrived, it was already half-melted.

6.3e   Abbreviations in Footnotes and Bibliographies

In footnotes and bibliographies, abbreviate the names of states, days of the week, and months of the year. Consult the dictionary for preferred forms of these abbreviations.

The following conventions of abbreviations apply only to footnotes and bibliographies. (See Section **6.8b** for proper footnote form.)

chapter, chapters	ch., chs.
edition, editions	ed., eds.
editor, editors	ed., eds.
line, lines	l., ll.
note, notes	n., nn.
number, numbers	no., nos.
page, pages	p., pp.
revised	rev.
revision, revisions	rev., revs.
volume, volumes	vol., vols.

Exercises

In the following exercises use abbreviations where convention requires or allows and spell out all inappropriate abbreviations.

1. At exactly ten o'clock Ante Meridian, on Tues., Apr. 15, the rocket will be launched from Cape Canaveral in Fla.

2. The Dr. told me to take two tbs. every four hrs. (i.e., half a bottle per day), but at that rate all my $ will soon be gone.

3. The Rev. Wm. Andrew Smith gave the sermon on the first Tuesday before Xmas at the Church of Saint John near the corner of 3rd Ave. and Mott St. Rev. Smith based his text on the nature of love.

4. Prof. Jamison's name appears in the new ref. bk. published by the Amer. Bk. Co. You can look it up in Ch. 5, p. 86 (that is, the chapter on abbreviation).

5. The standard of living in the U.S. exceeds that of the Union of Soviet Socialist Republics because of our private industry (e.g., the Ford Motor Co.) and our labor unions, such as the AFL-CIO, etc.

6.4 Conventions for Numbers (nos)

Except in tabular material, professional writers prefer to use words for numbers whenever they can do so efficiently. From a practical point of view, this convention means that those numbers or amounts that can be expressed in two words or less are usually spelled out.

6.4a Measurements

Spell out numbers or amounts of less than one hundred. Use figures for larger amounts:

Extremes of human height fall between **nine** feet for the tallest giants and **twenty-three** inches for the smallest dwarfs.

In my high school class, **583** out of **625** went on to college after graduation.

Spell out numbers that come at the beginning of a sentence:

One thousand-sixty-nine-pound Robert Earle Hughes was the heaviest man in the world. When he died at the age of thirty-two, his measurements were the largest on record.

Experienced writers will often rewrite a sentence to shift figures away from the beginning, particularly if rewriting will permit them to treat nearby numbers alike. Either figures or words are used throughout passages so that numbers can be presented in a consistent style.

Robert Earle Hughes weighed **1,069** pounds a few months before his death at the age of **32.** His measurements (waist, **122** inches; chest, **124** inches; and upper arm, **40** inches) were the largest ever recorded.

Use figures and units of millions or billions to refer to very large round numbers:

The Soviet Union, with **8.6 million** square miles of territory, has by far the largest area in the world. Canada, with **3.8 million** square miles, is a distant second.

Use figures to express fractions, decimals, and percentages:

> The thigh bone is the longest of the 206 bones in the human body. In a 6-foot-tall man, it measures **19¾** inches (or **27.5** percent) of his height.

When a unit of measure is shown by an abbreviation or a symbol, use figures:

> The Russian author Ivan Turgenev possessed the heaviest brain ever recorded. His brain weighed **4 lbs. 6.96 oz.** The brain of the noted French author Anatole France weighed only **2 lbs. 4 oz.**

6.4b Addresses

Use figures in addresses:

> Send me the check at **1422** Highland Boulevard, Hayward, California **94542.** If I am not at home, the mail will be forwarded to my summer residence at **24** Federal Hill Road, Milford, New Hampshire **03055.**

6.4c Dates

Use figures for dates and exact times:

> In **1973,** Jackie Stewart won the Monaco Grand Prix with an average speed of 80.963 mph in **1** hour, **44** minutes, **57** seconds.

Do not use *-st, -d, -rd,* or *-th* after figures showing the day of the month:

> July **4,** 1956, was wet but memorable. The third and the fifth were ordinary days, but in between came the heaviest rainfall ever recorded.

Note that references only to days of the month are spelled out.

6.4d Parts of a Book

Use figures to refer to specific page numbers and sections of books:

> My partner suggested that I read **Chapters 7** and **8** in *Poker for Fun and Profit* before I played another hand. I read both chapters, and then I memorized the glossary of terms beginning on page **174.**

6.4e Plural and Inclusive Numbers

The plurals of figures and decades are formed by adding an *s:*

> The contestants were all quite young; I think the oldest was in his late twenties. Among the leading golf scores were two **265s** and three **267s.**

In figures of four or more digits, units of thousands are separated by commas: 1,296; 23,500,000:

> Many record collectors can point to over **5,000** of these early blues recordings.

Inclusive numbers (*41–45*) have a hyphen between the beginning and ending figures. Include both digits in the ending figure when the numbers fall between 1 and 99. Include only the last two digits when the numbers fall in the same hundred:

> The best parts of the book appear on pages **76–77** when Vampirella, the friendly vampiress, meets her archenemy, the Cobra Queen. Afterwards, on pages **103–11,** there is nothing but conventional male heroes doing battle because of honor or duty or pride.

Never use a hyphen between numbers when they are preceded by *from* or *between:*

> World War I was fought **between 1914 and 1918** [not **between 1914–1918**].
> **From 1918** to 1919, the nation rejoiced the end of the war.

Exercises

In the sentences below, correct inappropriate abbreviations and numerical style as necessary.

> **1.** Edward ("Bozo") Miller, who stands five ft. seven and one-half inches tall and weighs two hundred eighty–300 lbs., is the world's greatest trencherman. He consumes up to 25,000 calories a day (more than 11 times the total recommended) and has a fifty-seven in. waist.
>
> **2.** The record for potato-chip eating was set by Paul G. Tully of Brisbane, Australia. In May 1969, Tully ate 30 two-oz. bags in twenty-four mins. and 33.6 seconds. Paul Hughes, 13, ate thirty-nine jam-and-butter sandwiches, each measuring 5 × three × ½ inches. And Tom L. Cresci ate 262.6 yards of spaghetti at Dino's Restaurant in San Diego, Calif., in 1971.
>
> **3.** Flight Major (later Colonel) Yuri Alekseyevich Gagarin completed a single orbit of the earth in record time.
>
> **4.** The stirrup bone, in the middle ear, measures from 0.10 to 0.17 of an inch in length and weighs from three hundredths to sixty-five thousandths of a gram.
>
> **5.** Enormous demand for credit in the face of a restricted econ-

omy pushed mortgages above nine % and the banks' prime rate above ten percent during 1974 and part of 1975. Even the federal government must now pay over 8% on a medium-term note issue.

6.5 Conventions of Spelling (sp)

Many beginning writers mistakenly consider spelling a minor concern of writing. From the reader's standpoint, however, a piece of writing strewn with spelling errors becomes a real chore to read. The professional writer recognizes the importance of consistent, accurate spelling. An exceptionally poor speller will consult a dictionary to check the spelling of every single word on a page, if necessary. And under no circumstances will he sacrifice the most efficient word for one that is easier to spell.

Even good spellers need to consult a dictionary on occasion for the spelling of a particular word. Poor spellers should have a paperback dictionary as their constant companion and should thumb it often rather than trusting to luck. In a course or job that requires a great deal of writing on a particular subject, it is a good idea to keep a handy list of the most frequently used and most difficult-to-spell words in that subject. Practice those common words that give the most difficulty and review the major spelling conventions.

6.5a *I* before *E*

One perfectly reasonable complaint about English spelling is that the same sound is often spelled in half a dozen different ways. The sound at the end of the word *me,* for example, is found in *eve, sleeve, grieve,* and *deceive.* Confusion between the *ie* and *ei* spellings accounts for a number of misspellings. The general rule is:

Place *i* before *e* except after *c* or when sounded like *a* as in *neighbor* and *sleigh.*

The rule is simple and straightforward, but the exceptions to the rule are not. Among these exceptions, some of the most common ones are:

financier	seize
species	weird
foreign	
height	
leisure	
neither	

6.5b Plural Spellings

The general rule for forming the plurals of English nouns is quite clear:

Singular nouns ending in a sound that cannot join smoothly with the soft sound of *s* to form the plural takes *es* instead. For nouns ending with the letter *y* and preceded by a consonant, change *y* to *i* and add *es*:

Singular	*Plural*
book	books
singer	singers
toy	toys
bus	buses
church	churches
tax	taxes
brandy	brandies
category	categories
seventy	seventies
sky	skies

There are exceptions, of course. Some words that look as if their plurals would be formed by adding *s* take *es* instead:

Singular	*Plural*
hero	heroes
potato	potatoes
tomato	tomatoes

A few nouns have singular and plural forms that look and sound alike:

Singular and Plural
deer
fish
sheep

There are also a few nouns that are singular in meaning, even though they happen to look like plurals because of a final *s*:

Singular, No Plural Form
mumps
physics
statistics

213

6.5c **Prefixes and Suffixes**

Most prefixes (such as *pro-*, *re-*, and *un-*) and many suffixes (such as *-est*, *-ize*, *-ly*, *-ment*, and the plural endings) are pronounced and spelled regularly. Spelling problems usually arise when the addition of a prefix or a suffix is not reflected in the pronunciation. The following guidelines are helpful in avoiding the most common prefix and suffix spelling errors.

When to Drop a Final *E*.

Drop a final *e* before a suffix beginning with a vowel. Do not drop a final *e* before a suffix beginning with a consonant:

please + ure = pleasure	arrange + ment = arrangement
ride + ing = riding	trouble + some = troublesome
guide + ance = guidance	sincere + ly = sincerely
locate + ion = location	hate + ful = hateful

Do not drop a final *e* before a suffix beginning with the vowels *a* or *o* if the final *e* is used to show the soft sound of a preceding *c* or *g*:

change + able = changeable
notice + able = noticeable

Some words drop a final *e* before the suffixes *ful, ly,* or *ment*:

awe + ful = awful
judge + ment = judgment
true + ly = truly

When to Change *Y* to *I*.

Change a final *y* to an *i* except before a suffix beginning with an *i*:

defy + ance = defiance
forty + eth = fortieth

But

fly + ing = flying

When to Double a Final Consonant.

Words of one syllable and words accented on the last syllable that end in a consonant preceded by a single vowel double the consonant when adding a suffix that begins with a vowel:

plan + ing = planning
forbid + en = forbidden

But

$$\text{keep} + \text{ing} = \text{keeping}$$
$$\text{benefit} + \text{ed} = \text{benefited}$$

Sound-alike Prefixes and Suffixes. Frequently, the vowels in prefixes and suffixes are "reduced" in normal conversation until they all sound alike. For example, the vowel *e* in the prefix *des-* is usually not stressed when it is pronounced. Thus, words like *despair* and *description* are often misspelled *dispair* and *discription*. Unstressed, "reduced" vowels also cause many writers to confuse the suffixes *-able* and *-ible*, *-ant* and *-ent*, *-ance* and *-ence*, because in each case the vowels *a*, *e*, and *i* sound exactly the same:

Correct	*Incorrect*
attendant	attendent
dependent	dependant
indispensable	indispensible
irresistible	irresistable
persistence	persistance
resistance	resistence

6.5d Homonyms

The writer who depends entirely on his ear to spell correctly runs into the problem of *homonyms*—words with exactly the same sound but with different spellings and different meanings. Homonyms like those listed below can be distinguished only on the basis of meaning or by making an association of some kind between the problem word and the one the writer knows how to spell.

Homonym	*Definition*
altar	a stand used in sacred cere-monies
alter	to make a change
ascent	an upward slope; the act of ris-ing
assent	agreement; the act of agreeing
capital	wealth; an official seat of gov-ernment
capitol	the building that houses a state legislature or the U.S. Con-gress
council	a group of people organized to advise and consult

215

counsel	advice; a lawyer
dyeing	the act of imparting new color
dying	present participle of *die*
principal	a person with controlling authority
principle	a law, rule, or code of conduct
stationary	fixed, unchanging
stationery	writing or typing paper
threw	past tense of *throw*
through	preposition (*I drove through town*)
weather	climatic conditions
whether	a conjunction indicating alternatives

In addition, there are several groups of three homonyms that cause spelling problems even though the difference in meaning among the members of each group is clear. Following are some of the most commonly confused three-word groups:

Homonym	*Definition*
cite	to quote or refer to formally
sight	vision
site	location
right	the state of being correct; privilege; opposite of *left*
rite	a ceremonial act
write	to communicate by placing words on paper
their	possessive pronoun (*their book*)
there	adverb of place
they're	contraction of *they are*
to	a preposition indicating movement, direction, contact, or proximity
too	synonym for *also;* intensive (*too much*)
two	the sum of one plus one

6.5e The Apostrophe (')

Several troublesome spelling problems involve the use of the apostrophe ('). The apostrophe has two uses: (1) to show the omission of a letter or letters from a contraction, and (2) to show the possessive case of nouns and indefinite pronouns. Beginning writers seem to have a particularly difficult time distinguishing between the contracted and possessive forms for the personal pronouns *you, he,* or *she,* and *they* and the relative pronoun *who.*

Contracted Form	*Possessive Form*
you're (*you are*)	your
he's, she's (*he is, she is*)	his, hers
it's (*it is*)	its
they're (*they are*)	their
who's (*who is*)	whose

One method that often helps writers choose the correct form is to replace the missing letters represented by an apostrophe. For example, if *it is* would make sense within the context of the sentence to be written, then the contraction *it's* is appropriate. But if *it is* would not make sense, then the possessive form *its* should be used.

Twenty Frequently Misspelled Words

Most writers not only misspell the same few words often, but they misspell them in exactly the same way. The most effective way to handle this problem is to study and master these words individually. Here are twenty of the most frequently misspelled words:

Correct	*Incorrect*
across	accross
all right	alright
benefit	benifit
definitely	definately
divide	devide
forty	fourty
grammar	grammer
misspell	mispell
necessary	necesary
noticeable	noticable
occasion	ocassion
pursue	persue
receive	recieve
separate	seperate
success	sucess
surprise	suprise
tragedy	trajedy
truly	truely
victim	victum
villain	villan

In each case, the writer must rely on habit and the dictionary until he develops an educated vision that makes every incorrect combination of letters look wrong, no matter how similar it is to the correct spelling.

Exercises

1. In each line below, one of the four words contains a common spelling error. Check each line as though proofreading a paper, locate the error, and correct it.

a. alright, recommend, species, vacuum

b. holiday, arguement, absence, separate

c. drunkeness, coolly, grammar, irresistible

d. financier, pronounciation, superintendent, necessary

e. surprise, definitely, repetition, wierd

f. undependable, insistant, category, churches

g. license, exhilarate, embarassing, courageous

h. ecstacy, benefited, whiskey, twelfth

i. sergeant, thier, fortieth, stepping

j. developement, occasion, receive, indispensable

2. Each sentence below contains one misspelled word. Rewrite each sentence to correct the misspelling.

a. Late that evening, a leaf brushed my sleeve as it fell, decieving me momentarily.

b. The first tomatos of the season were small and mealy.

c. Her efforts to succeed are scarcely noticeable, but I sincerely believe she will improve.

d. The hawk screamed it's defiance and persistence as it flew into the freezing weather.

e. Hovering overhead, eyes moving from right to left to catch sight of a panicky victim, the hawk was nearly stationery in the morning sky.

6.6 Hyphenation (-)

Hyphens are used to form compound words and to divide words at the end of a line. Compound words are sometimes written solid (*taxpayer*), are sometimes hyphenated (*up-to-date*), and are sometimes written open (*life preserver*). For compound words such as these, there are no practical conventions that tell when and when not to hyphenate. To find out if a compound word is hyphenated, solid, or open, consult a good dictionary or word-division book.

Although some compound words do not fit any special rule for hyphenation, and although hyphenation practices are changing all the time, there are several guidelines for the use of the hyphen. These conventions are given below.

6.6a   Compound Words

Hyphenate compound modifiers before a noun:

> The **gray-brown, coarse-grained** wood *shutters* had been left un-painted for twenty years. But the new tenant painted them a **bluish-green** *color* with the help of a **ten-foot** *stepladder* and a **do-it-yourself** *book* on home repairs.

Do not hyphenate when the first word of a compound modifier is an adverb ending in *ly:*

> It is a well-known fact that **poorly painted** *wood* begins to crack and peel. Soon **freshly painted** *areas* look older and more worn than they did before.

> The neighborhood is part of a **quickly growing** *community.*

Hyphenate to avoid an ambiguous meaning or an awkward combination of letters:

> Was it a slow moving van or a **slow-moving** van?

> She had a clear, **bell-like** voice.

Hyphenate spelled-out numbers from twenty-one through ninety-nine:

> When I am **thirty-five,** I expect to have a very good year.

> **Ninety-nine** out of one hundred young people would say the same thing.

> He finished in the **eighty-first** percentile in his college boards.

Hyphenate to separate the numerator and the denominator in fractions that are spelled out:

> **Two-thirds** of our class did better than I did on the final exam, but who's keeping score?

> More than **one-half** the marriages begun this year will probably end in divorce.

Hyphenate words with the prefixes *self-, all-,* and *ex-* and with the suffix *-elect:*

219

6.6b Divided Words

> Our **ex-president** and **secretary-elect** was a **self-appointed** expert on everything an **ex-all-American** might be expected to know.

Hyphenate words with other prefixes only when the element following the prefix is capitalized, is a numeral, or is more than one word:

> For many years it was considered **un-American** for U.S. citizens not to support their government. Today, more people are beginning to think such support **unnatural,** and **antigovernment** feelings abound in this country.

> The **pre-World** War I society was still quite **unsophisticated.** The **prewar** period was relatively prosperous.

> There were many **non-ablebodied** volunteers; a few of them were **nonviolent** as well.

6.6b Divided Words

Hyphens are also used to break a word between syllables at the end of a line. Questions about the proper place to break a word can be answered by consulting the dictionary. In the entry for each word, the raised period (·) indicates the syllable division:

> hy·phen·ate

However, it is not always acceptable to break a word at the end of a line. Some general guidelines for end-of-line word breaks are given below.

Do not divide words of one syllable:

> Just as I turned the last corner and peered **thr-**
> **ough** the foggy windshield, the car began to sputter and slow down. I realized the gas tank was empty.

Through should not be divided.

Do not divide a word so that a single letter remains at the end of a line or two letters appear at the beginning of a line:

> The real-estate agent told us that our land—one **a-**
> **cre**—had doubled in value. But we had already **decid-**
> **ed** not to sell until the value had tripled.

Acre should not be divided, and *decided* should be divided only after the first syllable, *de-*, or not at all.

If a prefix or suffix contains three letters or more, it may be divided from its root:

Since no one could explain the sudden **disappear-
ance** of the child, a search party was organized
immediately.

Do not divide proper nouns or the initials of a proper name:

Before joining the company, Martha attended **Vas-
sar** College.
I have decided to write about the poet **A.
E. Housman** for my master's thesis.

Do not divide a word at the end of a page and carry it to the
next page.

Exercises

Copy the passage below and hyphenate, combine, or leave the
italicized words as they are.

The *life long* dream of many *self made* Americans is realized
when they acquire a *nine room, split level* house with four *bed
rooms,* three baths, and a *two car* garage. When they choose an
automobile, they tend to forget that a *well tuned* engine is more
important than *white wall* tires, *racing stripes, four on the floor,*
or other *pseudo sporting* decorations. The very rich tend to live
more casually and spend their money more carefully. Learning to
live like the children of the industrialists or the *Wall Street* finan-
ciers could be a *well chosen* strategy for most of us. We would
enjoy unpretentious *well being* and *casually planned life styles.*

6.7 Conventions of Documentation and Quotation

When using sources in your writing, accurate and honest quotation and footnoting (called *documentation*) is a moral and practical
necessity. Give credit where credit is due. Passing off a section or
the whole of another writer's work as one's own—*plagiarism*—is not
simply bad manners, it is a form of theft. In some cases it is subject
to legal prosecution. The writer who deliberately plagiarizes knows
it. In this matter, no fine distinctions are necessary. However, the
appropriate and effective use of sources, so necessary in many writing tasks, can cause difficulties. Conventions and strategies are available to the writer for quoting and documenting efficiently and
accurately.

221

6.7a When to Document

The first decision the writer must make when dealing with source material is when to footnote. He should acknowledge the facts discovered or reported by another writer as well as ideas, opinions, or conclusions that are not his own: (1) when the material includes special information unique to his source, and (2) when the material is not within the common knowledge of his readers. If the material is common knowledge, then it is usually also public property. For example, the writer does not need to acknowledge the statement that Columbus discovered America or that the discovery took place in 1492.

After deciding which source material requires acknowledgment, the writer must decide how he will use this raw material in his finished product.

6.7b Informal Documentation

Direct quotations, charts, diagrams, and summaries of facts and ideas require formal acknowledgment. However, many interpretations, opinions, and conclusions that the writer has not arrived at independently also require acknowledgment, although perhaps not in the form of a footnote. Writers often acknowledge these sources informally by mentioning the source of the information (a person's name, the title of a book, etc.) in passing. In the paragraph below, for example, the writer has informally documented St. Augustine's statement about astrology by referring to the work in which St. Augustine made that statement:

```
    For thousands of years, the intricate, impressive
theories of the astrologers have attracted believers who
subsequently renounce their belief when they discover
that the theories simply do not account for the hard
facts of life. Over one thousand years ago, for example,
St. Augustine stated in his Confessions that he had
stopped believing in astrology when he learned that a
wealthy landowner and a slave on the same estate had
been born at exactly the same time.
```

The choice between formal and informal documentation depends on how the writer wants to use the source material and how he thinks his readers will want to use it. If he is citing sources that readers might want to see in the originals, formal documentation in the form of a footnote is appropriate. However, if he means only to credit or identify the originator of an idea, the writer can simply mention the source in passing, as was done in the preceding example.

6.7c How to Quote Prose

Notice that in the example above, St. Augustine's statement about astrology was paraphrased—his thoughts were used, but they were expressed in the writer's own words. Paraphrased material is run into the text and is never enclosed in quotation marks.

A *direct quotation* is an exact restatement of a writer's or a speaker's words. A direct quotation is always attributed to its source, usually by means of a footnote—unless it is a common proverb or a saying that is considered public property. Short direct quotations are always enclosed in quotation marks. Longer direct quotations are indented five spaces from the right and left margins and typed single spaced. Unless there are quotation marks in the original, none are used to signal the beginning and end of the quotation; the indentation and single spacing set off the quotation sufficiently.

Many beginning writers assume that acknowledging outside sources will somehow detract from the thoughts and opinions they contribute to the piece; they fear they will be considered unoriginal. In fact, the discovery, selection and accurate presentation of source material can be an accomplishment in itself. And no convention requires the writer to hold his source material in esteem or even to agree with it. Professional writers often document material they disagree with in order to present what they believe is more accurate information or more sensible opinions of their own. The art lies, not in how much material they collect or how impressive their lists of quoted authors are, but in what they do with their sources after they have found them.

The sample paragraph on page 224 is followed by examples that illustrate the various ways this source can be used effectively in writing. A writer wishing to use the information in this paragraph would probably not quote it in its entirety. The passage is more than fifty words long, the suggested limit for direct quotations, and it is too complete in itself.

The writer's job is to incorporate the source material into his own work without changing the author's meaning or intention. Analysis, evaluation, and argumentation are all methods by which writers

223

> The key question remains: Does astrology work, or is it merely superstitious hogwash? Pure astrologers point to some astonishing auguries. For instance, every 20 years the planets Saturn and Jupiter come close together in the heavens, an event known as a conjunction. For 120 years, every U.S. President inaugurated in the year of this conjunction has died in office: William Henry Harrison (who took office in 1841), Lincoln (1861), Garfield (1881), McKinley (1901), Harding (1921), Franklin Roosevelt (1941), Kennedy (1961). Four out of the seven were murdered. . . .
>
> But even true believers have never really got around what is called "the twin problem." Why do so many fraternal twins, endowed with identical horoscopes, develop such strikingly different personalities?[1]
>
> ———————
>
> [1] "Do You Believe in Astrology?" The Saturday Evening Post (January/February, 1974).

can use sources accurately to reach original conclusions while keeping the ideas of the original writer intact.

A direct quotation from the paragraph might be worked into one's own material as shown at the top of page 225.

If the writer wishes to incorporate a direct quotation into an original sentence of his own, he can arrange his material in a way similar to the example at the bottom of page 225. Building a direct quotation into the sentence can improve the presentation of sources by making the quotation seem less mechanical. Handled correctly, this technique would be perfectly acceptable even if the writer used it several times within a single paragraph, as shown at the top of page 226.

Whether the quotations are direct or paraphrased, they must be used accurately. For example, the original paragraph, on page 226, was carefully neutral in summarizing the interest in astrology. But in the example at the top of this page, the source material is being

It is well known that there is a conjunction of the planets Saturn and Jupiter every twenty years. But the remarkable events that seem to coincide with the conjunction make one wonder if there is more to this planetary occurrence than is generally assumed:

> For 120 years, every U.S. President inaugurated in the year of this conjunction has died in office: William Henry Harrison (who took office in 1841), Lincoln, (1861), Garfield (1881), McKinley (1901), Harding (1921), Franklin Roosevelt (1941), Kennedy (1961). Four out of the seven were murdered.[2]

If astrologers were consulted more frequently, such tragedies could be predicted and perhaps avoided.

---

[2] "Do You Believe in Astrology?" The Saturday Evening Post (January/February, 1974).

used to develop an argument against astrology. By eliminating the reference to the series of presidential disasters and other circumstantial evidence, the neutral tone of the original is nearly lost. There is nothing wrong with using someone else's work to support an argument or opinion, but when a writer does so, he should be sure not to distort the purpose of the original.

In an analysis of the renewed popular interest in astrology, one writer points out that the "key question" has remained unchanged since the time of St. Augustine: "Does astrology work, or is it merely superstitious hogwash?"[3]

---

[3] "Do You Believe in Astrology?" The Saturday Evening Post (January/February, 1974).

225

Astrologers often come up with predictions that the editors of The Saturday Evening Post called, in a recent article, a series of "astonishing auguries." However, these predictions often raise more questions than they answer. In the same article, the editors wondered: "Why do so many fraternal twins, endowed with identical horo-scopes, develop such strikingly different person-alities?" Of course, astrologers can provide no satis-factory answer to such questions, as every serious student of astrology has probably recognized. Unfortu-nately, most people are so eager to know what is in store for them concerning their jobs, financial statuses, love lives, health, and so on that they readily accept even the most unlikely forecast as inevitable fact. From my own analysis of the current interest in astrology, I would agree with the Post editors that the "key question" facing astrologers today is: "Does astrology work, or is it merely superstitious hogwash?"[4]

[4] "Do You Believe in Astrology?" The Saturday Evening Post (January/February, 1974).

6.7d   How to Paraphrase

Many writers are under the mistaken impression that if they make minor alterations in a quotation—such as changing a word or two or changing the active voice to the passive—they have para-phrased. Nothing could be farther from the truth. Paraphrasing entails more than making minor changes; it means completely re-phrasing the quotation so that only the core, the central idea, of the original is retained. Even when paraphrasing, however, a foot-note is required. In the example at the top of page 227, notice that the paraphrase leaves out much of the information of the original source and changes the sequence in which the information was presented. The information that remains is common knowledge that is not unique to this source; but here the source of information is acknowledged because the writer uses it to make a similar point.

Since William Henry Harrison was inaugurated in 1841, seven U.S. presidents have died in office, four of them by murder. Astrologers explain this fact readily: The seven men were inaugurated at twenty-year intervals during the conjunction of Saturn and Jupiter. The unfavorable planetary influences had apparently doomed the chief executives. But astrologers have not been able to explain why fraternal twins, born under exactly the same astrological influences, do not share similar fates or develop similar personalities. Astrology critics have used this fact to raise the key question facing astrologers today: Is astrology a science or merely a superstition?[5]

[5]"Do You Believe in Astrology?" The Saturday Evening Post (January/February, 1974).

6.7e How to Quote Poetry

Poetry is rarely paraphrased. It is generally quoted directly and either run into the text if it is short (no more than two lines) or set off if it is longer. When poetry is incorporated directly into the text, the writer should enclose the excerpt in quotation marks. In addition, the poet's style of capitalization should be followed, and each line of the poem should be separated with a slash mark (/):

William Butler Yeat's poems about love are often bittersweet; love is desirable but difficult to understand. In "Brown Penny" he writes: "There is nobody wise enough/To find out all that is in it [love]."[1]

[1]The Collected Poems of W. B. Yeats (New York: The Macmillan Company, 1956), p. 96.

When presenting a longer poetry excerpt, do not use quotation marks. Indent the excerpt on both sides, single space each stanza, double space between stanzas, and follow the poet's presentation conventions exactly:

When American poets speculate about the end of the world, their prophecies are grim but not very dramatic. In his poem "Fire and Ice," Robert Frost approaches the subject of doomsday in a very matter-of-fact way:

>   Some say the world will end in fire;
>   Some say in ice.
>   From what I've tasted of desire
>   I hold with those who favor fire.
>   But if I had to perish twice,
>   I think I know enough of hate
>   To know that for destruction ice
>   Is also great
>   And would suffice.[2]

Like most modern poets, Frost takes a psychological approach to the subject of doomsday. He equates fire with desire, or human passion, and ice with human hatred. From his understanding of human nature, Frost pessimistically suggests that we are capable of putting an end to ourselves in at least two different ways.

---

[2]Collected Poems of Robert Frost (New York: Henry Holt & Co., Inc., 1939), p. 268.

Exercises

1. Use the paragraph below as source material. Explain why you agree or disagree with the opinions expressed by using the following techniques: (1) direct quotations presented as excerpts, (2) direct quotations, built into your own sentences, and (3) paraphrases.

> Biofeedback training is based on the premise that we can modify or gain control over a range of bodily functions once thought to

be totally automatic. In many instances—if we want to relax a back muscle at will, or move a paralyzed arm, say—we cannot carry out the intention. Either nature has not provided us with a feedback mechanism, giving us signals we can use to learn that skill, or disease has destroyed a feedback system. Now, however, researchers have developed a host of sensory instruments that can help bridge the gap. The list of chronic ailments being treated—experimentally, at least—with biofeedback includes asthma, epilepsy, stroke paralysis, back pain, migraine and tension headache, to name a few. The technique is still in its infancy. "The potential is quite encouraging, and some early results are truly amazing, especially in treating neuromuscular problems," says Dr. Joseph Brudny, director of the new Sensory Feedback Therapy Unit at the ICD Center. "But I see it as a useful adjunct to our present medical tools, not as a panacea."

"It may not always work," a New York University professor of neurology, Dr. Julius Korein, says. "But it doesn't seem to have any harmful side effects—something you can't say about many drugs or surgical treatments."

"Teaching Your Body to Heal Itself," *Family Health*
(January/February, 1974)

2. Rewrite the following passages to correct errors in conventions of documentation.

Despite the anger and violence of the sixties, the so-called flower children of that era were hopeful for the future of humankind. Their optimism was frequently reflected in such songs of the times as the *Age of Aquarius,* which includes these lyrics: "Harmony and understanding/Sympathy and trust abounding/No more falsehoods or derisions/Golden living dreams of visions/Mystic crystal revelation/And the mind's true liberation." With this idyllic view in mind, the flower children believed the furor of the sixties would resolve itself into an era in which:

Peace will guide the planets
And love will steer the stars.

6.8   How to Footnote

Conventional footnote forms have been developed so that the writer can put into a footnote everything that the reader needs for seeing quickly and clearly where the information or quotation came from. Whether the documentation appears at the bottom of the page (*foot*notes) or at the end of a manuscript (*notes*), the same format is followed. (See Section **6.3e** for abbreviated words in footnotes.) **229**

However, a particular subject—psychology, for example—may have a footnote form different from the forms presented below. It is always a good idea to check with the instructor on the appropriate method for footnoting subjects.

Information to Include in Footnotes

From the reader's standpoint, the conventions governing the content of a footnote make perfect sense. To fully understand a writer's use of source material, the reader needs to know the author and title of the material. And, if he wants to obtain an original copy of the source the writer has used, the reader will also need to know the name of the publisher and where and when it was published. With this much information he can order the book from the library, a bookstore, or the publisher. Then, of course, he will need to know where in the source the passage he is interested in occurs. Writers present this information in roughly the order just described.

6.8a Building a Footnote

The following guidelines outline, step by step, the information that must be included in a footnote and the format in which it should be presented.

Author's Name and Title. Give the author's name in its full form. Having the full name can save someone a lot of time.

A shortened form of an unusually long book title may be used, but the first few words should be given exactly as they appear on the title page (*not* on the cover). Titles of articles in periodicals (magazines, journals, newspapers) should be given as well as the title of the periodical:

Book   [1] Timothy Crouse, *The Boys on the Bus*

Magazine [2] Benjamin DeMott, "Reforming Graduate Education," *Change*

Editor and Edition. Many books have editors as well as authors, and many books appear in more than one edition. If there is an editor, give the editor's name and the number of the edition directly after the title. Abbreviate editor and editors, edition and editions, as *ed.* and *eds.* Use arabic numerals for the edition:

[3] John Keats, *Complete Poems and Selected Letters*, **ed.** Clarence D. Thorpe

⁴ Robert G. Noreen and Walter Graffin, **eds.** *Perspectives for the 70s.*

⁵ David Popenoe, *Sociology,* **2nd ed.**

Facts of Publication. For a book give the city (and state, if necessary to avoid confusion) of publication followed by a colon, the publisher's name followed by a comma, and the year of publication. Place this information in parentheses. Do not place any punctuation before the facts of publication; follow the enclosed material with a comma:

⁶ Timothy Crouse, *The Boys on the Bus* **(New York: Dell Publishing Co., 1973),**

For a magazine or a newspaper give only the date of publication, followed by a comma:

⁷ Brian C. Weare, Richard Temkin, and Fred M. Snell, "Aerosol and Climate: Some Further Considerations," *Science,* **November 29, 1974.**

⁸ *The New York Times,* **13 July 1947,**

For a journal, see below.

Volume and Page Numbers. For a book, volume numbers are given in Arabic numerals followed by a comma:

⁹ Edward McNall Burns and Philip Lee Ralph, *World Civilizations,* 4th ed. (New York: W. W. Norton & Co., 1969), **Vol. 2,**

For a journal, volume numbers are given in Arabic numbers followed by the date of publication in parentheses. Do not use the abbreviations *vol.* or *vols., p.* or *pp.,* when both volume and page numbers are given:

¹⁰ Rictor Norton, "An Interview with Eric Bentley," *College English,* **36** (November 1974), **291–94.**

6.8b   Forms for Footnotes

The most frequently used footnote forms are listed below. Notice that in each case the information can be read as though it were a complete sentence: The footnote information begins with a capital letter and ends with a period. If the information already appears in the text and no confusion would result, the author's name may be omitted.

For a book.
[1] Rudolph Arnheim, *Visual Thinking* (Berkeley: University of California Press, 1969), p. 14.

For an edited book.
[2] Peter Schrag, "The Decline of the WASP," in *Leap into Reality,* ed. Richard Peck (New York: Dell Publishing Co., 1973), pp. 37–53.

Multiple authorship or editorship.
When more than three authors or editors are listed, give only the first name followed by the abbreviation *et al.* (and others). The abbreviation is not preceded by a comma:

[3] Burton Marcus et al., *Modern Marketing* (New York: Random House, 1975), p. 703.

For a magazine.
[4] Philip G. Zimbardo, Paul A. Pilkonis, and Robert M. Norwood, "The Social Disease Called Shyness," *Psychology Today,* May 1975, pp. 69–72.

For a journal.
[5] Mark W. Lipsey, "Research and Relevance: A Survey of Graduate Students and Faculty in Psychology," *American Psychologist,* 29 (July 1974), 541–53.

For a newspaper.
[6] Isadore Barmash, "Retail Jewelry Sales Rebound Sharply," *The New York Times,* 29 July 1975, p. 35.

For Subsequent Citations.   After citing a work the first time, follow the form below for all subsequent citations of the same work:

Book	Arnheim, *Visual Thinking,* p. 79.
Edited Book	Schrag, "The Decline of the WASP," p. 38

In subsequent citations, it is proper to cite only the author's last name and the page number. However, if there are citations to more than one work by the same author, the title must be repeated in subsequent citations to avoid confusion.

Other Footnote Citations.   Sometimes the writer finds it necessary to digress from his main discussion. For example, if he is using source material that is in opposition to other authorities, he may want to add his own qualifying remarks or compare his source with another. In some cases the writer may find that his source requires background information that is either too technical or simply too far afield from his main discussion. Adding this material to his basic footnote makes the information available to readers while not interrupting the coherence of the presentation:

> [1] Arthur G. Kennedy and Donald B. Sands, *A Concise Bibliography for Students of English,* 4th ed. (Stanford, California: Stanford University Press, 1960), pp. 393–438. The authors list detailed sources for early British history (p. 407), medieval and renaissance Britain (p. 409), and Britain from the eighteenth century to the present (p. 412). But they omit the influential studies of seventeenth-century Britain. Perhaps the best general source is the second edition of Richard D. Altick and Andrew Wright's *Selective Bibliography for the Study of English and American Literature* (New York: The Macmillan Company, 1963).

In a paper in which the writer refers time and again to only one or two sources, he may include his citations in the text. The citation should be enclosed in parentheses and placed directly after the reference or the quoted material:

> In her introduction to her book, *Women, Resistance and Revolution* **(New York: Vintage Books, 1974),** Sheila Rowbotham observes that "women have come to revolutionary consciousness by means of ideas, actions and organizations which have been made predominantly by men" **(p. 11).**

Citations to literary or other specialized works may also be placed in the text, after all the publication information has been given in footnote form the first time the source is used. Subsequent references are limited to identifying page or line numbers, references to specific acts or scenes, or particular sections of the whole source. These shortened citations are placed directly after the reference or quoted material and are not numbered. Here is an example of such a reference to Shakespeare's *The Merchant of Venice:*

> But then, in one of his most-often quoted speeches, Shylock asks: "If you prick us, do we not bleed? if you tickle us, do we not laugh? if you poison us, do we not die? and if you wrong us, shall we not revenge?" (act 3, scene 1, line 65)

By working in citations as shown in the preceding examples, the writer avoids awkward, repetitive footnotes and still gives the readers identifying information about the sources.

Exercises

The following footnotes have all the required information, including punctuation. But the material is not in the proper sequence, so the notes are difficult to read and use. By referring to the models in the preceding section, unscramble each footnote.

[1] *An Anthology of Writings from the Women's Liberation Movement: Sisterhood Is Powerful,* Robin Morgan, ed. (1970, Vintage Books; New York) p. 61.

[2] *Sisterhood Is Powerful,* "Oppressed Women," Robin Morgan, ed., pp. 372–75, Women's Collective of the New York High School Students' Union (Vintage Books, New York: 1970).

[3] Thomas Yoseloff, Ltd., Cranbury: New Jersey, 1969 (*General Washington and the Jack Ass,* J. H. Powell), p. 119.

[4] Bergen Evans and Cornelia Evans. p. 23 (*A Dictionary of Contemporary Usage,* 1957: Random House, New York.

[5] 2d ed., John M. Blum et al. (Harcourt Brace Jovanovich: 1968, New York), *The National Experience: A History of the United States.*

[6] "Health Occupations Education: Will the Profession Respond?" 1652–1654, Jean K. Kintgen, 74 *American Journal of Nursing* (September 1974).

[7] *Saturday Review/World,* Roger M. Williams, "What's Happened to the Communist Party in the USA?", pp. 10–14, 46, February 23, 1974.

6.9 Bibliography Form

Increasingly, professional writers, teachers, and editors prefer to combine the footnotes they use and the list of works cited in their papers into one set of notes attached to the end of the manuscript. In some situations (scholarly writing, for example), a bibliography may be required. Such a bibliography may be an alphabetical list of the works actually cited; or it may include every work looked at in the course of research. Sometimes a bibliography is *annotated,* which means that each of the listed sources has been evaluated by the writer.

When required to present a bibliography, use essentially the same information and format as in a footnote—with the following exceptions:

Author's name. Footnotes use the normal order; bibliographies reverse the order for alphabetizing (*Keats, John*).

Title. Footnotes may omit a subtitle or shorten the end of a long title; bibliographical entries must be complete.

Publication information. Footnotes enclose the city, publisher, and date in parentheses whereas bibliographies express these elements as a separate sentence with no parentheses. Bibliographies omit the page numbers of books, but page numbers are included in entries for periodicals.

content inspection, proofread a second time and concentrate on the conventions of presentation. During the second reading, look first for errors or inconsistencies in punctuation, grammar, capitalization, italics, spelling, and abbreviation. Then check end-of-line word division by reading up and down the right-hand margin. As a final check, read the material out loud, since fragments, run-on sentences, and idiomatic errors often are heard rather than seen.

How to Make Corrections

Mark and correct errors by using the standard proofreaders' symbols (see back inside cover of this book). Some errors in word division, spelling, and abbreviation will require further checking in the dictionary. In addition to information about individual words, the dictionary provides charts and tables that summarize the standard conventions of presentation.

If there are five or six changes on a page, retype or rewrite that page. Many professional writers retype a page with only three errors. But in most situations, if corrections are made neatly, a page can be submitted with more than three corrections.

Proofread each retyped page by reading each sentence separately, starting with the last and ending with the first. This technique allows any typing errors to be spotted quickly.

REVIEW EXERCISES

1. Rewrite the two passages below, making corrections according to the conventions of presentation discussed in this chapter. Keep a record of the number and type of changes made.

a. "Revolution" was probly not an accurate descriptive title for dr. Atkins' diet. The familiar *Drinking Man's Deit,* published in 1964, was also based on a low carbohydrate scheme—with added attractions, of course. And before that, another low-carbohydrate entry was the diet advocated by Doctor Herman Taller, in "Calories Don't Count," published in 1961. it sold well over a million copies, and many of the copies no doubt were bought by those who interpreted the title to mean tha t the deiters could eat all the food they wanted. These byers were disappointed. Dr. Taller advocated

Proofread and Corrected Page

On halloween, 1938, a radio broadcaster sat down before a microphone and proceeds to give an "eye-witness account" of an invasion by strange creatires from mars. Included in the report were discripsions of military resistance, property destruction, and public hysteria.

Actually, the broad cast was Orson Welles' radio adaptation of the H. G. Wells novel, War of the worlds. However, litseners who missed the opening announcment of the program believed that an invasion really was occuring and many panicked. This incident illustrates the extent to which we may be influenced by the mass media, even when the message is a phony. We tend to beliey what we see and hear over the media and to consider them authoritatative sources of information.

Although mass media communication has certain drawbacks and limitations, its very extensiveness makes it a unique and valuable mehtod of communication. Today we can speek to someone in another part of the world by tlephone, listen to stereo phonic sounc, watch the Olympic Competitions live via satellite. Clearly, the media have expanded our range of communication. we are now able to communicate more messages to greater number of poeple than ever before.

237

6.9f For a Public Document

U.S. Bureau of the Census. *Statistical Abstract of the United States: 1973.* Washington, D.C.: Government Printing Office, 1973.

6.9g For Unpublished Material

Rodkin, David A. "The Alliterative Devices of the Early Scotch Lowlands Poets." Diss. New York University, 1975.

Exercises

Unscramble the bibliographical entries below and rewrite them as a complete bibliography.

1. *The Journals of Claire Clairmont.* Ed. Marion Kingston Stocking, Harvard University Press: Cambridge Massachusetts, 1968.

2. Benjamin S. Bloom et al., eds. *Taxonomy of Educational Objectives: Handbook 1, Cognitive Domain,* New York, David McKay Company: 1956.

3. William Flint Thrall, Hibbard, A., and C. Hugh Holman, *A Handbook to Literature.* New York: The Odyssey Press, 1960.

4. Gruner, Charles R., Cal M. Logue, Freshley, Dwight L., and Richard C. Huseman, *Speech Communication in Society.* Allyn & Bacon, Inc.: Boston, 1972.

5. Octave Mannoni. *Freud.* Renard Bruce, translator. New York: Pantheon, 1971.

6. Brick, Allan R. "*Wuthering Heights:* Narrators, Audience and Message" College English (21) 1959, 80–86.

Proofreading

The final task of the writer is careful reading of the manuscript to catch and correct as many errors and inconsistencies in thought and convention as possible. After the struggle of writing a manuscript, proofreading can be a wearisome task, but the reader expects the finished product to be as error free as possible. Remember that from the reader's point of view, the writer is invisible. All the reader sees is the finished page—in every detail. And errors that interrupt the activity of reading will annoy and confuse him.

How to Proofread

Read the material once to check for logic and accuracy. Check quotations and footnotes at the same time. If the material passes this

Format. Do not indent the first line of a bibliographic entry, but indent all other lines from the left.

6.9a For a Book

One Author	Arnheim, Rudolf. *Visual Thinking.* Berkeley: University of California Press, 1969.
Two or Three Authors	Schwartz, Berthold Eric, and Ruggieri, Bartholomew A. *You Can Raise Decent Children.* New Rochelle, N.Y.: Arlington House, 1971.
More than Three Authors	Marcus, Burton, et al. *Modern Marketing.* New York: Random House, 1975.
An Edited Book	Lange, Victor, ed. *Modern Literature.* Vol. 2. Englewood Cliffs: Prentice-Hall, Inc., 1968. **(Editor as author)**
	Roosevelt, Theodore. *Writings of Theodore Roosevelt.* William H. Harbraugh, ed. New York: Bobbs-Merrill Company, Inc., 1967 **(Author and editor)**
A Translated Book	Marx, Karl. *The Grundrisse.* Trans. by David McLellan. New York: Harper & Row, 1972.
More than One Edition	LaPlace, John. *Health.* 2d ed. Englewood Cliffs: Prentice-Hall, Inc., 1976.
More than One Volume	Morison, Samuel E. *Growth of the American Republic.* 3d ed. 2 vols. New York: Oxford University Press, 1969.
Book with No Author	*A Manual of Style,* 12th ed. Chicago: University of Chicago Press, 1969.

6.9b For a Chapter from a Book

Aron, Raymond. "First Dialogue," in *Marxism and the Existentialists.* New York: Harper & Row, 1969.

6.9c For an Article from a Magazine

Weare, Brian C., Tempkin, Richard L., and Snell, Fred M. "Aerosal and Climate: Some Further Considerations." *Science,* November 29, 1974, p. 827.

6.9d For a Journal Article

Lipsey, Mark W. "Research and Relevance: A Survey of Graduate Students and Faculty in Psychology." *American Psychologist,* 29 (July 1974), 541–53.

6.9e For a Newspaper Article

Barmash, Isadore. "Retail Jewelry Sales Rebound Sharply." *The New York Times,* 29 July 1975, p. 35.

235

far afield from his main discussion. Adding this material to his basic footnote makes the information available to readers while not interrupting the coherence of the presentation:

> [1] Arthur G. Kennedy and Donald B. Sands, *A Concise Bibliography for Students of English,* 4th ed. (Stanford, California: Stanford University Press, 1960), pp. 393–438. The authors list detailed sources for early British history (p. 407), medieval and renaissance Britain (p. 409), and Britain from the eighteenth century to the present (p. 412). But they omit the influential studies of seventeenth-century Britain. Perhaps the best general source is the second edition of Richard D. Altick and Andrew Wright's *Selective Bibliography for the Study of English and American Literature* (New York: The Macmillan Company, 1963).

In a paper in which the writer refers time and again to only one or two sources, he may include his citations in the text. The citation should be enclosed in parentheses and placed directly after the reference or the quoted material:

> In her introduction to her book, *Women, Resistance and Revolution* **(New York: Vintage Books, 1974),** Sheila Rowbotham observes that "women have come to revolutionary consciousness by means of ideas, actions and organizations which have been made predominantly by men" **(p. 11).**

Citations to literary or other specialized works may also be placed in the text, after all the publication information has been given in footnote form the first time the source is used. Subsequent references are limited to identifying page or line numbers, references to specific acts or scenes, or particular sections of the whole source. These shortened citations are placed directly after the reference or quoted material and are not numbered. Here is an example of such a reference to Shakespeare's *The Merchant of Venice*:

> But then, in one of his most-often quoted speeches, Shylock asks: "If you prick us, do we not bleed? if you tickle us, do we not laugh? if you poison us, do we not die? and if you wrong us, shall we not revenge?" (act 3, scene 1, line 65)

By working in citations as shown in the preceding examples, the writer avoids awkward, repetitive footnotes and still gives the readers identifying information about the sources.

Exercises

The following footnotes have all the required information, including punctuation. But the material is not in the proper sequence, so the notes are difficult to read and use. By referring to the models in the preceding section, unscramble each footnote.

[1] *An Anthology of Writings from the Women's Liberation Movement: Sisterhood Is Powerful,* Robin Morgan, ed. (1970, Vintage Books; New York) p. 61.

[2] *Sisterhood Is Powerful,* "Oppressed Women," Robin Morgan, ed., pp. 372–75, Women's Collective of the New York High School Students' Union (Vintage Books, New York: 1970).

[3] Thomas Yoseloff, Ltd., Cranbury: New Jersey, 1969 (*General Washington and the Jack Ass,* J. H. Powell), p. 119.

[4] Bergen Evans and Cornelia Evans. p. 23 (*A Dictionary of Contemporary Usage,* 1957: Random House, New York.

[5] 2d ed., John M. Blum et al. (Harcourt Brace Jovanovich: 1968, New York), *The National Experience: A History of the United States.*

[6] "Health Occupations Education: Will the Profession Respond?" 1652–1654, Jean K. Kintgen, 74 *American Journal of Nursing* (September 1974).

[7] *Saturday Review/World,* Roger M. Williams, "What's Happened to the Communist Party in the USA?", pp. 10–14, 46, February 23, 1974.

6.9   Bibliography Form

Increasingly, professional writers, teachers, and editors prefer to combine the footnotes they use and the list of works cited in their papers into one set of notes attached to the end of the manuscript. In some situations (scholarly writing, for example), a bibliography may be required. Such a bibliography may be an alphabetical list of the works actually cited; or it may include every work looked at in the course of research. Sometimes a bibliography is *annotated,* which means that each of the listed sources has been evaluated by the writer.

When required to present a bibliography, use essentially the same information and format as in a footnote—with the following exceptions:

Author's name.   Footnotes use the normal order; bibliographies reverse the order for alphabetizing (*Keats, John*).

Title.   Footnotes may omit a subtitle or shorten the end of a long title; bibliographical entries must be complete.

Publication information.   Footnotes enclose the city, publisher, and date in parentheses whereas bibliographies express these elements as a separate sentence with no parentheses. Bibliographies omit the page numbers of books, but page numbers are included in entries for periodicals.

a highfat, low carbohydrate diet, excluding not only sweets and starches but also most fruits and vegetables. The "Right kind of fat," Dr. T. clai med, "Was vitally important." Poly unsaturated fatty acids supposedly "soften" body fat so that it can melt away *easily.*

Consumer Reports, "Reducing Drugs and Devices,"
in *The Medicine Show*

b. Dying stars more massive than the sun suffer a dramitic fate. The story ofthat fate is illumanated by 2 events moreth an 9 centuries apart. The first was a celesti al spectacle that burst on the morning of Jul. 4th, 1054 A D. On that day, astronomers in China recorded a brillant new star—Today we call i t a *supernova*—that shone more brightly than venus. For several weeks, it was visable in daylight, and it did not fade from the night sky for more thana year. The 2d event occurred in nineteen sixty-seven atthe *Mullard Radio A stronomy Observatory* of the Univ. of cambridge in England. Astronomer Antony Hewish and a Research Student, jocelyn bell, we re examining strip-chart recordings from a new antenna highly sensative to fluctuating radio Energy. The y discovered misterious signals at a particular Part of the sky. "It looked ridiculous," Prof. Hewish told me later when he showed me the historic reading. " you just don't get pulses like that from the sky."

Kenneth F. Weaver, "The Incredible Universe"

2. Decide which of the following words are divided incorrectly and why. Then correct the division.

B./F. Skinner
po-ol
a-cross
writ-ing
lar-ge
Washing-ton
gener-al
diction-ary
a-bout
sli-de
answer-ed
outsi-de
e-xcess
spe-ech
incident-ally

3. In three paragraphs of your own, use the source material below as an excerpt, as a paraphrase, and as a series of phrases built into your own sentences. Use as many sentences as you need, but take only the material that is most useful for your purpose.

James Hunt ("le Pilote") and Lord Alexander Hesketh ("le Patron") have burst into the ultra-serious world of Grand Prix racing like a breath of fresh air. Hunt has already been hailed as a future World Champion, having finished fourth in the British GP, third in the Dutch GP, second in the United States GP and eight overall in the World Championship—all this in his first season. At Wellington College, Berkshire, England, Hunt lived for sports and passed all his exams on the strength of his intelligence. "That's what kept me at Wellington," he said. "I love sport, I was to go to medical college as a surgeon: it wasn't something I really wanted to do, just the least of the evils available." Then James, the son of a well-to-do family, discovered motor racing.

David Phipps, "Profile: James Hunt," *Road & Track*

7

Punctuation

Marks of punctuation give the reader information about the relationships among words and sentences. The conventional signals that punctuation marks convey to the reader must be both precise and accurate for these relationships to be clear. Since the effectiveness of the whole communication depends upon the clarity of its parts, punctuating for meaning contributes to effective rhetoric.

PUNCTUATE FOR THE READER'S EYE

Recently a group of printers got together to improve the efficiency of our punctuation system. They came up with a new sign: the *interrobang* (?), a cross between the question mark and the exclamation point (called a *bang* in printer's jargon). The interrobang was designed to identify sentences that have the form of a question and the function of an exclamation—such as, "What is *that*?" Unfortunately, most people who saw the interrobang asked the same question.

Readers are slow to accept innovation in the printed language (no new punctuation mark has been invented since the introduction of quotation marks at the end of the seventeenth century). Still, as we shall see, the printers who introduced the interrobang were responding to a real problem, at least from the point of view of writers who have to use a limited number of punctuation marks for a wide variety of writing tasks.

Each punctuation mark (or lack of one) is a visual sign that shows the reader how words within a sentence and sentences within a paragraph are related. These signs provide the reader's eye with information that makes the structure and meaning of the sentence more visible and, therefore, easier to understand. In a way, everything on this page that is not a letter or a number functions as a punctuation mark—including the indentations that signal each new paragraph. Even the spaces between the words in a sentence and the capital letter that signals the beginning of a sentence can be thought of as visual signs indicating how parts of a composition are related.

The punctuation marks used most frequently, however, are fewer than a dozen: the period (.), the comma (,), the semicolon (;), the colon (:), quotation marks ("/"), parentheses ((/)), brackets ([/]), the dash (—), the question mark (?), and the exclamation point (!).

If each punctuation mark invariably had just one use, the writer would need only to decide whether the situation called for using that particular mark and add or omit it accordingly. But note the different uses of the comma in the paragraph below:

> George Washington was *not* first in the hearts of *all* his country-men. Soon after he became President, the freedom-loving, hot-tempered, hard-working Scotch-Irish who lived beyond the Allegheny Mountains in Pennsylvania concluded that the American Revolution had merely traded the oppression of one George for that of another. Because Washington listened to his dynamic young Secretary of the Treasury, Alexander Hamilton, instead of taking the advice of more cautious statesmen such as his Secretary of State, Thomas Jefferson, the Union almost came apart in the second decade of its existence.
>
> Iola B. Parker, "Whiskey Creek Keeps Running, But Only with Water," *Smithsonian*

The first comma is used to separate a beginning clause from the main body of the sentence; the next two to indicate a series; and the next two to set off an appositive (a name or description that repeats in different words a preceding name or description). Each comma joins or separates the words in the sentences for a slightly different purpose and sends a different signal to the reader about those words.

On the one hand, then, the printers were justified in thinking that each writing situation should have its own distinctive punctuation mark. But, on the other hand, such a system would require both writer and reader to memorize hundreds of marks and would still leave the writer with the problem of deciding when to use each mark.

Although each mark may be used in a variety of punctuation situations, each has a definite meaning when it is seen in context. For example, readers are familiar with the conventional meaning of the period at the end of a sentence, just as mathematicians are familiar with the meaning of the minus sign. And when the words surrounding the signal make up the type of structure readers expect to see, they hardly notice the punctuation at all. However, if the signal were to be changed or used out of context (for example, a comma instead of a period ending a sentence), readers would become confused. Obviously, then, the first step in using punctuation

243

without confusing the reader is to learn what each mark means and the context or contexts in which readers are accustomed to seeing it.

The second step is to learn to punctuate with consistency. While it is true that most basic conventions should be followed by every writer, there are situations in which the writer can choose whether or not to use punctuation:

> **In 1937** Leo C. Rosten did a scholarly survey of the 127 main Washington correspondents and found that only half of them had finished college. **With few exceptions** these reporters were inter-changeable drones who wrote the same formula stories day after day.
>
> Timothy Crouse, *The Boys on the Bus*

In these sentences, the comma can be omitted after the introductory phrases because the omission does not cause the reader to misread. However, after reading a composition for a while, the reader will become so used to seeing such comma omissions that he will note the difference should one suddenly appear after a short introductory phrase. Inconsistent punctuation of this kind is as annoying to the reader as inconsistent spelling.

The third step in using punctuation efficiently is to learn to use it not as an afterthought but as an important ingredient in the communication. Beginning writers often sprinkle the various marks into their finished sentences with little thought to their function—a teaspoon of commas, a dash of semicolons, a pinch of dashes.

Creative punctuation allows the writer to subordinate, coordinate, and show the reader the relationships among ideas. In the first of the two following paragraphs a lack of active punctuation makes the basic thought difficult to follow:

> The really great confrontation in our present world is between those who have and those who do not. This confrontation is not too likely to change in the next two decades. The confrontation is true within any society we know of. It applies to nations as well as individuals. We live in a technological milieu in which we can produce all the physical things that anyone in the world needs if we desire. We can produce what we need but not what we want. The confrontation becomes a sort of make-believe imagery in such a technological milieu. This is because we still act on an imprint that goes back to a much earlier time. This imprint is summed up in the expression that the poor we shall always have with us. We will have the poor just as long as we consider it in our interest to keep them that way.

244   In the second paragraph, the writer has made good use of punctuation to coordinate and subordinate and so avoids the problems apparent in the first version:

> The really great confrontation in our present world, and one not too likely to change in the next two decades, is between those who have and those who do not. This is true within any society we know of, and it applies to nations as well as individuals. In a technological milieu in which we can—if we desire—produce all of the physical things that anyone in the world needs (not wants, *needs*), this confrontation becomes a sort of make-believe imagery, because we still act on an imprint that goes back to a much earlier time: "The poor we shall always have with us." We will have the poor just so long as we consider it in our interest to keep them that way.
>
> Don Fabun, *The Dynamics of Change*

The complexity of the thoughts communicated is difficult enough for the reader to grasp without his having to struggle through the choppy sentences in the first version. We might argue, in fact, that the exact thought being presented is communicated successfully only because of the writer's ability to punctuate creatively. For example, in the third sentence the writer qualifies *can* with the phrase *if we desire* and the word *needs* with the phrase *not wants, needs*. With punctuation, these qualifications of individual words are effectively placed in the sentence. Without interrupting the flow of thought, the qualifications add punch to the main point: We have the technological capability to do away with absolute poverty, but we do not do so because we still believe that poverty is a necessary condition for many people, or we desire that it should be. Note also that the writer uses two separate conventions—dashes and parentheses—for inserting the qualifications. Dashes may have been used in one place and parentheses in another only to avoid cluttering the sentence with too many dashes. Or perhaps the writer intended to point up the first qualification rather than the second, since material in parentheses generally receives less attention than material within dashes.

Many more pages could be spent in discussing the writer's use of punctuation in the preceding sample paragraph, and the reader might even discover that he disagrees with certain of the writer's decisions. But the basic point is clear: accurate, creative punctuation is part of the writer's craft. Before being able to practice the craft, however, it is necessary to know what can be done with individual marks of punctuation within the conventional requirements. The following sections review the most common uses and abuses of punctuation.

245

INTERNAL PUNCTUATION (int p)

While all punctuation contributes significantly to the meaning of a composition, writers seem to have the most difficulty using *internal punctuation*—the marks that fall *within* sentences. For this reason, we will begin the section on punctuation conventions with a review of those governing internal punctuation.

Internal punctuation is used to show the relationship between a word or group of words and the sentence in which they appear. The five punctuation marks most frequently used within sentences are: the comma (,), the semicolon (;), the colon (:), the dash (—), and parentheses ((/)). Each mark is used primarily for clarity—to make the sentence a little easier to read. But internal punctuation is also used to indicate the relative importance of the various sentence parts. By using punctuation skillfully, the writer can guide the reader in interpreting sentences, thereby communicating the precise shade of meaning or the exact amount of emphasis intended. Internal punctuation, then, is not just a matter of mechanics but of rhetoric as well.

7.1 The Series

Whatever the information a writer wishes to communicate, often the most efficient method of presentation is to make a list. A summary of a person's accomplishments, a description of a social problem, a set of instructions for operating a typewriter—each can be presented as a *series,* a list of three or more elements arranged so that each element is recognizable as part of a longer list. The greatest advantage of a series is its simplicity and efficiency. Difficult or abstract ideas become clearer when they are organized in a straightforward list. In addition, a series avoids repetition of key words and allows the writer to communicate masses of information rapidly:

> In its short heyday, the nickelodeon theater was a pioneer movie house, a get-rich-quick scheme, and a national institution that was quickly turned into a state of mind.
>
> Russell Merritt, "Nickelodeon Theaters," *AFI Report*

The sentence would be cumbersome if the author had added "the nickelodeon theatre was" before each item in the series.

The following conventions for the use of punctuation in series cover the most common situations the writer meets.

7.1a   **The Comma (,)**

Use commas to separate three or more items in a series. When a conjunction separates the last two items, use a comma before the conjunction:

> There are rituals for birth, marriage, death, **and** much that occurs in between—graduations, engagements, retirements, etc.—but still no set way for dealing with the breakup of a marriage.
>
> Joseph Epstein, "Divorced in America," *New York Post*

If the items in a series are long phrases or clauses, or if punctuation is used within one or more items, a stronger mark than the comma is needed to prevent confusion.

7.1b   **The Semicolon (;)**

Use semicolons to separate items in a series if the items are unusually long or if punctuation is used within one or more of the items:

> Not long ago, a divorced man or woman was thought to be weak or wicked. Perhaps these stereotypes have begun to crumble because of increased social tolerance; because of an increased awareness of the needs of individuals; or (and this is more likely) simply because more and more people have become divorced.
>
> Adapted from Joseph Epstein, "Divorced in America," *New York Post*

7.1c   **The Colon (:)**
A colon tells the reader that a series is to follow.

Use a colon to introduce a series (numbered or unnumbered) when the subject matter is relatively formal or technical:

> A couple contemplating divorce would be wise to follow a three-step course of action: (1) communicate their disappointments in the marriage to each other openly, honestly, and, if possible, calmly; (2) consider realistically all the pros and cons of dissolving the marriage; and (3) seek professional counseling.

7.1d   **The Dash (—)**
When a series interrupts the main thought of a sentence, a colon cannot sufficiently set the series off. For clarity, the dash is used in such situations to indicate the beginning and end of the series.

Use a dash before and after a series interrupting the main thought of a sentence:

> With the advent on the contemporary scene of a large new cast of family members—ex-wives, second and third husbands, stepfathers, stepchildren, half-brothers, and half-sisters—divorce, ironically, seems almost to be recreating a family unit on the order of the old extended family of aunts, uncles, grandparents, and cousins of distant remove.
>
> Joseph Epstein, "Divorced in America," *New York Post*

Use a single dash to set off summarizing series at the beginning or end of sentences:

Beginning Series	Alimony, custody, visitation, and shared property —these are the ties that bind the new extended family.
Ending Series	Instead of being tied by blood, as the old extended family was, this new extended family is tied by decree—alimony, custody, visitation, and shared property binding them all together. Joseph Epstein, "Divorced in America," *New York Post*

Exercises

Where necessary, use commas, semicolons, colons, or dashes to punctuate the series in the following sentences.

1. Broken promises petty rivalries and police harassment such were the obstacles they encountered.

2. The most powerful politicians Thompson DiNapoli and Greenberg were watching the election returns in the dark and smoke-filled room.

3. American writers who have created philosophies of life are Hawthorne Melville Emerson and Thoreau.

4. In the far reaches of the universe there are places where a teaspoon of matter weighs as much as two hundred million elephants where a tiny whirling star winks on and off thirty times a second and where a small and mysterious object shines with the brilliance of ten trillion suns.

5. The state hospital urgently needs the following specialists physicians paramedical workers and vocational counselors.

6. In London's Covent Garden, the street urchins converse in rhyming slang flower girls drop by to stock up on fresh baskets of daisies and primroses and nuns patiently collect alms and vegetables in the tumult and commotion of a thriving outdoor market.

7.2   Phrases and Clauses

Although every simple sentence contains a subject, a verb, and an object or complement, these basic sentence parts need not always appear in the same order (subject-verb-object). In fact, shifting the order of sentence parts often allows the writer to create variety and interest that might otherwise be lacking. Especially in complex sentences, internal punctuation can be used creatively to separate phrases and clauses for clarity, emphasis, and variety.

7.2a   Introductory Phrases and Clauses

Frequently, a phrase or dependent clause is shifted to the beginning of the sentence to introduce the ideas conveyed by the main clause. Such an introductory element is generally separated from the body of the sentence by commas. The punctuation is simply a sign that the normal word order of the sentence has been altered.

Use a comma to separate an introductory phrase or clause from the main clause of the sentence:

For four months, archeologists carefully excavated the funnel-shaped pit. At the bottom, 52 feet down, on a carpet of 26 bamboo mats, stood a massive wooden box.

Alice J. Hall, "A Lady from China's Past," *National Geographic*

By arranging the sentence parts so that phrases containing references to time and place come first, the author of the preceding paragraph organizes her material so the archeological discovery is dramatic. The beginning of each sentence leads the reader down through the earth to the discovery waiting beneath the ground. Each of the introductory elements could be shifted to other positions in the sentences they begin. As they appear, however, each opening phrase provides an interesting and efficient transition from one sentence to the next.

If the introductory element is short, the comma may be omitted:

For four months archeologists carefully excavated the funnel-shaped pit. **At the bottom** stood a massive wooden box lying on a carpet of twenty-six bamboo mats.

Since short introductory elements may be written with or without   **249** a comma, particular care must be taken to control the clarity of sentences with allowable comma omissions. Although sometimes the comma is clearly unnecessary, other situations require a comma to prevent misreading. If an introductory sentence element can be misread, the comma must be retained:

Clear:	On Thursday morning, the archeologists returned home.
Clear:	On Thursday morning the archeologists returned home.
Unclear:	When they returned home was dull.
Clear:	When they returned, home was dull.

Because situations do occur in which the absence of a comma after an introductory element can confuse the reader, many writers prefer to retain the comma to separate all introductory elements. To do so is more conservative usage, but it guarantees that all such sentences will be read accurately and that the comma convention for this situation will be used consistently.

7.2b Restrictive and Nonrestrictive Modifiers

A dependent clause, phrase, or other modifier may also be located within the body of the sentence, directly after the noun it modifies. These sentence parts frequently, though not always, begin with one of the relative pronouns (*who, whom, whose, that, which, what, whoever, whomever, whichever,* and *whatever*). Modifying clauses may be *restrictive* or *nonrestrictive.* Restrictive modifiers provide *essential* information for identifying or defining the noun they modify. Nonrestrictive modifiers supply *extra* information that could be omitted without changing the basic meaning of the sentence.[1]

Do not set off restrictive noun modifiers with punctuation:

The source **that I found most helpful in preparing my paper on the American Civil War** was *The American Story,* edited by Earl Schenk Miers.

In this sentence, the modifying clause provides information that, if omitted, would leave the sentence incomplete in meaning.

Use commas to set off nonrestrictive noun modifiers:

[1] Many writers prefer to use *that* instead of *which* to introduce restrictive modifiers, and *which* in place of *that* for nonrestrictive modifiers. Because this distinction further assists the reader in distinguishing between restrictive and nonrestrictive modifiers, it is a style worth adopting.

John Hay, **who was Lincoln's secretary and observed him at close range all the time he was in the White House,** insisted that it was "absurd to call him a modest man."

Edmund Wilson, "Abraham Lincoln," *Patriotic Gore*

Here the modifier only supplies additional information. Although it adds color and interest, the sentence, in context, would be understandable without it.

Use dashes or parentheses to set off a nonrestrictive noun modifier from the sentence in which it appears when the modifier contains internal puntuation:

Ulysses S. Grant—who was self-reliant to a fault, indifferent to tradition, and interested mainly in what the future held in store—typifies the pioneers.

The self-reliant Ulysses S. Grant typifies the pioneers (who were likely to be running farms, setting up businesses of their own, or otherwise supporting themselves independently).

When a modifier includes internal punctuation, the dashes assist the reader by showing where the modifier begins and ends. Parentheses are used to set off nonrestrictive modifiers for clarity when the information they provide is something of an afterthought, mentioned in passing.

Both restrictive and nonrestrictive modifiers may appear without their relative pronouns. In either case, the same punctuation conventions apply as for modifiers that begin with a relative pronoun:

Restrictive	The subject **[that] I chose** was an interpretation of the contrasts between Ulysses S. Grant and Robert E. Lee.
Nonrestrictive	Grant, **[who was] the son of a tanner on the western frontier,** was everything Lee was not.

An important point to remember about noun modifiers is that often they can be either restrictive or nonrestrictive, depending on the writer's intention:

Restrictive	Grant believed that frontier people **who were self-sufficient** stood for democracy because they had grown up in the middle of it and knew how it worked.
Nonrestrictive	Grant believed that frontier people, **who were self-sufficient,** stood for democracy because they had grown up in the middle of it and knew how it worked.

251

In the first sentence, the writer is referring to a particular group of frontier people (those who were self-sufficient), not to frontier people in general. Because the writer wants to point up this important distinction, he does not set off the modifier with punctuation. In the second sentence, however, the writer wants "frontier people" to refer to that group as a whole. Since in this instance the modifier represents secondary, nonessential information, it is set off with commas.

7.2c Restrictive and Nonrestrictive Concluding Phrases and Clauses

A restrictive and nonrestrictive concluding phrase or clause may qualify, comment on, or restate in other words information contained in the body of the sentence. The punctuation conventions for these concluding sentence parts are the same as those for other such modifiers. The punctuation serves to identify the concluding material by separating it from the main body of the sentence. Concluding modifying phrases and clauses frequently begin with *although, because, since, while,* or one of the other subordinators.

Do not set off restrictive concluding phrases or clauses with punctuation:

> An increasing number of families from all economic strata of society have cut down on meat **since the drastic rise in food costs.**

As an integral part of the sentence above, the restrictive concluding phrase could not be removed without taking away from the meaning of the sentence.

Use a comma to set off a nonrestrictive concluding phrase or clause:

> I am not a vegetarian—yet. Neither is anyone else in my family. But we are considering it quite seriously, and so are many of our friends, **because it has finally dawned on us that eating meat at our normal rate contributes directly to famines in many parts of the world.**
>
> Maya Pines, "Meatless, Guiltless," *The New York Times Magazine*

Here a comma is necessary to separate the nonrestrictive concluding clause because it signals a sharp break in the continuity of thought.

In most instances, a comma is used to signal a nonrestrictive concluding phrase or clause. However, dashes and parentheses are sometimes used instead. Although both marks signal a more definite break than is indicated by the comma, parentheses usually enclose information not directly related to the subject or structure of the sentence.

Use a dash or parentheses to separate a concluding phrase or clause when there is a sharp break in the form or content of the sentence:

> The human body needs fresh supplies of protein every day for growth and for healthy functioning—.36 grams of protein per pound of body weight, or 46 grams for a 128-pound woman and about 56 grams for a 154-pound man are the recommended daily allowances.
>
> Maya Pines, "Meatless, Guiltless," *The New York Times Magazine*

> Our first radio broadcasts, expanding through space at the speed of light, are now about fifty light-years away—the outer limit for any intelligent beings who may be listening in and wondering what on earth we are talking about. The number of these intelligent beings could be truly astronomical (if one assumes that other galaxies have on the average as many stars and planets as the Milky Way).

Exercises

1. Decide whether or not to punctuate the introductory phrases or clauses in each of the following sentences. State your reasons.

a. According to an ancient legend an emperor's consort, by watching silkworms in the garden, learned to spin and weave fine cloth.

b. Hidden by barriers of time and space unknown and unexplained the stellar collision might have remained forever beyond the reach of science.

c. Out of the laboratory in Peking stepped a short man in a white smock.

d. Resting casually on his arm was the priceless antique vase.

e. Having convinced himself of his own moral superiority Goodman Brown rejected the rest of mankind.

f. Whether or not he dreamed the meeting his life thereafter was full of gloom.

g. As a result of his rejection of the devil Goodman Brown denied his essential humanity.

h. Emotionally drained and spiritually exhausted Goodman Brown lives on in misery.

253

2. Decide whether each modifier is restrictive or nonrestrictive and punctuate accordingly. Explain each decision you make.

a. The old man sitting restlessly before the fire opened his eyes slowly and glared at the women who were all rocking comfortably back and forth.

b. The courtroom at Appomattox where Grant accepted Lee's surrender is thé only historical monument and the only courtroom for miles around.

c. The Grant who won the Civil War seems almost to have been a different man from President Grant who ran his administration with little regard for political corruption.

d. A so-called black hole which is the end product of the collapse of an extremely large star is the ultimate concentration of matter that was predicted by Einstein's theory accepted for years as a theoretical possibility but only recently confirmed as a near certainty.

e. The possible confirmation comes from an experiment which was conducted at the University of Maryland that appears to reveal powerful gravitation waves similar to those that would be expected when matter is drawn into a black hole and that are apparently coming from the center of our galaxy.

f. The hyphen used to show the combination of two or more words into a single term that represents a new idea looks exactly like the hyphen used to show the division of a word at the end of a line.

3. In the following sentences, select the concluding phrase or clause and punctuate it accordingly, using the comma, the dash, or parentheses as convention suggests. Explain each decision you make.

a. Nathaniel Hawthorne was primarily interested in the connection between guilt and sin although his characters were occasionally afflicted with madness as well.

b. Both Nathaniel Hawthorne and Edgar Allan Poe explored the psychology of guilt one from the point of view of sin and the other from the point of view of insanity.

c. Now the problem was out of her hands and out of her mind or so she thought at the time.

d. Ernest Hemingway was wounded during World War I in Italy while he was serving as an ambulance driver.

e. Paul Cudahy was astonished when he heard the terms of the proposal a repeal of the Fourteenth Amendment and most of the recent reform legislation including legalized abortion.

f. Cudahy said he would win because his opponent was tired although everyone was tired by that time because no one had stopped talking for three hours.

7.3 Appositives

The *appositive,* a noun modifier, repeats the meaning of a preceding noun or pronoun, but in more specific terms. For example, the expression *a noun modifier* in the preceding sentence is an appositive. The appositive is a handy descriptive tool for bringing a subject quickly and efficiently into focus. Since appositives add extra information to a sentence, they are generally nonrestrictive and are enclosed in commas.

7.3a Midsentence Appositives

Use commas to set off an appositive that appears in the middle of a sentence:

> Dracula, **the Prince of Wallachia,** was given a bad press by his political opponents.

The appositive in the sentence above amplifies the subject, *Dracula,* in more specific terms.

Use dashes to set off an appositive in the middle of a sentence if the appositive includes internal punctuation:

> Dracula's victims were generally boyars—**wealthy, rebellious feudal landowners**—although he reportedly impaled tens of thousands of ordinary citizens, generally in a spirit of righteous indignation.

Note that the appositive set off by dashes in the preceding example defines the noun it follows, *boyars.* Dashes are used to replace the commas at the beginning and end of the appositive simply to make the construction, which contains internal punctuation, more visible.

Use parentheses to set off an appositive in the middle of a sentence if the appositive includes technical or background information:

> Dracula **(or *Draculae,* to give the more accurate spelling)** inherited his name, which means *son of the devil,* without having much to say about it.

7.3b End-of-Sentence Appositives

An appositive appearing at the end of a sentence is often set off with a comma or a dash.

255

Use a comma before final appositives that contain no internal punctuation and that are closely related to the thought of the main sentence:

> Scholars point out that Vlad II probably acquired the name *Dracul* after he was initiated into the Order of the Dragon and was obliged at all times to wear the order's insignia, **a dragon.** It would be difficult for the citizens of Wallachia to avoid the implications of the dragon, **a medieval symbol for Satan.**

Because the final appositives in the preceding example provide extra information directly related to the nouns they follow (*insignia* and *dragon*), they are set off with commas.

Use a dash to set off final appositives that include internal punctuation or that represent a sharp break in the continuity of the preceding thought:

> To the modern mind the only creature associated with death by impaling is the vampire—**a mythical, blood-drinking being who rises from the grave in search of victims.**

Occasionally, an appositive is restrictive—that is, it provides information essential to the meaning of the sentence. In this case the appositive should not be set off with punctuation:

Incorrect   The American novelist, Mark Twain, was really named Samuel Clemens. [Mark Twain is not the only American novelist.]

Correct   The American novelist Mark Twain was really named Samuel Clemens.

Incorrect   Twain's novel, *Huckleberry Finn*, was written from the point of view of a young boy discovering life. [Twain wrote other novels.]

Correct   Twain's novel *Huckleberry Finn* was written from the point of view of a young boy discovering life.

Exercises

Punctuate the appositives in the following sentences according to the preceding conventions. Explain your decisions.

1. Brandy our old Irish setter has never missed and never won a fight.

2. Half blind and lame, the old dog is hardly able to locate her most frequent opponent Fifi the poodle next door.

3. Eric Hoffer a sensitive and thoughtful longshoreman is self-educated.

4. The *Herald-Star* a leading newspaper is read by 1.7 million people daily.

5. The best-selling nonfiction book for last month was *Clean Genes* a book about genetic pollution.

6. Many of the most controversial issues will be handled by the so-called sensitive government agencies the State Department, the Defense Department, the Environmental Protection Agency, and the Atomic Energy Commission.

7. The uninterrupted increase in government spending as a percentage of the gross national product the total of goods and services produced each year may have reached a point of no return.

8. Oaxaca a city in Mexico that is pronounced "wa-Ha-ca" has been the scene of festive preparation for several weeks.

9. The folk singer, Janis Ian, is currently making a comeback.

7.4 Parentheticals

By definition, parentheticals are not directly connected to the sentences in which they occur. They are interrupters that modify a sentence or a part of it and may be set off with commas, dashes, or parentheses, depending on the writing situation:

Dracula, **according to one story,** once nailed spikes into the turbans of several Turkish envoys who for religious reasons had refused to remove their hats.

According to another story, Dracula once invited the nation's misfits to a great feast at his castle. He then asked the multitude—**the beggars, the old, the sick, and the poor, who had gorged themselves and were quite drunk**—if they wanted to be free from all worldly cares. When they answered affirmatively, he ordered the castle boarded up and set on fire. No one escaped.

Sir Thomas Malory **(1395–1471)** wrote *Morte d'Arthur.*

Samuel Clemens **(Mark Twain)** wrote *Huckleberry Finn.*

Parenthetical elements are another of the writer's tools for condensing, creating variety, and adding information.

Exercises

Decide whether each parenthetical expression in the sentences below requires commas, dashes, or parentheses. Explain the reasons for your choices.

1. Many dress designers expected some actually demanded that women become dissatisfied with last year's fashions.

257

> **2.** Their president on the other hand defended or rather tried to defend his policy of not spending money appropriated by the legislature.
>
> **3.** The cost of the dinner five dollars including tax and tip was a good value.
>
> **4.** The facsimile edition the experts predict it will soon be sold for over $100,000 is only four by five inches.
>
> **5.** As far as I know and I would like to stress the fact that I have not been personally involved the final report will definitely not be ready for several months.
>
> **6.** The ceiling of the Sistine Chapel it required 700 square yards of plaster and took Michelangelo four years to complete working flat on his back suspended forty feet above the ground gives you an idea of what a great artist can accomplish and what he can put up with in the name of art.

7.5 Coordinating Conjunctions

Words, phrases, clauses, and sentences that are grammatically equal are said to be *coordinate*. Usually, coordinate constructions also have meanings that are equal in weight or value. These constructions are often joined by one of the *coordinating conjunctions (and, but, or, nor, so, yet)*, and the resulting sentence patterns express addition, contrast, conclusion, alternative, or cause and effect.

> His early books were presented in a **repetitious and heavy-handed** style, **but** they contained many **fresh and impressive** ideas.

The adjectives *repetitious* and *heavy-handed* are coordinate, as are *fresh* and *impressive*. Both sets of adjectives are connected by the coordinating conjunction *and*. In addition, the sentence is composed of two coordinate clauses ("His early books . . . style" and "they contained . . . ideas") linked by the coordinating conjunction *but* and punctuated with a comma to show the sentence structure. The conventions for punctuating the most common types of coordinate constructions are given below.

7.5a Coordinating Conjuctions with the Comma

Use a comma before a coordinating conjunction that connects two main clauses:

> Until recently, most astronomers believed the universe began in one huge explosion, **and** they believed it has been expanding ever since. Others admitted that the universe is expanding, **but** they denied the original "big bang" theory.

Note that each main clause in the coordinate sentences above could appear alone:

> Until recently, most astronomers believed the universe began in one huge explosion.
> They believed it has been expanding ever since.
> Others admitted that the universe is expanding.
> They denied the original "big bang" theory.

The purpose of the commas and the conjunctions *and* and *but* is to combine the sentences into structures that allow the reader to grasp the ideas and relationships more rapidly.

7.5b   Coordinating Conjunctions with the Semicolon

Use a semicolon before a coordinating conjunction connecting two main clauses if one of them is unusually long or contains other punctuation:

> The universe began when, about 13 billion years ago, a primordial mass exploded, took shape as a fireball, cooled into gas clouds as it expanded, and began to form into celestial bodies. The universe may continue to expand forever**; or** it may collapse in on itself after 40 billion years, when gravity slows and halts the original expansion.

Notice that the semicolon replaces the comma before *or*. Since the second of the two main clauses already contains a comma, a semicolon is necessary to separate the clauses more distinctly. However, even when there is no internal punctuation in one or both clauses, the semicolon is needed to distinguish one complete sentence from another. (See Section **7.6** on main clauses.)

7.5c   Coordinating Conjunctions without Punctuation

Do not punctuate coordinating conjunctions when they join two words or two phrases or when they begin a sentence:

> Scientists continue to **speculate and search** for clues that will explain the mystery of the universe. There are still many questions about the **origin and future** of the universe. **But** not all the questions that are being asked by the experts have answers.

Occasionally, the punctuation may be omitted between two coordinate clauses if both clauses are short and if their meaning is clear when they are read together:

> We may eventually learn the answers **or** we may have to learn to live without them.

7.5d Coordinate Modifiers

With a series of two or more modifiers, the writer must decide whether the modifiers are coordinate and need punctuation or are not coordinate and require none.

When Commas Are Required

Use commas to separate each modifier in a series if the modifiers are coordinate—that is, if each modifies the noun separately. Do not use a comma after the last modifier in a coordinate series:

> Rep. Shirley Chisholm of New York ran for President to break the tradition of the **white, middle-class, male-dominated** political system. She lost, but in *The Good Fight* she tells how her struggles to pry open a closed door jolted many people to a new political awareness. Cracking that door meant battles with everyone from **chauvinistic black male** politicians to liberal George McGovern supporters.
>
> Barbara Morrow Williams, *Psychology Today*

The first series of modifiers is coordinate; each of the adjectives modifies the words *political system:*

> the white political system
> the middle-class political system
> the male-dominated political system

The second series of modifiers is not coordinate and should not be punctuated. In this case, each adjective modifies the one following it, not the noun *politicians.* This distinction makes it possible to change the order of the modifiers without causing confusion.

A convenient way to check a modifying series for coordination is to reorder the modifiers. If the reordered series makes sense, the modifiers are coordinate. If the series cannot be reordered without disturbing its meaning, the modifiers are not coordinate. For example, the first series of modifiers in the examples above could be reordered without consequence to read: "the middle-class, white, male-dominated political system." However, the same cannot be said of the second series: "male black chauvinistic politicians."

When Commas Are Not Required

Do not use a comma to separate a modifier from a compound noun (a group of words that function as a single noun, such as *boy friend*):

> The ski instructor is a large, good-looking man with **flaming red hair** and a **tremendous energy drive.** To some he is an earnest, honest, sincere guy; to others he is the resort's **greatest con man.**

In the first of the three series of modifiers, *flaming* modifies *red hair,* not just *hair.* Readers think of the description *red hair* as a total idea, just as they do *energy drive* and *con man.* Since these word groups represent complete concepts, they can be treated as single nouns and should not be separated from their modifiers by a comma.

7.6   Main Clauses

Main clauses, although grammatically able to stand alone as complete sentences, often are more effective when joined together to form larger, more complex constructions. These constructions help writers to balance and coordinate their writing and to give their readers variety that would otherwise be missing. Sometimes a comma is sufficient to separate main clauses. (See Section **7.5a** on coordinating conjunctions.) Other times a semicolon must be used instead. The most common writing situations involving a semicolon with main clauses are given below.

7.6a   Main Clauses without a Coordinating Conjunction

Use a semicolon to separate two or more main clauses that are closely related in form or in content:

> Children begin by worshipping their parents; they mature by judging them; they become adults by learning to forgive.
>
> Her parents were always aware of human guilt; the awareness came from their fascination with the way a sense of guilt can influence a child's behavior from the cradle to the grave.

Notice that the semicolons in the first example replace the coordinating conjunctions and commas. Readers understand the connection between the three main clauses because the clauses are parallel and balanced. The similarity in form encourages readers to see a similarity in meaning.

In the second example, the second main clause is an explanation of the first. Here a comma would not separate the two clauses sufficiently, and making two separate sentences out of them would interrupt the thought. A semicolon allows the main clauses to be joined smoothly, yet it provides enough separation for ease in reading.

261

7.6b Main Clauses with a Conjunctive Adverb

Use a semicolon to separate main clauses joined by a conjunctive adverb (e.g., *however, nevertheless, moreover, therefore, furthermore, consequently*):

> Crime statistics have been increasing rapidly; **therefore**, a demand for law and order has become a political issue.

Like coordinating conjunctions, conjunctive adverbs are transitional words that carry a thought from one main clause to the next.

Exercises

Use commas or semicolons where necessary to punctuate the modifiers and to separate the main clauses in the following sentences. State the reason for each punctuation mark you add.

1. The new elevator operator has been on the job for three days but he already knows each of the tenants in the luxurious high-rise apartment building on a first-name basis.

2. She is a heavy red-faced sandy-haired woman with a menacing mysterious smile and a quick sure touch on the machine she operates at work.

3. Many futurists believe that our society is changing faster than ever before but most people are unaware of the basic changes that are taking place in their lives.

4. They seem to be involved with social change but their main interest, in spite of the widespread concern with ecology and the equal-rights movement, has been in making money.

5. The worst is over but we have yet to find a solution.

6. Many scientists believe that marijuana is less harmful than alcohol nevertheless alcohol is legal and marijuana is not.

7. She writes one chapter each morning by sitting down at the typewriter and staying there for three hours without a break.

7.7 Transitional Words and Expressions

In writing, to move from one thought to another smoothly and logically is never easy, but the ability to do so and to punctuate transitions efficiently is an asset to any writer. Transitional words and expressions (such as *however, therefore, nevertheless, furthermore, similarly, on the other hand, consequently, in fact, also, in addition*) help to indicate the direction of the writer's thought and the relationships among his ideas. Transitionals may appear at the beginning, middle, or end of a sentence. Usually, they are set off from the rest of the sentence by a comma or a pair of commas. The following conventions for punctuating transitionals are those writers are most likely to use. Note that some of these words and expressions are, in different contexts, conjunctive adverbs and need a semicolon. (See Section **7.6b.**)

Use commas to set off transitional words from the body of a sentence:

> The speech community of English, comprising all those who use it as their regular means of communication, numbers over three hundred million persons, any one of whom can converse (admittedly sometimes with difficulty) with any other. **In addition,** large numbers of people whose native speech is not English go to the trouble of learning it in order to be able to communicate with the native English speakers—or in some cases, with each other.
>
> W. Nelson Francis, *The English Language: An Introduction*

> People may argue over whether or not whales are fish or spiders are insects. Such arguments, **however,** are wholly within the conventional field of language.
>
> W. Nelson Francis, *The English Language: An Introduction*

Do not set off *however* with punctuation when it is used to indicate quantity or degree rather than a transition:

> **However** much I love chocolate, I love a clear complexion more. [Degree]
>
> **However,** as much as I love chocolate, I love a clear complexion more. [Transition]

Exercises

1. Add an appropriate transitional word or expression to the following pairs of statements. Punctuate according to the preceding conventions.

a. The afternoon psychology class was full. I was able to register for the one given in the morning.

b. Many of Shakespeare's characters reflect such universal human qualities as greed, jealousy, and pride. His characters are believable even today, centuries after the plays were written.

263

c. It is uncanny how accident prone my brother is. Five years ago he broke his leg in an automobile accident, three years ago he broke his arm in a fall, and just last year he cut his foot severely when he stepped on some broken glass at the beach.

d. The research team neglected to complete the third step of the experiment. Their conclusions could not be fully proven.

2. Add or correct the punctuation around the transitionals in the following sentences.

a. Home economics used to be a course taken only by young women. Today however many young men enroll as well.

b. I thought the film *The Exorcist* was unnecessarily gory in parts. On the other hand it was fascinating to see what can be done today with make-up and special effects.

c. However, difficult it may be to learn to drive a car, most people are glad to have this skill.

d. Today, people who want to buy first homes often cannot obtain mortgages, and they are forced therefore to renew their apartment leases.

7.8 Introducing Long Amplifications and Quotations

The *colon* (:) is a punctuation mark used primarily to direct the reader's attention forward. It is a convenient device for introducing additional information to the reader without having to use extra, cumbersome words. The result is a smoother, more streamlined presentation that is easier for the reader to grasp. The conventions below show typical writing situations that call for a colon.

Use a colon to set off a long or formal statement that summarizes or explains what has come before:

He came back a new man: his hair was dyed to remove every trace of gray; his face was lifted; his nose was shortened; his ears were pinned back; and his height was increased three inches by elevator shoes.

Use a colon to introduce a long or formal quotation:

Ralph Nader has said: "Crime statistics almost wholly ignore corporate or business crime; there is no list of the ten most wanted corporations; the law affords no means of regularly collecting data on corporate crime; and much corporate criminal behavior (such as pollution) has not been made a crime of corporate opposition."

Ralph Nader, *America, Inc.*

7.9 Punctuating to Avoid Ambiguity

A writer will sometimes find that punctuation is needed to avoid ambiguity. If it is impossible to arrange a sentence to avoid ambiguity, punctuate so that the reader can grasp the meaning on first reading.

Use a comma to separate two identical words:

| Unclear | Whatever is is right. |
| Clear | Whatever is, is right. |

Use a comma to separate a sequence of two or more names or numbers:

Unclear	To Billy the Kid Pat Garrett was a sneak.
Clear	To Billy the Kid, Pat Garrett was a sneak.
Unclear	In 1968 1,959 authors attended our seminar.
Clear	In 1968, 1,959 authors attended our seminar

Use a comma to separate a sequence of two words that could be misread without punctuation:

Unclear	Ever since her anniversaries have been remembered.
Clear	Ever since, her anniversaries have been remembered.
Unclear	When racing thoroughbreds are protected by blinders.
Clear	When racing, thoroughbreds are protected by blinders.

7.10 Avoiding Overpunctuation

Often, beginning writers punctuate whenever they want to indicate a pause, as in speech. However, it is as inefficient to overpunctuate as to underpunctuate. While too little punctuation can cause ambiguity and misreading, too much punctuation results in a choppy presentation that distracts the reader from the content of the writing. The following conventions help writers avoid overpunctuating their work.

Do not separate a verb from its complement unless there are intervening words that require punctuation:

| Incorrect | The members agreed, that school busing was a dangerous innovation. |
| Correct | The members agreed, **after many long and heated discussions,** that school busing was a dangerous innovation. |

265

In the first example, there is no need to separate the verb *agreed* from its complement, introduced by *that*. However, in the revision the adverb phrase *after many long and heated discussions* intervenes and must be punctuated with commas.

Do not separate a modifier from a noun that directly follows it:

Incorrect	He was an untrustworthy, disloyal, unhelpful, Boy Scout who became a bespectacled, boyish, scoutmaster.
Correct	He was an untrustworthy, disloyal, unhelpful Boy Scout who became a bespectacled, boyish scoutmaster.

In the first example, punctuation should not separate the adjectives *unhelpful* and *boyish* from their nouns. Punctuation is used only to separate coordinating modifiers from one another. (See Section **7.5d.**)

Do not separate two words or phrases connected by a coordinating conjunction:

Incorrect	She was extremely honest, and courageous.
Correct	She was extremely honest and courageous.

Exercises

Correct the internal punctuation in the following sentences where necessary.

1. The best way to go on a diet, is to review your objectives carefully before beginning.

2. Too many ecology freaks are scaring us, by publishing doomsday predictions, about pesticides that they say will inevitably destroy our farmland.

3. The hidden truth about urban renewal, becomes obvious once you accept that fact that the projects, frequently, build new slums, to replace the old.

4. The same Mr. Goldberg, who was once U.S. ambassador to the UN, was also an associate justice of the Supreme Court.

5. Television advertisements directed toward young children sell the idea that material goods will make you healthy, wealthy, and wise, adults.

6. She is basically honest, and patient, but her mother, and her aunts have had a bad influence on her.

7.11   End Punctuation (end p)

Few writers hesitate when they capitalize the first word of a sentence. The convention is so habitual that they capitalize automatically. But the following conventions for end punctuation still cause some problems for many beginning writers.

7.11a   The Period (.)

Do not use a period to show the end of a sentence that is parenthetically included in another sentence:

> Varied and well-planned vegetarian diets are quite safe. And when one includes milk, cheese, and eggs (that is called a *lacto-ovo-vegetarian diet*), one runs very little risk of being poorly nourished. (Of course, vitamin B-12 supplements are easily available.)
>
> Maya Pines, "Meatless, Guiltless" *The New York Times Magazine*

Notice that the period is placed *inside* a final parenthesis used to enclose an independent sentence. When the parenthetical element occurs at the end of a sentence, the period is placed outside the final parenthesis:

> The new vegetarians include the Hare Krishna chanters, various yoga sects, and health-food addicts (not to mention hundreds of thousands of otherwise ordinary young adults).

7.11b   The Question Mark (?)

Do not use a question mark at the end of an indirect question.

> Incorrect   Mr. Clark asks his readers if our government can hope to meet its ideals and obligations by reacting to social unrest with anger and with force?
>
> Correct   Mr. Clark asks his readers if our government can hope to meet its ideals and obligations by reacting to social unrest with anger and with force.

Place a question mark inside quotation marks or parentheses only when the question is a part of the quoted or parenthetical expression:

> When Basil was introduced to the CIA agent (had they met somewhere before?), he turned to Glenda and demanded, "Why didn't you tell me our phone was bugged?"

7.11c (!)

The Exclamation Point (!)

A skilled writer will communicate strong emotion more effectively through the choice and arrangement of words and phrases than by an exclamation point. Instead of helping to emphasize a statement, the exclamation point causes the reader to focus on the mark itself. Check your own reactions when you suddenly learn the sentence you just finished reading was supposed to be expressing strong emotions. How could you have missed the excitement! It is right here on the printed page!

Exercises

Rewrite the following sentences, adding or correcting the appropriate end punctuation.

1. Will all the delegates please remain seated while the roll is being called?

2. The meeting will begin promptly tomorrow morning, without fail!

3. If family planning has worked in Japan, isn't it likely to be just as successful in India.

4. The Press Secretary exclaimed, "What on earth is that"

5. The reporter and the campaign manager (they were overheard by other passengers as they boarded the plane.) were complaining bitterly.

6. The manager maintained that it was unsafe to release the information (a totally erroneous idea)

7. Ellen Levy, a cub reporter, wondered why the other reporters claimed the campaign was running so smoothly?

8. One reason for the confusion was the limited time for preparation—only three days!

7.12 Quotations ("/")

The most common writing situations that require quotation marks are listed below. (See Section **6.7c** for conventions governing long quotations.)

7.12a Direct and Indirect Quotations

Use quotation marks to enclose direct quotations, the exact words someone has spoken or written:

"One curious consequence of the current boom in science," writes Martin Gardner, author of *Fads and Fallacies in the Name of Science*, "is the rise of the promotor of new and strange scientific theories. He is riding into prominence, so to speak, on the coat-tails of reputable investigators."

The critics have said Gardner's book is "an excellent study in human gullibility."

Do not use quotation marks for indirect quotations that tell in your own words what someone else has written or said:

Incorrect   Gardner explained that "most of his research was done in the New York Public Library, which has an extensive collection of crank literature."

Correct   Gardner explained that most of his research was done in the New York Public Library, which has an extensive collection of crank literature.

7.12b   Titles of Published Works

Use quotation marks to enclose the titles of songs and paintings; radio and television programs; newspaper and magazine articles; and poems, short stories, and other material that is part of a longer published work. (See Section 6.2 for titles that are italicized.):

"Mona Lisa" is the title of a country and western song as well as the name of a famous painting by the Italian artist Leonardo da Vinci.

One of my favorite chapters in *The Scarlet Letter* is Chapter 16, "A Forest Walk."

"The Easy Chair," a section of informal literary discussion and review, no longer appears in *Harper's*.

7.12c   Special Use of Words and Phrases

Use quotation marks around a word or phrase to indicate (1) an attitude of reserved judgment or disbelief on the part of the writer, or (2) the use of an informal expression in a formal discussion:

Some of the "best" students think nothing of exchanging course papers with their peers.

Our sample showed that a typical response to marijuana was an increased awareness of colors and a general euphoria—what a dope user would call being "stoned."

Professional writers, however, do not use quotation marks to apologize for a word. Instead, they make every effort to use words that fit their needs exactly:

7.12d Placement of Other Punctuation

Poor	Experienced writers know that the "quotation marks-around-an-inexact-word" technique is no substitute for using the correct word in the first place.
Improved	Experienced writers know that placing inexact words in quotation marks is no substitute for using the correct word in the first place.

7.12d Placement of Other Punctuation

Place a comma or a period inside quotation marks:

> "Marriage partners want many things," the psychiatrist explained. "But what they need is companionship and understanding."

Place a semicolon or a colon outside the quotation marks:

> The noted author claimed that he writes books for children because "they love interesting stories, not commentary or rationalization"; however, this can be said about most adult readers as well.

> The following discussion deals with the problem of "future shock": insufficient awareness of the rapidly changing present and inadequate preparation for the imminent future.

Place a dash, question mark, or exclamation point inside the quotation marks when this additional punctuation is part of the quoted material. Place the additional punctuation outside the quotation marks when it is part of the entire sentence:

> My husband began by saying, "Drive carefully—" but then changed his mind and said, "Why don't you let me drive this time?" What do you think he meant by "this time"?

7.12e Quoting Within a Quotation

Use single quotation marks ('/') to enclose a quotation within a quotation:

> According to Joseph and Lois Bird, the modern marriage is a paradox that "has been described in terms of the Biblical words 'that two shall become one.'"

7.12f Using Brackets in Quotations ([/])

Direct quotations should always be presented *exactly* as they appear in the original. (See Section **6.7c.**) Although writers may correct or comment if absolutely necessary to clear up an ambiguity, to provide missing information that the reader would need to understand the quotation, or to fit in the material grammatically, such additions should be placed in brackets. The quotation itself should always represent the source word for word.

Use brackets to enclose corrections or comments when they must be inserted into a quotation to prevent misunderstanding:

> The lawyer explained his position: "In the dual school system, which was struck down by *Brown* vs. *Topeka* [*Brown vs. Board of Education of Topeka, 1954*], the aim was clearly to segregate students by race."

> The diary continued: "Well, if Mr. L[loyd] won't leave, I'm sure Mother and I will find a way to convince him."

When quoting directly, the writer should avoid expressing his personal scorn or doubts by using exclamation points or question marks enclosed in parentheses. Such personal opinions should be written out and presented separately before or after the excerpt.

7.12g   Ellipses (. . .)

Use ellipses to indicate the omission of one or more words within a sentence of quoted material:

```
According to the translator:

    That the publication of One Day in the Life of
    Ivan Denisovich was an important event, no one in
    his right mind could possibly doubt. It was,
    after all, the first public treatment of a sub-
    ject which had been central in Soviet life for
    well over two decades . . . yet which had re-
    mained the great unmentionable.¹
    _____

    ¹Alexander Solzhenitsyn, One Day in the Life of Ivan
Denisovich, trans. Ralph Parker (New York: Fawcett,
1963), pp. xiii-xiv.
```

Do not use ellipses at the beginning or end of quoted material that is run into the text:

> Incorrect   According to the translator, the book was ". . . the first public treatment of a subject which had been central in Soviet life for well over two decades. . . ."

> Correct   According to the translator, the book was "the first public treatment of a subject which had been central in Soviet life for well over two decades."

Use ellipses preceded by a period to indicate an omission from (1) the end of a sentence within a quoted passage or (2) an omission of more than one complete sentence:

According to the translator:

It was, after all, the first public treatment of
a subject which had been central in Soviet life
for well over two decades. . . . In the last several years Soviet writers had come closer and
closer to the concentration camp question. . . .
But it was only with Solzhenitsyn's <u>One Day</u> that
there appeared in print concrete specific descriptions of actual life in a Soviet concentration camp under Stalin.[1]

---

[1]Alexander Solzhenitsyn, <u>One Day in the Life of Ivan
Denisovich</u>, trans. Ralph Parker (New York: Fawcett,
1963), pp. xiii–xiv.

Exercises

Correct the following passages or add quotation marks.

1. To analyze Edna St. Vincent Millay's poem Renaissance, it is necessary to know something of the woman and her background.

2. 'Mel would tease Sid incredibly,' says Larry Gilbart, who worked with Brooks on "Caesar's Hour" in the mid-1950s, as did such gag-writing luminaries as Woody Allen and Neil Simon. 'Mel would make fun of his clothes, his shoes, his jewelry. Sid loved it, because he knew he *owned* all that cleverness. He once grabbed Mel by the head and said, "This is *mine*!" And Mel grabbed Sid's wallet and said, "This is *mine*."

Paul D. Zimmerman, "The Mad, Mad Mel Brooks," *Newsweek*

3. An article on water pollution in the February 17, 1975, issue of *Newsweek* contains a statement by an unnamed senior official of the Environmental Protection Agency that says, in essence, that "the water we drink does not measure up to former standards."

4. No sooner was the guilty John Raymond behind bars than the real murderer confessed.

5. When I asked the stranger when the next train would arrive, he turned slowly, paused, and replied," . . . Not for another three hours, I'm afraid. . . ."

REVIEW EXERCISES

1. Explain what each punctuation mark tells the reader in the paragraphs below.

a. The elements of a fire are fuel, air, and heat. Fuel and air are intimately mixed almost everywhere in the environment, but a fire does not start unless a spark or friction ignites a fuel-oxidizer system. A fire spreads because the heat feeds into new fuel and raises it to the ignition point. To extinguish a fire one removes one of the elements: by cooling the hot fuel or by separating the fuel and the air.

Howard W. Emmons, "Fire and Fire Protection,"
Scientific American

b. If all else fails to prevent a fire, the best hope is to detect it soon after it starts. The detection devices now available operate by hot gas, by a high rate of rise in temperature, by a flicker of flame, by obscuration of light by smoke, or by the presence of smoke particles. None of these methods is entirely satisfactory. In almost every area of measurement man's instruments are superior to his senses, but not in fire detection. No practical detector now made can distinguish reliably between tobacco smoke, wood smoke, and smoke from an electrical appliance with anything like the acuity of the human nose. One can anticipate, however, that advances in solid-state electronics will eventually result in detectors that are sensitive, reliable, and inexpensive.

Howard W. Emmons, "Fire and Fire Protection,"
Scientific American

2. Rewrite each paragraph below, adding or correcting punctuation according to the conventions covered in this chapter.

a. To many couples marriage means little more than just living together. But others succeed in establishing a true union which involves sharing an entire life as well as a home. In the book *Marriage Is for Grownups* Joseph and Lois Bird analyze the problem areas common to most marriages and ask the question are you grown-up enough to handle it.

The authors who have years of experience in marriage counseling offer no instructions instead they encourage each partner to examine his or her own fears demands values and defenses in order to decide where the marriage relationship should go and how to reach that goal. As the Birds point out this is not a marriage cookbook providing pat answers that would one hopes apply to all but that never do.

Whether they discuss communication problems finances sex inlaws children or religion they do so on a realistic level. Notice how they approach the question of religion in We All Have Mixed Marriages the final chapter in their book.

b. Ever since Magellan sailed around the globe in 1519 few have doubted that the earth is round. Yet three eccentric theories of the earth's shape have each won a surprising number of converts in the present century Voliva's flat-earth view the hollow-earth doctrine of John Cleves Symmes a retired Captain in the U.S. Infantry and most incredible of all the theory that we are living on the inside of a hollow sphere.

c. Wilbur Glenn Voliva a paunchy baldish grim-faced fellow who offered $5,000 to anyone who could prove to him that the earth was spherical made several trips around the world lecturing on the subject. In his mind of course he had not circumnavigated the globe he had merely traced a circle on a surface he described as being flat as a pancake. Here is what Voliva has to say about the earth and the sun the idea of a sun millions of miles in diameter and 91 million miles away is silly. The sun is only thirty-two miles across and not more than 3,000 miles from the earth. It stands to reason it must be so God made the sun to light the earth and therefore must have placed it close to the task it was designed to do.

d. Captain Symmes first announced his hollow-earth theory by distributing a circular asking one hundred men he called brave companions to join him on an expedition to the opening at the North Pole which he believed to be over a thousand miles wide. The more Symmes's Hole as it soon became known was ridiculed the angrier he became and the more energy he spent finding supposed facts to support his views. The most complete descriptions of these views which are quite remarkable are to be found in two books one published in 1826 by James McBride the Captain's number-one convert gives hundreds of reasons for believing the earth to be hollow. The reasons are drawn from physics astronomy climatology the migration of animals and the reports of travelers. Symmes's son Americus argues in the other book which was published in 1878 reason common sense and all the analogies in the natural universe conspire to support and establish the theory.

e. However Symmes's beliefs made no dent whatever on the science of his day but they did leave a strong mark on science fiction. Edgar Allan Poe's novel entitled *Narrative of Arthur Gordon Pym* was intended to describe a voyage similar to the one Symmes was unable to make. If the Symmes theory produced good science fiction think about the effect of an even more preposterous view that was formulated in 1970 by another American Cyrus Reed Teed. For thirty-eight years with unflagging energy Teed lectured and wrote in defense of the theory that the earth was hollow *and* that we were all living on the inside.

8

Grammar

> Although grammar can be an interesting subject in itself, the writer's main concern is with its practical applications—the ability to meet the readers' expectations about the rules of conventional grammar required in the written language. A knowledge of grammatical terms and conventions and an ability to discuss them can simplify this task.

THE NATURE OF GRAMMAR

Every language has a *grammar*—the conventional patterns of changing the form of words and arranging them to accomplish different intentions:

They heard cries of **"Help!"**
They **helped** each other.
The **helpings** are always generous.
Competent hired **help** is difficult to find.

By five years of age, children usually know most of the basic sounds and patterns of their language and use them proficiently in speech, although it is not uncommon to hear a child exclaim, "I can run *more better* than my sister can" or "*I holded* Mommy's hand when I crossed the street." Usually, accepted word order seems to be established in the child's mind before such matters as comparative forms or verb tenses, which require more sophistication.

The grammar of speech in one's native tongue is, generally, not taught formally, as reading is, but is acquired by living with the language and using it to adapt to the social environment. *Formal grammar,* on the other hand, must be studied to be learned. Formal grammar refers to the systems that describe how the language works. Before studying formal grammar, a native speaker of the language is already knowledgeable about grammatical matters. When he has mastered certain principles of formal grammar, he becomes aware of the *reasons* for the habitual choices he makes from among the various speech patterns. In essence, he becomes conscious of his language as language.

276 Formal grammar has two sides: *descriptive grammar* and *prescrip-*

tive grammar. *Descriptive grammar* is to language as physics is to nature; in each case a method is used to describe and communicate how something that already exists happens to work. In nature, photosynthesis is a process described by the formula: water + carbon dioxide $\xrightarrow{\text{sunlight}}$ oxygen + organic compounds. The formula does not make the process; it merely communicates what happens in the process. In English, "ain't" and "isn't" are contractions, each composed of an inflection of the verb "to be" with the negative "not." Again, this knowledge of the language pattern does not make the pattern but describes it. Descriptive grammar does not assign values to the patterns of language. It does not say one form is good grammar and the other poor. Although "ain't" may be called a variant form, it is not rejected as nonstandard or illiterate. It is noted as a form people do use.

Prescriptive grammar concerns itself less with how the language actually is used than with how it *should* be used. Prescriptive grammar sets standards and establishes values. "Do not use a singular subject with a plural verb" and "Never split an infinitive" are typical of the standards set by prescriptive grammar. And, according to prescriptive grammar, "ain't" is simply unacceptable.

One of the most influential early grammar texts spells out the idea of proper English grammar quite clearly:

> The Principal design of a Grammar of a Language is to teach us to express ourselves with propriety in that Language; and to enable us to judge of every phrase and form of construction, whether it is right or not.
>
> Robert Lowth, *A Short Introduction to English Grammar*

As this statement illustrates, conventions of capitalization and sentence construction have changed over the years. So, too, have ideas about the nature and seriousness of correct and incorrect grammar. Although the tendency still exists to evaluate a person's education, knowledge, class, and even morality on his use of grammar, such judgments do not have the power and significance they once had, when to say "they was" was nearly a sin.

The suggestion that prescriptive grammar has lost some of its foothold must be qualified: Although the loosening of the "rules" in speaking has been rather rapid, the guidelines in writing have not changed nearly so quickly. Several reasons account for this situation. In the first place, readers are accustomed to written material being more grammatically correct than the spoken word and are therefore less tolerant of deviations from conventional practices.

Second, writing itself is a more formal activity than speaking because writing has permanence. And since writers are able to revise their work, they are expected to produce polished results. Finally, and most important, grammatical oversights barely apparent in speech can be truly confusing in writing. In terms of the writer's purpose—to inform, persuade, and please—it is to his advantage to master certain conventions of prescriptive grammar. The ability to follow such conventions increases the writer's chances of meeting the reader's expectations.

This chapter provides a review of grammatical terminology (where descriptive grammar applies) and a glossary of high-frequency grammatical errors (where conventions of prescriptive grammar apply).

USING GRAMMATICAL TERMS

We said earlier that descriptive grammar has the practical use of enabling those who know the description to communicate efficiently about their writing. Consider this situation:

Writer: What's wrong with my style?

Editor: Every sentence starts with an article. The constructions tend to be passive and your sentence subjects are always imprecise.

If the writer had no knowledge of the system for discussing grammar, the editor would have to respond differently:

Editor: Everything between the beginning capital letter and the period starts with *a, an,* or *the.* You always write "it was done to him," or "the constitution was written by," or "there are many people who read," or. . . .

When we know the system, we can discuss the principles more precisely.

8.1 A Review of the Parts of Speech

Traditionally, we recognize eight parts of speech: *nouns, pronouns, adjectives, verbs, adverbs, prepositions, conjunctions,* and *interjections.* The parts of speech are word classes—the basic categories into which words can be divided and arranged for study. Terms like *noun* and *pronoun* identify large numbers of words that share distinctive characteristics. Each part of speech is based on (1) grammatical function, (2) grammatical form, and (3) meaning. For example, classifying a word as a noun means that it has a certain function—as the subject of a sentence, for instance; a certain form—such as a plural *s* ending; and a certain meaning—that is, the name of a person, place, or thing:

> The plants died from lack of rain.

In this sentence, *plants* is a noun. It functions as the subject of the sentence; its form is plural; and it names a particular thing.

Nouns

A *noun* is a word that names a person, place, or thing. It most often functions in the sentence as the subject or as an object of a verb or preposition. Nouns are subdivided into two major classes: *proper nouns* and *common nouns.* Proper nouns are capitalized and name specific persons (*William*), places (*Detroit*), or things (*General Motors*). Common nouns name general classes of people (*boys*), places (*cities*), or things (*companies*). (See Section **8.2b** for how nouns change their form.)

Pronouns

A *pronoun* is a word that takes the place of a noun and therefore can perform the same functions. In written English, *it,* for example, has only the meaning it acquires from its reference to another word or words, called its *antecedent:*

> **Senior citizens** are frequently made to feel **they** have no purpose in **it.**

In this sentence *they* clearly refers to the antecedent *senior citizens,* but we cannot possibly understand what *it* refers to without some previous reference:

> **Society** often makes senior citizens feel they have no use in **it.**

There are eight classes of pronouns, and each pronoun is placed in one or more categories depending on its function.

1. *Personal pronouns* refer to particular people, objects, qualities, and so on (*I, me; you; he, him; she, her; it; we, us; they, them*):

> **She** has never been one of my close friends.
> **We** decided to play tennis instead of golf.

279

2. *Relative pronouns* relate one group of words to another (*who, whose, whom, which, that, what, whoever, whichever,* and a few others):

> People **who** take themselves too seriously often end up making fools of themselves.
>
> The Super Bowl is the game **that** ultimately decides the national football championship.

3. *Interrogative pronouns* are used to ask questions (*who, which,* and *what*):

> **Who** is the king of rock?
>
> **What** is the best book you have read this year?

4. *Demonstrative pronouns* point out (*this, that, these, those,* and others):

> **That** is an absurd suggestion.
>
> **This** was one of your better days.

5. *Indefinite pronouns* act like nouns and require no antecedent (*all, both, it, each, anybody, anything,* and others):

> **Anything** you want to do will be fine with me.
>
> **Anyone** can ride a bicycle.
>
> **It** is raining.

6. *Reciprocal pronouns* express mutual relationships (*each other, one another*):

> A marriage can hardly be called successful if the two people constantly hurt **each other.**
>
> An unwillingness to share often interferes with young children's ability to play with **one another.**

7. *Intensive pronouns* add emphasis to the word they refer to (*myself, yourself, herself, themselves,* and others):

> All Shakespeare's plays were written by Shakespeare **himself.**
>
> I **myself** copied down the license number of the hit-and-run truck.

8. *Reflexive pronouns* have the same meaning as the subject and are used when the action of the subject passes back to it (*himself, ourselves,* and others):

> The fender did not dent **itself.**
>
> What is freedom is a matter we decide for **ourselves.**

Note that the form of a pronoun can change because of the reference it makes and the relationship it has to other words in the sentence. (See Section **8.2c.**)

Adjectives

An *adjective* is a word that describes or modifies a noun or pronoun. Adjectives are classified according to three degrees: positive, comparative, and superlative:

Positive	Chris is a **good** tennis player.
Comparative	Chris is a **better** tennis player than Sue.
Superlative	Chris is the **best** tennis player on the team.
Positive	tall, beautiful, good
Comparative	taller, more beautiful, better
Superlative	tallest, most beautiful, best

(To see how adjectives are changed to form the comparative and superlative, consult Section **8.4**.)

Verbs

A *verb* expresses an action, a condition, or a state of being. It is the major element of the *predicate* of a sentence—the part of the sentence that makes an assertion about the subject:

Action	In some states the price of gas **increased** by 50 percent.
Condition	Hester Prynne **suffered** under Puritan restrictions.
State of Being	I **am waiting** to see the results of my driving test.

Depending upon the changes the verb undergoes for different contexts, it can be classified as regular or irregular.

(For a discussion of changes in verb forms, see Section **8.3**.)

Adverbs

An *adverb* is a word that modifies a verb, an adjective, or another adverb. Adverbs are frequently divided into four major groups:

1. adverbs of place (He strolled **outside**)
2. adverbs of time (She left **early**)
3. adverbs of manner (She spoke **slowly**)
4. adverbs of frequency (The club meets **regularly**)

A subclass of adverbs, sometimes called *adverbs of degree,* is composed of words such as *even, extremely, just, more, much, only, quite, surely, too,* and *very.* (See Section **8.4** for a discussion of the changes in adverb forms.)

Prepositions

A preposition is a word that shows the relationship between a noun or pronoun (called the *object of the preposition*) and some other word in the sentence. Common prepositions are *after, at, before, by, for, from, in, of, on, to,* and *with:*

Writers look **to** their editors for guidance.

She placed the letter **on** the table.

Jim and Louise traveled **from** New York **to** London.

Conjunctions

A *conjunction* is a word that connects words, phrases, or clauses. Conjunctions are divided into three subclasses:

Coordinating Conjunctions	*Subordinating Conjunctions*	*Correlative Conjunctions*
and	after	either. . . or
but	although	neither . . . nor
for	as	both . . . and
or	because	not only . . . but also
nor	before	
	how	
	if	
	since	
	while	
	when	
	whether	
	why	

Coordinating conjunctions connect items of equal grammatical value:

The ballerina **and** her partner received thunderous applause.

In this sentence the nouns *ballerina* and *partner* are functioning together as the subject.

Some dieters are easily tempted, **but** others are not.

Here the conjunction *but* joins two independent clauses.
Subordinating conjunctions join subordinate clauses and main clauses:

Most students found the exam extremely difficult, **although** they had studied diligently.

If you make reservations sixty days in advance, you receive a $100 discount on your airfare.

In both examples the subordinating conjunction introduces the subordinate clause.

282

Correlative conjunctions operate in pairs and join elements of equal grammatical value:

> The customer decided to buy **either** the 1974 Dodge **or** the 1974 Plymouth.
>
> **Both** Linda **and** Peter are qualified doctors.

A fourth group of conjunctions, called *adverbial conjunctions* or *conjunctive adverbs,* function primarily to connect main clauses or complete sentences. Included in this class are *consequently, therefore, furthermore, however, likewise, moreover, nevertheless, thus:*

> One year my father waited until April 20 to file his tax return: **consequently,** he had to pay a penalty for lateness. **However,** because he learns from his mistakes, my father has never filed a late tax return again.

Interjections

Interjections—such as *oh, well,* and *yes*—are words that express strong feelings or emotion and may be inserted in a sentence without being grammatically connected to the other sentence elements:

> With food shortage a growing concern to people worldwide, we may be forced to tap other resources; and, **yes,** we all may be eating synthetic hamburger one day soon.

The ways in which we establish the traditional parts of speech leave many questions about the language structure unanswered. It is not always clear how words are actually assigned to the proper class. Words like *handshake, perseverance,* and *cattle* are easily recognized as nouns. Yet the meaning of *handshake* seems to refer to an action rather than to a thing. The meaning of *perseverance* is slightly clearer: it refers to an abstract quality or concept. But *perseverance* does not have a plural form, one of the basic requirements for nouns. *Cattle,* on the other hand, does not have a singular form. Many words appear to be nouns by some criteria, but not by all. Nevertheless, the traditional methods of classification, as illustrated in the labels attached to words in their dictionary definitions, do serve adequately when discussing the types of writing problems that may arise when one is using them. The important point is to have a clear sense of which words belong in which category—whether or not the criteria can be explained in terms of a formula.

Some words seem to be different parts of speech in different contexts. *Run,* for example, is a noun in the sentence "He hit a home *run.*" But *run* is also a verb: "She can *run* like a deer." The *-ing* form of this verb can also be a noun in some circumstances: "*Running*

283

is good exercise." In other circumstances the -*ing* form is an adjective: "He gave a *running* account of the retreat."

Other word endings are used regularly to change the part of speech to which a word belongs, or, to put it another way, to change the function of the word. A word like *care,* for example, functions either as a noun ("*Care* is the watchword of the wise") or as a verb ("I *care* whether she is happy or sad"). Adding such endings as -*ful* or -*less* will change the noun to an adjective: "She is a *careful* worker"; "He is a *careless* driver." The -*ly* ending creates an adverb: "She *carefully* proofread her work"; "He parked the car *carelessly.*" Adding -*ness* will create a noun: "Her greatest asset is *carefulness*"; "His *carelessness* has caused several accidents." With few exceptions, our sense of how word endings change the parts of speech is sufficiently developed at an early age to allow us to make such changes and to recognize them without formal study. Ultimately, what is important to the writer is not what "dictionary" class a word belongs to but how it is being used in a sentence.

Exercises

1. Complete each sentence below by filling in the blank with an appropriate word or expression. Name the part of speech of the words or expressions you add.

> Example   A *conjunction* is a word that joins words, phrases, or clauses. (noun)

> **a.** Nouns are _____ into two major classes: proper nouns and common nouns.

> **b.** A pronoun is a word that takes the place _____ a noun.

> **c.** Adjectives are words that modify a noun _____ a pronoun.

> **d.** Some adjectives use the words *more* and *most* to show their _____ and superlative degrees.

> **e.** Interjections such as *oh, well,* and *ouch* are _____ difficult to define.

2. Without checking the dictionary, list all the parts of speech that each of the following words might fall into and use each in a sentence.

> brave   elastic   interest
> watch   jet   brew
> set   hit   before

284   3. For each group of sentences below, change the italicized word from the first sentence so that it is in the appropriate form for each of the following sentences. List the part of speech of the words you supply.

Example   Although the Americans and British both speak English, their *idioms* differ.

Idiomatic expressions are not meant to be taken literally. (adjective)

a. They are learning how to *grow* avocadoes.
The _____ rate of the world's population increased dramatically.
Our avocadoes are _____ nicely.

b. *Photography* is an important art form of the twentieth century.
The _____ at the current Associated Press Exhibition are some of the finest I have seen.
A skilled _____ is as much of an artist as a portrait painter.

c. Their *final* exams begin next week.
The exams were _____ corrected and graded.
The winners will meet in the semi-_____ .

d. She inherited a small *fortune* at the age of twenty-one.
She is more generous now to the less _____ .
_____ , she can afford to be generous.

e. *Health* foods are becoming more popular every day.
I hope to be _____ , wealthy, and wise.
The doctor tried to restore the patient's _____ by prescribing huge doses of vitamins.

f. She took off her coat and started to *warm* her hands at the fire.
Dress _____ when you leave the house.
The fire gave a cheerful light and a much-needed _____ .
The weather report said that it will be fair and _____ .
There are varying degrees of coolness and _____ throughout New England.

DEFINITION OF INFLECTION

We have been referring to and illustrating the ways some parts of speech—nouns, pronouns, verbs, and adjectives—change their form for different functions and meanings within the sentence. This process is called *inflection.*

To inflect literally means "to bend or curve," and it is important to language because it enables the writer or speaker to indicate to an audience his relationship to an object, time of action, degree of

285

modification, and so on. For example, *"raining"* and *"rained"* give information valuable for planning a picnic. And there is certainly a difference between being *"good"* and being *"better."*

Although inflection is not the only tool in the English language for indicating relationships (others will be illustrated later), it is one of the most fundamental. Following is a brief discussion of various terms that are important for understanding the implications of inflection in English.

Case

Case refers to the inflectional forms given to a noun or pronoun in order to indicate its grammatical relationship to other words. There are three cases in English: *subjective* (or nominative), *possessive* (or genitive), and *objective* (or accusative):

> I [subjective] gave **my** [possessive] lawyer all the records, and **she** [subjective] used **them** [objective] effectively to win the case.

In this sentence *I* is the subject of its clause; *my* shows possession of *lawyer; she* is the subject of the second independent clause; and *them* is the object of the verb *used.*

With changes in language over the centuries, English has lost most of the inflections that show case. The difference between nouns used as subjects and those used as objects is shown today by word order, not by inflectional endings. However, the personal pronouns and the relative pronoun *who* show all three cases, even though two pronouns, *you* and *it,* do not distinguish between subjective and objective case. (See the discussion of inflection of pronouns, Section 8.2c.)

Mood

The term *mood* refers to distinctions in the form of a verb that show the writer's attitude toward the actions represented by that verb. There are three categories of mood: *indicative* (a statement or question), *imperative* (a command, request, or direction), and *subjunctive* (conditions contrary to fact; suppositions, recommendations, wishes, demands, and resolutions):

> Indicative   The personnel director asked, "When did you **join** the Army?"
>
> My cousin **joined** the Army in 1970.

Imperative	The first time I drove alone, all I could remember from my instructor was the warning "**Be** careful."
	As a child, I was always told, "Please **keep** your elbows off the table during meals."
	To use the photocopy machine, **turn** the switch to "on," **place** the page to be copied in the proper position, and **press** button A.
Subjunctive	The lawyer recommended that I **plead** guilty.
	Before paying the bill, Jane demanded that the store **itemize** her purchases.
	If I **were** married, I would insist on sharing the household duties with my spouse.
	I wish my grades **were** better.

Of the three moods the indicative is the one used most frequently. The subjunctive has largely disappeared from English and is used primarily in formal writing situations. (See Section **8.3** on inflection of verbs.)

Number

Number is a term that refers to the grammatical distinction between the singular and plural forms of nouns, pronouns, verbs, and demonstrative adjectives (*this, that, these, those*):

Singular	The old **woman** always **wears** black and **attends** every **funeral** in our **church,** whether or not she **knows** the deceased. **This** practice **is** called official mourning.
Plural	**People** who **attend funerals** of **persons they** do not **know are** called official **mourners. These people** often **wear** black daily.

All nouns and pronouns, except the relative and interrogative pronouns (*who, which, that*), have forms that distinguish the singular from the plural number. However, most verbs change form to show number only in the present tense, third person. (See the discussion of person below and Section **8.3** on inflection of verbs.)

Person

Person refers to the grammatical distinctions between speaker (first person), person spoken to (second person), and person spoken about (third person). The inflectional system for showing person is limited to personal pronouns and verbs:

First Person	**I am** about to begin college.
	We know college will offer new and challenging experiences.
Second Person	**You are** about to begin college.
	You know college will offer new and challenging experiences.
Third Person	**He is** about to begin college.
	They know college will offer new and challenging experiences.

(See Section **8.2** on inflection of nouns and pronouns and Section **8.3** on inflection of verbs.)

Tense

Tense refers to those distinctions in verb form that place the actions expressed by the verb in a certain period of time. There are six tenses in English—present, past, future, present perfect, past perfect, and future perfect. They are formed by inflection and by the addition of helping verbs, called *auxiliaries.* The following are some of the various tenses of the verb "to sing":

Past Tense	Enrico Caruso **sang** until the day he died.
Present Tense, First Person	I **am singing** this song especially for you.
Present Tense, Third Person	He **sings** too loudly.
Future Perfect Tense	Beverly Sills **will have sung** that opera fifty times after tomorrow's performance.

(For a full discussion of the various tenses see Section **8.3a**.)

Voice

Voice refers to distinctions in verb form that show whether the subject acts (active voice) or is acted upon (passive voice):

Active	Jonathan **informed** the senator.
Passive	The senator **was informed** [by Jonathan].
Active	She **gave me** the correct answers.
Passive	The correct answers **were given** to me.

288   (See Sections **4.8** and **8.3c**.)

INFLECTION AND ENGLISH USAGE

The English language has lost most of its inflections. Whereas in Old English almost every word was inflected to show its grammatical function in a sentence, only five major inflections are left in modern English:

1. The addition of *-s* to nouns to form plurals and possessives
2. The addition of *-s* to verbs to form the present tense, third person, singular number
3. The addition of *-ing* to verbs to form the present participle
4. The addition of *-d* or *-ed* to verbs to form the past tense
5. The addition of *-er* and *-est* to adjectives to form the comparative and superlative forms

There are other inflections, of course. Some nouns form their plurals with an ending other than *-s* (*child/children; man/men; die/dice*), and some verbs form their past tense by some means other than adding *-d* or *-ed* (*go/went; know/knew; run/ran*). But the five inflections listed above are the only "living" inflections—that is, the ones used when new words enter the language.

One important consequence of the long process of simplifying inflections is that writers now increasingly rely on word order to show the way a word is used in a sentence. Rather than changing the form of the word, modern English changes the order in which the words are arranged. For example, since nouns have no special endings to show case, the position of a noun before or after the verb in a sentence indicates whether it is functioning as a subject or an object:

Unemployment [subject] creates **recession** [object].
Recession [subject] creates **unemployment** [object].

Possession can be indicated not only by a possessive inflection but also by the preceding preposition *of:*

The origin **of** the war has never been fully understood.

Unfortunately, the process of inflection loss has not been systematic, and some of our inflectional system is potentially confusing. Notice, for example, the multiple uses we make of the inflectional ending *-s*. We use the same letter ending to indicate the plural of nouns (*kings*); the possessive singular and plural of nouns (*king's, kings'*); and the third person present singular of verbs (*He wears the*

289

crown). Originally, different forms were used for these functions. The areas of inflectional change in which the forms are irregular or in which similar endings are used for different signals are precisely those areas in which the majority of difficulties in conventional usage occur.

The following sections illustrate in detail the inflection of various parts of speech.

8.2   Inflection of Nouns and Pronouns

The inflection of nouns and pronouns, called *declension*, is used to indicate variations in (1) number, (2) case, and (3) person. Pronouns are inflected to indicate each of these three forms, whereas nouns are inflected to show only number and case.

8.2a   Number

Most nouns change their singular form to plural by adding -*s* —although, of course, there are a number of words borrowed from other languages (*alumnus/alumni; phenomenon/phenomena*) that do not do so. Other exceptions are illustrated by such words as *tooth/teeth, mouse/mice,* and *sheep/sheep*. When in doubt about plural forms, consult the dictionary.

(For inflections of pronouns to show number, see Section **8.2c**.)

8.2b   Case (ca)

Nouns are inflected to indicate the possessive case by the use of *'s*. Carelessness can result in the confusion between the *plural number* of nouns and their *possessive case*. The following inflections of the common nouns *student* and *child* illustrate this point:

Singular	student, child
Singular Possessive	student's, child's
Plural	students, children
Plural Possessive	students', children's

(For inflections of pronoun case, see Section **8.2c**.)

8.2c   Person

Although nouns are not inflected to show variations in person, pronouns are. The following table shows the inflection of personal pronouns in number, case, and person:

SINGULAR

	Subjective	Possessive	Objective
First Person	I	my, mine	me
Second Person	you	your, yours	you
Third Person	he, she, it	his, her hers, its	him, her, it

PLURAL

	Subjective	Possessive	Objective
First Person	we	our, ours	us
Second Person	you	your, yours	you
Third Person	they	their, theirs	them

The relative pronoun *who* is not inflected to show number, but it is inflected to indicate case:

Subjective	Possessive	Objective
who	whose	whom

8.3 Inflection of Verbs

The inflection of verbs, called *conjugation,* is used to show changes in tense, person, number, mood, and voice.

To discuss verbs, it is useful to know that their *principal parts* are the primary inflected forms from which all other variations are derived. The English language traditionally recognizes four principal parts: present infinitive, past, past participle, and present participle. These inflected forms are used singly and with other words to change the nature of the verb in the various ways noted above. The following list shows the principal parts of the common verbs *play* and *throw:*

Present Infinitive	play, throw
Past	played, threw
Past Participle	played, thrown
Present Participle	playing, throwing

Play forms its past and past participle by the addition of *-ed.* Such verbs (including those that add just *-d*) are called "regular," or "weak," verbs. *Throw,* inflected by a vowel change, is called an "irregular," or a "strong," verb. The present participle of all verbs is formed by adding *-ing* to the present infinitive. Principal parts of all verbs are given in the dictionary. Even commonly used verbs sometimes need to be looked up.

291

8.3a (t)

8.3a   Tense and Mood (t)

The six English tense forms can be defined as follows:

Present tense expresses a present or habitual action and utilizes the present infinitive form of the verb:

> They **play** ball every day.
>
> He **is throwing** the ball hard.

Note that the second sentence illustrates the common *progressive* form of the present tense of the verb *to throw,* which is formed by joining the present participle *throwing* with an auxiliary, *is,* indicating present time.

Past tense expresses an action completed in the past and utilizes the past form of the verb:

> They **played** ball yesterday.
>
> He **threw** the ball hard.

Future tense expresses an action to come and utilizes the present form of the verb with the auxiliary *shall* or *will:*

> I **shall play** ball tomorrow.
>
> He **will throw** the ball hard.

Present perfect tense expresses an action begun in the past but finished or being continued in the present. It utilizes the past participle of the verb and a present form of *have:*

> They **have played** ball every day this week.
>
> He **has thrown** the ball hard consistently all week.

Past perfect tense expresses an action completed before some other action. It utilizes the past participle of the verb and the past tense of *have:*

> Even before the backstop was installed they **had played** ball on that field.
>
> He **had** not **thrown** anything but strikes until he walked the fourth batter.

Future perfect tense expresses an action that will be completed before a future time. It utilizes the past participle of the verb, *shall* or *will,* and *have:*

> By Sunday, I **shall have played** ball on that field for exactly two years.
>
> He **will have thrown** five innings of hitless ball if the next man makes an out.

The subjunctive *mood* shows distinctive forms only in the present tense of *be* (If I *be;* if you *be;* if he, she, it *be;* if we *be;* if you *be;* if they *be*); in the past tense, first and third person singular of *be* (If I *were;* if he *were*); and in the third person singular of all verbs (I demand that he *tell* everything he knows).

8.3b Person and Number

All verbs, except *be,* are inflected to show person and number only in the present tense, third person, by adding -*s:*

Singular	I play; you play; he, she, it plays
Plural	We play, you play, they play

Conjugation of the verb *be* in the present and past tenses is as follows:

Singular	I am; you are; he, she, it is
Plural	We are, you are, they are
Singular	I was; you were; he, she, it was
Plural	We were, you were, they were

Auxiliaries such as *can, could, will,* and *would* are not inflected.

8.3c Voice

Depending upon certain inflections, a verb is said to be in the *active* or *passive* voice. The passive inflection of a verb is shown by a form of the verb *be* followed by its past participle:

Active	The spider **spins** an enormous web.
Passive	An enormous web **is spun** by the spider.

The passive voice can be formed only with verbs that can take objects in the active voice. In the sentences above, the object of *spin* (*web*) becomes the subject in the conversion to passive voice.

8.4 Inflection of Adjectives and Adverbs (ad)

The inflection of adjectives and adverbs is called *comparison* and shows different degrees of quality or quantity through the positive, comparative, and superlative forms.

8.4a Positive

The *positive* expresses a basic quality or quantity:

Adjective	Many people believe that Ann Landers offers **wise** advice.
Adverb	They feel she advises them **wisely**.

293

8.4b Comparative

8.4b Comparative

The *comparative* expresses a greater degree than the positive form, or it makes a comparison between two persons, places, or things. Comparative adjectives are formed by adding -*er* to the positive form or by placing *more* before adjectives of three or more syllables. Comparative adverbs are usually formed by placing *more* before them but sometimes by adding -*er* to the positive form:

Adjective	When calamity strikes, Jane is always **calmer** than I.
Adjective	I became **more hysterical** than she.
Adverb	When our car was hit by a truck last year, she was able to speak **more calmly** to the police than I was.
Adverb	When our car was hit by a truck last year, I shouted **louder** at the driver than she did.

8.4c Superlative

The *superlative* shows the greatest degree of quality or quantity or compares three or more persons, places, or things. It is formed by adding -*est* to the positive form or by placing *most* before it:

Adjective	The one we thought was so quiet was the **loudest** fan at the game.
Adjective	Of all the ballerinas, the one in blue tights was the **most beautiful.**
Adverb	Of all the fans at the game, the one sitting next to me yelled the **loudest.**
Adverb	Of all the ballerinas, the one in blue tights danced the **most beautifully.**

Some comparisons are irregular:

Positive	good, bad, little, much
Comparative	better, worse, less, more
Superlative	best, worst, least, most

Exercises

In the following sentences, indicate the appropriate inflection of the word in parentheses. Name its part of speech and describe the nature of the inflection.

Example When we (return) to our old address on Weaver Street, all we found was a vacant lot. [*returned,* verb, past tense]

1. The salesperson told me the long-sleeved red sweater (be) on sale next week.

2. The chairperson of the committee does (many) of the work.

3. She was bruised yesterday while (try) to squeeze through the closing subway door.

4. By the time the rush begins, we (leave) the concert hall.

5. She learned French (quickly) than I.

6. My sister vowed not to have (many) than two children.

7. People would read more if television (invent).

8. Alice swims (good) than I.

9. By next spring, we (own) our house for one year.

10. Jack's Diner serves the (good) chili I have ever eaten.

THE GRAMMAR OF THE SENTENCE

From a functional point of view, writing sentences involves putting down on paper a group of words designed to express a complete thought. We accomplish this purpose by choosing, arranging, and inflecting words so that the reader will accept them as a complete thought. Given a particular situation, we usually know which arrangement of words fulfills our expectations and which does not. Consider, for example, the following sentences:

1. Not long ago the largest family sedans were about the size of today's so-called intermediates or mid-sized cars.

2. Colorless green station wagons sleep furiously.

3. It was raining.

4. Wise consumer shop careful for credit.

5. The federal government has set minimum standards for the safety of water supplied by local water systems.

Few readers would have difficulty accepting sentences 1, 3, and 5 as complete thoughts. However, sentences 2 and 4 are clearly in need of revision to make them meaningful. Readers and writers alike have developed a kind of grammatical sense—an intuitive knowledge of English grammar—that enables them to distinguish those classes of words that can appear together from those that cannot.

Sentences that fit traditional expectations of grammar usually are those consisting of a *subject* (typically a noun, a noun phrase, or a pronoun) followed by a *predicate* (a verb or verb phrase and its object or modifier):

295

Subject	Interest rates
Predicate	have gone up.
Subject	Many savings institutions
Predicate	specialize in loans backed by savings accounts.
Subject	The interest assessed on your unpaid balance each month
Predicate	becomes part of the balance against which interest is charged each month.

Saying that a sentence has a subject and a predicate, however, is hardly the end of the matter, because subjects and predicates may themselves be composed of many smaller constructions. No matter how complex they become, English sentences tend to follow the subject–predicate order and tend to be understood as combinations of complete subjects and predicates.

To sum up, readers expect to read sentences in which the writer has:

1. included the necessary elements—a complete subject and a complete predicate
2. placed the elements in a conventional grammatical order
3. used the appropriate inflectional forms of all the words
4. used words and constructions that produce a statement, question, command, or exclamation that is understandable.

From the writer's point of view, the key to effective sentence making and revision is to keep in mind the basic structure of each sentence and a clear sense of its meaning.

Exercises

1. In each sentence of the following paragraph, underline the complete subject once and the complete predicate twice.

Example   The convenience of credit cards ultimately places consumers in an economic bind.

Consumer credit has been an American way of life since Colonial times, when farmers borrowed against their crops and bought most of their furniture on the installment plan. Credit cards, "no-bounce" checking accounts, and sophisticated methods of computing interest have altered credit techniques a bit, but the basic theory has remained the same over the centuries: Lenders rent money to those who need it. Money is thus a commodity, and someone who borrows, or rents, money pays for the privilege. The interest rate is the rental price of money. A prospective borrower must always remember that lenders are in the business of credit, not in the business of doing favors. If lenders offer easy repayment terms, they are not doing it just to be nice; they are doing it to increase their sales volume. Easy credit terms have swelled the amount of consumer credit. By the end of 1974, Americans owed more than $188-billion (excluding mortgages) and were using about 16 percent of their take-home pay for that debt.

"How to Shop for Credit," *Consumer Reports*

2. In each sentence of the following paragraph, cross out every word not necessary to form a complete sentence. Check yourself by reading the remaining words aloud or by writing them on a separate piece of paper and supplying the appropriate punctuation. Each combination of subject and predicate that remains should sound or look like a complete sentence. The first sentence has been done for you.

~~Closed-end~~ credit, ~~which includes installment loans~~, is ~~commonly~~ used to finance ~~such items as~~ cars or appliances. In a closed-end loan, a specific amount is borrowed and repaid over a specific time period, usually in equal monthly installments. Open-end credit, which includes department-store charge accounts and bank credit cards, is more flexible. Generally, the monthly repayments required are lower than with installment loans; and consumers can, within certain limits, elect how much of their bills they wish to pay at any one time. The first step in shopping for credit is to compare the interest rates charged by different institutions. The Truth-in-Lending Act, passed in 1968, requires lenders to quote the cost of credit in terms of the annual percentage rate. This is the effective rate a person pays for credit; it includes the basic finance charge as well as any additional fees, such as credit-investigation fees, service charges, or mandatory insurance premiums. Studies made last year by various public interest research groups have found that some institutions were still quoting "add-on" or "discount" rates instead of annual percentage rates. These rates are ones used internally by banks and are approximately half the equivalent annual percentage rate. The Truth-in-Lending Act prohibits creditors from quoting these misleading low rates to the public.

"How to Shop for Credit," *Consumer Reports*

GLOSSARY OF GRAMMATICAL TERMS

Grammar is actually a language about language. By knowing the names of the common grammatical terms and constructions, the writer can place himself at a distance from the writing problems. This distancing enables him to gain insights into the conventions of writing and the techniques for communicating effectively.

The terms discussed in the following section are those commonly used by writers and readers alike, not because they are uniquely precise or efficient but because they are widely understood to describe the English language. Terms are listed alphabetically for easy reference.

Absolute A grammatically independent construction within a sentence. A *nominative absolute* is the term often used to describe an absolute phrase and usually consists of a noun followed by a participle:

| **The party being over,** we left for home.

Active The voice expressed by the verb in a sentence when the subject is linked with its verb or acts upon its verb.

| Ultraviolet light **is** potentially lethal.
| The ozone shield constantly **breaks down** and **re-forms.**

There are no special endings indicating the active voice. All sentences not in the active voice are said to be passive. (See Section **8.3c.**)

Adjective A word used to describe or limit the meaning of a noun or pronoun. (See Sections **8.1** and **8.4.**)

Adverb A word used to modify a verb, adjective, or other adverb. (See Sections **8.1** and **8.4.**)

Agreement The correspondence in form among the parts of speech in sentences. (See Section **8.9.**) For example, a subject noun or pronoun must agree in person and in number with its verb:

| This **plan itself,** which **is** ten years old, **is** still quite useful.

If the subject, *plan,* is changed to *plans,* a series of other changes must follow so that all the parts agree:

| These **plans themselves,** which **are** ten years old, **are** still quite useful.

Sometimes confusion results when the verb precedes the subject in a sentence:

| There **is** many **causes** for inflation.

In this case, the subject, *causes,* needs to be located and the correct verb form supplied:

298 | There **are** many **causes** for inflation.

A plural verb is used when a sentence has two or more subjects joined by *and:*

| Mary **and** her *friends* were at the party.

When two or more subjects are joined by *or* or *nor,* the verb agrees with the subject nearest it:

| Neither Mary **nor** her *friends* **were** there.

A pronoun must agree in person, number, gender, and case with the word to which it refers (*antecedent*):

| The **cans,** whose chemical components are known as "freons," typify the premium we have placed on convenience, but **they** may also symbolize the high price that convenience brings.

They must be plural to agree with the plural antecedent *cans.*

A demonstrative adjective must agree in number with the noun it modifies:

| **These** aerosol **chemicals** may be breaking down the stratosphere.

Antecedent A word or group of words to which the pronoun refers.

| As a dedicated **teacher, he** always gave his students individual attention.

The noun *teacher* is the antecedent of the pronoun *he.* Since the pronoun must agree with its antecedent, the third person singular pronoun, *he,* must be used.

Words used as the second element include the personal pronouns (*I, you, he, she, it, we, they*), the relative pronouns (*who, which, that*), the reflexive pronouns (*myself, yourself, himself, herself, itself, ourselves, yourselves, themselves*), and the demonstrative pronouns (*this, that, these, those*):

Relative	Although the **book** was well known, **it** was rarely read.
Personal	**The man who** wrote the economics textbook was not well known.
Reflexive	Some **authors** do not involve **themselves** enough in the marketing of their books.
Demonstrative	**These** second **reviews** are more flattering than the first reviews.

A pronoun whose antecedent appears in previous sentences should agree with that antecedent:

299

> The true intellectual is interested not only in books but also in sports, politics, finance, farming—in short, everything. None of **these** interests is alien to him.

Appositive A *substantive* (a word or group of words used as a noun) placed beside another substantive and denoting the same person or thing:

> **One** of my best friends, an **ophthalmologist,** recently performed a successful operation on Harrison Sewell, the **mayor** of the city.

Ophthalmologist is in apposition with *one* (*of my best friends*), and *mayor* is in apposition with *Harrison Sewell.*

Most appositives need to be set off by commas. Only when the appositive is essential to the meaning of the sentence is it not set off by commas:

> | Not Essential | **William Faulkner,** a renowned American **writer,** won the Nobel Prize for Literature. |
> | Essential | The American **writer William Faulkner** won the Nobel Prize for Literature. |

(For a fuller discussion of punctuating appositives, see Section **7.3.**)

Auxiliaries "Helping" verbs—a subclass of verbs used before the main verb in a sentence to express tenses other than present or past, to show passive voice, and to add other dimensions of meaning to the main verb. The irregular verbs *be, have,* and *do* are often used as auxiliaries:

> Gorillas **have been found** in ever fewer numbers for several years.
> Soon tourism **will bring** motorcycle drag strips to Balinese beaches.

Other auxiliaries are *can, could, shall, should, will, would, may, might,* and *must:*

> If the spread of tourism is not regulated, it **may destroy** its own reason for being.
> We **could see** Central Park from our hotel window.

Case The inflectional form of nouns and pronouns showing their relation to other words in the sentence. (See Section **8.1.**)

Clause A group of words with a subject and a predicate. (For the conventions of punctuation for phrases and clauses, see Section **7.2.**)

A *main* clause, or *independent* clause, makes an independent assertion and can stand alone as a sentence. Every complete sentence must contain at least one main clause:

300

After refusing to install an expensive burglar-alarm system, **we were robbed twice during the year.**

Subordinate, or *dependent,* clauses cannot stand alone. They function as nouns, adjectives, or adverbs.

A *noun clause* is a group of words with a subject and a verb that functions as a noun. It can serve, therefore, as subject or object of a verb or occupy virtually any other sentence position that a noun can occupy:

That fluorocarbons are stable is one of their biggest advantages. [subject]

Viola had recently read, however, **that they were harming the environment.** [object]

An *adjective,* or *relative,* clause is used to modify a noun. It appears after the noun and is usually introduced by one of the relative pronouns, of which the most common are *who, which,* and *that:*

The chemical engineers were trying to find a new freezing substance **that was neither poisonous nor flammable.**

The people **who witnessed the accident** were all willing to testify in court.

An *adverb clause* is used to modify a verb, an adjective, an adverb, or an entire main clause. It is often introduced by one of the subordinating conjunctions (*when, if, because, after, since, although,* and others):

When they are pressurized slightly, fluorocarbons liquefy.

They make an ideal refrigerant **because they also withstand a large amount of heat before breaking down.**

Complement A word or words that complete the meaning of a verb. Complements include nouns or pronouns functioning as direct or indirect objects:

Direct Object   Competition among suppliers passes **benefits** along to consumers.

Indirect Object   Monopoly gives **them** extreme wealth.

Predicate nouns and adjectives can function as subjective complements—that is, by defining or describing the subject:

The market **system** is a cultural **barometer.**

The **economy** is **declining.**

301

A predicate noun *barometer* can take the place of the subject *system*. The adjective *declining* describes the subject *economy*.

Predicate nouns and adjectives can also function as objective complements:

> Many people make private wealth their primary **goal.** Others believe public benefits to be **unnecessary.**

The predicate noun *goal* can replace the object *wealth*. The predicate adjective *unnecessary* describes the object *benefits*. (See also **Objects.**)

Conjugation A term used to describe the changes in the inflectional forms of a verb to show tense, voice, mood, person, and number. (See Section **8.3.**)

Conjunction A word used to connect words, phrases, and clauses. (See Section **8.1.**)

Coordination A grammatical device, often using the coordinating conjunctions, for creating constructions of equal rank. The two main clauses of a compound sentence may be coordinate:

> **The market system is efficient,** but **it may not take wider social issues into account.**

Two or more single words or phrases may be coordinate:

> **Supply** and **demand** are key economic concepts.

> Many people are still undecided about whether to believe **those economists who are optimistic about the future** or **those who are pessimistic.**

Correlatives Conjunctions used in pairs to coordinate sentence elements. Correlative conjunctions include *either . . . or, neither . . . nor, both . . . and,* and *not only . . . but also.* Each correlative is generally followed by a word, phrase, or clause of equal grammatical rank:

> You may **either** pay your bill in full at the end of each month **or** pay a percentage of your total expenditures at an interest rate of 3 percent.

> **Neither** the concept of wealth **nor** the concept of progress is strictly a matter of economics.

Correlative structures should be used only when they fit sensibly into the sentence:

> **Either** I will complete the report **or** next week will be chaotic.

> Sharon **not only** is an expert carpenter **but also** uses only the best quality wood.

In the examples at the bottom of page 302, correlatives are inappropriate because they do not lend themselves to the sense of the sentences. In both cases, it is necessary to revise:

> If I do not complete the report, next week will be chaotic.
>
> Sharon is an expert carpenter and uses only the best quality wood.

Declension   A term referring to the inflectional changes of nouns and pronouns. (See Section **8.2.**)

Dependent Clause   See **Clause.**

Direct Object   See **Complement** and **Object.**

Gerund   See **Verbals.**

Independent Clause   See **Clause.**

Infinitive   See **Verbals.**

Inflection   Variation in the form of words to indicate change in meaning and function. (See Sections **8.2–8.4.**)

Interjection   A word used to express emotion. (See Section **8.1.**)

Linking Verb   (or *copula*, Latin for "link")   Establishes an equation between the subject of a sentence and the property or quality expressed by the predicate:

> Physics **is** my best subject.
>
> Chocolate **is** fattening.

In the first sentence, *is* links one noun, *physics,* with another, *subject.* Note that the sentence may be reversed without loss of meaning: "My best subject is physics." In the second sentence, *is* links the noun *chocolate* with the adjective *fattening,* a quality often associated with it. In modern English, subject and adjective may not be reversed. Objects and qualities on each side of the linking verb must be truly linked, either logically or by convention.

Be is by far the most common and the most important linking verb. Others include *become* and verbs of the senses (sometimes called "sensory verbs"), such as *seem, appear, look, feel, taste,* and *smell.* Linking verbs are followed by nouns or adjectives, not by adverbs:

> In a relatively short time, she **became** a superstar.
>
> The dress **looked** good [*not* **well**] on her.
>
> The two materials **feel** the same, but they **look** quite different.

Modification   The use of a word of one class, such as an adjective, to limit the meaning of a word of another class, such as a noun,

303

by making the meaning more exact. The word with such a limited meaning is called the *head* of the construction in which it appears. The other word or words are called *modifiers.* The relationship between the head and the modifiers is called *modification.* A modifier may be a single word or a series of individual words, such as adjectives, used to modify a noun:

Our company has several openings for **skilled** *engineers.*

A massive hydroelectric *project* is under way in Quebec.

Finally, the **backbreaking, thankless, messy** *job* was over.

Modifiers may also be phrases or clauses that modify a noun:

Prepositional Phrases	The rolling arctic-alpine *tundra* **of the Yukon** dances **with wild flowers in early summer** and turns scarlet **in the fall.**
Relative Clauses	The *women* **who helped develop the American West** and **who otherwise contributed to the growth of the United States** are largely ignored in textbooks.

In addition, modifiers themselves may be modified:

The *house* **on the corner plot, which measures one acre square,** was sold last week.

In this sentence, the noun *house* is modified by the prepositional phrase *on the corner plot.* The prepositional phrase is, in turn, modified by the relative phrase *which measures one acre square.*

Mood Distinctions in the form of a verb to show the writer's attitude toward the action of the verb. (See Section **8.3a.**)

Noun A word that names a person, place, or thing. (See Section **8.1.**)

Number The form of a noun, pronoun, verb, or demonstrative adjective to indicate singular or plural. (See Section **8.2a.**)

Object A general term for a word or group of words that follows the verb or preposition. Personal pronouns and the relative pronoun *who* appear in the objective case when used as objects.

A *direct object* names the receiver or the immediate goal of the action expressed by a transitive verb:

She *paid* **the waiter** and *left* **the restaurant** in a rush.

She *liked* **the food** but *hated* **the service.**

An *indirect object* names a person or thing that is indirectly acted upon, or to which something is given, said, shown, or done. Indirect objects are followed by direct objects:

> The waiter brought **her** the wrong order.
> She gave **him** a small tip.

Object Complement Completes the statement begun by the verb and direct object. Object complements appear after a direct object and refer to the same person or thing as the direct object:

> She did not consider the waiter to be **a skilled professional.**
> The waiter called her **an overdemanding customer.**

Object of a Preposition Prepositional phrases, consisting of a preposition plus its object, are used to modify the subject or the predicate of a sentence:

> She left **through the lobby.**
> The waiter angrily carried the dishes **to the kitchen.**

Participle See **Verbals.**

Parts of Speech Classification of words according to their grammatical function, grammatical form, and meaning in a sentence. (See Section **8.1.**)

Passive The voice expressed by the verb in a sentence when the subject is acted upon:

> Pat **was given** a season ticket to the Mets on December 21.
> Only a short while ago, fluorocarbons **were considered** environmentally safe by scientists and manufacturers.

(See also Section **8.3c.**)

Phrase A group of related words lacking a subject and verb. Phrases are used as nouns, adjectives, adverbs, or verbs:

> The architect **with the blueprints** stared gloomily **at the construction site.**

In this sentence the subject is *architect* and the verb is *stared.* The prepositional phrase *with the blueprints* functions as an adjective modifying the noun *architect.* A second prepositional phrase, *at the construction site,* functions as an adverb modifying the verb *stared.*

Predicate The part of a sentence that makes a statement or asks a question about the subject. The predicate must be linked to its subject by agreement in number and person. It may consist of a single verb:

> She **talks.**

The predicate may also contain auxiliary verbs and modifiers:

305

| She **had been talking on the phone all morning.**

The predicate may also contain nouns, noun phrases, or pronouns functioning as objects or as predicate nominatives:

| She **had been talking all morning on the phone to her grandson in Nebraska.**

Each of these constructions may themselves be modified:

| She **had been talking all morning on the phone downstairs in the lobby to her grandson, who had recently moved with his family to Nebraska.**

Predicate Nominative A predicate as subjective complement. See **Complement.**

Pronoun A word that takes the place of a noun. (See Section **8.1**.)

Sentence A group of words, grammatically complete and independent, which expresses what a reader recognizes as a complete thought and contains (except for imperative sentences) a subject and predicate combination. Sentences are classified by structure as follows:

A *simple sentence* has one main clause:

| The pilot's wife drove.

A *compound sentence* has two or more main clauses:

| **He flew to Aspen** and **she drove to Topeka.**

A *complex sentence* has one main clause and one or more subordinate clauses:

| Because the pilot's wife was afraid to fly, she drove her car.

The subordinate clause begins with *because,* and the main clause begins with *she.*

A *compound-complex sentence* has two or more main clauses and one or more subordinate clauses:

| He flew to Aspen, and she drove to Topeka because she was afraid to fly with him.

The two main clauses begin with *he* and *she,* and the subordinate clause begins with *because.*

Subject The part of a sentence that tells what the sentence is about. The subject names the person, place, or thing about which the predicate makes a statement or asks a question. A personal pronoun appearing as subject takes the nominative case:

They knew they had nothing to lose.

The subject, when given in more detail, may contain modifiers before or after the head word:

The elderly couple downstairs who gave the information to the police knew they had nothing to lose.

Each of these modifiers may itself be modified:

The elderly retired couple downstairs who gave the necessary information to the first police lieutenant to arrive at the scene of the hold-up knew they had nothing to lose.

In addition to nouns and noun modifiers, subjects may be composed of *gerunds*—the present participle of a verb—and used with other words to form a noun:

Knowing they had nothing to lose prompted the **elderly** couple to give the necessary information.

Subjects may also be composed of phrases and clauses:

That the police lieutenant received the necessary informatiom was undeniable.

Subordination   A grammatical device for creating structures that are dependent upon the main clause of a sentence. The dependent clauses in a complex or compound-complex sentence are subordinate:

If the beauty of the globe itself is the first victim of progress at any price, tourism and the travel industry will be the second.

The dependent clause begins with *If,* and the main clause begins with *tourism.* Other clauses, such as relative clauses and phrases, are logically subordinate because they depend on the main clause of a sentence and cannot appear alone.

Subordination as a grammatical device for stylistic efficiency, clarity, and grace is discussed in Sections **4.3, 5.6d,** and **5.6e.**

Tense   The time expressed by the action of the verb. (See Section **8.3a.**)

Verb   A word or phrase used to assert an action, condition, or state of being. A *transitive verb* takes an object:

I **hit** the ball.

An *intransitive verb* does not take an object:

| The choir **performed** well.

Two pairs of verbs, *lie/lay* and *sit/set,* are often confused. In each pair one of the verbs can be intransitive only, the other transitive only:

Intransitive	When I am tired, I **lie** down.
Transitive	Please **lay** the book on the table.
Intransitive	We will **sit** close to each other on the bus.
Transitive	If you **set** the packages down, you might forget them.

The principal parts of these verbs are:

Present Infinitive	lie, lay, sit, set
Past	lay, laid, sat, set
Past Participle	lain, laid, sat, set
Present Participle	lying, laying, sitting, setting

Verbals A word derived from a verb but used as a noun, adjective, or adverb. There are three kinds of verbals: *gerund, infinitive,* and *participle.*

A *gerund* is·an *-ing* form of the verb used as a noun:

| **Running** is good exercise, but I prefer **swimming.**

Running, a noun, serves as a subject, while *swimming* becomes a direct object.

An *infinitive* is a verbal usually preceded by *to* and used as a noun, adjective, or adverb:

| I like **to read.** [noun, direct object]
| It is time **to read.** [adjective, modifying *time*]
| We were eager **to read.** [adverb, modifying *eager*]

The subject of an infinitive takes the objective case:

| I took **her** to be her sister.

Her is the subject of *to be.*

Either a present participle or a past participle is a form of a verb used as an adjective:

| The tree **blowing** in the wind may fall.
| **Blown** to one side, the tree fell.

308   In both instances the participle modifies the noun *tree.*

Exercises

1. Study the italicized elements in each of the sentences below. Tell how the element as a whole is related to the sentence in which it appears. Then explain how each word within the element is related to the other words.

Example   Each person *that you claim as a dependent* must satisfy certain requirements.

The clause *that you claim as a dependent* is known as a *relative clause.* It is used to modify the noun *person* by adding information that makes the meaning of *person* more exact. The modifying clause refers to persons who must satisfy certain tests in order to be claimed as dependents. The clause is introduced by the relative pronoun *that.* The personal pronoun *you* is the subject of the clause, appears in the second-person singular, and is in the nominative case. It refers to the reader of the sentence. The verb *claim.* . . .

a. The repairs *could have been finished by the workers.*

b. *Although the desert landscape of the Baja Peninsula was well known,* it was not widely traveled until recently.

c. *The city planner with the most foresight* regarded the new shopping mall with alarm.

d. Marcia's classmates *might have been mistaken.*

e. The ozone shield exists *in a delicate balance in the stratosphere.*

f. Aerosol cans illustrate the importance of convenience, *but they may illustrate the price of convenience as well.*

g. The chairman of the science department *gave the dean a letter of resignation.*

h. The old man has gone, but he will return tomorrow—*if he can remember the address.*

2. For each of the following sentences write two sentences in which you expand the original sentence so that it makes sense and contains (1) exactly ten words and (2) more than twenty words.

Example   History is dull.

Exactly 10:   The careful study of history is dull for some students.

More   Although the study of history is dull for most college
than 20:   students, surprisingly we find that they are fascinated
              by historically based movies from Hollywood.

a. They may elect him chairman.

b. He will give his son a Rolls Royce.

c. Big Bill plays the acoustic guitar.
d. Night fell.
e. They remained our friends.
f. The burglars were desperate.
g. Food stamps are not the answer.

COMMON GRAMMATICAL ERRORS

The grammatical errors that most frequently turn up in writing occur (1) in the construction of a sentence (fragments, run-on, shifts), (2) in agreement (subject-verb, antecedent), or (3) in the use of the appropriate grammatical form (particularly with pronouns and verbs). From the reader's point of view, such lapses detract from the rhetorical effectiveness of the communication.

8.5 Sentence Fragments (frag)

A *sentence fragment* is a sentence part presented as though it were a complete sentence, with an initial capital letter and final sentence punctuation:

The names of many rock groups show originality and imagination. **Such as the group called** *Mandrill.* *Earth, Wind and Fire* is another good example.

Fragments Caused by Omitting the Verb

Sentence fragments are often the result of omitting the verb, as in the second and fourth word groups below:

In *The Great Gatsby,* the green light becomes a go-ahead signal. **The signal to go after Daisy.** And in the end, it is seen as a beacon of hope for all to follow. **A yet unobtained dream.**

Generally, such fragments simply produce the effect of carelessness or haste. This type of fragment can be avoided by incorporating the material into the preceding sentence by using a colon or dash to signal a long or dramatic pause:

In *The Great Gatsby* the green light becomes a go-ahead signal—**a signal to go after Daisy.** And in the end it is seen as a beacon of hope for all to follow: **a yet unobtained dream.**

Using the wrong verb form in a sentence may inadvertently create a sentence fragment. The error is easy to overlook unless the sentence is read over carefully:

> Dante uses the idea of poetic justice in *The Inferno*. The various layers of Hell **corresponding** to the severity of the sin and the punishment to be suffered.

It is usually not necessary to attach this type of fragment to preceding or following sentences. A simple change in verb form will solve the problem:

> Dante uses the idea of poetic justice in *The Inferno*. The various layers of Hell **correspond** to the severity of the sin and the punishment to be suffered.

Fragments may also be caused by *confusing a dependent clause with an independent clause:*

> Although taxes cause people with large incomes to complain and people with small incomes to go without bread.

Here the subordinating conjunction *although* makes the group of words following it a dependent clause and, thus, a fragment. The subordinating clause requires another statement to complete its meaning:

> Although taxes cause people with large incomes to complain and people with small incomes to go without bread, **no one can deny the need for additional improvements in public transportation and public safety.**

8.6 Comma Splice (cs)

A *comma splice* occurs when two main clauses are joined without a coordinating conjunction between and with only a comma separating them:

> The job requires long hours, the salary is generous.

There are several ways to correct a comma splice:

1. A *period or semicolon* may be inserted between the two main clauses (see also Sections **7.6a** and **7.6b**):

> The job requires long hours. The salary is generous.
> The job requires long hours; the salary is generous.

311

2. A *coordinating conjunction* preceded by a comma may be inserted between the two main clauses (see also Sections **7.5a** and **7.5b**):

| The job requires long hours, **but** the salary is generous.

3. One of the clauses may be made subordinate:

| **Although the job requires long hours,** the salary is generous.

8.7   Run-on, or Fused, Sentences (fs)

A *run-on*, or *fused, sentence* is composed of two or more main clauses combined without punctuation:

| In times of fuel shortages, it is essential that we learn to use less fuel in personal transportation. **This is where the motorcycle is useful with its low fuel consumption it uses less fuel and gets more miles per gallon than any car.**

The same methods for correcting the comma splice can be used to correct run-on sentences:

1. Insert a *period or a semicolon* between the two main clauses:

| This is where the motorcycle is useful. With its low fuel consumption, it uses less fuel and gets more miles per gallon than any car.
| This is where the motorcycle is useful; with its low fuel consumption, it uses less fuel and gets more miles per gallon than any car.

2. Insert a *coordinating conjunction* preceded by a comma between the two main clauses:

| Run-on | Parking is no problem you can fit even where a "bug" can't squeeze in. |
| Revised | Parking is no problem, **for** you can fit where even a "bug" can't squeeze in. |

3. Change one of the clauses to a subordinate construction:

| Run-on | You do not have to worry about the security of your motorcycle, it is small enough to store in a number of places. |
| Revised | **Because your motorcycle is small enough to store in a number of places,** you do not have to worry about its security. |

8.8   Illogical Use of the Linking Verb (Copula)

What follows the linking verb should be a restatement of what precedes it:

| Illogical | In *The Great Gatsby,* the green light **is** Gatsby's view of his relationship with Daisy. |
| Revised | In *The Great Gatsby,* the green light **symbolizes** Gatsby's view of his relationship with Daisy. |

A green light cannot *be* a view, but it can *symbolize* one. By substituting a more specific verb for *is,* the sentence is made logical and clear.

8.9 Agreement (agr)

Agreement is the relationship between the form of a subject and its verb or between the form of a pronoun and its antecedent or the word it modifies.

8.9a Subject-Verb Agreement

In every subject-verb combination, the form of the subject controls the form of the verb:

I spend 20 percent of my take-home pay on bills.

They were spending too much.

Errors in subject-verb agreement generally appear in complicated sentences. They often occur either (1) because the writer makes the verb agree with the closest noun rather than with the true subject, or (2) because the writer has not properly determined the number expressed by the subject:

Faulty Subject Agreement	Several short *breaks* during a writing assignment **is** more beneficial than one long rest period.
Revised	Several short *breaks* during a writing assignment **are** more beneficial than one long rest period.
Faulty Number Agreement	*Economics* **are** more difficult for me than English.
Revised	*Economics* **is** more difficult for me than English.

8.9b Agreement with Subjects Connected by *And*

A compound subject, in which two or more nouns or pronouns are connected by *and,* is plural even though each part is singular in form:

| Faulty | According to many used-car dealers, the 1965 *Buick Sky-lark* and the 1965 *Ford Country Squire station wagon* **is** the best **buy** available. |

> Revised   According to many used-car dealers, the 1965 *Buick Skylark* and the 1965 *Ford Country Squire station wagon* **are** the best **buys** available.

8.9c   Agreement with Subjects Connected by *Or* or *Nor*

Words in a compound subject connected by *or, but,* or *nor* have the same number that an individual word would have if it appeared alone. If two singular nouns are connected, the complete subject is singular. If two plural nouns are connected, the complete subject is plural. If one singular and one plural word are connected, the complete subject takes its number from the word nearest the verb:

> Faulty   The president or the *vice president* **are** going to make the announcement regarding taxes.
>
> Revised   The president or the *vice president* **is** going to make the announcement regarding taxes.
>
> Faulty   Neither the President nor his *aides* **was** concerned about the distribution of farm subsidies.
>
> Revised   Neither the President nor his *aides* **were** concerned about the distribution of farm subsidies.

8.9d   Agreement with Collective Nouns

Collective nouns (*audience, class, team*) are singular in number when they refer to a single group or a single collection of objects. When a collective noun is thought of not as an entity but as a number of individuals who act independently of one another, the noun is plural. Agreement thus depends, in part, on the writer's intention:

> When he addressed the *audience,* **they** shifted uncomfortably in their seats.
>
> He could see **it** was a restless *audience.*

Most collective nouns, however, are conventionally taken as singular:

> Unconventional   The *city council* **are** appointing a committee to study the economic implications of migration from the cities to the suburbs.
>
> Revised   The *city council* **is** appointing a committee to study the economic implications of migration from the cities to the suburbs.

8.9e   Agreement with *Each* and *Every*

A singular pronoun is used to refer to antecedents containing the words *each* and *every* because the words are grammatically singular, even though they are commonly used with a plural meaning in everyday speech:

Faulty	The chairperson asked *each* member of the board to make **their** own decision.
Revised	The chairperson asked *each* member of the board to make **his** own decision.
Faulty	*Every* corporate executive needs some independence, even though **they** work as part of a close-knit team.
Revised	*Every* corporate executive needs some independence, even though **he** works as part of a close-knit team.
Faulty	There is general agreement that *every* department must be responsible for **their** own internal economy.
Revised	There is general agreement that *every* department must be responsible for **its** own internal economy.

8.9f Agreement with Interposing Modifiers

Single words or participial and prepositional phrases that come between the subject and the verb of the sentence have no effect on the agreement between subject and verb:

Faulty	*The horde* of admirers jamming the convention hall, clapping their hands, and stamping their feet **do** not dismay the experienced entertainer.
Revised	*The horde* of admirers jamming the convention hall, clapping their hands, and stamping their feet **does** not dismay the experienced entertainer.
Faulty	At any performance, I find that *the first few minutes* of the show **is** the most exciting.
Revised	At any performance, I find that *the first few minutes* of the show **are** the most exciting.

8.9g Agreement with *There Is* and *There Are*

When the verb precedes the subject of a sentence, as it does in sentences beginning with *there is* or *there are,* particular effort must be made to locate the true subject. The subject controls the form of *be* that follows the word *there. There* has no effect on the agreement between subject and verb:

Faulty	**There are a series** of studies indicating that among young drivers the rate of accidents climbs steeply between the ages of eighteen and nineteen and then falls sharply at the age of twenty.
Revised	**There is a series** of studies indicating that among young drivers the rate of accidents climbs steeply between the ages of eighteen and nineteen and then falls sharply at the age of twenty.

315

> Faulty   **There are** ample **evidence** to suggest that most young drivers are mature enough at twenty to combine driving skill with an awareness that **there is,** in fact, **dangers** on the road.
>
> Revised   **There is** ample **evidence** to suggest that most young drivers are mature enough at twenty to combine driving skill with an awareness that **there are,** in fact, **dangers** on the road.

In these writing examples, the number expressed by the verb is controlled by the subject: *a series* (singular) *of studies, ample evidence* (singular), and *dangers* (plural).

8.9h   Pronoun-Antecedent Agreement

Personal pronouns must agree in gender, number, and case with their antecedents. The relative pronoun *who* must agree in gender and case with its antecedent. The demonstrative and reflexive pronouns must agree in number with their antecedents:

> Faulty   The author **who** I admire is Mark Twain.
>
> Revised   The author **whom** I admire is Mark Twain.
>
> Faulty   Women are forbidden to speak with the female offender or to associate with **them** in any way at the risk of being put in *tebreya* **herself.**
>
> Revised   Women are forbidden to speak with the female offender or to associate with **her** in any way at the risk of being put in *tebreya* **themselves.**

In the first sentence, the relative pronoun should be in the objective case, *whom,* not the nominative case, *who.*

The antecedent of the personal pronoun in the second sentence is *female offender.* The pronoun should show the female gender, singular number, and objective case—*her.* In the same sentence, *women* takes the plural reflexive pronoun *themselves.*

8.10   Shifts in Point of View (pv)

A shift in point of view involves inconsistency in subject and voice, person and number, or tense and mood. Shifts in these sentence elements are liable to confuse the reader, thereby reducing the efficiency and effectiveness of the communication.

8.10a   Shifts in Subject and Voice

Do not shift the subject of a sentence or the voice of the verb:

Wolves or wild dogs could be heard in the distance as we entered the forest. No one seemed worried by the strange sounds, but the dark shadows made the children alarmed. After flashlight beams were sent dancing through the thick branches of the trees, everyone relaxed a little.

Notice that within each sentence two or more different subjects are used and the verbs alternate between active and passive voice. Revision entails choosing either the active or passive voice for each sentence and beginning each sentence with the subject of the main clause:

We heard wolves or wild dogs in the distance as we entered the forest. No one seemed worried by the strange sounds, but the children were alarmed by the dark shadows. Everyone relaxed a little after we sent the flashlight beams dancing through the thick branches of the trees.

8.10b Shifts in Person and Number

Do not shift person or number. Either type of inconsistency is a sign that the writer has not clearly focused his material:

Faulty	If **you** want **your campfires** to be pleasant and practical, **he** has to build **it** carefully.
Revised	If **you** want **your campfires** to be pleasant and safe, **you** have to build **them** carefully.

The second-person singular *you* shifts to the third-person singular *he*, and the plural *campfires* shifts in number to the singular pronoun *it*.

8.10c Shifts in Tense and Mood

Needless shifts in tense only confuse the reader. It is therefore generally more efficient to use one tense consistently in a paragraph:

Shift in Tense	The old cabin **was** set back in a grove of pines. As we **approach,** we **saw** the broken windows and the holes in the walls.
Revised	The old cabin **was** set back in a grove of pines. As we **approached,** we **saw** the broken windows and the holes in the walls.

In this paragraph, the tense shifts from the past to the present and then back to the past again. Revised, the past tense is used consistently throughout the paragraph.

Shift in Mood	The cabin looked as though it **were** missing its front teeth. Soon we would catch sight of our first elk, if fate **is** willing.
Revised	The cabin looked as though it **were** missing its front teeth. Soon we would catch sight of our first elk, if fate **were** willing.

8.11 (mix)

The mood in this paragraph shifts from the subjunctive to the indicative. However, the revised paragraph uses the subjunctive mood consistently.

8.11 Mixed Constructions (mix)

Much of our conversation is sprinkled with *mixed constructions*. False starts or shifts in sentence strategy midway through a sentence are quickly forgotten in spoken English, but they are strikingly obvious when they appear in writing. One sentence construction should be used consistently and should be completed before another begins:

> **As a professional ecologist,** making money from the environment is by far the most serious problem in America today. **Take,** for one example, **in** the proposed strip mining in Montana, the landowners stand to make millions. As a result, every few feet **a test sample of the surface dirt a chunk** is gouged out and analyzed, measuring the distance from "pay dirt." Later on, when men or wildlife attempt to use the adjoining territory, **it leaves a big wound in the ecology.** If we cannot live in harmony with the environment, **we cannot expect that the environment will let us live peacefully.**

The elements in bold type indicate the false starts—the incomplete constructions that have been abandoned or partially blended in with other incompatible sentence elements. Revision entails choosing one construction and completing each construction that is begun:

> As a professional ecologist, **I would say that** making money from the environment is by far the most serious problem we face in America today. For example, the proposed strip mining in Montana will make millions for the landowners. As a result, **a test sample of the surface dirt is gouged out** every few feet and analyzed to measure the distance from "pay dirt." Later on, when men or wildlife attempt to use the adjoining territory, **they will face a big wound left on the surface of the earth.** If we cannot live in harmony with the environment, **we cannot expect that the environment will let us live peacefully.**

8.12 Split Infinitives

The *split infinitive*—the intervention of an adverb or other expression between the word *to* and the plain form of the verb—is not necessarily an error. However, most writers avoid the construction where possible, because the intervening words tend to disrupt the flow of the sentence:

Faulty	After final exams, the dean asked me **to as quickly as possible bring** my grade-point average up to the minimum.
Revised	After final exams, the dean asked me **to bring** my grade-point average up to the minimum **as quickly as possible.**
Faulty	I promised **to immediately finish** my two incompletes and **to in the future contact** my academic adviser if I had any problems.
Revised	I promised **to finish** my two incompletes **immediately** and **to contact** my academic adviser **in the future** if I had any problems.

However, writers invariably use the split infinitive where avoidance would create awkwardness:

Acceptable	**To just miss** the bus is a frustrating way to start the day.

8.13 Dangling Constructions (dgl)

A modifier is said to dangle when it modifies nothing in the main clause of a sentence or when it seems to modify a word to which it is not logically related:

Dangling	**Convinced that the voters were not well informed about the candidate's speaking engagement,** advertisements were distributed announcing the new schedule.
Revised	**Because he was convinced that the voters were not well informed about the candidate's speaking engagement,** *the campaign manager* distributed advertisements announcing the new schedule.
Dangling	**Entering the auditorium late,** 300 disgruntled members of the audience could be heard shifting restlessly in their seats.
Revised	**Entering the auditorium late,** *we heard* 300 disgruntled members of the audience shifting restlessly in their seats.

As these examples illustrate, most problems with dangling modifiers can be resolved by expanding the main clause. (See also Section 4.11f.)

REVIEW EXERCISES

1. Eliminate the ineffective sentence fragments by combining them with the main clause or making them into complete sentences.

a. My mother shook her head sadly and walked out of the room. Which was her way of avoiding the question.

b. Kidnapping is becoming a tool of political dissent. Chiefly because no individual can ignore the personal threat implied.

c. The two leading candidates have identical platforms. But different parties.

d. Many young people are still considering the Peace Corps as an alternative to a boring job at home. Not just for the chance to travel, either.

e. The audience at the singer's funeral services was a mixed one. Rich and poor, black and white, young and old, all sitting side by side and sharing their grief.

2. Combine each of the following pairs of sentences into a single sentence. Supply appropriate punctuation, coordinators, subordinators, or sentence modifiers where necessary.

a. Poker, he often confessed, was his first love. Bridge had won his heart only recently.

b. Publishing, I grant you, has much to offer. Public relations, certainly, has much more.

c. We saw no easy exit. There was no easy exit close enough to where we were seated.

d. What is needed is the reality and not just the name of a liberal education. This college must strive to provide such an education, sooner or later.

e. The two men cleared away the brush. Then they pitched their tent and spread their army blankets.

3. Revise the fragments and run-on sentences in the passage below according to the method that produces the clearest and most efficient expression.

In Shakespeare's day there was no system of copyright as it exists today and authors did not receive royalties from their books. Normally a work being sold outright to a publisher for a lump sum. Early regulation of the book trade was not designed to protect the rights of authors, it was rather intended to prevent the publication of "seditious books," and the spreading of "great and detestable

320

heresies." No real recognition of author's right was established until after the Copyright Act of 1709 and the numerous legal contests that clarified it during the 18th century. There was, however, regulation of the book trade in Elizabethan England and it was established in 1557 by the creation of the Company of Stationers. The Company, or Guild, was granted power to restrict printing to its qualified members and was authorized to seize or destroy prohibited books or to imprison anyone printing contrary to its orders. The Company, through its officers, enforced rules by levying fines, in extreme cases it destroyed a press entirely. Also requiring that books should be registered with the Company before publication. Such registration established the copies as the property of certain members and book pirates who ignored these priorities were subject to punishment by Company officers. The written registers of the Company survive and they are among the most valuable of the sources of information, about early printing and publishing.

4. Adjust the sentences below in which the linking verb is used illogically.

   a. What they did was to publish their poems anonymously.

   b. Disgrace was her greatest fearfulness.

   c. Time is money.

   d. You are either part of the problem or part of the solution.

   e. Their greatest strength was to undertake the impossibility.

   f. Unlimited control is my dream.

   g. Water is life.

   h. The pursuit of glory was what they did best.

   i. The injustice was to keep struggling unsuccessfully.

   j. Love is all you need.

5. Copy each sentence and write the appropriate form of the verb in parentheses in the blank space.

   a. The agency _____ (have) approved your petition.

   b. Clyde's shooting and our tight four-man defense _____ (be) keeping our Class-B team within a few points of the state champions.

   c. There _____ (be) only one old Mercury and a new Fiat on the lot today.

   d. She could see the planes, like a flock of great birds, _____ (bank) and _____ (turn) suddenly to the south.

   e. He was one of the soldiers who _____ (seem) always to be where there is no bloodshed.

321

    f. Amelia is one of those executives who never _____ (stop) planning and revising.

    g. Freud _____ (do) not understand the full powers of the subconscious mind.

    h. A sundae, loaded with syrup, marshmallow, whipped cream, chocolate sprinkles, and nuts, _____ (be) always too much for my stomach.

  6. Copy each sentence and revise it so that every pronoun agrees with its antecedent.

    a. The home economics instructor asked each student to create their own dinner menu.

    b. If either the banker or the grocer were unqualified, they would not be able to keep their jobs.

    c. Her family has carried on bravely in spite of their tragedies.

    d. Everybody has their own answer to the problem of inflation.

    e. Each person should sign those petitions and exercise their right to protest government spending.

    f. None of the novelists were willing to read their latest novels aloud.

  7. Revise each sentence below by eliminating all unnecessary shifts in subject or voice.

    a. Before we heard her story, many questions were asked.

    b. He put epoxy glue around all the wooden surfaces, and then the broken toys were repaired.

    c. After a hot fire was built by the explorers, they dried their wet clothing.

    d. While Mexico leads in silver mining, the most plentiful supply of gold is found in South Africa.

  8. Revise each sentence below to eliminate all unnecessary shifts in person or number.

    a. Everyone should be able to learn about birth control, if their religious conviction permit.

    b. If one is dissatisfied with the way television commercials are being aired, you should write to the network brass more often.

    c. Mary McCarthey once said of the Boston Pops that they were second to none.

    d. I tried cigar smoking but they made my head ache.

  9. Revise the following sentences by eliminating all unnecessary shifts in tense or mood.

a. The master sat down with his cello and begins to play the most beautiful music I will ever hear.

b. She would be delighted to attend if her husband might accompany her.

c. The store manager decided to offer some free samples, and suddenly the place is jammed with new customers.

d. Now you say you prefer to travel by plane, but if the weather was bad, you would be happy to go by bus.

10. Correct the various shifts in the following passages and state the nature of the shift that occurs in each (subject or voice, person or number, tense or mood).

a. A person who wants to get something out of his classes must do more than simply the required amount of work. You can often pick up a degree by doing just the minimum, but one cannot get an education that way.

b. When I first read Hemingway's story, I thought he was mostly interested in the two killers who come into the restaurant and inquire about Ole. They are revealed through their clipped speech and their attempts to bully the boys in the diner. Most of the story seems to concern them. Nick did not speak very often.

c. After Spike had reported on his investigation and they had weighed the chances of getting caught against the possibilities of a substantial haul, it was decided to go home and make the attempt some other time.

11. Eliminate any mixed construction in the following sentences by rewiting as necessary.

a. As a mecca for the financial leaders, most young stockbrokers yearn to live in New York.

b. By introducing consumer education in the elementary school, young people could approach their adult role as consumers with confidence and maybe they would get ahead more quickly.

c. In every effort the secretary made to explain her problem to her friend got her more confused.

d. I tried to explain the cause of inflation to my parents who from their expressions one would think they were still living during the Great Depression.

12. Revise the following sentences by eliminating awkward split infinitives.

a. The police officer tried to quietly and quickly separate the two women.

323

b. The owner of the store asked the boys to immediately produce proof of their age.

c. The president vowed to, if the budget permits, have the minutes of the club meeting published.

d. The leading powers might suddenly decide to one day in the near future drastically reduce their nuclear stockpiles.

13. Combine each sentence below with the introductory modifier suggested for each. Leave the modifiers as they are, but revise the sentences so the combinations are clear and logical and do not dangle. Change the voice of the verb if necessary.

a. Having turned off the light. Ominous shadows were seen in the corner by Maria.

b. While trailing his fingers carelessly in the water. A five-pound bass was caught by Sandy.

c. To prove that there were no hard feelings. A victory banquet was given by the losing candidate.

d. Playing the last ten minutes with a broken finger. The sonata was completed by Roberta with a flourish.

e. After watching for an hour and ten minutes. The missing jewels were finally discovered by us.

f. Being unable to obtain materials. The new product was scrapped by her father's company.

14. Revise the following sentences to rid them of dangling modifiers.

a. Trying to climb through the dormitory window at midnight, the Dean of Women caught her and had her suspended.

b. Being afraid of almost everything that moves, we were not impressed with his threats.

c. Although he was only pretending to shoot, the pistol went off suddenly with a loud explosion.

d. At the age of nine, my father's interest in old coins was already evident.

e. Every promise had been broken by the new government, causing widespread dissatisfaction.

f. On approaching the city, the transmitter on top of the sky-scraper is the only point above the horizon.

Research and the Library Paper

The rhetorical processes involved in preparing the library paper are essentially the same as those required for other writing assignments. In the library paper, however, the writer is concerned not only with his own experiences and ideas but also with those of others. The library paper is more likely to be a success if the writer has a system for recording, arranging, and using the research and is familiar with the library tools available for doing the research.

THE RESEARCH PROCESS

The word *research* refers to a diverse group of activities, each centered around the investigation of facts by careful study and analysis of a subject. Each of the following tasks requires searching for and studying information:

1. A reporter wants to find out what construction companies receive the largest number of school building contracts. He goes to the city records bureau.
2. A scientist at the National Bureau of Standards is asked to find out if aluminum wire is more hazardous than copper wire. She sets up a series of laboratory experiments.
3. A personnel director is puzzled about why a particular division of the furniture plant has a higher absentee record than other divisions. He interviews workers in his office and at their homes.
4. A lawyer needs to find precedents for suing the government for failure to enforce equal-opportunity laws. He looks up cases in the law library.
5. A student is puzzled about why prejudice against women is so difficult to eliminate despite changes in the laws. She goes to the library and reads books and articles about the problem of prejudice.

Although the activities listed above may require different methods of investigation and will be pursued in different places, all are based on the same process—the gathering of information to answer a question. The question may never have been asked before; it may have been asked and answered satisfactorily; it may have been asked but not answered satisfactorily. Whatever the results of the investigation into the subject, however, the research activity will usually lead to some type of written report. The conventional form for presenting this report will vary with the profession: the investigative reporter's *article;* the scientist's *laboratory report;* the lawyer's *brief;* the student's scholarly research *essay.* Each is presented differently. However, the essay based on library research—the particular focus of this chapter—is not very different from other research and writing activities. In fact, although the particular methods for researching and presentation may be special, the basic principles are the same:

1. Thorough and accurate collection of information.
2. Objective and logical evaluation of the evidence.
3. Unity, coherence, and clarity in presentation.

While readers may rightfully expect any communication to reflect these qualities, they expect writing based on research to be more thorough than a shorter communication (editorial, essay, examination, and so on), which usually requires less time and information gathering to prepare.

Originality and Research

Some research will lead to fresh insight into the material investigated; some will not. Although originality for the sake of originality is not the purpose of research, the process of immersing oneself in the subject area will, in fact, often lead to new ways of viewing the subject or to interesting ways of communicating the results.

However, without thorough research, the writer is unlikely to become involved enough to discover new and interesting ways to present his data. For example, an essay based on two or three hours of library reading, presented as a collection of undigested and undeveloped facts and quotations, is unlikely to contain fresh insights or to be interesting reading. Nor is it likely that research done to back up a totally preconceived notion, one the writer could have formulated without leaving the desk, will lead to a fresh contribution to the subject. A library paper based on undigested and unanalyzed facts and opinions is dull; one based on unexamined personal opinions is likely to be misleading, since the writer will tend to search for and use only that information that backs up his own opinion.

A library paper more likely to be informative, reliable, and interesting is the result of a process that occurs something like this:

1. The writer formulates a general idea about a rather large subject.
2. The writer begins to search for information touching on the subject area.
3. From preliminary data, the writer forms a hypothesis about the subject and begins to search for additional information that will confirm or disprove the hypothesis.
4. As the amount of collected information increases, the writer uses each set of facts and information to narrow the hypothesis until it becomes sharply focused and restricted to the limits of time and space available for the research assignment.
5. This process of using more and more information to produce a smaller and smaller research subject continues until the writer can assert confidently that the subject of the paper and the thesis—what the writer wants to say about the subject—can be presented thoroughly within the limits of the assignment.

In practice, to be sure, the writer's progress is seldom quite so smooth during the process of preparing a library paper (or any research project, for that matter). However, immersing oneself in a subject area, analyzing and questioning information, abandoning false leads or hypotheses, rethinking ideas—all these are the activities most likely to yield results useful to both the writer and the reader. At the heart of the research process is the interplay between the writer's ideas and the information required; the information will often lead to new ideas, which themselves require supporting information, or to a change in those ideas that started the research. Although the writer can be given useful techniques for organizing and pursuing the research (the purpose of this chapter), there are no shortcuts for the most important part of the research process: the continual questioning and searching.

PREPARING FOR LIBRARY RESEARCH

A library paper makes special demands on a writer's ability to collect, organize, and evaluate information. To prepare the way, the writer should have a grasp of the following:

1. How to select a suitable subject and focus it until the outlines of a workable project are revealed.
2. How to develop methods for researching.
3. What research tools are available within libraries.

328   In the following sections, each technique will be discussed in turn.

Choosing and Focusing a Subject

Finding a subject is usually not a problem. Nothing in human experience can fail to yield a topic worthy of research when basic questions are asked about it:

1. How did it happen?
2. How does it work?
3. What does it consist of?
4. What is its significance?
5. How does it relate to other things?

When a writer approaches any subject or experience by asking one or more of these questions, the problem becomes not what to research but how to limit the research. Choosing a subject, then, is really a matter of focusing in order to assure maximum coverage within the time and space limits available to the writer. Subjects like "The Nature of Prejudice" or "Feminism: A Sociological and Psychological Study of the Woman Question from Ancient Times to the Present Day" would take years, if not a lifetime, to research, analyze, and write about. These subjects could not be adequately covered in ten or twenty pages. But both could be starting points for a much better focused research project.

The principles discussed in Chapter 2 for focusing a subject and thesis are essentially the same for library projects. Moreover, focusing the research topic helps to limit and organize not only the subject but also the research to be done. Trace, for example, the way in which the author of the research paper at the end of this chapter may have focused both the topic and the investigation. The general subject area is *prejudice*. The focusing may well have begun with a series of questions the writer could answer only by finding specific information:

What characterizes prejudice?
How does prejudice affect people?
Why is it so difficult to eliminate prejudice?

At some point the writer would choose one of the questions listed above as the most interesting to her. Assume she chose the last one. The writer could have started researching at this point, but she chose to focus the topic even further by applying the question to a particular group:

329

Why is it so difficult to eliminate prejudice against women?

For a ten-to-twenty-page essay this question is still too broad, and after some preliminary reading and careful thought, the writer narrowed the focus even further:

Could it be that the very nature of the English language makes it difficult to eliminate prejudice against women?

The preceding process is hypothetical, of course, and the writer's interest in the topic may well have started with a personal observation. For example, recalling a phrase from the Declaration of Independence which states that all *men* are created equal, the writer may have wondered whether the word *men* in such a context could reflect a long-standing attitude toward women. In this case, she would have arrived at the topic from a specific observation which is directed toward the general question.

However the author arrived at the topic, at some point the focusing process led her to determine the type of information required to prove that prejudice against women is indeed built into the language. Among the thousands of books, reports, and articles about language and prejudice, which ones should she read? Focusing will not provide the list, but it will guide the writer through the mass of information available to those bits that might actually be useful. From a list of article titles, such as the following, the writer could make a reasonable choice about the ones likely to contain information or statements about her topic:

"Women Writers and the Double Standard"
"The Most Important Women Writers in America"
"Women's Styles Through the Ages"
"Language and Women's Place"
"Women in a Sexist Society"

The second and third articles could easily be eliminated from the topic; the fourth and fifth articles certainly should be looked at; and the first article might be worth skimming over. The titles of the articles chosen for reading indicate that they probably are in the author's topic area, since the expressions "double standard," "women's place," and "sexist" directly or by implication signal that the material is about prejudice.

Although the information in the first books or articles read might never appear in the final essay, it can be used for further focusing. The writer finally reaches a point where the subject is so clearly focused that the statement of the subject is actually a hypothesis:

To prove: The nature of the English language causes prejudice against women.

At this point, if the writer does not yet have in hand information that is much more specific, she will need to collect more data about:

1. how the English language is actually used to distinguish between men and women.
2. how language directly affects our social attitudes.
3. the instances of prejudice against women that can be directly and logically related to the English language.

And if the evidence gathered did not support the hypothesis, the writer would have to reshape the hypothesis or write a report about negative findings (which can be valuable and interesting to a reader if they correct a possible misconception). The focusing process, then, does not determine the final results. It only makes the subject and research manageable.

Exercises

1. Assuming that you have a maximum length of ten pages available, evaluate the following subjects as research topics. Are they too narrow or too broad? Too general or too complex? Could they be adequately researched in a month?

a. How to shop for consumer goods economically.

b. The applications of computer technology to education.

c. Television as a threat to literacy.

d. A modern viewpoint about success.

e. The lace-making machine and the development of female American taste.

f. The meaning of Shakespeare's *Hamlet*.

g. Varieties of communal living in the American counterculture today.

2. Choose one of the topics above that you have considered too broad and show how it might be narrowed to fit the ten-page limit (if necessary, reread Chapter 2, pp. 32–36). What sort of specific information would you need to write about the topic?

ORGANIZING THE RESEARCH

Like other human activities—from sports to business—research requires setting up an efficient system to accomplish the job with a minimum of wasted effort. For library research there is a tested method used for organizing a bibliography and for note taking.

Although any *consistent* method will do, it is worth following the suggested procedures not only because they are ready-made but also because past researchers have found them effective.

Preparing and Using Bibliography Cards

Since a writer may begin actual library research while he is still choosing and focusing a subject, he should immediately begin collecting a *bibliography*—a list of books, magazines, newspapers, and other material on the subject. The researcher usually gathers the bibliography from two types of sources:

1. Published lists of works about a subject, called *bibliographies*. (See pp. 339–43.)
2. Footnotes and bibliographies in works the writer reads for general or specific information.

The writer should have a system for storing this information so that it can be easily referred to, added to, and organized (most often alphabetically or by topic). Most investigators find that a system of lined or unlined cards (usually 3-by-5 or 4-by-6 inches) fulfills all these requirements. Each bibliography entry is kept on a single card so the writer can arrange the articles and books alphabetically or by topic and subtopic, as the need arises. Researchers avoid placing two items on a single bibliography card, for although doing so might save a few seconds of time and a few square inches of space, the saving is not worth the cost, later on, of having to look for an item buried at the bottom of a card.

An individual bibliography card should be made for everything the researcher reads, no matter how casually or quickly. Every researcher at one time or another has located an article or book that seemed unimportant at first glance but that later proved to be necessary. And most researchers have experienced the difficulty and frustration of retracing their steps to locate information that could not be easily found because the bibliography card was not filled out, was filled out incompletely, or was lost on the reverse side of another bibliography card.

Format for Bibliography Cards

Researchers follow a standard form in filling out their bibliography cards. A *book card* looks like this:

BOOK CARD

```
301. 41, 2          Bibliography
1 7 6 m               └─ 1. Type of Card
                       ─ 2. Call Number
                       ─ 3. Author
Millett, Kate  ←      ─ 4. Title
Sexual Politics ←    ─ 5. Publication Data
New York: Doubleday, 1970


              Important book
```

Item 1 is merely a brief reminder to the researcher that the card is a bibliography card. Item 2 is placed on the card when the book is looked up in the card catalog. (See pp. 337–39.) By placing the call number on the card, the researcher avoids having to look it up a second time. Items 3 through 5 should be as complete and accurate as possible, since they may be used to construct either footnotes or a bibliography at the end of the library paper. No matter which source (bibliography, footnote, card catalog) originally led him to the book, the researcher should make a new bibliography card when he has the book itself in hand, since the original information may not be precise or accurate. Except for the copyright date, which is found on the back of the title page, the information on the new card should be taken only from the title page—not from the cover of the book. Finally, the researcher often finds it helpful to jot down a quick note about the usefulness of the book, such as "not useful," "too general," "important." Such notes remind him whether he has looked at the book and whether it is of value for his purposes.

The form for magazine and newspaper cards is basically the same as for a book, except that, since newspapers are ordered from the stacks by title, no call number can be entered. As on the book card, the information should be as complete as possible. For a magazine or journal, the volume and date of publication should

333

be given completely and with particular care, because this information is the only way of telling one issue from another. The volume number is located on one of the first inner pages of the publication. Also included on the bibliography card are the inclusive page numbers (and column number for a newspaper), because these will be needed if the library paper requires a bibliography. Again, the researcher should not trust the accuracy of the source that led him to the article or newspaper. A new bibliography card should be made from the material actually in hand.

If the principle of one unit of information per card is adhered to, the resulting card bibliography can be referred to quickly, stored easily, and expanded and revised efficiently. Expansion and revision are essential, because the cards made during preliminary research are often used primarily to find the material that will actually be read and considered for the final bibliography.

The Note-taking System

The basic principle for note taking is for the researcher to select one system and to use it consistently. Many researchers find it most efficient to use note cards of a single size and to write on one side only. It is difficult to organize a collection of notes taken on different size cards and sheets of paper. The particular fact or quotation needed during writing may be buried in a mass of other material on a page of notes, or on the back of a note card already used and filed away. In the long run, it saves time to use a consistent system in which each note has its distinct place.

As in preparing the bibliography cards, the researcher should be sure to place all the needed information on each card:

1. Each piece of information or quotation is entered on a separate card (or, if necessary for longer quotations, a series of numbered cards).
2. The source is briefly identified on each card.
3. The page or pages on which the information or quotation appears is placed on each card.
4. Quotations are put in quotation marks and are checked against the original quotation for accuracy.
5. If material is summarized or paraphrased, the fact is indicated on the note card.

334 Typical note cards might look like this:

SAMPLE NOTE CARDS

Masculine Terminology

Terms like "man" are meant to refer to both sexes, but the mental image evoked is usually male, not female.

Millett, pp. 54-55

Society Viewed as Male

Freud discusses primal man and <u>his</u> relationship with <u>fellow workers</u>: "After primal man. . . . The Other. . . fellow worker." No mention of primal women workers.

Freud, p. 46

How much note taking should be done depends not only upon the particular research project but also on the specific stage of the project. As the research progresses, the writer may know more precisely which information is needed and, therefore, will often need to take fewer notes than were needed earlier in the research process. Although there are no guidelines for the number of note cards needed, the following suggestions can ease the note-taking burden:

1. Since an author will frequently sum up forcefully or clarify an initial position toward the end of a piece, researchers may read an entire article or chapter of a book before returning to take notes.
2. When an article or extensive section from a book appears to be particularly useful for the project, researchers may save time by photocopying the material on the machines now provided in most libraries. The researcher, however, still makes out a bibliography card and a note card containing a summary or a reminder that he has the material in hand.
3. Although the researcher may expect to use directly in the report only a small percentage of his notes, he saves time in the long run by including too much information rather than too little. It is particularly frustrating to have to return to the library for a specific date, statistic, name, or other fact that would have taken only a few moments to jot down initially.
4. When an idea occurs in reading, the researcher will write it on a note card and possibly work in a quotation from the source that sparked the idea. The simple fact or quotation in isolation from its context will frequently fail to start the same chain of reasoning at a later date. In effect, by putting down the reason for choosing to copy the information, the researcher is beginning to write the draft.

Whatever techniques the researcher uses, the basic principle is to have a well-thought-out method before starting to gather information. Constructing a system for the bibliography and note taking after beginning to research may lead to lost material and backtracking. In brief, emphasis should be placed on the preparation for research.

USING THE LIBRARY

The researcher's actual work in the library occurs in the following stages:

1. Becoming familiar with the resources and organization of the particular library to be used as well as libraries in general
2. Collecting information for a preliminary bibliography
3. Ordering and reading research material

If only to reduce fatigue, frustration, and time, the researcher should know the library tools available. In addition, asking the librarian specific rather than general questions such as "can you help me to find material about prejudice?" will prove to be time saving for both the researcher and librarian. Finally, it is impossible for the librarian to know every subject in detail, and any books to which he sends the researcher are likely to be the most general. Therefore, part of the researcher's job is to become his own librarian.

Library Systems

Every library will be organized a little differently from every other one and will contain lesser or greater amounts of material, but the resources and facilities will be basically the same. Libraries have three types of research material:

1. A general collection of books, usually available for borrowing up to a period of one month.
2. A collection of reference materials for use only in the library reference section.
3. A collection of periodicals, bulletins, pamphlets, microfilm, and other special publications and documents for use only within the library.

Before the first research session, the researcher learns the location and layout of the various elements of the library: the reference rooms; the card catalogs; the copying facilities; the microfilm readers; and the books, magazines, and other research materials. If the library has open stacks (allowing the researcher to go directly to where the materials are stored), the researcher can get most of the material himself. If the stacks are closed (that is, restricted to library personnel), the researcher will need to know the procedure for ordering the types of material he needs from the librarian. (See p. 339.)

Card Catalogs

The heart of a library is its *card catalog*—an alphabetical listing of all library holdings. Libraries with large collections may have separate card catalogs for books, magazines and journals, manuscript collections, and other special collections. Whether the library has one or many card catalogs, the materials will be filed by one or more of the following systems:

1. Alphabetically by author
2. Alphabetically by the first word of the title (except for *a, an,* or *the*)
3. Alphabetically by the major subject area (e.g., Microbiology, England, Literary Criticism)

337

Because the subject classifications are usually broad and may be incomplete, they are likely to be useless for the purpose of starting a preliminary bibliography. For example, the subject cards in the catalog may not include the periodicals devoted to the subject. Periodicals themselves will be listed only by title. For a guide to the contents of periodicals by subject and author, the researcher must refer to one of the various indexes of periodicals and other bibliographies. (For a discussion of these tools, see pp. 340–41.) The card catalog, therefore, is the place the researcher goes to in order to determine whether the library has a specific book, magazine, or other material he needs.

Each card in the catalogs has a *call number* that shows where the material is located. In addition to the call number, the researcher needs only the author's name and the title. (As noted on page 333, the call number should be placed immediately on the researcher's bibliography card.) Much of the other information on a catalog card is not relevant to the immediate task. However, the card will indicate whether the book in question has a bibliography that may provide additional sources in the topic area. The Arabic numerals on the card indicate the various headings under which the book is classified. The Roman numeral simply indicates that a book listed by author is also filed by title:

SAMPLE CATALOG CARDS

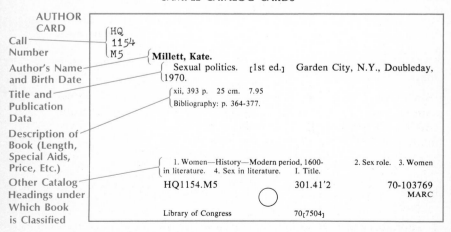

Note that title and subject cards are similar to author cards except that the additional information is placed above the author's name. (See page 339.)

If the library has open stacks, the researcher uses the call number to locate the material on the shelves. If, however, the stacks are

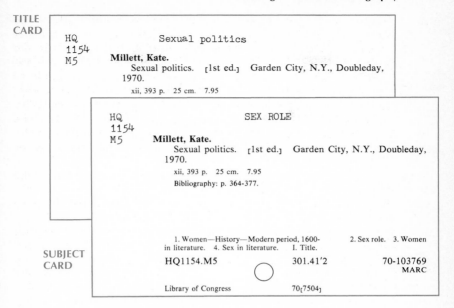

TITLE CARD

HQ
1154
M5   Sexual politics

        Millett, Kate.
            Sexual politics. ⌐1st ed.⌐ Garden City, N.Y., Doubleday,
        1970.
            xii, 393 p. 25 cm. 7.95

HQ
1154
M5   SEX ROLE

        Millett, Kate.
            Sexual politics. ⌐1st ed.⌐ Garden City, N.Y., Doubleday,
        1970.
            xii, 393 p. 25 cm. 7.95
            Bibliography: p. 364-377.

SUBJECT CARD

            1. Women—History—Modern period, 1600-   2. Sex role.   3. Women
        in literature.   4. Sex in literature.   I. Title.
        HQ1154.M5   301.41′2   70-103769
                                                                            MARC

            Library of Congress   70⌐7504⌐

closed, an additional step is necessary. The researcher fills out a *call slip* and presents it to the librarian in charge of getting material from the stacks.

Building an Efficient Bibliography

The variety and number of books, magazines, microfilms, government documents, manuscripts, and other printed and visual material would be overwhelming if the researcher had to start from scratch and sort out the specific items he wished to look at. Fortunately, lists of these materials are readily available. Such lists can be general, covering a wide range of works and subjects; or they can be specific, covering a narrow segment of a large topic area. For example, *The Reader's Guide to Periodical Literature* is a reference work that lists by subject, author, and title the articles in over 150 general periodicals (magazines appearing one or more times a year). However, reference works like *Language and Language Behavior Abstracts* list only articles on a particular subject (although the articles are drawn from numerous journals relating to the subject).

Simply knowing that somewhere there is likely to be a useful list or lists enables the researcher to avoid endlessly pulling books from shelves, leafing through countless magazines, and searching through countless pages in newspapers or microfilm rolls in the hope that something helpful will turn up.

A valuable source for finding what bibliographies are available is *Guide to Reference Books* (8th ed., 1967), by Constance Winchell, and its three supplements. This work is a bibliography of bibliographies (a reference work about reference works). It lists the various books in which the researcher can find the reference sources he will need for building his own bibliography. Listed (and often described) are not only the most general bibliographies but also extensive lists and descriptions for specific subjects in the humanities (English, history, philosophy, and so on), the social sciences (psychology, sociology, government, and so on), and the physical sciences (biology, chemistry, physics, and so on).

On the other end of the scale is the bibliography devoted to a particular subject within a field. For example, Joan Aldous and Reuben Hill's *International Bibliography of Research in Marriage and the Family* (1900–64) lists resources for a narrow aspect of the field of social work.

Whether broad or narrow, reference bibliographies fall into two categories: (1) *basic bibliographies,* covering a subject up to a certain date, and (2) *current bibliographies,* listing material for a specific time period, often year by year.

1. *Guides and Manuals.* Such works provide researchers with an overview of the major bibliographic sources in a particular field. For example, Roger Cletus Smith's *Guide to the Literature of the Zoological Sciences,* 6th ed. (1962) could be used for an overview of how to do library research in zoology. Frank A. Rice and Allene Guss's *Information Sources in Linguistics: A Bibliographical Handbook* (1965) is a selective bibliography that lists available literature in linguistics and related fields. Such works are guides that point the way to the major reference resources in a field.

2. *Bibliographies.* These references can be of the broadest sort, listing books that cover all aspects of a subject area. For example, the *Cambridge Bibliography of English Literature* (1941–57), 5 vols. (with supplements) lists works written by and about all major writers and some minor ones. The *MLA (Modern Language Association) International Bibliography* (1969–) is an annual three-volume survey of (1) the books and articles written about modern literatures, literary criticism, and linguistics, and (2) the books and articles written about all major and minor literary figures. Prior to 1969 this bibliography was a part of *PMLA (Publications of the Modern Language Association).*

3. *Indexes.* These reference works list a variety of sources, including periodicals; journals; book reviews; and anthologies of essays, plays, short stories, and poetry. For example, the *Social Sciences and Humanities Index* (1907–date) lists not only articles from magazines covering such subjects as sociolinguistics and American literature but also books or individual essays in books on a given subject, such as women in literature. Other, special indexes, such as *The Education Index* (1929–date) concentrate entirely on a particular field.

4. *Encyclopedias.* Universal encyclopedias, such as the *Encyclopedia Britannica,* 24 vols. (with annual supplements) provide general and specific information about many subjects. At the end of the longer articles, brief bibliographies of the topic may be given. There are also special encyclopedias—such as Philip L. Harriman, ed., *Encyclopedia of Psychology* (1946)—devoted to a single subject area that would make up only a portion of a universal encyclopedia.

Encyclopedias vary in quality and should be used with care. (See also pages 342–43.)

5. *Handbooks.* These reference tools provide the researcher with miscellaneous statistical, historical, and literary data. For example, Alexander Campbell Martin and William D. Barkeley's *Seed Identification Manual* (1961) has photographs, identification clues, a selected bibliography, and an index. *Words into Type,* 3d ed., Completely Revised (1974) gives style guidelines followed by many writers, editors, printers, and others in publishing.

6. *Histories.* A basic, thorough history of a subject area not only provides more detailed subject background than an encyclopedia but also often contains valuable bibliographical information. Albert C. Baugh's *A History of the English Language,* for example, tells the story of the development of the English language and also gives bibliographies at the conclusion of each chapter.

7. *Biographical Dictionaries.* These reference works—whether general biographies of important persons, such as the *International Who's Who* (1936–date); or listings of persons in a special field, like the *World's Who's Who in Science* (1968)—can be valuable both for general background information and for compiling a bibliography. For example, the *Dictionary of American Biography* (*DAB*) (1928–37), 20 vols., with index and supplements, contains brief bibliographies after the entry for each major figure, as does the *Dictionary of National Biography* (*DNB*) (British) (1922), 22 vols. and supplements.

Part of the researcher's training thus consists in learning both the most general reference lists and the specific bibliographies in his subject.

When using a reference work such as the *Guide to Reference Books* (or the books it lists), the researcher may not immediately find titles that specifically refer to his library project. Subjects and titles will cover broad categories, and the researcher may need to look for material under more than one subject category. For example, reference books on the English language may be listed under "Linguistics" as well as "English Language." "Prejudice" and "Women's Rights" may appear in different bibliographies devoted to psychology, sociology, or other social sciences. And many interesting research topics, when fully developed, simply will not fall within one of the standard subject classifications. Often a research project necessarily crosses the boundary lines. For example, subject divisions such as linguistics or sociology (two of the areas covered in the sample library paper in this chapter) are broad categories whose primary function is to lead the researcher to other, more specific subject areas. Therefore, the researcher cannot rely on a handful of bibliographic sources but must know where to find additional necessary reference works.

Aside from the fact that a preliminary bibliography can be most efficiently gleaned from the seven classes of reference material discussed above, a major reason for using such works is that they are more likely than the card catalog to lead the researcher to relevant material. Subject cards, for example, may be incomplete and will always be extremely general. And the title of a book may not always fully reflect what subjects are covered in it. More important, since no library is complete, compiling a bibliography from reference works rather than from catalog cards may lead the researcher to an important work that, although unavailable in his own library, can be ordered from other libraries through a borrowing system called *interlibrary loan*. If the researcher has allowed himself sufficient time for his work, the library will arrange to borrow a copy of a book, an article, a magazine, a dissertation, or other material from another library.

In building the preliminary bibliography, the researcher must also be aware that no reference work can be totally complete or reliable. New information is always appearing that will not be listed until the reference work is brought up to date. Indeed, the compiler of the reference work may simply miss some items. One type of reference work must be used with extra caution—encyclopedias. Encyclopedias are useful for an overview of a subject, especially if the researcher is unfamiliar with a particular topic. However, such works—even particularly fine ones, such as the *Encyclopedia of Human Behavior*—will not always contain the most up-to-date information or theories. (By the time the work is put together and printed many years may have passed.) In any case, even the longest entry in an encyclopedia is relatively short and is intended as a summary of the subject. With rare exceptions, then, the researcher will use these works only for a quick run-through of a subject. The research paper itself will be founded on material gathered from other, more comprehensive sources.

There is no substitute for actually looking at reference bibliographies themselves, learning their organizations, and discovering their limitations. Reading about them is of little use; therefore, no list is included here. However, some of the more frequently used reference works are listed as part of the following exercise.

Exercises

1. Each of the questions below can be researched and answered by consulting one of the following common references, found in the library reference section:

Books in Print
Current Biography
Dictionary of American Biography (DAB)
Dictionary of National Biography (DNB)
Education Index
Encyclopedia Americana
Encyclopaedia Brittanica
Library of Congress Card Catalog
Oxford English Dictionary (OED) (originally, *The New English Dictionary*)
Readers' Guide to Periodical Literature
Social Sciences and Humanities Index
The New York Times Index
Union List of Serials
World Almanac

Answer the questions in any order that seems convenient. Be prepared to explain why each source is suitable and how a researcher could use each source to provide specific answers to the questions.

a. Who wrote "Deadly Innocence: Hawthorne's Dark Women," found in volume 41 of the *New England Quarterly,* June 1968?

b. Where are the Fang (a Bantu tribe) located?

c. How many articles under the subject heading "Women's Libera-

343

tion" and having to do with sexism in the English language were published between December 1963 and January 1974?

d. What was the name of Carry Nation's alcoholic husband?

e. What did the word *knight* mean in medieval England?

f. Who is the president of India?

g. In what year did Paul Simon and Art Garfunkel dissolve their partnership?

h. Which American libraries contain all the issues of *Naturalists' Circular?*

i. Who was responsible for printing Elizabeth Barrett Browning's poem *Battle of Marathon* and in what year was it printed?

j. What is the price and who is the publisher of *Linguistics and English Grammar?*

2. In Constance Winchell's *Guide to Reference Books,* find a reference book that would supply a source in which to look up the following:

a. The Russian translations for English chemical terms

b. Published American dissertations in linguistics

c. An annual list of books and articles about American and British literature and literary figures

d. A history of the English language

e. A list of leading psychologists

f. A collection of Renaissance paintings

g. Special terms in photography

h. A history of dance

i. A list of books and articles on economics

j. A book of major plays by Irish playwrights

EVALUATING SOURCES AND BEGINNING TO WRITE

The preliminary bibliography and later additions to it lead the writer to his material, but they do not evaluate it. Although it may be tempting to rely upon the sources for facts and opinions, the researcher must constantly judge them. Recording and presenting to a reader a collection of facts and quotations is not likely to be interesting or informative. The reader could get as much or more from the original.

To evaluate his material intelligently, the researcher constantly keeps in mind the following questions:

1. *When was the work written?* The older a fact, the more likely it is to be outdated. Judgments based on such facts may, in turn, be obsolete. For example, opinions formed in 1870 about the ability of women to pursue professions are likely to have been based on narrow experience and would hardly be good evidence for an antifeminist article written today.
2. *What was the writer's purpose?* Except for simple presentation of facts (and even these may be selected with a bias), most authors have a point of view, a group of assumptions about their material. These assumptions, whether implied or stated, shape the author's facts as well as his conclusions. The researcher must discover the writer's assumptions and evaluate them.
3. *What was the author's intended audience?* A book or article—on language, for example—intended for a general audience may stress sensational conclusions or facts. Or, a popular article may water down the complications of a subject. On the other hand, a scholarly article may become so heavy with the complications that it misses the most meaningful aspect of a fact or subject.
4. *Did the writer present other points of view?* Material that is too one-sided about an issue is automatically suspect. The writer may have suppressed information in order to push his own thesis.
5. *If the writer makes a generalization, does he support it with data and examples?* When the writer makes only the vaguest acknowledgment of the work of others or fails to support his statements with specific illustrations, the researcher should be especially wary of the material and examine it with care.

The researcher should be prepared to make these evaluations before, during, and after reading. Sometimes, in fact, the best research results from demonstrating how oversights have been handed down from one generation to the next by previous researchers who have not raised probing and evaluative questions. The researcher can correct the record or show the consequences of misinformation in order to demonstrate his own approach to good advantage.

When to Begin the First Draft

As the writer becomes familiar with the subject by reading and evaluating material, not only the future direction of the research but the thesis itself begins to come into focus. Even before the research is finished, a pattern begins to emerge. The source material begins to reveal the same basic point or points over and over, the issues or the arguments become similar, and the researcher begins to fit each new piece of information with earlier ones more quickly. He can almost predict the results of further research.

Even though the process of collecting and evaluating information carefully must continue, the first draft should be started when approximately 50 percent of the research has been completed. No one can anticipate precisely how much research will be needed ultimately, but the writing should not be postponed until the last book or article has been read and the last set of note cards completed. As the draft is being written, new facts or more complete documentation will be needed. The researcher will have to return to the source material for a fact or quotation he may have glanced at rather than taken down. The very process of writing may reveal areas of interest that will have to be researched. Because none of these possibilities can be anticipated, it is more efficient to combine the first stage of writing with the later stages of research.

Outlining

The researcher cannot begin to outline until he has a sense of where his research is leading him. Once he knows his general direction, however, an outline is useful for organizing the first draft. Some investigations are fairly brief, and the writer may need only an informal scratch outline. (See Section **2.5.**) A scratch outline is often sufficient for longer reports as well as for shorter papers, if the line of argument or the issues being analyzed are straightforward. In such situations, the writer assembles his note cards and bibliography cards in sequence and begins to write, using the scratch outline as a guide.

When a great deal of material needs to be organized and a number of involved points need to be made in a complex order, it is helpful to construct a *formal outline* in either sentence or topic format. The sample library paper (see pages 351–58) was organized according to the formal topic outline on the opposite page.

The formal outline helps the writer to foresee certain problems that may develop while the paper is being written. For example, in developing the outline, the writer may be led to new research if the material in his note cards is not sufficient for developing a point. However, although the outline is a valuable aid, the writer should not become wedded to it. The sample library paper, for example, follows the outline generally, but it does not follow the proportions indicated by the three main sections. The writer used the outline to keep on the right track and as an aid in the process

Sample Formal Outline

Sexism and the English Language

<u>Thesis</u> statement

People are now recognizing that our use of the English language both reflects and promotes a sexist orientation to society.

I. "Linguistic sexism" and where it is found
   A. The ways in which language and culture are inter-twined
      1. Language of the marriage ceremony
      2. History of <u>man</u> and the masculine pronouns
   B. Ways in which sexism operates in the structure of English
      1. Subsuming terms: <u>man</u> and <u>he</u>
      2. Sexist ambiguity
      3. Society viewed as male
      4. Work descriptions: compound words in <u>man</u>, feminine suffixes
   C. How language is used to perpetuate sexist stereo-types
      1. Standard descriptive tags for men and women
      2. Common sexist stereotypes
II. Why linguistic sexism is a social problem
   A. Intertwining of language, thought, and behavior
   B. Social effects of stereotyping
      1. False ideas about people
      2. Needless limitations on our lives
         a. Career aspirations of young girls and boys
III. How to combat linguistic sexism
   A. Personal guidelines
      1. Using sexual references carefully
      2. Refusing to think in terms of sexist stereotypes
      3. Dropping pejorative descriptive tags

of focusing the thesis of the essay but did not become too attached to the formal design. The writer uses the outline; the outline does not use the writer.

Handy Devices when Preparing the First Draft

Preparing the first draft is often the most hectic stage of a research project. Research is still going on; new note cards are being written; the writer is still clarifying the direction of the paper. There are several techniques that can save the writer time and energy in writing the first draft and in making future revisions.

1. Each time a quotation is incorporated into the draft, immediately place the footnote after the quotation. The footnote should be in the conventional form. (See Section **6.8b.**) This procedure saves the time of having to search through the bibliography cards and note cards later.
2. Insert every quotation or fact in the draft and check it for accuracy. In subsequent drafts, when a page with quotations is rewritten, cut out the quotation and footnote and paste or staple them to the new page. The chance of misquoting increases each time a quotation is rewritten or retyped.
3. Before inserting quotations that run a half or full page long, check to see if the point the writer wishes to discuss is buried within the quotation, as it often is. In such cases, shorten the quotation by paraphrasing statements that merely introduce the main point. Quote only the particular part of the passage that makes the point. (See Section **6.7c.**)
4. Before or after each quotation, add comments describing its relevance to the topic of the library paper. Often, quotations are not self-explanatory. (See Section **6.7c.**)
5. When two or three sources say essentially the same thing, distribute the quotations among the various authorities. Unless the subject is a single book, the reader may assume that constant references to one source mean there is only one source or that the researcher has discovered only one source.

In addition to easing the job of writing the first draft, these techniques will also make the first draft more useful when it is time to revise.

Revising the First Draft

When the first draft is completed, it is often a good idea to let it sit briefly. On returning to it for revision, the writer will be in a more objective frame of mind to evaluate the writing and research.

If the library paper is too much like the outline—that is, thin and lacking development—it will need to be filled in. A library paper requires more than a sound and logical organization. It requires specific details, examples, and illustrations to back up the writer's thesis. If more research is required, it is done with the same care as the original research.

Revision is also the time to delete unnecessary material from the paper. Excessively long quotations can be shortened and information not needed to demonstrate the writer's thesis can be eliminated. Even inherently interesting or unusually well-documented ideas that are not central to the thrust of the paper can distract the reader and should therefore be deleted.

The rhetorical principles used in revising the library paper are the same as those for any writing task. The paper should be revised for unity, completeness, and coherence; and the details should follow the conventions of writing. These principles (discussed in Chapters 1–8) will determine the success of the library paper as an effective communication.

The Final Draft

Although putting together the final draft must be attended to carefully, it is basically a mechanical process. The final draft should be proofread several times, and pages that have too many changes (five or six) should be retyped. (See pages 236–38.) Guidelines for preparing the title page and for documentation are given below. (For the conventions of margins and spacing, see page 195):

1. *Title Page.* The title is centered and placed one-third from the top of the page. Following the title, and also centered, are the writer's name, the course title and number, the instructor's name and the date, in that order.

2. *Documentation.* Notes may appear together at the end of the paper or at the foot of the page on which the cited material appears. The bibliography is listed on a separate page under the title "Works Cited." (See Sections **6.8** and **6.9** for the conventions of footnoting and listing bibliographic material.) Note that the bibliography usually consists of only the works actually used in the paper. If additional works that were studied but not incorporated are listed, the proper bibliography title would be "Selected Bibliography."

   (Note: Blank pages, fancy covers, decorative pictures or drawings, and other additions not an integral part of the library paper should not be included. A simple format is less likely to distract the reader.)

349

SAMPLE LIBRARY PAPER

Although the sample library paper that follows is successful in many ways, it is not flawless. By citing the positive qualities of the paper as well as its shortcomings, the accompanying commentary traces the writer's progress while evaluating her attention to the principles of effective writing discussed in this handbook.

Sexism and the English Language

Diane Berkowitz

English 100

Professor J. Davis

January 5, 1976

Sexism and the English Language

Recently a number of new, sex-related terms have entered our language: womens' liberation, male chauvinism, sexploitation. These words reflect the growing awareness that sexism[1] pervades our society. Events of the last few years demonstrate that people—men and women alike—are becoming aware of sexism in both private and public life. Popular magazine articles and books, feminist organizations such as the National Organization for Women (NOW), and even recent government legislation draw attention to the presence of sexism in social, economic, and political spheres of life. But sexism exists in less obvious places, too; sexism can be found in our everyday language, in the words we use to formulate and express our ideas and feelings.

> The first paragraph focuses on the general subject area—sex discrimination—and leads into the specific subject—linguistic sexism.

Once a speaker or a reader is attuned to the problem of sexism in language, it is not difficult to find its traces everywhere. Consider the words that conclude the traditional American marriage ceremony, "I now pronounce you man and wife." What is a man? A man, of course, is a male human being, the member of the couple who can grow a beard. The word man refers to a biologically determined subcategory of human. What is a wife? A wife, of course, is a woman who is married to a man. The state of being a wife is not biologically determined; the word wife is a socially determined designation through which the woman is defined in terms of the man. If a marriage ceremony were to be free of sexism, it would have to, among other things, conclude with the words "I now pronounce you man and woman" or "I now pronounce you wife and husband."

> The writer cites specific, detailed evidence of how prejudice against women is deeply imbedded in the English language.

The entire substructure of the English language rests on discriminatory distinctions between men and women, as the history of these two terms themselves indicates:

> The writer cites historical evidence of linguistic sexism but does not develop, comment on, or draw conclusions from the quotation.

But more evidence of the male dominance of the language lies in our lexicon of sexual words and words denoting gender. The word man originally meant human being, but males appropriated it; later they came up with the word wif-man (now woman) for the other half of the race. He, with different endings to show gender, was once the pronoun for all third persons, but men took over the root word; she was an afterthought.

----

[1] Webster's New World Dictionary, Second College Edition, defines sexism as "the economic exploitation and social domination of one sex by the other."

> For footnote form, see Section 6.8.

> Female came into Middle English as Old French femelle, a di-
> minutive of femina, but was soon corrupted into its present
> form through the process of (male) folk etymology.[2]

Today, when a writer wishes to refer to all humans, the term man or mankind is invariably used. But what about women? Are they meant to be included in these terms? Similar problems occur when the third-person-singular pronoun is employed. When speaking of someone whose sex is either unknown or irrelevant to the discussion at hand, a writer almost always says "he." Could this anonymous "he" really be, in fact, a she? Kate Millett has observed this linguistic practice and concludes:

> With the Indo-European languages this is nearly an inescapable
> habit of mine, for despite all the customary pretense that
> "man" and "humanity" are terms which apply equally to both
> sexes, the fact is hardly obscured that in practice, general
> application favors the male far more often than the female as
> referent, or even sole referent, for such designations.[3]

The English language itself, and Americans who use that language are guilty of furthering sexism. In a recent unpublished essay, Elizabeth Burr, Susan Dunn, and Norma Farquhar summarized some of the major ways our use of language both reflects and promotes a sexist orientation to the world.[4]

According to the essay, subsuming terminology consists of "masculine terms which are commonly believed to include or refer to females as well as males, but which, in fact, operate to exclude females."[5] The use of man for humans and the overuse of the pronoun he (as mentioned above) provide examples of subsuming terminology. References to "man-made improvements" or "man-made implements" similarly neglect women.

Burr, Dunn, and Farquhar also cite sexist ambiguity as a source of our sexist view of the world:

---

[2]Ethel Strainchamps, "Our Sexist Language," in Woman in Sexist Society, ed. Vivian Gornick and Barbara K. Moran (New York: Basic Books, 1971), p. 240.

[3]Kate Millett, Sexual Politics (New York: Doubleday & Company, Inc., 1970), pp. 54–55.

[4]Elizabeth Burr, Susan Dunn, and Norma Farquhar, "Guidelines for Equal Treatment of the Sexes in Social Studies Textbooks" (unpublished essay, 1973), pp. 5–12.

[5]Burr, Dunn, and Farquhar, p. 5.

Marginal notes:

Long quotations are set off from the text, indented from both margins, and typed single spaced. They are not enclosed in quotation marks. (See Section 6.7c.)

Short quotations are enclosed in quotation marks and run into the text. (See Section 6.7c.)

First footnote reference. (See Section 6.8.)

Subsequent footnote reference. (See Section 6.8b.)

3

Use of the words <u>man</u> (without a definite article) and <u>men</u> to represent human beings in general or adults in general is also objectionable on the ground that such usage is ambiguous. Since both <u>man</u> and <u>men</u> are also frequently used to denote males only, it often becomes a matter of making an educated guess as to whether the author means males and females both or males only. It is moreover possible that such terms are employed by the authors to conceal their lack of information concerning females.[6]

Viewing society as male is another practice cited in the essay as contributing to linguistic sexism.[7] Most writers and speakers act as though the whole world were male. Consider the following passage, taken from Freud's <u>Civilization</u> and <u>Its</u> <u>Discontents</u>:

After primal man had discovered that it lay in his own hands, literally, to improve his lot on earth by working, it cannot have been a matter of indifference to him whether another man worked with or against him. The other man acquired the value for him of a fellow worker.[8]

Although Freud goes on to discuss the origins of the family and the dependency of the female, his view of people in general is entirely male oriented. Did it not occur to him that primal woman worked, too? More subtle, though equally disturbing, examples of male orientation can be found in statements such as: "Compared with other men, he . . ."; "More than any other man, he. . . ." These references carry with them the implication that only males exist in the world.

Burr, Dunn, and Farquhar point to discrimination in work descriptions as a major way the English language makes known its pro-male biases regarding work.[9] Many job-related terms, for example, end in <u>man</u>, implying it is only men who perform in these roles: <u>fireman</u>, <u>repairman</u>, <u>salesman</u>, <u>cameraman</u>, etc. Certainly, women can and do work in these jobs. New words that more accurately reflect today's realities are needed here. <u>Salesperson</u> is now widely accepted, and <u>chairperson</u> is becoming the correct way to describe the leader of a meeting. In other cases, where adding

Discussion of the quotation is needed.

---

[6]Burr, Dunn, and Farquhar, p. 6.

[7]Burr, Dunn, and Farquhar, pp. 7–8.

[8]Sigmund Freud, <u>Civilization</u> <u>and</u> <u>Its</u> <u>Discontents</u>, ed. and trans. James Strachey (New York: W. W. Norton & Company, Inc., 1962), p. 46.

[9]Burr, Dunn, and Farquhar, pp. 11–12.

4

the suffix -person sounds awkward, it is still often possible to
avoid making a sexual determination: fireman can become fire
fighter; cameraman can be replaced with camera operator.

A second type of discrimination can be found in the addition
of feminine endings to neuter job-related terms: authoress, poetess,
aviatrix, laundress, sculptress, etc. These terms imply that
women become special and unequal examples of the neuter term. To
say that someone is a poetess makes us think that she is not a poet,
and we wonder why. Even more obnoxious than the -ess ending are
the labels female and lady before a job description. To say that
Emily Dickenson is a "female poet" or that Billy Jean King is a
"lady tennis player" detracts from their status as poet and
athlete and brings some unpleasant stereotypes to mind. If women
do a job, let the language describe their work—not their sex.

So far, we have been discussing the sexist underpinnings of
the English language that are so deeply ingrained and so well established that they have become almost imperceptible. But how is
language used to perpetuate and maintain sexist stereotypes?

People of all sexual persuasions seem to take great delight
in calling women names. Writers, journalists, and every guy on
the street has a list of terms with which to describe women.
Among the many popular disparaging terms for describing women,
writer Cynthia Ozick finds the following:

> One: she is sentimental, imprecise, irrational, overemotional,
> impatient, unperseveringly flighty, whimsical, impulsive un-
> reliable, unmechanical, not given to practicality, perilously
> vague, and so on. In this view she is always contrasted with
> man, who is, on the other hand, unsentimental, exact, rational,
> controlled, patient, hard-headed, mechanically gifted, a
> meeter of payrolls, firm of purpose, wary of impulse, anything
> but a dreamer. Description One accounts for why throughout
> her history she has been a leader neither of empires nor of
> trades nor of armies. But it is also declared that, her na-
> ture having failed her in the practical world, she cannot
> succeed in the world of invention either: she is unequipped,
> for example, for poetry in that (here is Description Two) she
> is above all pragmatic, sensible, unsentimental, unvisionary,
> unadventurous, empirical, conservative, down-to-earth, unspon-
> taneous, perseveringly patient and thus good at all the
> minutiae of mechanical and manipulative tasks, and essentially
> unimaginative. In short, she will wander too much or she
> will wander not at all. She is either too emotional or she
> is not emotional enough. She is either too spontaneous or
> she is not spontaneous enough. She is either too sensitive

The "unpleasant
stereotypes" re-
ferred to in the
paragraph are
not specified.
Elaboration is re-
quired for a
stronger conclu-
sion.

This transitional
paragraph does
not shift the
emphasis, as is
indicated, but
expands it. The
potential line of
development
should be hinted
at earlier.

The quotation is
presented in the
correct format
but is much too
long. It can be
shortened con-
siderably and
portions of it sum-
marized.

354

(that is why she cannot be president of General Motors) or
she is not sensitive enough (that is why she will never write
<u>King Lear</u>).[10]

As Ozick observes, women are stereotyped and pinned with linguistic
tags whether they want them or not. Often, as Ozick has noted,
women are put into a double-bind: they are damned for possessing
one "trait" and then damned for possessing its opposite.

The ridiculousness of sexist stereotyping can be seen when we
compare the different labels attached to men and women who exhibit
the same kinds of behavior. A man who chooses not to marry is a
"bachelor." This term conjures a vision of a gay, carefree person,
a playboy who enjoys relationships with many women but who has not
yet been "lassoed" into marriage. A woman, on the other hand, who
chooses not to marry is a "spinster" or an "old maid." Far from
being glamorous and carefree, we imagine her to be old, ugly, and
unhappy; we suppose that she teaches Sunday school while waiting
for a husband to appear.

Similarly, when we hear that a man is "assertive" we suppose
that he is strong, forceful, direct, and commanding. We think
that he would make a great businessperson. When we hear a woman
called "assertive," something entirely different comes to mind.
We may think that she is loud, bossy, and unpleasant; we almost inevitably conclude that she must be a "castrating bitch."

We have discussed the many manifestations of sexism in the English language, but we have not yet directly addressed the question
of exactly <u>why</u> linguistic sexism creates a problem in society.
There are two major reasons why sexism (like racism or any other
prejudice) in language becomes a social problem. The first reason
grows out of the relationship between language and thought. Lin-
guist Lev Semenovich Vygotsky believes that meaningful language
arises from the interaction between thoughts and words, that neither precedes the other, and that they come into existence together.[11]
If we apply this belief to linguistic sexism, we can conclude

_____

[10]Cynthia Ozick, "Women and Creativity: The Demise of the
Dancing Dog," in Gornick and Moran, p. 311.

[11]Lev Semenovich Vygotsky, <u>Thought and Language</u>, trans.
Eugenia Haufman and Gertrude Vakar (Cambridge, Mass.: MIT Press,
1962), p. 125.

The mention of
"two reasons" in
the beginning of
the paragraph
makes it neces-
sary to summa-
rize them briefly
before elaborat-
ing or to have
both reasons con-
tained within
the same para-
graph. Other-
wise, the writer's
train of thought
becomes vague.

6

that if our language is male oriented, our thinking will reflect this orientation—to the detriment of men and women alike. If, for example, our language, with its overuse of the pronoun he, implies that the whole world is male, that the norm is masculine, then women will implicitly think of themselves as oddities. If our language reflects sexist biases, there is no way our thinking can fail to do so as well.

The second reason sexist language creates social problems has to do with the effect of stereotyping on society. Stereotyping perpetuates false ideas about people and blinds us to realities. If we foolishly accept the idea that all women are weak, for example, and the idea that all men are unemotional, we shall neither recognize nor appreciate the strong woman or the sensitive man.

An even more harmful effect of stereotyping is that it places restrictions on our lives. For example, a girl who grows up seeing mail carriers, fire fighters, and doctors portrayed in the media as males is unlikely to see herself in any of these roles. Similarly, a boy who grows up believing that men do not cry, that males are always strong and silent, may become inhibited, ashamed to express his feelings. Eventually, the victim of such stereotyping may become an emotional cripple. In both cases, adhering to stereotypes restricts the individual from realizing his or her full potential.

There are many methods that can help to rid the English language of sexism. Individually, we can learn to become more careful with our language. In speech and in writing, we can watch our pronouns, using he only when we mean to refer explicitly to men. We can refuse to use sexist terminology; we can refuse to assume that the whole world is male, even if it means that we have to rewrite some of our sentences. Instead of saying, for example, "The average American drinks his coffee black," we can say, "The average American drinks black coffee," or, "Most Americans drink their coffee black."[12] Furthermore, we can refuse to think in terms of

---

[12] "'Man!' Memo from a Publisher," The New York Times Magazine (October 20, 1974), 106.

This paragraph and the one that follows are not focused. The writer does not explain why linguistic sexism becomes a social problem but cites effects of linguistic sexism on society.

The sentence about "emotional cripple" should be illustrated to verify the force of the expression.

7

sexual stereotypes and can drop from our vocabularies words that demean women.

Sexism in language, as in life, still exists, but one hopes it will not be around much longer. There is a growing awareness, among individuals and among institutions, of the distortions of thought and language that are caused by sexism. With awareness comes change, and with change comes growth--and liberation.

The concluding paragraph reads well but is weak. No firm conclusions are drawn based on the information gathered.

Works Cited

For bibliography
form, see Sec-
tion 6.9.

Burr, Elizabeth, Dunn, Susan, and Farquhar, Norma. "Guidelines
    for Equal Treatment of the Sexes in Social Studies Textbooks."
    Unpublished essay, 1973.

Freud, Sigmund. <u>Civilization and Its Discontents</u>. Ed. and trans.
    by James Strachey. New York: W. W. Norton & Company, Inc.,
    1962.

"'Man!' Memo from a Publisher." <u>The New York Times Magazine</u>, Octo-
    ber 20, 1974, 106.

Millett, Kate. <u>Sexual Politics</u>. New York: Doubleday & Company,
    Inc., 1970.

Ozick, Cynthia. "Women and Creativity: The Demise of the Dancing
    Dog," in <u>Woman in Sexist Society</u>. Ed. by Vivian Gornick and
    Barbara K. Moran. New York: Basic Books, 1971.

Strainchamps, Ethel. "Our Sexist Language," in <u>Women in Sexist
    Society</u>. Ed. by Vivian Gornick and Barbara K. Moran. New
    York: Basic Books, 1971.

<u>Webster's New World Dictionary</u>, Second College Edition. Cleveland:
    William Collins & World Publishing Company, 1974.

<u>Woman on Words and Images</u>. "Sex Stereotyping in Children's Read-
    ers." Princeton, N. J., 1972.

Vygotsky, Lev Semenovich. <u>Thought and Language</u>. Trans. by Eugenia
    Haufman and Gertrude Vakar. Cambridge, Mass.: MIT Press,
    1962.

REVIEW EXERCISES

1. Select one of the questions below and make a list of the types of information that would be needed to provide a full answer. Use this information (1) to define the subject area of a hypothetical library paper and (2) to narrow the subject area by the process of focusing by classes or by causes.

a. What evidence has been offered to document the presence of visitors from space during earth's prehistory?

b. Have employment opportunities improved over the last ten years for minority-group Americans?

c. Why did former-President Nixon visit China?

d. What significant changes have there been in the lifestyles and values of American youth since the 1969 Woodstock Rock Festival?

e. Will the automobile give way to television as a means of "commuting" to work within the next twenty years?

f. What techniques are available for solving the world's food (or population) problems? Can these problems be solved in time to prevent global catastrophe?

g. Within your lifetime can people expect to have personal computers that serve as auxiliary memories and problem-solvers?

h. What events during the 1920s would, if known, increase the reader's understanding of F. Scott Fitzgerald's *The Great Gatsby?*

2. Review the list of *Works Cited* in the specimen paper and suggest the probable bibliographic sources used to compile the preliminary bibliography. Consult two of these sources and supply five articles or books that also could have been used. Would this additional information encourage you to alter the specimen paper in any way? If so, why?

3. Using the outline for the specimen paper as a basis, evaluate the paper by writing a brief analysis and critique of the organization and research. In your analysis incorporate answers to the questions below.

a. Compare the introductory and the concluding paragraphs. Are the two related? In essence, what is the writer saying?

b. Locate and identify the major sections of the paper and the subtopics under each. How much space does the author devote to them? Does each section seem to be adequately developed? Why or why not?

c. Has the author adequately used detail and exemplification to support her points? Explain your answer.

359

d. Study the author's organization by looking at the transitions from one section to the next. Are they logical and clear? Why or why not?

e. Does the author clearly distinguish between evidence and opinion? Cite specific examples to support your answer.

f. Taking the specimen paper on its own terms (a semester project for a college class), has the writer done an adequate job of covering her topic and developing her thesis? If revision seems in order, what specific revisions would you recommend?

4. Write a brief analysis of the documentation in the specimen paper using the following questions as a guideline.

a. Have enough sources been consulted to support the conclusions?

b. What type of source material did the writer use? Are the sources used as examples of the writer's thesis or as authorities for the points made in the paper?

c. Do the sources seem sufficiently up to date?

d. Which author and which volume were cited most frequently? Why do you think the writer cited this particular source so often?

e. Explain the format used in the footnotes. (Refer to Section **6.8** if necessary.)

Glossary of

Usage

10

Most of the entries in the glossary refer to common misuses of English that even the most experienced writer may make. Many of these lapses are errors in diction (see Sections 5.5-5.15) or spelling (see Section 6.5). Others are colloquialisms—local speech habits brought into writing. The entries here are by no means a complete listing of usage problems. When in doubt, reach for the handiest tool available—the dictionary.*

About, Around   *About* and *around*, synonyms of *nearly*, are used interchangeably in speech, but *about* is preferred in writing. However, it is still preferable to give the reader precise details.

> Vague   Most four-year colleges require **about** (not **around**) 125 credits for graduation.
>
> Precise   Four-year colleges require from 120 to 130 credits for graduation.

Accept, Except   *Accept*, a verb, means "to receive with favor" or "to approve."

> Politicians who **accept** even small gifts from a lobbyist put themselves in a compromising position.
>
> Students learn quickly which teachers demand quality and which will **accept** anything handed to them.

Except, usually a preposition, means "with the exclusion of" or "the rejection of."

> The discussion of marriage in college health courses covers everything **except** the problems encountered by newlyweds.

Actually   *Actually*, an adverb, means "in fact" and is a synonym of "really." Like "really," it is so vague and overused that it is no longer effective.

> Vague   Actually, there are many different diets one can follow to lose weight.
>
> Precise   Once the decision is made to lose weight, the dieter is faced with a variety of philosophies and gimmicks.

*For further information on word usage, see Chapter 5, "Diction."

Advice, Advise *Advice,* a noun, means "recommendation" or "information given to aid."

| **Advice** is often given but seldom heeded.

Advise, a verb, means "to give the recommendation or aid."

| An arresting officer's first duty is to **advise** the suspect of his rights.

Affect, Effect These two words cause writers problems because both are used to express causal relationships. *Affect,* a verb, means "to influence" or "to modify."

| Injuring his knee **affected** the athlete's career.

Effect, usually a noun, means "the result" or "the change brought about by some influence or modification."

| The long-term **effects** of a football player's injuries cannot be determined until he is forty or fifty years old.

Effect can also be a verb meaning "to bring to pass," "to produce," or "to make."

| Howard Cosell helped **effect** Muhammed Ali's reinstatement as a boxer by openly befriending him.

Agree to, Agree with One *agrees to* actions but *agrees with* people.

| That Chamberlain **agreed to** compromise with Hitler does not mean he **agreed with** Hitler.

All of In most cases, when used to modify a noun, *all* by itself is sufficient.

| Wordy   **All of** the officers wore blue.
| Revised   **All** the officers wore blue.

Allude, Elude, Allusion, Illusion *Allude,* a verb, means "to refer to" or "to mention."

| Few coaches bother any longer **to allude** to the virtues of sportsmanship.

Elude, a verb, means "to avoid" or "to escape."

| The reason oil companies need to raise prices on American oil **eludes** most consumers.

An *allusion,* a noun, is the indirect reference made when one *alludes.*

| The **allusions** in the poem are to the biblical story of Moses.

363

An *illusion,* also a noun, is a mistaken, unreal, or misleading image.

> Many manufacturers still suffer under the **illusion** that Americans will buy anything that has style and gives status.

A lot   *A lot,* meaning many, should be spelled as two separate words, if used at all. *A lot* is vague and should either be replaced by a more specific word or dropped altogether.

> Vague   **A lot** of athletes receive enormous sums for a season's work.
>
> Precise   The stars on a professional team occasionally receive in excess of one hundred thousand dollars a year.

Alot is a misspelling of *a lot.*
Lot of, lots of, and *lots* are unacceptable abbreviated forms of *a lot.*

Already, All ready   *Already,* the adverb, means "previously."

> Most student nurses **already** have career objectives and therefore have little need of counseling.

All ready means either "all are ready" or "all is ready."

> The rocket was **all ready** to fire.

Among, Between   These prepositions have specific uses. *Between* is used when differentiating two items.

> There is no real difference **between** an A— and a B+.

Among is used to differentiate three or more items.

> Grading systems **among** teachers vary.

Amount, Number   *Amount* is used with items always taken as wholes.

> The **amount** of **time** children watch television affects their reading skills.

Number is used with items that are temporarily grouped together but that keep their individuality.

> The **number** of **children** who watch television excessively has increased.

(See also **Fewer, Less.**)

Anyways, Anywheres   *Anyway* and *anywhere* are preferred to *anyways* and *anywheres.*

> Awkward   Although I prefer to be near the water, I spread my blanket **anywheres** I can when the beach is crowded.

| Revised | Although I prefer to be near the water, I spread my blanket **anywhere** I can when the beach is crowded. |

Around See **About.**

As *As* is a vague substitute for the conjunctions *because, since, while, when, if, whether,* or *for,* all of which denote different meanings.

| | Diets are only beneficial to health **as** (if? when? because?) they are followed by the truly obese. |

As . . . as, So . . . as *So . . . as* is preferred for negative comparisons.

| | Interest rates are still **not so** low **as** they were in the Great Depression. |

As, Like *As, as if,* and *as though* are preferred to *like* for making comparisons or contrasts.

| Faulty | We often treat scientists **like** they were the saviors of humankind. |
| Revised | We often treat scientists **as if** they were the saviors of humankind. |

Aspect, Factor, Feature, Function Whenever possible, these vague nouns should be replaced with more specific nouns.

Vague	This **aspect** of the movie was well paced.
Precise	This **scene** of the movie was well paced.
Vague	Kicking is an important **function** in football.
Precise	A good kicker can help win games by making field goals and extra points.

As regards, In regard to Substitute a more precise word for these wordy phrases.

| Wordy | People who oppose football usually do so **in regard** to its violence. |
| Revised | People who oppose football usually object to its violence. |

As to, With respect to *As to* and *with respect to* are awkward substitutes for *about.*

| Awkward | Most people are concerned **as to** the bite inflation is taking from their incomes. |
| Revised | Most people worry **about** the bite inflation is taking from their income. |

Bad, Badly   The adjective *bad* and the adverb *badly* are often confused. *Bad* describes the subject; *badly* describes the verb.

| The *lasagna* tasted **bad** (*not* **badly**).

The taste of the lasagna (a condition) is being described, not the action of tasting.

| He *hammers* **loudly** (*not* **loud**).

The act of hammering is being described.

Because   See **Reason is (was).**

Because of the fact that, Being as, Being that   Phrases like these are wordy constructions that are awkward substitutes for *because* or *since* and should be avoided whenever possible.

Awkward	George Allen retired Sonny Jurgensen **because of the fact that** the quarterback's injuries caused him to spend so much time on the bench.
Improved	George Allen retired Sonny Jurgensen **because** the quarterback's injuries caused him to spend so much time on the bench.
Awkward	**Being as** how the newly rich need a visible symbol of their success, they buy a Cadillac.
Improved	**Because** the newly rich need a visible symbol of their success, they buy a Cadillac.

Between   See **Among.**

But what, But that   In negative constructions, *but what* and *but that* are ungrammatical substitutes for *that.*

| Faulty | Nixon doubted **but what** anyone would discover the tapes. |
| Revised | Nixon doubted **that** anyone would discover the tapes. |

Can, may   There is distinction between *can,* meaning "the ability to perform," and *may,* meaning "the possibility of performing."

| President Ford **can** veto the bill.

(He has the ability [right] to.)

| President Ford **may** veto the bill.

(Possibly he will use that ability [right].)

Capital, Capitol   *Capital* refers to financial assets, upper-case letters, and cities that are seats of government.

| Brown's Department Store will need more **capital** to avoid bankruptcy.

From far and wide, buses filled with tourists entered the **capital.**

Capitol refers to the building in which a legislature meets. In the case of the edifice in which the U.S. Congress meets, the term is usually capitalized.

Every year tourists mount the steps of the **Capitol** with smiles and cameras at the ready.

Certainly, Sure   Substitute *certainly* for the weak word *sure.*

Vague   Tennis is **sure** an interesting sport.

Improved   Tennis is **certainly** an interesting sport.

Precise   Tennis is a contest between individuals who not only must be skilled athletes but must also be able to plan their own strategies.

Cite, Sight, Site   The verb *cite* means "to refer to."

Eisenhower was fond of **citing** Washington's Farewell Address to his troops.

The verb *sight* means "to see."

Once the Puritans **sighted** the New World's bleak shore, they wondered if they might have been better off in England.

The noun *sight* means "a vision" or "what is seen."

The **sight** of dying fish has not been enough to move most citizens to lobby against water pollution.

The noun *site* means "a location."

The **site** chosen for building a factory must be close to water in order to provide cheap energy and convenient waste disposal.

Compare to, Compare with, Contrast to   A writer *compares* one thing *to* another to show their similarities.

Many writers start their **comparison of** Knute Rockne's career **to** Vince Lombardi's by pointing out that both died at the height of their careers.

A writer *compares* one thing *with* another to see if they are alike or different.

Consumer Reports **compared** the Pinto's miles per gallon **with** the Vega's.

Contrast to is used to show differences.

The structured blues stanza **contrasted to** the improvised jazz theme illustrates the difference between open and closed form.   **367**

Convince, Persuade   Use *convince* with ideas and *persuade* with action.

| Because college administrators are **convinced** they are parent substitutes they are not easily **persuaded** to eliminate curfews for coeds.

Could of, May of, Might of, Must of, Should of, Would of   In writing, substitute *could have, may have, might have, must have,* and *should have* for these slurred speech forms.

| Most dieters **could have** (*not* **could of**) avoided obesity by not eating between meals.

Criteria   *Criteria*, meaning "standards," is the plural of *criterion* and should take a plural verb and be replaced by a plural pronoun.

| In the 1950s the **criteria** for becoming adoptive parents **were** based on the assumption that the middle-class life is the best life.

Data   *Data* is the plural form of *datum* (evidence) and, therefore, takes the plural form of a verb or pronoun.

| No **data** *are* ever conclusive in themselves.

Deal with   Substitute a more precise verb for *deal with* if one is possible.

| Vague | Administrators of the late 1960s were unwilling to **deal with** students' demands.
| Precise | Administrators were unwilling to **negotiate with** students about their demands.
| Precise | Administrators were unwilling to **comply with** students' demands.
| Precise | Administrators were unwilling to **give in** to students' demands.
| Precise | Administrators were unwilling to **admit** that the students had legitimate demands.

Definite, Definitely   Both *definite,* an adjective, and *definitely,* an adverb, are vague terms meaning "having precise limits." Either drop them altogether or rewrite the sentence giving more precise detail.

| Vague | People **definitely** take more interest in their health than they used to.
| Precise | People have become more concerned with their health now that they know a poor diet, overeating, and a lack of exercise will eventually lead to heart disease.

Devise, Device *Devise,* a verb, means "to invent" or "to contrive."

> No one has ever **devised** a more effective method of losing weight than eating less.

Device, a noun, is a "scheme" or "a machine produced by devising."

> Of all the **devices** for losing weight, eating less is the best.

Differ from, Differ with Two things are different from one another.

> College **differs from** high school because the scholastic demands on the student are greater in college than in high school.

To differ with is *to disagree with.*

> Mets' fans often **differ with** the umpire's calls.

Different from, Different than The preposition *from* is preferred to *than.*

> European football (soccer) is as **different from** American football as cricket is **from** baseball.

Doubt but what See **But what.**

Due to, Due to the fact that, Owing to See **Reason is (was).**

Each, Every When writers want to keep the items separate, they use *each;* when they want them to be thought of as a group, they use *every.*

> **Each** diamond in the necklace was perfect.
> **Every** semester I begin each class planning to make straight A's.

Effect See **Affect.**

Either, Neither These correlations are used in references to one or the other of two.

> **Either** Alice **or** Walter will be voted class president.
> For me, learning a new language is **neither** easy **nor** pleasant.

Elude See **Allude.**

Etc. *Etc.,* meaning "and so forth," is vague. If the list is meant to give a few typical examples, the sentence should be constructed to indicate that fact.

> Vague   The government regulatory agencies are the FDA, AEC, ICC, **etc.**
>
> Precise The FDA, AEC, and ICC are some of the many government regulatory agencies.

369

Every   See **Each.**

Except   See **Accept.**

Except for the fact that   *Except for the fact that* is a wordy substitute for *but*.

Wordy	College and professional football are alike, **except for the fact that** professional teams play for money.
Revised	College and professional football are alike, **but** professional teams play for money.

Expect, Suppose   *Suppose,* meaning "to guess," is a vague substitute for *expect,* meaning "to anticipate."

Vague	He **supposed** he would receive a wage increase at the beginning of the year.
Precise	He **expected** to receive a wage increase at the beginning of the year.

Factor   See **Aspect.**

Fantastic   In writing, a more specific word or words than *fantastic* should be used to communicate the idea of "*better than good.*"

Vague	*The Invisible Man* is a **fantastic** novel.
Precise	*The Invisible Man* is an excellent novel because it links the experiences of a black man to the emptiness of the American dream.

Feel   In writing, use the more precise verbs *believe, think, argue* or *understand* instead of *feel*.

Vague	Some people **feel** that watching a game enables the spectators to release violent impulses in a socially acceptable manner.
Precise	Some people **argue** that watching a game enables the spectators to release violent impulses in a socially acceptable manner.

Fewer, Less   *Fewer* is used to describe nouns that are temporarily grouped but that keep their individuality.

Since Watergate, **fewer** legislators follow their party leaders without question.

Less, an adjective, is used to describe items always taken as wholes (money, work) or to describe values and degrees.

During an inflation, people must learn how to get along with money that is worth **less;** during a recession they must get along with **less** money.

Since Watergate, the Congress should be **less** inclined to rubber-stamp the President's programs.

(See also **Amount, Number**)

Firstly   *First* is preferred to *firstly*.

| Faulty | **Firstly,** one needs to know the exact time of his birth as well as his birth date if he wishes a truly accurate astrological chart. |
| Revised | **First,** one needs to know the exact time of his birth as well as his birth date if he wishes a truly accurate astrological chart. |

Fix   In writing, it is preferable to use a more precise noun than the colloquial *fix* to mean "an awkward situation."

Young couples should not run to their parents when they **have a problem** (*not,* **when they are in a fix**).

Function   See **Aspect.**

Funny   Replace the colloquial adjective *funny* with one that is more precise, such as *strange, comical, amusing,* or *absurd.*

Today, the concept of the divine right of kings seems **absurd** (*not* **funny**).

Good and, Good many   Both phrases are vague and should be avoided or omitted altogether in writing in favor of precise detail.

Vague	The value of the dollar has been going down **good and** fast.
Precise	The dollar has decreased in value by 15 percent over the last two years.
Vague	A **good many** people are out of work in Central City.
Precise	Sixty-two percent of the people in Central City are currently unemployed.

Good, Well   *Good,* an adjective, should be used only to modify a noun. *Well,* an adverb, should be used only to modify a verb, adjective, or adverb.

Good *health* is brought about by *eating* **well** and exercising regularly.

Grand, Great   *Great* and *grand* are vague terms meaning "excellent." They do not specify *why* the noun is *grand* or *great.*

| Vague | The automobiles of the 1950s were **grand** because they had **great** style. |

371

| Precise | The automobiles in the 1950s were long and low, and their sleek fins reminded one of a jet airplane.

Guess In writing, either *suppose* or *question* is preferable to the vague *guess.*

| Vague | Consumers now **guess** that a powerful engine is not necessary for most driving.
| Precise | Consumers **question** the necessity of a powerful engine for most driving.

Had better, Had best, Has got to, Had of, Had ought These colloquialisms should be avoided in writing and *should* or *must* used instead.

| People now realize that we **should** (*not* **had best**) start conserving resources.

Hardly, Only, Scarcely These words are negatives and therefore should not be combined with other negative constructions in a sentence.

| Once a college adopts an open-admissions policy, it **can hardly** (*not* **cannot hardly**) maintain its academic standards without a remedial program.

Idea A more specific noun, such as *plan, belief, theory,* or *premise* is preferred to the vague noun *idea.*

| Most diets are based on the **premise** (*not* **idea**) that fewer calories will automatically result in a loss of weight.

If, Whether Both *if* and *whether* are used to indicate possibility.

| Many students wonder **if (whether)** grades reflect learning.

But *whether* is used to indicate alternatives.

| Most teachers and students still believe learning must be measured, **whether** (*not* **if**) by standard grades *or* by a written evaluation.

Illusion See **Allude.**

Imply, Infer *Imply,* a verb, is a synonym for *suggest.*

| Some toothpaste commercials **imply** that brushing one's teeth is the only way to reduce cavities.

Infer, also a verb, means "to conclude from evidence."

| Critics, looking at the decreasing interest in baseball and the increased interest in football and hockey, **infer** that the popularity of contact sports is on the rise.

Individual, Party, Person *Individual* is used to single out one person, animal, or item from a group.

> Students at large universities complain that they are not treated as **individuals.**

Person refers to one human being.

> When a citizen needs a grievance redressed by the government, he often has trouble finding the **person** (*not* **party**) in charge.

Party refers to a group of people.

> The landing **party** at Plymouth found a landscape that was Edenlike in its beauty but threatening to the pilgrims' survival.

Infer See **Imply.**

In regard to See **As regards.**

Its, It's *Its* is the possessive case of *it. It's* is the contraction of *it is.*

> The most significant feature of the 1976 automobile is **its** compact design.

> An automobile is no longer a luxury item used for Sunday drives; **it's** a necessity used for travel to work, school, and stores.

Kind of, Sort of In writing, substitute *somewhat* or *rather* for *kind of* and *sort of.*

> Faulty   All grading systems are **sort of** arbitrary.
>
> Revised   All grading systems are **somewhat** arbitrary.

Omit *a* from such constructions.

> Faulty   One **kind of a** plant needs watering every day.
>
> Revised   One **kind of** plant needs watering every day.

Make *kind of* and *sort of* agree in number with their referents.

> Some **kinds of** *plants* can be killed by too much water.
>
> He was the **sort of** *person* who needed a lot of encouragement.

Lay, Lie *Lay,* a verb, means *to put* or *place,* and is done to something.

> The way one **lays** down a book can reveal his attitude toward it.

Lie, also a verb, means *to recline,* and is done to oneself.

> People who need **to lie** down periodically may be suffering from undiagnosed anemia.

The past tenses are formed as follows:

> The way my brother *laid* down the book revealed his attitude.
> After my older brother finished his last final, he came home and *lay* down.

The past perfect is formed as follows:

> The Dean *has laid* down the law on late papers.
> The broken statue *has lain* there for two years.

Less   See **Fewer.**

Let's   This contraction of *let us* should not be used in formal writing.

Lie   See **Lay.**

Like, As   See **As, Like.**

Literally   *Literally* means "without exaggeration" and should not be used as a synonym for *actually.* However, both words are vague and should be omitted whenever possible.

> Vague   Astrologers **literally** believe they can predict the future.
> Improved   Astrologers **actually** believe they can predict the future.
> Precise   Astrologers believe they can predict the future.

Loose, Lose   *Loose,* the adjective, means, "free, unattached."

> General Motors was forced to recall three models of automobiles when it found out the engine mounts were **loose.**

Lose, the verb, means "to cease having" or "not to win."

> Farmers **lose** money on every other steer they raise.

Lot of, Lots of, Lots   See **A lot.**

May   See **Can.**

Maybe, May be   *Maybe,* an adjective meaning "perhaps" or "possibly," should be distinguished from the verb form *may be.* Whenever possible, use precise detail instead of the vague *maybe.*

> Vague   **Maybe** Medicaid will help the elderly.
> Precise   Medicaid will help the elderly only if it pays for all medicine as well as for hospital bills.

May of   See **Could of.**

Media   *Media* is the plural of *medium* and, therefore, takes a plural verb and a plural pronoun.

The **media** *are* unjustly blamed for the news *they* are only reporting.

Might of   See **Could of.**

More important, More importantly   Substitute *more important* for *more importantly.*

> **More important** (*not* **more importantly**), we must find substitutes for fossil fuels.

Must of   See **Could of.**

Neither, Either   See **Either, Neither.**

Not . . . as, Not . . . so   See **As . . . as.**

Nowhere, Nowheres   In writing, use *nowhere* rather than the speech form *nowheres.*

> The money was **nowhere** (*not* **nowheres**) to be found.

Nowhere near   In writing, substitute *not nearly so* for the speech form *nowhere near as.*

> Little League is **not nearly so** (*not* **nowhere near as**) much fun as sandlot baseball.

Number   See **Amount.**

Off of   *Off of* is a redundant for *off.*

> Many college administrators are more concerned with keeping students **off** (*not* **off of**) campus lawns than with quality education.

Only   See **Hardly.**

Outloud   In writing, *aloud* is preferable to *outloud.*

> Learning to read for comprehension is more important than learning to read **aloud** (*not* **outloud**) with expression.

Outside of   *Outside of* is a redundancy. *Outside* is sufficient.

> Plants will gain strength if they are planted **outside** (*not* **outside of**) the house during the summer.

Outside of should not be used as a synonym of *except for.*

> **Except for** (*not* **outside of**) tennis, there are few spectator sports that I enjoy.

Passed, Past   *Passed,* the past tense of *to pass,* means "moved by or completed satisfactorily."

> Some drivers consider their cars extensions of themselves and do not like to be **passed** on the road.

Past, a noun, means "in former times."

375

During social crises people are often nostalgic about the **past.**

Person See **Individual.**

Personal, Personnel *Personal,* an adjective, means "private."

Many questions on job application forms are **personal.**

Personnel, a noun, means "a group of people employed by the same organization."

Factories with assembly lines have trouble keeping their **personnel** from becoming too bored to be efficient.

Persuade See **Convince.**

Practicable, Practical *Practicable,* an adjective, means "capable of putting into practice."

The plan to freeze the terminally ill until cures are found for their diseases is not yet **practicable.**

Practical, also an adjective, means "useful or sensible."

We often sacrifice the beautiful in modern architecture for the **practical** and efficient.

Real, Really *Real* and *really* are used colloquially to mean "very" and "extremely." Whenever possible, substitute a more precise word or add specific detail.

Vague	Most people are **really** afraid of inflation.
Improved	Most people are **extremely** afraid of inflation.
Precise	Most people fear inflation because it reduces their purchasing power.

Reason is (was) In writing, a clause beginning with *that,* not *because,* is usually required after *the reason is (was).*

The **reason** he sold his house **was that** (*not* **because**) his company transferred his department.

Respectfully, Respectively *Respectfully* means "with respect."

An audience should listen **respectfully** to a speaker, no matter how bored they become.

Respectively means "each in the order given."

Football and baseball draw the largest crowds in the winter and summer **respectively.**

376   Scarcely See **Hardly.**

Set, Sit *Set*, a verb, means "to put" or "to place" and is done to something.

> Only a government can successfully **set** the standard for a safe automobile.

Sit, also a verb, means "to be seated" and is done by someone.

> Too often one sees clerks **sitting** and gossiping while customers wait.

The past tenses are formed as follows:

> She **set** the papers on the desk and left them there for days.
> In the past students with problems **sat** outside the Dean's office for hours without being noticed.

Should of See **Could of.**

Sight See **Cite.**

Site See **Cite.**

So In writing, *so that* should be used instead of just *so*.

> Most incoming freshmen are attending college **so that** (*not* **so**) they can meet the requirements for an already chosen profession.

Substitute *because* or *since* for *so* in such constructions as the following:

> The designated-hitter rule was instituted **because** (*not* **so**) the opposing team was assured an easy out when the pitcher came to bat.

Somewhat See **Kind of.**

Somewheres In writing, use *somewhere* instead of *somewheres*.

> The company decided it had to economize **somewhere.**

Sort of See **Kind of.**

Such *Such*, used as a synonym for "very," is vague and should be replaced with precise detail.

> Vague   History is **such** an interesting subject.
> Precise   The study of history encompasses many fields, including literature, science, and art.

Suppose See **Expect.**

Sure and, Try and Do not use these speech forms in writing.

> Students **try to** (*not* **try and**) keep up with assignments, but teachers who assign papers at midterm undermine well-planned schedules.

(us glos) *Glossary of Usage*

Sure, Certainly See **Certainly.**

Terrible, Terribly Both words are vague synonyms for *very, bad,* or *badly.* Use more precise detail or drop the terms altogether.

| Vague | Infrequent, excessive exercise can be **terribly** bad for one's health. |
| Precise | Infrequent, excessive exercise can be **bad** for one's health. |

Than, Then *Than,* a conjunction, is used for comparisons or contrasts.

Most television commercials are more *annoying* **than** *amusing* to viewers.

Then, an adverb, means "next."

Once a working mother finds a job, she **then** has to find a reliable person or institution to care for her child.

That, The fact that *That* is preferred to the wordy construction *the fact that.*

Some instructors forget **that** (*not* **the fact that**) students take four or five courses in addition to their own.

That, Which, Who, Whom Use *that* or *which* to refer to things and animals; *who* or *whom* to refer to people. Use *that* to introduce restrictive clauses and *which* for nonrestrictive clauses. (See also Section **7.2b.**)

| Restrictive | The storms **that** occur in the summer are often the most violent. |
| Nonrestrictive | Garlic, **which** is used in the Mediterranean countries, is thought to benefit circulation. |

Use *who* when the pronoun is the *subject* of a verb.

Students **who** are *dissatisfied* with grades are sometimes unaware of the criteria used to evaluate their work.

Whom is used to refer to the *object* of a preposition or to the *indirect* or *direct object* of a verb.

The candidate **whom** the voters will vote *for* must project an honest image.

City planners can no longer be indifferent to those people **whom** *they displace* in order to build a highway or a school.

Their, There, They're *Their* is a possessive pronoun.

378 Voters are becoming disgusted with politicians who are only concerned about **their** own reelections.

There is sometimes an adverb showing places.

> **There,** at the foot of the Mississippi, the French founded the city that would become the birthplace of jazz.

Other times, *there* is an *expletive* (an introductory word or filler).

> **There** are professional athletes the public has never heard of.

They're is a contraction of *they are.*

> **They're** the players who do a consistently adequate job, but never break records.

Thing   Replace *thing* with a precise reference.

> Vague   Automobiles do many **things** that frustrate owners.
>
> Precise   When a tire is flat, a battery is dead, or a transmission is burned out, most people wish Henry Ford had never been born.

To, Too, Two   *To* is a preposition.

> People remain immobile when they watch television, but they do not just sit and listen to the radio.

Too is an intensifier.

> By midterm most freshmen are **too** tired to learn efficiently.

Two is a number.

> Listerine cleans your mouth in **two** ways.

Try and   See **Sure and.**

Want for, Want to   In such constructions as the following, *want* should be followed by an infinitive, not by the preposition *for:*

> Most nineteenth-century immigrants to America **wanted to give** (*not* **wanted for**) their children broader opportunities than they would have in their native countries.

Well   See **Good.**

When, Where   *When* refers to a time sequence; *where* to a place.

> **When** the fire subsided, rescue workers searched through the plane wreckage for survivors.

> Ambulances raced survivors to nearby hospitals, **where** they were treated for burns.

379

Do not use *is when* or *is where* for definitions.

> Faulty   A depression is **when** there is a period of economic slowdown.
>
> Revised   A depression refers to a period of economic slowdown.

Where, That   *Where* indicates place and should not be used as a substitute for *that*.

> Faulty   Some business students do not understand **where** physical education, music, and literature will help them in their careers.
>
> Revised   Some business students do not understand **that** physical education, music, and literature will help them in their careers.
>
> Correct   At Gettysburg, not only can tourists see **where** Lincoln gave his famous Gettysburg Address, but they can also walk in the open fields and have a picnic.

Whether   See **If.**

Which   See **That.**

While   The conjunction *while* shows a time relationship and is a synonym for *during*. However, *while* should not be used as a synonym for *but* or *although*.

> Faulty   **While** Ralph Nader made people aware of how unsafe their cars are, the Arab boycott made owners more concerned with how economically their automobiles can be run.
>
> Revised   **Although** Ralph Nader made people aware of how unsafe their cars are, the Arab boycott made owners more concerned with how economically their automobiles can be run.

Who, Whom   See **That.**

Whose, Who's   *Whose* is the possessive of *who*.

> The Alsace-Lorraine section of modern France has changed hands so often that no one knows **whose** it should be.

Who's is a contraction of *who is*.

> Psychologists never answer the question of **who's** to be held responsible for the crime—the criminal, his parents, his teachers, his friends, or his society.

With respect to   See **As to.**

Would of   See **Could of.**

Acknowledgments

Roger Angell, "Down the Drain" (June 23, 1975). Reprinted by permission of *The New Yorker*.

Roger Angell, *The Summer Game*, © 1972 by the Viking Press. Reprinted with permission.

George Arthur, "Capsule Reviews" (November 1974), © 1974 by *Crawdaddy* Publishing Co., Inc. Reprinted by permission. All rights reserved.

Thomas Bailey, *A Diplomatic History of the American People*, 9th ed., p. 52, © 1974. Reprinted by permission of Prentice-Hall, Inc., Englewood Cliffs, New Jersey.

The Benedictine Sisters of Peking, *The Art of Chinese Cooking*, © 1970. Reprinted with permission of The Charles E. Tuttle Co., Inc., Tokyo, Japan.

Lee R. Bobker, *Elements of Film*, © 1969 by Harcourt Brace Jovanovich, Inc. Reprinted with their permission.

Lee R. Bobker, *Making Movies*, © 1973 by Harcourt Brace Jovanovich, Inc. Reprinted with their permission.

"Brown Penny" from *Collected Poems of W.B. Yeats*, copyright 1912 by Macmillan Publishing Co., Inc., renewed 1940 by Bertha/Georgie Yeats. Reprinted by permission of M.B. Yeats, Miss Anne Yeats, and Macmillan of London & Basingstoke.

Kate Coleman, "Kung-fu." Reprinted by permission of *Women Sports* Magazine.

Nancy Axelrad Comer, "Waterworks: Five Women in Oceanography," © 1974 by the Condé Nast Publications, Inc. Reprinted by courtesy of *Mademoiselle Magazine*.

Adelle Davis, *Let's Cook It Right*, © 1970 by Harcourt Brace Jovanovich, Inc. Reprinted with permission.

"Do You Believe in Astrology?" © 1974 by The Curtis Publishing Company. Reprinted with permission from *The Saturday Evening Post*.

Howard Emmons, "Fire and Fire Protection" (July 1974). Reprinted by permission of *Scientific American*.

Joseph Epstein, *Divorced in America*, © 1974 by Joseph Epstein. Reprinted by permission of E.P. Dutton & Co., Inc., publishers.

Bergen Evans, "Grammar for Today," © 1960 by The Atlantic Monthly Company, Boston, Mass. Reprinted with permission.

Index

384

List of Sections